Badass Women and
Hashtagged Zombies

CONTRIBUTIONS TO ZOMBIE STUDIES

White Zombie: Anatomy of a Horror Film. Gary D. Rhodes. 2001

American Zombie Gothic: The Rise and Fall (and Rise) of the Walking Dead in Popular Culture. Kyle William Bishop. 2010

Back from the Dead: Remakes of the Romero Zombie Films as Markers of Their Times. Kevin J. Wetmore, Jr. 2011

Generation Zombie: Essays on the Living Dead in Modern Culture. Edited by Stephanie Boluk and Wylie Lenz. 2011

Race, Oppression and the Zombie: Essays on Cross-Cultural Appropriations of the Caribbean Tradition. Edited by Christopher M. Moreman and Cory James Rushton. 2011

Zombies Are Us: Essays on the Humanity of the Walking Dead. Edited by Christopher M. Moreman and Cory James Rushton. 2011

The Zombie Movie Encyclopedia, Volume 2: 2000–2010. Peter Dendle. 2012

Great Zombies in History. Edited by Joe Sergi. 2013 (graphic novel)

Unraveling Resident Evil: Essays on the Complex Universe of the Games and Films. Edited by Nadine Farghaly. 2014

"We're All Infected": Essays on AMC's The Walking Dead and the Fate of the Human. Edited by Dawn Keetley. 2014

Zombies and Sexuality: Essays on Desire and the Living Dead. Edited by Shaka McGlotten and Steve Jones. 2014

...But If a Zombie Apocalypse Did Occur: Essays on Medical, Military, Governmental, Ethical, Economic and Other Implications. Edited by Amy L. Thompson and Antonio S. Thompson. 2015

How Zombies Conquered Popular Culture: The Multifarious Walking Dead in the 21st Century. Kyle William Bishop. 2015

Zombifying a Nation: Race, Gender and the Haitian Loas on Screen. Toni Pressley-Sanon. 2016

Living with Zombies: Society in Apocalypse in Film, Literature and Other Media. Chase Pielak and Alexander H. Cohen. 2017

Romancing the Zombie: Essays on the Undead as Significant "Other." Edited by Ashley Szanter and Jessica K. Richards. 2017

The Written Dead: Essays on the Literary Zombie. Edited by Kyle William Bishop and Angela Tenga. 2017

The Collected Sonnets of William Shakespeare, Zombie. William Shakespeare and Chase Pielak. 2018

Dharma of the Dead: Zombies, Mortality and Buddhist Philosophy. Christopher M. Moreman. 2018

The Politics of Race, Gender and Sexuality in The Walking Dead: Essays on the Television Series and Comics. Edited by Elizabeth Erwin and Dawn Keetley. 2018

The Subversive Zombie: Social Protest and Gender in Undead Cinema and Television. Elizabeth Aiossa. 2018

Parenting in the Zombie Apocalypse: The Psychology of Raising Children in a Time of Horror. Steven J. Kirsh. 2019

Beyond the Living Dead: Essays on the Romero Legacy. Edited by Bruce Peabody and Gloria Pastorino. 2021

Reading the Great American Zombie: The Living Dead in Literature. T. May Stone. 2022

The Zombie Movie Encyclopedia, Volume 2: 2000–2010. Peter Dendle. 2022

Faith and the Zombie: Critical Essays on the End of the World and Beyond. Edited by Simon Bacon. 2023

Dead, White and Blue: The Zombie and American National Identity. Aaron W Clayton. 2023

Badass Women and Hashtagged Zombies

Gender in *The Walking Dead* from Screen to Social Media

ALLISON CHRISTINA BUDAJ

CONTRIBUTIONS TO ZOMBIE STUDIES

McFarland & Company, Inc., Publishers

Jefferson, North Carolina

This book has undergone peer review.

LIBRARY OF CONGRESS CATALOGING-IN-PUBLICATION DATA

Names: Budaj, Allison Christina, 1985– author.
Title: Badass women and hashtagged zombies : gender in The walking dead
from screen to social media / Allison Christina Budaj.
Description: Jefferson, North Carolina : McFarland & Company, Inc., Publishers, 2024. |
Series: Contributions to zombie studies | Includes bibliographical references and index.
Identifiers: LCCN 2024037369 | ISBN 9781476691572 (paperback : acid free paper) |
ISBN 9781476654676 (ebook) ∞
Subjects: LCSH: Walking dead (Television program) | Women on television. |
Social problems on television. | Online social networks. | LCGFT: Television
criticism and reviews.
Classification: LCC PN1992.77.W25 B83 2024 | DDC 791.45/72—dc23/eng/20240828
LC record available at https://lccn.loc.gov/2024037369

BRITISH LIBRARY CATALOGUING DATA ARE AVAILABLE

ISBN (print) 978-1-4766-9157-2
ISBN (ebook) 978-1-4766-5467-6

Front cover image: © N. Steele/fotogestoeber/Shutterstock

Printed in the United States of America

*McFarland & Company, Inc., Publishers
Box 611, Jefferson, North Carolina 28640
www.mcfarlandpub.com*

Acknowledgments

I thank my understanding parents, Betsy and Jerry, and Dennis and Wanda. All four of you raised me to be independent and follow my dreams, even if it meant writing a dissertation and now a book on zombies. Without each of you and the support of my family, I would not be here today. To Sarah and Lauren, I am so fortunate to have you as sisters.

I am especially indebted to three illustrious scholars: Chelle, Gina, and Misti. I will never forget our many shenanigans during residency, traveling nationwide for conferences, and our much-needed Skype chats. You three keep me going.

To my Cincinnati framily, you are the support group I never knew I needed and am so thankful to have in my life!

Words cannot express my gratitude and appreciation for my chair, Dr. Chris Voparil, and my committee members, Dr. Diane Allerdyce and Dr. Elizabeth Aiossa. Thank you for encouraging me to "flesh out" my thoughts, watching the series, and embarking on this journey with me. Thank you, Dr. Aiossa, for blazing a trail for zombie culture and being a constant source of inspiration.

I am also exceptionally grateful to my colleagues for supporting my decision to pursue a doctoral degree, writing letters on my behalf, and tolerating my countless discussions about zombies. Thank you, Shari, for your friendship. You are always offering help and constant encouragement. Thank you, Marian, for inspiring me, being a dear friend, and going to Walker Stalker! Thank you, Greg, for proofreading the many (horrible) draft papers I sent to you over the years.

Lastly, I would like to thank my partner, TR Gormley. Your patience knows no bounds, your humor relieves these many stressful days, and you give the best hugs. I love you more than words can express.

Table of Contents

Preface

If I had to guess, my interest in zombies started when I first encountered the arcade game *The House of the Dead*. I was hooked, whether it was the light gun in my hand or the simulated fight for survival that drew me in. I am trying to remember exactly how old I was at this first encounter, but I do remember seeking out this game every time I set foot in an arcade. My love of this horror game eventually evolved into an interest in horror films, largely thanks to my father, an avid film buff with a penchant for "collecting" movies, and I will leave it at that. We constantly had access to what seemed to be an unlimited assortment of VHS tapes. His interests ranged from war to biographical to romantic comedies to, you guessed it, horror. Suppose my sister inherited my father's stubbornness. In that case, I must have inherited this interest in visual narratives as I spent the entirety of my undergraduate, graduate, and eventually doctoral degree studying media, especially the horror genre.

Fast-forward to 2020, an eerily apocalyptic time when the world experienced a complete shutdown as we barricaded ourselves in our houses and practiced social distancing to prevent the further spread of Covid-19, I successfully defended my dissertation focusing on AMC's *The Walking Dead*. As only the second person in my doctoral program at Union Institute & University to write a dissertation on zombies (shoutout to the badass trailblazer who started the trend, Dr. Aiossa), my interest in horror seemed to reach the pinnacle of my writing endeavors. That is, until this book.

Like my experience with *The House of the Dead*, I cannot recall precisely when I started watching *The Walking Dead*. I remember hearing people talking about it; the premise sounded right up my alley. However, working two jobs while pursuing a master's degree meant I was studying, working, or (if possible) sleeping. It was not until I started working full-time as a college professor that I could enjoy leisurely activities such as exercising, because as Columbus (Jesse Eisenberg) in *Zombieland* (2009) reminds us, the first rule is cardo, or watching television. From my initial viewing of "Days Gone Bye," I became obsessed with this narrative.

1

As the most-watched series in cable history, *The Walking Dead* attracted millions of spectators thanks to a rabid fanbase dedicated to the original graphic novel (also named *The Walking Dead*), the amiability of characters, and the formatting of the series presenting a never-ending story about zombies. Outside of character likeability, I often engaged in conversations about various annoyances or theories about the series with my partner at the time, coworkers, and anyone who would listen. Indeed, some characters were clear standouts. Other characters I found exceptionally troubling.

Once I started my doctoral program and narrowed my dissertation focus, I found I was not alone in my frustration. Numerous scholars zeroed in on the circumscribed social representations that appear in the series, especially the contributions made by women in the post-apocalypse. Significant analyses by researchers such as Elizabeth Erwin, John Greene, Michaela Meyer, Amanda Keeler, Dawn Keetley, Cynthia Vinney, Caryn Wiley-Rapoport, and countless others identified the distinct gender divide where the women dutifully cook, clean, and tend to children, while the men exultantly hunt, protect, and lead without question. Despite these in-depth investigations, scholars have neglected how the prolonged run of the series affords specific characters time to adapt, evolve, and shatter conventions. It is here that I wanted to make my mark. Initially, I wanted to examine the transformations of women such as Carol Peletier (Melissa McBride) and her evolution from battered homemaker to the Queen of the Kingdom. As the only remaining female character from the first season, Carol is undoubtedly a powerhouse. Still, I needed to expand my reach, especially considering my goal was to write a dissertation.

So, I turned to characters such as Maggie Rhee (Lauren Cohan), who leaves behind her sheltered life on the family farm to lead the Hilltop Colony. There is also Michonne Hawthorne (Danai Gurira), who distances herself from self-imposed isolation to become head of security and the First Lady of the Alexandria Safe-Zone (@AngelaKang). Even though there are several scholars focused on Michonne as a prominent Black character, few have been able to track her progression across her entry and exit from the series. Additionally, new characters entering the narrative continue to defy the heteronormative dominance so focused upon by scholars. There are women like Tara Chambler (Alanna Masterson), who, as the first openly gay character in the television series, challenged the troubling "bury your gays" trope. And for Rosita Espinosa (Christian Serratos), who, as the first prominent Latina woman, evolves beyond a sexualized commodity.

Finally, I found Enid (Katelyn Nacon) to be a perplexing and yet exciting contribution to the narrative since this person comes into the storyline as much a mystery as Michonne. To be one of the few characters to survive on her own for an undetermined period, I wanted to explore her character progression more. And as scholars quickly noted the rampant focus on White male authority in the series, I wanted to examine how the start of the ninth season and beyond disrupts such preeminence with the promotion of the first female showrunner and subsequent focus on female-centric storylines. But my journey did not end there. To my delight, my exploration into *The Walking Dead* expanded to include its spinoffs, especially considering how a unique tale chartered new territory as blank slates for *The Walking Dead* Universe to develop, deepening my exploration of the tensions, anxieties, and fears that plague society.

There is one last part of this story I wanted to include, that of the fans. Realizing I am only one voice applying my assumptions and analysis of this series, I thought other voices needed to be heard. Taking inspiration from a few of my fellow scholars and after reading *Textual Poachers* by Henry Jenkins, I decided to focus on what Jenkins dubbed "participatory culture" in this journey. Thankfully, fans do not sit idly by as the nearly 200 episodes of *The Walking Dead* aired on television. Using *Twitter*, now known as *X*, to give reactionary comments in a lively fashion and turning to platforms such as *Reddit* to discuss thoughts, air grievances, and offer speculation, fans demonstrated a more nuanced understanding of this series. By integrating analyses of social media commentary from these dedicated viewers, I demonstrate how *The Walking Dead* Universe as a popular culture icon has inspired pervasive debates about gender roles in this apocalyptic narrative and actively challenged producers of the series to include more representation. To the fans of *The Walking Dead* Universe, I am forever grateful for your diligence.

Introduction

Imagine, if you will, a person awakes from a coma to an empty hospital room. Surveying the space for any signs of life, they reach over to touch the dried, brittle bouquet of flowers left at their bedside for who knows how long. The clock on the wall stopped at exactly 2:17. Slowly, the person rises from their bed only to fall immediately to the ground from their weakened state. After managing to get to their feet, they stumbled into the darkened hallway of what appears to be an abandoned hospital, or so they thought. Finding a door chained shut and spray painted "Don't Open Dead Inside," something or someone on the other side pushes against it, grayish fingers extending out through the widened gap between the doors. Turning to the other direction, they come upon a stairwell and eventually make their way outside to find a parking lot lined with bodies wrapped in white hospital sheets. Just over an embankment, a military base camp appears deserted. Not a soul in sight. There is no noise other than crickets chirping. The world has gone silent and is now filled with the dead.

While I was not one of the over five million viewers to watch the pilot episode of *The Walking Dead* when it aired on October 31, 2010, I do remember how I felt watching this episode for the first time. I wondered how I might react if I awoke to a world I no longer recognized and where the dead now roam. Would I make my way back home in search of my family? Would I even make it out of the hospital? How would I react to seeing a zombie for the first time? If I did make it home, how long would I last? Where would I go? So many questions and so many possible answers. I suppose that is the beauty of a post-apocalyptic horror narrative like *The Walking Dead* and its various spinoffs. Viewers are invited to contemplate their own actions and reactions to what they see unfolding within the storyline, but they are not limited to just discussing the series at the company water cooler or with their viewing companions. Thanks to social media, fans across the globe could post their thoughts in real time, hashtagging their comments to categorize their posts with other those from other viewers. Debates about next actions, theories about certain characters' fates, cheers and dissent all happening in rapid-fire fashion online.

The Walking Dead *Universe Explained*

As impossible as it might be to predict the rampant success of *The Walking Dead* beyond its graphic novel roots, the adaptation of the novel evolved into what creator Robert Kirkman himself envisioned for his narrative, that of a "'zombie movie that never ends'" (quoted by Jenkins, "How to Watch Television: The Walking Dead"). Kirkman admitted his own doubts about the original graphic novel lasting more than 12 issues (Colucci). Much to his and surely others' surprise, the graphic novel extended to more than 30 story arcs when Kirkman closed in on issue 200 and two connecting novels highlighting the origin story of a noteworthy antagonist of *The Walking Dead* (other than the zombies), Philip Blake (David Morrissey) a.k.a. The Governor (Crecente; Proctor 8).

Even more impressive, *The Walking Dead* spread beyond its graphic novel roots to spawn a digital visual narrative universe, aptly titled *The Walking Dead* Universe online. Within this sprawling televised and digitized apocalyptic narrative world comes the host network's first live aftershow (*Talking Dead*) (Ng), a slew of webisodes serving as paratexts for the main series (*The Walking Dead: Webisodes*) (Opie "The Walking Dead Timeline"), a prequel narrative told through "the lens of [a] high school guidance counselor" (*Fear the Walking Dead*) ("Fear the Walking Dead"), a limited run miniseries described as "the first generation to come-of-age in the apocalypse" (*The Walking Dead: World Beyond*) (@Shudder), and an anthology series featuring both new and existing characters within the established walker-laden realm (*Tales of the Walking Dead*) ("About Tales of The Walking Dead"; Moore).

Intensifying the expanse of *The Walking Dead*'s relentless spread came three more highly anticipated televised spinoffs: *The Walking Dead: Dead City* chronicling the journey of two iconic foes turned what we will call "friends" for now, Maggie Rhee and Negan Smith (Jeffrey Dean Morgan), *The Walking Dead: Daryl Dixon* storyline focusing on its namesake character (because, if you following anything relating to *The Walking Dead* on social media, if Daryl dies, we riot), and *The Walking Dead: The Ones Who Live*, a series that will (hopefully) bring closure to those ever lively debates about the fate of the shipped #Richonne pairing (Acuna "The Long-Awaited Rick and Michonne"; Ramos). Along with the eleventh (and final) season of the original series adaptation under the direction of showrunner Angela Kang, *The Walking Dead* Universe appears as unstoppable as the undead it so brilliantly features.

It's Not About the Zombies Anymore

Recalling my hypothetical curiosities about my ability to exist in the post-apocalyptic world of *The Walking Dead* flagship series, I contemplated the implications of such questions. Am I capable of surviving such an event, or would I "opt out"? Are there others like me in the series pondering their own abilities and mortality? Would there be a character with whom I could identify, follow along with, and even champion their survival? In the article, "Locating Zombies in the Sociology of Popular Culture," Todd Platts concludes, "We can learn much about a culture by understanding how it scares itself and the zombie's 'blank slate' is perfect for this endeavor" (553). Though I understand Platts' application of zombies serving as a blank slate for us to place our anxieties on, I wondered more about what scares and motivates us in a series such as *The Walking Dead*. As the seasons progressed, it became quite clear that the dead were no longer the scariest part of this world. While the pesky undead still make survival challenging, the living within the series faced grave uncertainties like food scarcity, housing instability, fuel shortages, sufficient access to medicine, and even war on top of a mysterious and lethal illness. All very real needs; all very scary conditions. Still, despite the odds and not always easily, the survivors managed to overcome. Taking a deeper look, I thought more about how other fears manifest in this post-apocalyptic narrative world. Turns out, there is more than just the fear of meeting our basic needs that manifest. With each iteration of *The Walking Dead* Universe, it became more apparent how the spinoffs diverged from the flagship narrative, especially when promoting storylines focusing away from the heteronormative and patriarchal dominance showcased in *The Walking Dead*'s initial seasons. The narratives evolved to emphasize women in positions of power, body autonomy, divergent sexual identities, blended families, increased gender representation, differing abilities, struggles with mental health, death and mortality, and even drag queens, which I found myself wanting to investigate deeper.

Outside the blank slate zombies provide us to place our fears on, the complexity of the characters within *The Walking Dead* and beyond offer more than just viewing enjoyment. Though John O'Brien asserts, "we can learn about ourselves by understanding [zombies] better," and thus reflect "the culture that produced them," I firmly believe we can learn more by ourselves by exploring and understanding the living better, especially if these narratives are reflective of the culture that produced them (3:45–3:52).

Audience members watch and discuss why the individuals in the world no longer reminiscent of our own act in ways that defy convention. Beyond social commentary and companionship formulated by the plethora of social media conversations happening in real-time, Stephen Kirsh identifies the uses and gratifications zombie narratives offer audiences through mediated storytelling. In *Parenting in the Apocalypse*, Kirsh names escapism, catharsis, fear reduction, sensation seeking, morbid curiosity, and vicarious experiences as ways viewers of zombie narratives fulfill various needs. He continues by illustrating the importance of zombie entertainment to meet one or more of these needs at any given time during the narrative (Kirsh 13).

Thus, while *The Walking Dead* can and often does present numerous heart-pumping moments when the main characters seem pitted against inexplicable odds enticing our morbid curiosity, they can engage in conversations about "what ifs" and debate the actions of the characters. Even Kirkman acknowledges how zombies can offer a reflection of ourselves as a form of social commentary, admitting how while zombie narratives "show us gore and violence and all that cool stuff too … there's always an undercurrent of social commentary and thoughtfulness" (Introduction). While zombies relentlessly hunt for the survivors in the series, these survivors must consciously act to ensure their existence.

Since zombie narratives typically fall under the horror genre umbrella, a genre known to reinscribe stereotypes, understanding the roles of the living is essential to discerning how a television series about zombies speaks volumes about social anxieties, especially those experienced by oppressed demographics. For instance, the depiction of gender in the horror genre and its penchant for typecasting women as the "helpless virgin" or "damsel in distress," fearful, helpless, incapable of surviving on her own, but still somehow always managing to look pretty. Indeed, there are exceptions to such typecasts. *Carrie, Halloween*, the *Alien* franchise, and, more recently, *Hereditary* offer examples of dominant female roles in a genre overtly labeled as misogynistic (Bertram). For the most part, women on both the big and small screen become objects for viewing pleasure and specimens subject to fierce criticism for scholars and viewers alike. From their clothing to hairstyles, partner selection, age, and language, every aspect of a female character becomes a target for ridicule. The first few seasons of *The Walking Dead* flagship series did little in the way of promoting any positive depictions of women overshadow any potential for positive representation. Still, I have a theory about these portrayals. What if *The Walking Dead* did this purposefully to elicit audience outrage and challenge those immediate reactions and assumptions as each character matures and evolves over the full extent of the narrative? In this way, *The Walking Dead* serves as a social commentary on the pre-apocalyptic world and the roles women tend to play within, as well as demonstrates how media portrays and typifies female characters on screen.

In this book, I aim to explore more than just the zombies by digging into more about the anxieties that plague us. In essence, I want to investigate the fears that play out amongst the living in *The Walking Dead* Universe. Though I completely agree with Elizabeth Aiossa and her argument that "the zombie apocalypse is not an automatic fix for a flawed society" in her work *The Subversive Zombie*, the formatting of the series and its spinoffs as a continual narrative unraveling through a television series presents viewers a unique opportunity for observation and discussion (128). As active contributors through participatory culture, viewers not only witness significant character transformations but can also explore how a series can inspire audience members to involve themselves in conversations regarding the existence of and divergence from convention using social media platforms. More specifically, while this book references theoretical foundations, such as film and gender studies, my primary focus in this exploration is to offer and analyze a collection of discussions held by fans across various social media platforms about the various fears showcased in *The Walking Dead* and beyond.

With an abundance of episodes open for analysis, there exists plenty of space for fans such as me to contemplate the social issues made apparent in *The Walking Dead*, especially when considering its extensive time on air. From the earlier days of the series featuring characters such as Maggie Rhee becoming the family matriarch after the death of her father to the character Carol Peletier making the difficult, if not a cringe-worthy, decision to kill a duo of sickened individuals before a mysterious and deadly contagion infects her surrogate family, characters in the series progressively and decisively act in ways that test boundaries. Each installment of the series permits time for the protagonists to adapt and evolve in their new environment. Therefore, key episodes become ideal specimens for in-depth character analysis as their pre-apocalyptic ways of being, including any prescribed stereotypes, fade into the past. As noted by Paul Vigna in *GUTS: The Anatomy of the Walking Dead*, this series reflects a "new reality.... The natural disaster of the zombie apocalypse forces these precarious communities to do away with any of the old prejudices" (29). With eleven seasons (relatively 200 episodes) of content, the days leading up to the fall die away for a new world in *The Walking Dead*.

Social Zombies

Previously, I mentioned how my exploration of *The Walking Dead* Universe not only references theoretical foundations but primarily focuses on contextualizing scholarship pertaining to the concept of the fan-scholar and participatory culture. Starting with its television debut back on Sunday, October 31, 2010, *The Walking Dead* Universe has always existed in a time where viewers can discuss collaboratively using social media platforms. Online forums and tweets create a digital space for viewers to develop their own perceptions about the series, including the societal issues presented within the narrative. Since its inception in March 2006, the microblogging site known as *Twitter* (now known as *X*) has offered users a platform for exchanging information, sharing memes, and even commenting on television shows. After its television debut, *The Walking Dead* flagship series dominated cable television rankings and tweets. Viewers utilize hashtags, a digital marker that "turns any word or group of words that directly follow it into a searchable link" (Hiscott), compiling tweets about the series able to be followed in real time. Besting *Sunday Night Football* and inching out powerful dramas such as Fox's *Empire* and HBO's *Game of Thrones*, *The Walking Dead* became one of the most tweeted about series of the 2015–16 season, averaging 435,000 tweets per episode ("Empire, Walking Dead Top TV Tweets, Data Shows"; Lynch 8).

With such a rabid fanbase, the post-episode show *Talking Dead* often compiles user comments from social media for discussion with series actors and crew, special guests who also happen to be fans of the series, and, at times, a few select fans make their way to the couch to engage in post-episode banter, teasers, and perhaps my favorite aspect of the show, highlighting the deaths from various episodes, a subject that I discuss in more detail later. Taking engagement one step further, host Chris Hardwick often provides viewers with an on-air call to action by inviting them to use social media or phone into the series and ask questions, thus combining fan excitement surrounding the series and inside commentary from those closest to the show.

Of the conversations taking place about *The Walking Dead* on social media, discussions regarding the expectations of specific characters highlight a deepened understanding these viewers have about concepts such as gender normative roles. Though women often act in unconventional, often violent, ways to protect their makeshift families, these actions are not only deemed justifiable or necessary by viewers, but viewers openly champion such actions. As one viewer comments, "I love that when shit hits the fan they're gonna be shocked when carol goes rambo mode again" (Comment on "Diversity and gender roles"). Comments such as this show how gender performances, such as Carol's mastery in regressing into her submissive housewife persona, demonstrate a keen understanding of normalized gender expectations. Nevertheless, the series, and those watching it, often remind us how actions have consequences. In *The Walking*

Dead, acts of violence can be interpreted as more than just operating on instinct or for protection, especially for women. As Dawn Keetley notes in the introduction to *The Politics of Race, Gender and Sexuality in* The Walking Dead, these acts of violence align many survivors with masculine traits since violence, even if committed by women, is often correlated as a masculine trait (3). Therefore, Keetley concludes that *The Walking Dead* is not necessarily focused on performative gender roles. Instead, the series becomes a "hypermasculine fantasy" as anyone willing to engage in violence is rewarded with authoritative positions (Introduction 3). However, unlike Rambo, characters like Carol do not necessarily pursue glory or recognition but merely do what is necessary to protect others.

Unfortunately, Keetley is not alone. In "'Look at the Flowers': Meme Culture and the (Re)Centering of Hegemonic Masculinities Through Women Characters," Tiffany Christian supposes "however often the show's writers and producers might attempt to complicate its characters and storylines, fan reception has a tendency to fixate on celebrating the masculinity, even hypermasculinity, of characters" (67). Despite the humor implied through various memes representing Michonne giving Chuck Norris nightmares, referring to the popularity of Chuck Norris jokes popular years before the debut of *The Walking Dead*, Christian argues that such memes, perhaps unconsciously, disparage feminine traits. In other words, by reveling in Michonne's skill with a katana or cheering Carol's solo assault on Terminus with a rocket launcher, viewers of the series forget, even deny, the fact that these strong characters identify as women. However, these very actions transform women beyond their preconceived gender limitations. Most notable is Carol's transformative moment setting Terminus ablaze to rescue her group from the "Termites," a resident group of cannibals, in the fifth season of *The Walking Dead* flagship series. Rather than condemning or questioning her predilection of setting her enemies on fire (as she would do again in later episodes), Carol is heralded as a badass by fans (Champagne; Pugh; Rowles; Tabrys; Tassi).

Effectively using the aggregating power of social media, viewers collaboratively discuss aspects of the series, such as gendered roles and expectations. Though only sometimes in agreement about these perceptions, social media undoubtedly provides viewers a place to unite based on this mutual interest. Similarly, movements such as the #MeToo movement united individuals across the world because of hashtags. Initiated by Tarana Burke in 2006 as a means to help victims of sexual violence, "Me Too" gained considerable attention on social media when actress Alyssa Milano tweeted a call to action asking victims of sexual violence to respond with the phrase "me too." The following days resulted in nearly 325,000 responses to Milano's initial tweet (*Chicago Tribune* Staff and KT

Hawbaker; Oliver). The use of social media allows for a virtual alliance of the masses, thanks in no small part to the incorporation of hashtags. Used while watching television, social media offers viewers a chance to express their admiration or even condemnation of character actions and representations. As Erica Burman urges,

> We need to subject [performances] to analytical scrutiny, rather than allowing them to figure implicitly, or presuming some shared understandings in their taken-for-granted character. Since, within current social arrangements, we are all in some way sexed or gendered, there is a reflexive or countertransferential character to any discussion of gender and sexuality. Each of us approaches these questions from our own histories and opinions—and the fact that it is rare for anyone not to have fairly elaborate and pronounced opinions on these matters is surely an indication of how important they are [19].

Thus, using social media to openly voice opinions about character development and representation demonstrates the power of such a publicly accessible forum. Viewers cannot and will not take these series at face value. With their wide distribution on television and streaming online, series such as *The Walking Dead* and its spinoffs open themselves up for interpretation. As the numerous threads, tweets, posts, and a dedicated series talk show prove, fans of *The Walking Dead* Universe have much to say.

Let's Hear It for the Women

When I initially set out to write about *The Walking Dead*, my primary focus was on one character, Carol Peletier. But as I continued to watch and analyze the series, I found myself in awe of so many of the women in the series. Though I do not know if I have the gumption of Carol or the stamina of Michonne, I could identify with various aspects of several of these extraordinary female characters. As these female protagonists continue to develop over eleven seasons, I navigated how fans digitally catalog reactions to and debate about a narrative where the survivors must willingly perform in ways beyond any pre-apocalyptic gender role expectations. As a result, less prominent are limitations placed upon the fierce women of *The Walking Dead* through gender-laden identifiers associated with a world where the dead walk. The behaviors exhibited by the women of *The Walking Dead*, such as acting in ways not generally ascribed to their gender, not only demonstrate the capability of these characters but offer viewers powerful characters to empathize with and admire.

In particular, the evolution of women in the series from domesticated housewives to those ready and able to act mirrors the increasing number of public movements calling for equality, acknowledgment of oppression, or bringing awareness to rampant sexism. The women of *The Walking Dead* continuously demonstrate progressive growth and maintain incredible self-awareness despite constant threats posed by both the dead and the living. This conscious knowledge indicates that these women are defying expectations; they are decisive in their ability to engage in acts of violence and understand the implications of these actions. While answering fan questions during a panel discussion for a New York Comic Con, Kirkman confessed a reluctance to eliminate Carol as his "attempt to show, like, just how broken an individual can become from the zombie apocalypse ... is made stronger by all of the actually more horrible things that happened to her" ("Robert Kirkman's The Walking Dead Panel" 35:13–35:40). Elizabeth Erwin notes how "readings of the text rely heavily upon scene analysis" as they "fail to take into consideration full character arcs" (78). For Carol, her evolution from meek to mighty transpires over several seasons, which brings into focus the importance of analyzing full character arcs.

Thanks to the protection of the preliminary group, Carol eventually evolves to rely on her cunning, as demonstrated by the solo assault on Terminus. To this point, Carol Memmott argues how the "men of zombie-overrun post[-]apocalyptic America are borderline crazy and in desperate need of a reality check ... the women are focused, fearless, and walking tall" ("Among the Walking Dead, Women Stand Tall"). Though the men of *The Walking Dead* initially put up a strong front in the beginning, the women (eventually) start running the show. As viewers and scholars, we need to give them time to do so.

Over the last decade, the presentation of what of scares us has changed significantly in ways never imagined. These women and their evolving performances deserve serious discussion and exploration. With intense complexity and depth, these characters diverge tremendously from the submissive women first depicted in the series. Instead of fulfilling an expectation to bear children, these women consciously choose motherhood despite the dangers present. Instead of being disregarded, these women are incredibly cognizant of their being and capabilities. While the conversations within scholarly zombie-focused books such as *The Politics of Race, Gender and Sexuality in* The Walking Dead are wide-ranging, very few speak to these emerging positive representations of gender roles. The series continues to introduce new faces with each season on the air, such as Tara Chambler, Rosita Espinosa, and Enid or new personalities introduced in the ninth season and beyond, such as Magna (Nadia Hilker), Yumiko (Eleanor Matsuura), sisters Connie (Lauren Ridloff) and Kelly (Angel Theory), and Juanita Sanchez known commonly as Princess (Paola Lázaro), numerous character arcs and stories of survival are still open to examination. Moreover, with the promotion of Angela Kang as the first female showrunner in the show's history ahead of the ninth season, these newly introduced characters offer new and exciting levels of competence and increased diversity, including the first deaf character in the series.

The women of *The Walking Dead* are decisive, commanding, and worthy of serious contemplation for how they transcend, shatter, and destroy normative expectations of their gender. No longer meek, scared, or needing a man for protection, these women have come a long way from their duties or paying attention to washing clothes in the first few seasons. In this post-apocalyptic world, the "only 'right' action is the one that keeps you alive" (Vigna 41). For the women of *The Walking Dead*, keeping alive means acting in ways considered to be uncharacteristic of their ascribed gender roles. With each episode, a new challenge or battle ensues to test the ability of the survivors to make decisions, even violent ones, if necessary. These scenarios lead Keetley to observe that these women are rewarded for their choices to commit acts of violence, with their actions providing more fuel for the "hypermasculine fantasy" (Introduction 2). Instead, I see these actions as stepping stones for these individuals to assert their dominance in a world formerly controlled by men and now roamed by the shambling husks of former friends and loved ones. The answer is clear: the female characters I focus on in this book do not perpetuate any hypermasculine fantasy but instead maintain control of their abilities as strong and fierce individuals without a vendetta or seeking any reward or glory. *The Walking Dead* provides a break from normative roles to enter a place where women survive because of their wit and ability instead of their looks or biology.

Offering refreshingly deviant perspectives, the women I discuss beyond prescribed tropes and destroy stereotypes commonly associated with the horror genre. Women such as Carol Peletier, Maggie Rhee, and Michonne evolve from roles of submission and isolation to leading others. Moreover, these women also decide when to take on partners and choose motherhood even in the most trying times—disrupting stereotypes, Tara Chambler, Rosita Espinosa, and Enid progress away from limitations placed upon them by orientation, sexuality, and immaturity to dominant and valued roles in their respective communities. The ninth season brings increasingly diverse roles in ability and strength by introducing more divergent characters and even initiates the first female antagonist into the series. Continuing into the eleventh and final season, a new edition to the narrative presents a refreshing look at isolation and hope in the apocalypse.

During a 2015 TEDxStolkholm speech entitled "The Apocalypse Worth Spreading," Herman Geijer poses an interesting question, "Why is the zombie apocalypse relevant today?" (00:14–00:18). Given my previous discussion about representation and continuing into the subsequent chapters I aim to bring further clarification to this very question. In watching such a series, I demonstrate Geijer's assertation of how in a cataclysmic event such as an apocalypse, "our true selves can emerge" and how we can "*be the people we really want to be*" ("The Apocalypse Worth Spreading" 05:20–05:27; emphasis added). Regardless of the limitations previously placed upon identifiers such as gender, identity, or ability, each character in this book emerges anew in this televisual apocalyptic narrative. Clay Routledge echoes this notion, stating how "[in] a brutal and bloody struggle to survive in a world full of zombies, some people would find their true meaning and purpose" (251). An apocalypse, as dim as it might seem, represents an opportunity for these characters to experience a rebirth—a chance to live a different life.

Noticeably during the TEDTalk given by Geijer, our speaker changes the narrative from a man waking up in the apocalypse to use a more general term, person. Along with replacing gender, Geijer offers the following conclusion to the true purpose of zombie narratives: "I believe it's about *hope*[,] and maybe it's always been about *hope*" ("The Apocalypse Worth Spreading" 14:55–15:01; emphasis added). Hope in an apocalypse is not so absurd when considering zombie visual narratives' long history. Hope reportedly led even the greatest of all zombie narrative film directors, George A. Romero, to change the original ending to the iconic 1978 film *Dawn of the Dead* (Bailey; Rick K; Smith). In his chapter "Dawn of the Shopping Dead," Matt Bailey explains how *Dawn* experienced a change as Romero recognized exactly how "consumerism's promise of more for all (in the mall) seemed hollow" to the extent that the film's two main protagonists, Peter (Ken Foree) and Francine (Fran) (Gaylen Ross), kill themselves in the original ending (206). However, this disparaging ending changed during production to provide audiences with "*a glimmer of hope*" (Bailey 206; emphasis added). Though uncertain, the somewhat ambiguous ending leaves the audience with just that, a glimmer of hope. For Peter, Fran, and her unborn child escape in a helicopter from their former stronghold in the local mall.

Capitalizing on the Romero zombie archetype, *The Walking Dead* extends the zombie universe to incorporate the quality of blockbuster cinematography and the undercurrent of social issues into a narrative made for an elongated television narrative. For viewers of *The Walking Dead*, this extension in the storyline provides ample opportunities for strong and skilled characters to emerge. With their continuous evolution from season to season, the women of *The Walking Dead* offer hope in a world no longer held captive by a pre-apocalyptic patriarchal society. Hope drives the protagonists to keep living, doing whatever is necessary to make this happen. Hope motivates audiences to cheer on the protagonists of these narratives to keep fighting. And as for hope, Jens Manuel Krogstad declares, such narratives must imbue "a sense of optimism that suggests hope will always remain so long as goodness is not allowed to flicker and die" (par. 10). Even narratives about the zombie apocalypse, such as *The Walking Dead*, offer audiences a glimmer of hope as the story progresses and the characters persevere. As Henry Jenkins surmises, narratives persevere because stories "are meaningful to those who produce and consume them, because they satisfy our sense of what it means to be a human living in a particular cultural context" (1062). Whether verbally or visually disseminated, hope keeps the audience holding on for something. Perhaps that something is finding a cure for a rapidly spreading disease that kills and later reanimates the dead. Alternatively, perhaps, something is seeing characters, regardless of their gender, overcoming adversity and oppression to kick ass in the apocalypse.

Despite the obviously heavy focus on gender, I wanted to expand my initial research into these roles to touch upon other seldom discussed yet incredibly significant aspects of this series. Beyond women coming to dominate the storyline, other tensions, anxieties, and fears manifest in a series like *The Walking Dead* and its spinoffs. I mentioned a number of these previously, but they are worth reiterating again. Not only due women emerge in diverging roles but so does ableism, blended family dynamics, divorce, sexual orientation and identity, body autonomy, drag, addiction, abortion, death and dying, dependency on technology, and to some keen-eyed fans, references to Big Pharm. Though I'd love to cover each anxiety that makes its way into the series, my primary goal is to focus on often neglected portrayals on screen. The characters presented across *The Walking Dead*'s expensive time on screen are rich in representation and worthy of our attention. Zombies, in this regard, are not the only blank slate on which we can place our societal anxieties or tensions.

What Is This Book's Purpose?

This book focuses on how audiences engage in discussions about societal issues presented through the scripted narrative world of AMC's *The Walking Dead* and its spinoffs using social media. The social media platforms *X* and *Reddit* are essential due to their timeliness and content-rich nature. These platforms allow fans to engage in a participatory culture surrounding the series and its spinoffs during live runs and long after episodes air on television. From interpretations of character action and character development to approving or dissenting comments regarding the narrative's progression, fans offer considerable, and, at times, exceptionally poignant commentary often ignored unless you are part of the fanbase. The conversations focused on *The Walking Dead* with specific attention paid to certain series characters within the narrative emphasize the significance of fan-based interactions because of the ability for viewers to not only offer their interpretations but also can make personal connections through self-disclosure. As author Henry Jenkins explains in *Textual Poachers*, participatory culture "transforms the experience of media consumption into the production of new texts, indeed of a new culture and a new community" (39). Through social media, fans of the series not only engage in conversations about apparent societal issues such as gender roles but insert themselves and their experiences into these conversations.

The new culture created out of *The Walking Dead* manifests in the active disclosure of its fans through character analysis matched with personal experience. For myself, watching *The Walking Dead* culminated in heated debates with colleagues and long conversations with my significant other over potential outcomes of events and theories regarding the development of characters. For fans, online conversations compare the situations inside the narrative and correlate these moments with events in the real world. On *Reddit*, one viewer pinpoints the impact of one scene from "The Grove" when Carol executes Lizzie Samuels (Brighton Sharbino) and how such events, though highly dramatized, speak to difficult choices made. They state how:

> I found that episode, culminating in that scene of course, symbolic. We all have to do some really fucked up shit IRL, even though we're good people, shit that noone wants to, and in an ideal world wouldn't have to. But it's not an ideal world, and it's not in our power to make it one. OK, so the real-life fucked up shit isn't executing children, but it's just on a smaller scale [cosmic_punk].

Considering this comment, viewers demonstrate how conversations taking place online about this series dig deeper into the human condition. Also, debates manifest about the unbelievable decisions, such as participating in egregious acts of violence, these characters make to survive and protect in this apocalyptic world.

With the ascension of Angela Kang to showrunner just before the production of the ninth season, *The Walking Dead* emphasizes the ability of characters beyond gender roles and allowed more diversity to present a more inclusive cast more reflective of the audience watching the series. Uniting social media conversations focused on interpreting, giving voice, and negotiating character analyses fueled by my own curiosity about the various interpretations and applications made by viewers of the series. As

Jenkins writes, "the difference between watching a series and becoming a fan lies in the intensity of their emotional and intellectual involvement ... evok[ing] different viewing competencies than more casual viewing of the same materials" (56). Thus, I find myself an active participant in a digital zombie-fueled debate about how these fictional scenarios manifest in the real world outside of fictional narrative television.

In this book, I include "my fellow fans as active collaborators" in the exploration and analysis of this visual narrative phenomenon (Jenkins 7). By recognizing fans to be an essential aspect of interpreting popular culture texts, I allow viewers to "speak of 'artists' where others can see only commercial hacks, of transcendent meaning where others find only banalities, of 'quality and innovation' where others see only formula and convention" (Jenkins 17). After all, the series does not only fall upon the investigative eyes of scholars and academics. As recipients, audience members are not only active participants but, as Jan Teurlings notes, incredibly sophisticated commenters. According to Teurlings, an analysis of viewer comments posted to *X* and *Tumblr* demonstrates how "the interpretation of audience's worlds and professional knowledge has reached high levels, with viewers frequently talking about and assessing series the way an industry professional would" (220). The debates, conclusions, and the like about the series offered by the audience demand attention due to the dedication spent writing about and discussing the series and the incredible level of depth offered by viewer insight.

To execute this analysis of the series and conversations from fans about *The Walking Dead* Universe, my textual artifacts include: (1) Select episodes from the main series and its spinoffs that aired on the host network *AMC* and streamed to date; (2) Using exclusive series hashtags (i.e., #thewalkingdead, #TWD, or #richonne, the clever mashup of Rick and Michonne after the establishment of their romance in the sixth season) *X* or *Reddit*-based comments associated with the characters identified within this book; and (3) Opinion pieces incorporating various social media and other fan commentaries from viewers posted on various websites such as *UPROXX* or *ComicBook.com*. I feel it is critical to note that fan commentary included in this book is captured exactly as they appear online. The inclusion of these direct quotes not only helps with authenticity, but I feel it captures the very spirit of what Jenkins's meant by the participatory culture surrounding a series. It is not enough to watch an episode. Viewers devote time to discussing, analyzing, theorizing, and even arguing about what they see and interpret about the events and the characters on their screens.

The justification for using opinion pieces from websites offers a synthesized collection of viewers' comments without necessarily having to comb through the innumerable remarks left on various social media platforms such as *X*. As Jeremy Adolphson notes in their dissertation, "'We'll Get through This Together': Fan Cultures and Mediated Social Support on AMC's *Talking Dead*," a report generated from the website *RiteTag* calculated there were over 3,000 unique tweets per hour after *The Walking Dead*'s broadcast on Sundays (8). Additionally, per a Nielsen report, *The Walking Dead* averaged 435,000 tweets per episode during its third season alone (Umstead 31). Alec Bojalad reported on the website *Den of Geek* that there are more than 400,000 registered users on *The Walking Dead* subreddit (within the *Reddit* website, subreddits are subsidiary threads or categories that collectively focus on a particular topic or in this case, can focus on a television show), which make for ample discussions to analyze in the publicly accessible forum ("The Walking Dead: How AMC Harnessed"). Therefore, considering the length of the series, matched with the average given above, this book relies on a selection of compiled or archived comments given by viewers. Also, considering how opinion pieces are subject to publication restrictions, *Reddit* and *X* comments provide uncensored commentary for consideration.

By opening this analysis to include the voices of my fellow fans, matching their insight with my own interpretations through the lens of my fan experience, and backing this discussion with research, I aim to balance these two sides as part of this journey. As Matt Hills reminds us, "fan and academic identities can be hybridised or brought together not simply in the academy but also outside of it" (15). Engaging with my fellow enthusiasts in reading and cataloging their comments, I understand the role of this social media space is not only to discuss altering roles but also for the viewers to insert their perceptions and reflections of themselves in these dynamic characters. After all, without viewers continuously returning each week, streaming previous seasons, commenting on social media, attending conventions, and so forth, the show, just like the rotting dead themselves, would decay and disappear.

Chapter Overview

Chapter 1 provides an overview of the existing discussions centering on societal issues explored in this book such representations of gender in television and horror. Additionally, this chapter discusses previously chronicled debates centered on gender and sexuality, death and dying, mental health, and participatory culture surrounding *The Walking Dead* and other zombie visual narratives. Considering the expanse of *The Walking Dead* Universe, the importance of altered perceptions of societal issues like gender roles and representations of sexuality has yet to be fully appreciated or explored in a book like this one. Still, I find it essential to review the work of my predecessors to understand how *The Walking Dead* fits into a larger conversation about its usefulness as a popular culture artifact.

Chapter 2 discusses the character arcs of three dominant female leads from the series: Carol Peletier, Maggie Rhee (née Greene), and Michonne. These women not only rose to prominent ranks amongst the three main colonies but also were in full possession of agency as they made their own decisions about motherhood and relationships. However, while united in their power and choice to become mothers, each character presents a unique opportunity for analysis, given their drastically different storylines and development within the series. Interwoven through this chapter are viewer comments with my own observations of both the narrative and comments from viewers.

Chapter 3 continues with Tara Chambler, Rosita Espinosa, and Enid. Each of these characters offers quite differing personas while presenting distinct representations of sexuality, body autonomy, and breaking gender-laden norms. Despite evolving into three powerful female characters, these women embody very different representations of sexuality in *The Walking Dead* and are noticeably absent. Amongst my analysis of these three characters are viewer comments providing specific discussions about the representation of the LGBTQ+ community, the sexualized female body, and how these characters defy gender normative expectations.

Chapter 4 focuses on pays specific attention paid to the developments apparent from the start of the ninth season after the promotion of Angela Kang to showrunner, the first female to hold this role in the history of *The Walking Dead* television series. The ninth season reintroduces Judith Grimes (Cailey Fleming) as a Colt Python-wielding sage-like preteen focused on seeing the good in all humans. Born in the third season, Judith represents hope for a future as the only known child in this narrative to be born in the apocalypse. This season also brings a new crop of survivors to the Alexandria Safe-Zone, including new and diverging characters: Magna, Connie, Kelly, and Yukimo. Unique to this time in *The Walking Dead* is the introduction of Alpha (Samantha Morton), the leader of the Whisperers, a hostile group of survivors who disguise themselves with the skin of the undead and mimic their actions to blend in with them, and an exception to the predominant male antagonists of the series. Continuing into its tenth season, *The Walking Dead* introduced Princess, a vibrant character who suffers from crippling depression and loneliness, thus presenting another level of complexity to very relatable anxieties faced by characters in the series. Under the direction of showrunner Angela Kang, viewers overwhelmingly voice their sentiments, applauding and dissenting, regarding changes made in the narrative during this season and beyond.

Chapter 5 deviates slightly from an overarching analysis of societal issues to consider the representation of death and dying in *The Walking Dead*. Despite its ubiquitous and ever-persistent presence in *The Walking Dead* Universe, how death is faced by specific characters is not equal. Referencing the discussions of melancholy and melancholia by prominent neurologist and founder of psychoanalysis Sigmund Freud and philosopher and gender theorist Judith Butler, I explore specifically the demise of memorable characters and how the depiction of death is dependent on their gender. Of note in this chapter are the actions and reactions of Rick Grimes (Andrew Lincoln) and Morgan Jones (Lennie James) compared to the treatment of death and dying by the characters discussed throughout this book. From this analysis, while it is apparent death comes for all, the way these characters encounter death very much depends on their gender.

Chapter 6 expands beyond the preliminary visual narrative of *The Walking Dead* with the varying success of *The Walking Dead: World Beyond* and *The Walking Dead: Daryl Dixon* as original variations of *The Walking Dead* Universe. For these spin-offs, there is excellent potential to correct some wrongs exhibited in typecasting specific character roles. Not to say these spin-offs are utterly void of tropes, but their blank slates as series are not beholden to the storyline presented in the original graphic novel. With *The Walking Dead: World Beyond* focusing on adopted sisters, Hope (Alexa Mansour) and Iris Bennett (Aliyah Royale), and Felix Carlucci (Nico Tortorella), a close family friend of the Bennett sisters and part of a same-sex biracial couple. *The Walking Dead: Daryl Dixon* introduces the character Coco as a drag queen in a fully operational French nightclub hidden within the Paris Catacombs. Paloma, winner of *Drag Race France*, stars as Coco, and was personally asked to join the cast by Daryl Dixon actor Norman Reedus. As with previous chapters, analysis of these narratives interwoven with viewer commentary on social media provides insight to fan speculation, opinions, and evaluations of these additions.

Chapter 7 explores the potential for a series like *The Walking Dead* to join the ranks of cult television along with other prominent horror-themed serial narratives such as *Buffy: The Vampire Slayer* and *Supernatural*. What is more, the extensions of *The Walking Dead* Universe allow fans to continue favoring surviving characters, such as Daryl, or offer fans a chance to revisit previous characters and become familiar with new characters. By taking a deeper look at the trajectory of *The Walking Dead* Universe and the practices of fans, the more apparent is its status as a cult television phenomenon.

Finally, the Conclusion presents an outlook for the changing face of societal issues in the apocalypse as "survival is predicated upon the living being able to make choices that test their previous constructions of what it means to be human" in *The Walking Dead* (Balaji xi). *The Walking Dead* Universe does not appear to be stopping its spread anytime soon, as evidenced by various dovetailing series spin-offs already on air and those soon to come. Keeping an optimistic mind about the potential of these series, I add my hopes for these spawning series and the various directions they *could* take when considering the foundations laid by the original series.

1

Speaking of Zombies…

Speaking directly to the flagship series, *The Walking Dead* is arguably one of the most impactful renditions of a zombie visual narrative to date as it continued to draw millions of viewers through its finale after eleven seasons on the air (Bradley, "Spin-off"; Mathews). Joining the ranks of other notable zombie narratives to come before it, *The Walking Dead* gained considerable attention for those watching it to scrutinize, rip apart, and dissect. Given the near impossibility of addressing the entirety of this seemingly endless catalog of zombie narratives preceding and succeeding the series, let me highlight several key zombie visual narratives that have emerged in what Kyle William Bishop terms the "'Zombie Renaissance'" (*American Zombie Gothic* 12; Introduction 5). Specifically, films such as Capcom's *Resident Evil* and Danny Boyle's *28 Days Later*, which essentially jumpstarted the Zombie Renaissance in the late–1990s, are worth noting due to their status as popular culture artifacts (Bishop *American Zombie Gothic* 16; Platts "From White Zombies" 230). Jumping ahead to what Bob Burnett calls "America's Lost Decade," a decade that experienced horrors such as the attacks on September 11, a massive financial depression, Hurricane Katrina, and outbreaks such as West Nile, Anthrax, SARS, and H1N1, and considering the two hundred zombie narratives emerging in that time, zombies garnered a valuation of $5 billion (Balaji; Moran-Perez; Ogg; "2000–2009: America's Lost Decade").

On October 31, 2010, *The Walking Dead* introduced 5.345 million viewers to the post-apocalypse with brilliant simplicity in the story matched with an incredible cinematic quality (Vigna; Welch). Episodes dedicated to developing female-centric storylines emerged with Angela Kang at the helm as the series continued into its ninth season. As *Comic-Book.com* contributor Cameron Bonomolo reports, "the train is now 'being driven by women' under the stewardship of showrunner Angela Kang, who pushed for stronger and better represented female characters" ("'The Walking': Jeffery Dean Morgan Responds"). However, the promotion of Kang to showrunner in January 2018 did far more than

23

offer diverging narratives from the original comic to the television series ("Angela Kang–Showrunner"; Bonomolo, "'The Walking Dead's Michael Cudlitz"). Kang herself diverges from convention as the only female showrunner in the history of the series (Bowman). Though a contributor writer on the show, Kang's promotion to showrunner ahead of the ninth season marks a triumphant step forward in combatting the significant underrepresentation of female showrunners in television.

Dedicating more attention to developing female protagonists not only diverges from the long history of horror narratives following the triumphs of men, but women of all backgrounds and abilities come to the forefront. By presenting more diversity in the cast through new character introductions, *The Walking Dead* continues to depart from the tropes habitually associated with horror visual narratives. From its onset, *The Walking Dead* focused primarily on the actions and decisions made by men. Most notably, the first season presented men hunting, scavenging, and protecting the group while the women incessantly tended to laundry. In the second season, displaced from Atlanta, the women continued tending to laundry, making dinner, and caregiving, while men continued protecting the group now situated at the Greene family farm. Not until the third season, when the group found refuge in an abandoned prison, did the series show how roles changed as the women more frequently wielded weapons and were often called upon to make decisions as part of a council protecting the West Georgia Correctional Facility, otherwise known as the Prison. The women featured in *The Walking Dead* have progressively gained dominant roles, culminating in the departure of lead male protagonist Rick Grimes during the ninth season. With every change made to the series, *The Walking Dead* distances itself not only from its graphic novel origin but also the dominant trope typified in the horror genre: a young, White, primarily blonde, virgin female in need of a strong, cunning, non-disabled (predominately White) male rescuer.

The purpose of this chapter is to provide an overview and critical analysis of academic scholarship focusing on the representation of gender in horror. The section "Gender in Horror Visual Narratives" offers a historical context for women in horror films. Paying particular attention to Carol Clover and her notion of the "final girl," women in these narratives only seem redeemable and worth saving because of their special status as virgins. Looking more directly at *The Walking Dead*, the section "Gender and *The Walking Dead*" analyzes how scholars interpret and critique the representation of gender. Additionally, this section brings attention to notable absences in literature focused on the series, most notably the need for more analysis after Rick and the core group entered Alexandria in the fifth season. For the section "Performative Gender Roles," I discuss how the women featured in this book, more specifically Carol, are often overlooked or neglected for their contributions by other characters within the narrative. Whether we blame this neglect on gender or lack of respect by other characters, women such as Carol often act in courageous ways but receive little, if any, acknowledgment. In the last section, "Participatory Culture and the Undead," I analyze existing scholarship focused on the use of social media and *The Walking Dead*. No other scholarship has looked at *The Walking Dead* throughout the eleventh and final season. Instead, scholars often focus on a single season, or even just a single episode, for analysis, leaving behind several crucial moments in character development and discussion from fans.

Gender and the Female Body in Zombie Visual Narratives

Without insight into the cause of the apocalypse, nor any notion of its end, these characters perform familiar tasks in traditional roles until they acquire knowledge essential for survival. In this way, *The Walking Dead* departs from conventional horror films by how women gain the necessary survival know-how and through the transformation of traditional gender roles through prolonged character survival and adaptation to their apocalyptic world. Nevertheless, these changes take some time to manifest. In "Tough Women of the Apocalypse: Gender Performativity in AMC's *The Walking Dead*," Brooke Bennett argues, "it would be quite silly to assume that since the apocalypse happened about a month or so before…, social norms would drastically have altered" (88). Considering how little time separates the beginning of the apocalypse until viewers find the group camping outside the city of Atlanta in the first season, one needs to consider the previous lives and roles these characters hold to this point. Andrea Harrison (Laurie Holden), a former civil rights attorney, comes equipped with a gun given to her by her father but lacks the knowledge of its operation. For Carol, a former housewife and a mother, her expertise is restricted to performing domesticated tasks. And the list continues.

The Walking Dead further differentiates from conventional horror visual narratives in its revisioning of the "final girl" trope. Devised by Carol Clover in her work *Men, Women, and Chain Saws: Gender in the Modern Horror Film*, the "final girl" is a character who possesses many features similar to a man, from her practical nature to her name. However, she is the "only character to be developed in any psychological detail" (Clover 44) and exhibits astuteness, readiness, and sensibility. Additionally, this character presents an "'active investigating gaze'" (Clover 48), an ability typically reserved for men. That is, the "final girl" vigorously pursues, even tracks, the killer while, along the way, the audience witnesses through her eyes as she pursues the antagonist. As *The Walking Dead* progresses from season to season, the women featured in the show exude many of these characteristics with exceptionally in-depth psychological detail. From murdering two fatally ill survivors to prevent the spread of disease during the fourth season to staking out the Sanctuary in hopes of assassinating Negan, leader of the Saviors, and preventing a war between the survivor colonies in the seventh season, the women of *The Walking Dead* demonstrate careful thought about their actions, even while risking ostracism or, potentially, death.

However, despite the numerous similarities, the women of *The Walking Dead* depart from Clover's theory in many ways, especially regarding their sexuality and ability. As Clover describes,

> The Final Girl is boyish, in a word. Just as the killer is not fully masculine, she is not fully feminine—not, in any case, feminine in the ways of her friends. Her smartness, gravity, competence in mechanical and other practical matters, and sexual reluctance set her apart from the other girls and ally her, ironically, with the very boys she fears or rejects, not to speak of the killer himself [17].

Considering this description, many women of *The Walking Dead* should not have survived through all eleven seasons. This statement is especially true when considering how many engaged in some taboo sexual activity, a few becoming mothers after the apocalypse, and in the case of Rosita, employing her sexuality as a tool to gain knowledge about mechanics or other valuable skills. Furthermore, while the women work tirelessly to protect their loved ones, none of them showcase fear of their opponent, either alive or dead. Keeping their feelings concealed, such as with Carol by using her kill diary from the seventh season, or with Michonne secluding herself to talk to both the departed Rick and son Carl Grimes (Chandler Riggs) as seen in the ninth season, the women of *The Walking Dead* maintain a composure often lost on their male counterparts, a sign of incredible strength and control.

Framing *The Walking Dead* as a zombie culture icon should not obscure that *The Walking Dead* is just a tiny part of a much longer history of zombie visual narratives, especially the revolution of the modern-day zombie story by George A. Romero. Kirkman himself acknowledges the extraordinary impact *Night of the Living Dead* had on the creation of *The Walking Dead* by stating how the "'level of social commentary tucked effortlessly into that flawless horror film was awe-inducing, and is sadly still extremely relevant today'" (qtd. in Davis). Interestingly, Davis brings attention to the coincidental naming (or not) of *TWD*'s character Duane Jones (Adrian Kali Turner), son of Morgan Jones in the series, and the name of the actor who portrayed the iconic character Ben (Duane Jones) in *Night of the Living Dead*. Undoubtedly, as Kirkman recognizes, issues of racial tension and gender Romero wove so seamlessly into *Night of the Living Dead* still resonate with audiences and scholars alike even five decades after the debut of this iconic film.

Beginning with *Night of the Living Dead* and evolving into the subsequent films making up the *Dead* franchise, the female characters featured within these Romero narratives progressively develop into autonomous survivors, thus coaching the audience for "presentations of human women as active and even violent agents," as Stephen Harper notes in his work "'They're Us': Representations of Women in George Romero's 'Living Dead' Series." In *Night of the Living Dead*, Barbra (Judith O'Dea) actively and resourcefully manages on her own until finding safety with other survivors (Aiossa 29). However, where Barbra becomes almost catatonic when around others and later perishes at the hands of the ghouls, *Dawn of the Dead* presents Fran as a fully engaged and eager female lead. From her agreement to weapons training to learning how to pilot the helicopter, Fran refuses to succumb to prescribed gender expectations, showing a distinct progression compared to Barbra in *Night of the Living Dead* (Aiossa 56; Harper). In *Day of the Dead*, Dr. Sarah Bowman (Lori Cardille) quickly emerges as a commanding leader with her authority, another progression beyond the depictions of both Barbra and Fran from the first two films (Aiossa 63). Scholars such as Elizabeth Aiossa, in her book *The Subversive Zombie*, show examples of female progression beyond gender stereotypes that continue with each installment of these Romero films.

Given the near impossibility of addressing the entirety of this seemingly endless catalog of zombie narratives preceding and succeeding Romero, let me highlight several key zombie visual narratives that have emerged in what Kyle William Bishop terms the "'Zombie Renaissance'" (*American Zombie Gothic* 12; Introduction 5). Specifically, films such as Capcom's *Resident Evil* and Danny Boyle's *28 Days Later*, which essentially jumpstarted the Zombie Renaissance in the late–1990s, are worth noting due to their distinct representation of female characters (Bishop *American Zombie Gothic* 16; Platts "From White Zombies" 230). *Resident Evil*, a loose adaptation of Capcom's video game *Biohazard*, is an especially compelling artifact given its part in an impressive worldwide earning of "$1.2 billion to date" and its ranking as part of the franchise of the "highest-grossing film series ever based on a video game" (Andreeva). The first film installment (and the series in general) follows the lead female protagonist, Alice (Milla Jovovich), as she battles the aftermath of the Umbrella Corporation and the detrimental results of an infection caused by the T-virus (*Resident Evil*). In following a lead female protagonist, *Resident Evil* effectively departs from its zombie narrative predecessors. Though not following a female protagonist, Danny Boyle's *28 Days Later* presents a dynamic portrayal of a Black female survivor, Selena (Naomie Harris), and thus "moors itself in the toughness of the strong-black-woman stereotype" (Brooks 471). Selena's continuous survival speaks to her ability and is doubly significant, given her identity as the only Black woman in this film (Aiossa 73). In particular, Selena rescues lead protagonist Jim (Cillian Murphy) after he awakens from a coma almost a month after a disastrous invasion of a laboratory by animal rights activists to find the world overrun by those infected by the "Rage" virus (*28 Days Later*). Notably, as Kinitra Brooks points out in her essay "The Importance of Neglected Intersections: Race and Gender in Contemporary Zombie Texts and Theories," Selena's maternal instincts, along with her weapon of choice and resilient persona are what associate Selena as the strong Black woman (471).

Nevertheless, while both Selena and Alice manage to survive due to their skill and, especially in the case of Selena, lack of trust in others, Alice develops almost superhuman fighting capabilities as a direct result of becoming infected, a skill she uses to combat the infected (*Resident Evil*). In contrast, Selena must survive on her wit and non-genetically manipulated (i.e., more human) ability. Even though *The Walking Dead* and *Resident Evil* succeeded as adaptions of zombie narratives, *The Walking Dead*'s storyline mirrors *28 Days Later*. Both stories introduce the apocalypse through the patriarchal lens of a lead male protagonist waking from a coma to the concept of blended apocalyptic families as survivors form groups together in the narrative. Both narratives even depict a strong Black woman wielding a blade to combat the antagonists. Though Michonne embodies many of the same characteristics as Selena, her solo entry into *The Walking Dead* narrative and perceptible silence lead those around her to grow suspicious. Despite such apprehension, Michonne becomes a vital part of the core group after disclosing her past to Carl, with whom Michonne develops a robust maternal bond (discussed more thoroughly in the next chapter).

Though a plethora of subsequent films and television shows made their way to screens following the debut of these films, few (if any) can match the Box Office success of the *Resident Evil* franchise or take credit for the resurgence of zombie narratives as with *28 Days Later*. The 2009 film *Zombieland* surpassed the 2004 Zack Snyder remake of *Dawn of the Dead* as the "top-grossing zombie film in the United States" until Marc Forster's *World War Z* was released in 2013 (Gray; Nilles). Interestingly, both *Zombieland* and Snyder's *Dawn of the Dead* present diverging portrayals of female survivors, while *World War Z*, a successful adaptation from Max Brooks' book by the same name, continues the perpetuation of

White male dominance in the apocalypse. In many ways, Snyder's remake follows in the footprints of its namesake by establishing the narrative inside a typical American shopping mall and the few survivors escaping to an unknown fate. Taking the place of Fran is Ana (Sarah Polley), a head-strong nurse who survives to the end of the narrative and does so without her need to defend any future offspring. As a zombie comedy (aka the Zom Com), *Zombieland* departs from the homogenous genre of horror associated with the zombie narratives released in the United States. However, sisters Wichita (Emma Stone) and Little Rock (Abigail Breslin) find themselves in a similar predicament as Barbra in *Night of the Living Dead*. In both films, these female protagonists appear fully competent in their ability to survive until they intermingle with groups of men.

How to Be a Woman in The Walking Dead

As noted in the introduction of this book, academic scholarship dedicated to character development has yet to examine *The Walking Dead* through to the eleventh and final season. By failing to analyze all nine seasons, the existing scholarship only considers part character arcs demonstrating radical progression, especially for women. *The Walking Dead* departs from its graphic novel roots, but the series diverges from limitations reducing women to subservient roles. Overwhelmingly negative, existing scholarly analyses of gender roles in *The Walking Dead* describe women as weaker, demeaned, and submissive due in no small part to routinely being seen performing cooking, cleaning, and caregiving tasks. Nevertheless, with time, fixed gender roles have faded as women rise to prominence in the group. Indeed, generous scholarship focuses on the often described subservient or regressive roles of the wife, homemaker, and mother (Baldwin and McCarthy; Barkman; Bennett; Cady and Oates; Franklin; Garland et al.; Gavaler; Greene and Meyer; Erwin; Hagman; Keeler, "A Postapocalyptic Return to the Frontier"; Keeler, "Gender, Guns, and Survival"; Lavin and Lowe; Sugg; Zidarević), as well as the stereotypical representation of the "angry Black woman" (Abdurraqib; Aiossa; Brooks; Christian; Garland et al.; D. Johnson).

Moving further away from their former meek and submissive selves, the women in *The Walking Dead* progress into hunters, protectors, and killers, demonstrating their ability to adapt and move beyond conventions while at the same time maintaining an incredible self-awareness and agency. Unless I "missed the memo," as Amy Harrison (Emma Bell) so sarcastically quips to Jacqui (Jeryl Prescott Sales) in the episode "Tell It to the Frogs" during the first season, a zombie apocalypse has yet to happen;

these characters must resonate with audiences in some way. Including recognizable identities such as policemen, a pizza delivery boy, an attorney, doctors, and teachers introduce characters who are "so common as to almost be stereotypical" and enable the audience to identify with these individuals (Vigna 5). In *Triumph of The Walking Dead: Robert Kirkman's Zombie Epic on Page and Screen*, an anthology of essays by various authors about all things *The Walking Dead*, Bishop continues the conversation about the potential for the series to develop over the long-term run of a television series. His chapter, "The Pathos of *The Walking Dead*: Bringing Terror Back to Zombie Cinema," which emphasizes both pathos and ethos in the series, concludes how the audience "actually feels something during horror, and these psychological and physiological responses parallel those experienced by the depicted characters, creating the mirroring effect that defines the genre" (K. Bishop 3). Therefore, for *The Walking Dead* to serve as a societal mirror for who we are, the characters of *The Walking Dead* must represent who we are.

Moreover, despite the bias toward male protagonists such as Rick Grimes early in the series, other characters embark on grander evolutions in character development. As Danee Pye and Peter O'Sullivan note, the series is not just the journey of Rick but the development of multiple characters. In their chapter "Dead Man's Party," the authors argue that "taken in combination the show and the comics demonstrate that gender is a social construct, that it can be constructed differently, and that in clinging to outmoded ideas of gender roles the survivors increase the likelihood of their falling prey to the ravenous undead" (Pye and O'Sullivan 107). As for the zombies themselves, Pye and O'Sullivan observe that while the zombies are genderless, they carry the symbols of the biological sex and prospective gender distinctions, such as clothing (107–108). While the dead have no care for gender, the living reinforcing binaries or marking of gender is hardly new.

Even in George A. Romero's epic film *Night of the Living Dead*, there are notes of gender identification placed upon the undead. The various tensions characters within the modern zombie genre experience are only part of a much grander series of societal tensions. In particular, *Night of the Living Dead* not only brings to mind the racial tensions of the 1960s but also the apparent reliance female characters have on their male counterparts. Additionally, as scholar Elizabeth Aiossa highlights, such narratives manifest an overt dependency on identifying gender to humanize the undead. One example of gender identification in the film occurs when Barbra is told by Ben, "'Don't worry about him' ... 'I can handle him'" (28). Though Ben outlives Barbra and other survivors as the dead infiltrate the once-fortified homestead, his shocking death demonstrates significant negligence by those unwilling to see beyond differences such as race or gender. Michael Levine and Damian Cox note how zombies represent lingering reminders of the past, of a world that once was, and adding a familiarity, such as a recognizable face, can enhance the drama and intensity of the story. As they write,

> An uncanny reminder of the human can take numerous forms, but in the most influential zombie films, zombies are not merely uncanny remainders; they are projections of a despised and frightening aspect of ourselves. They disturb us, not merely by haunting us (i.e., the survivors we identify with as an audience) and menacing us, but by representing a despised and frightening feature of our natures. For this reason, zombie narratives need to be understood in terms of the psychological defense model of prejudice [Levine and Cox 88].

Thus, if zombies no longer care for gender, the living can reinscribe normative and limiting roles. Still, as Dawn Keetley offers in the introduction to *The Politics of Race, Gender and Sexuality in* The Walking Dead, "The characters are caught in the stark binaries of predator and prey, of living and (un)dead—the only differences that matter now" (1), binaries still exist in the series. The difference, however, is in which binaries remain. In the next section, I discuss performative gender roles and their place in *The Walking Dead* narrative. Though once a limitation for some, as scholars note, gender roles transition from restriction to an intelligent tool for survival.

Playing House in the Apocalypse

At the outset of my time watching *The Walking Dead*, quite a few moments made me squirm with disdain. While the blood and guts never bothered me, as I spent many hours watching horror films with all levels of gore, my contempt stemmed from specific actions directed at and performed by women. For instance, in the second season, when Andrea shows a preference for learning about guns, Lori Grimes (Sarah Wayne Callies) verbally confronts Andrea for failing to adhere to gender-laden tasks of cooking or cleaning while staying at the Greene family farm. Another instance appears in the first season when Shane Walsh (Jon Bernthal) quickly dismisses Carol and her offer to help the group escape from the Centers for Disease Control and Prevention (CDC) confines in Atlanta. As if reinforcing gender traditions, these scenes provide examples of how *The Walking Dead* opposes conventional roles while simultaneously demonstrating how gender roles are presumed as a limitation of ability and skill by characters in the series. Early on, Carol exemplifies a battered homemaker, Michonne exudes distrust with her constant silence,

Maggie embodies the obedient daughter, Tara assumes the tough-talking lesbian role, Rosita is the sexualized Latina, and so on.

Nevertheless, as the series progresses and characters have ample time to develop their sense of self in their new world, the audience sees these women act in ways necessary for the group and evolve beyond the expectations placed upon them by their gender. As Judith Butler asserts in *Gender Trouble*,

> Gender ought not to be construed as a stable identity or locus of agency from which various acts follow; rather, gender is an identity tenuously constituted in time, instituted in an exterior space through a stylized repetition of acts. The effect of gender is produced through the stylization of the body and, hence, must be understood as the mundane way in which bodily gestures, movements, and styles of various kinds constitute the illusion of an abiding gendered self [191].

In other words, characters such as Carol "perform" in ways others expect of her gender. By donning pastel sweaters and asking if she can join a Junior League–like organization within Alexandria, Carol plays to the assumptions of others, which allows her to gain the advantage of appearing non-threatening ("Remember").

Still, the representations from the various analyses of female characters do not necessarily or accurately depict women in this post-apocalyptic narrative. From negotiating with other survivor colonies as Maggie did with Georgie (Jayne Atkinson) in the eighth season to Michonne and the council at Alexandria deciding to allow a newly-introduced group of survivors led by Magna into their fortified walls during the ninth season, these life and death decisions come as a far cry from seemingly tame conversations about coffee makers and vibrators in the first season. In the article "No Clean Slate: Unshakeable Race and Gender Politics in *The Walking Dead*," Kay Steiger highlights blogger Courtney Stoker's application of the Bechdel-Wallace Test to the pilot episode of *The Walking Dead*. According to the report, the episode failed the test "'*hard*'" despite its hour-long run (qtd. in Steiger 104). This failure, as Stoker concludes, demonstrates a severe lack of equality for women in the series. Named after cartoonist Alison Bechdel and friend Liz Wallace, the concept originated from the 1985 comic *Dykes to Watch Out For*, as the characters within the comic strip laid the foundation for critiquing male-dominated visual narratives (Garber; Jusino). The Bechdel-Wallace Test (commonly referred to as the Bechdel Test) encompasses three questions that, for some researchers, identify evidence of male bias and gender inequality (Agarwal et al. 830). The questions in this test include: "(T1) are there at least two named women in the movie? (T2) do these women talk to each other? and (T3) do these women talk to each other about something besides a man?" (Agarwal et al. 830).

Pulling movies from the *Internet Movie Script Database* website, Agarwal et al. present a strong correlation between passing the Bechdel-Wallace Test and the level of importance the role of women played within the visual narrative (838).

However, while I admit the first episode of *The Walking Dead* would fail "hard" based on these criteria, I am reluctant to apply this determination to the entire series, and for a good reason. If *The Walking Dead* means to be this never-ending zombie movie, a judgment about the series cannot depend on a single episode. Instead, each episode is a chapter in a more extended and ever-changing zombie visual narrative. In *American Zombie Gothic*, which became available the same year as *The Walking Dead* aired on television, Bishop speaks about his hope for a prolific zombie graphic novel turned television series. Written by Robert Kirkman and directed by Frank Darabont, using a "'long-haul' approach," Bishop comments how at a minimum, "such a production, if realized, would finally give the zombie narrative the time it needs to map out the complicated human relationships that would result from a zombie infestation that ends normal society" (*American Zombie Gothic* 206–07). Stating how this zombie narrative is no longer about the zombies themselves, Bishop believes *The Walking Dead* is about human character and, speaking about Rick Grimes specifically, chronicles his life in the wake of an apocalypse (*American Zombie Gothic* 206). However, culminating in eleven seasons on the air, *The Walking Dead* moves beyond just one person's journey to a narrative dominated by complex character development, loss, and struggle. For some of these characters, this struggle means shedding the past ways and moving toward a brighter, hopefully safer, future. For audiences, watching these character evolutions on-screen provides instances of positive progression for women in a post-apocalyptic narrative.

Death and Dying in The Walking Dead

While *The Walking Dead* presents a thought-provoking case of melancholy, an exploration into the origins of melancholia needs to be considered. Before going further into Butler and the application of melancholy, attention must be paid to the work of Sigmund Freud. Additionally, along with the contemplation of Freud, additional authors will be reviewed for their interpretation and analysis of Butler's application of melancholy. From this and shifting back to the incorporation of *The Walking Dead*, a few scenes from the series will be analyzed for the appearance of melancholia.

In his chapter "Mourning and Melancholia," Sigmund Freud opens with a discussion of the peculiarity between melancholia and mourning. As he writes, "Mourning is regularly the reaction to the loss of a loved person, or to the loss of some abstraction which has taken the place of one, such as one's country, liberty, an ideal, and so on" (Freud 243). As an experience, when mourning takes hold of a person, it can cause a deviation from expected behavior. However, the severity of the deviation does not create a situation in which the sufferer may seek medical assistance for their condition. Melancholia, on the other hand, deepens the severity of pain for the sufferer to the point that there is a profound loss of interest. Freud elucidates on the peculiar mental characteristics of melancholia as "profoundly painful dejection, cessation of interest in the outside world, loss of the capacity to love, inhibition of all activity, and a lowering of the self-regarding feelings to a degree that finds utterance in self-reproaches and self-revilings and culminates in a *delusional expectation of punishment*" (244; emphasis added). It seems that in the case of melancholia, the sufferer internalizes and self-imposes blame for their intensely troubled state of being. In the exemplars presented in this chapter, blame manifests in various ways depending on the character. The "punishment" each character inflicts also differs as they feel the need to atone for their actions or the loss of their loved ones.

Despite their differences in definition, Freud points out their distinctly similar characteristics, from emotions experienced to lack of interest. To Freud,

> Profound mourning, the reaction to the loss of someone who is loved, contains the same painful frame of mind, an equal loss of interest in the outside world—in so far as it does not recall him—the same loss of capacity to adopt any new object of love (which would mean replacing him) and the same turning away from any activity that is not connected with the thoughts of him [244].

While Freud does disclose the lack of disorder of self-esteem being the only real difference between the two conditions, he does include the ability for one to explain the sensation as a determining factor for what falls closer to pathological (244).

From this notion, Freud furthers the discussion of mourning by describing how the one experiencing loss undergoes instances of fantasy. He explains how "clinging to the object through the medium of a hallucinatory wishful psychosis" causes the sufferer to purposefully discard reality instead of reveling in these fleeting moments (Freud 244). As the sufferer attempts to navigate their way through the loss, they eventually must realize that it is not the person themselves. Instead, mourning is stimulated by what is missed about the person (Freud 245). Therefore, as Freud continues, "melancholia is in some way related to an object-loss which is withdrawn from consciousness, in contradiction to mourning, in which there is nothing about the loss that is unconscious" (245). The difficulty then lies in being able to see what the person who is experiencing melancholia sees. It is an internal struggle, which the sufferer must bear alone and often, in *The Walking Dead*'s case, is dissociative. As Freud explains, the world surrounding a person in mourning becomes empty, whereas a person experiencing melancholy encounters an emptiness of their ego. From this point, the person suffering internalizes the loss and redirects the blame to themselves (Freud 246–47).

Returning to *Gender Trouble*, Butler furthers Freud's discussion of melancholy. She summarizes Freud's conclusion of the ego's integration of melancholy. Butler writes how in experiencing the loss of another, especially one that is loved, Freud argues, "the ego is said to incorporate that other into the very structure of the ego, taking on attributes of the other and 'sustaining' the other through magical acts of imitation" (78). An impression of the lost loved one becomes a way to find a connection to something recently severed. Unfortunately, by retreating into the ego, the person succumbs to melancholy, and their identity becomes inextricably tied to this new way of being. Furthermore, as explained previously by Freud, it is an internal struggle. As Butler reminds us, this struggle is an essential task of the ego as it seeks recognition (78).

Butler further explains how sadness and mourning work together to survive the experience of loss. According to Butler, "Freud suggests that the internalizing strategy of melancholia does not *oppose* the work of mourning, but may be the only way in which the ego can survive the loss of its essential emotional ties to others" (79). From here, after the internalization of loss, gender takes a formation as it tries to navigate away from the taboo and deflects this desire to another member of the opposite sex, one that does not violate the incest taboo. She goes on to include the discussion of the Oedipal complex as a young boy seeks identification by his father while also fearing castration by his father. In this dynamic, the boy chooses heterosexuality and, to avoid the taboo of incest, places his desire on a member of the opposite sex who is not his mother (Butler 79–80).

Later in the same chapter of her work *Gender Trouble*, Butler refers to an argument by Nicholas Abraham and Maria Torok, which asserts that an object is not only lost but a loss is acknowledged. This process, what the authors refer to as introjection, is the opposite of incorporation, in which the loss is retained in some way (Butler 92). Incorporation, as Butler explains, "belongs more properly to melancholy, the state of disavowed or suspended grief in which the object is magically sustained 'in the body' in some way" (92). Additionally, as a cultural institution, heterosexuality is deemed standard. Identifying as anything else would violate the cultural structure of what is the norm (Butler 96). Unfortunately, as far as *The Walking Dead* is concerned, it is normative behavior that leads to death and loss. In his chapter "A Zombie Among Men: Rick Grimes and the Lessons of Undeadness," Scott Kenemore defines normal as "an idea we invented to make ourselves feel better" than we were before (192). Specifically, Kenemore concludes that accepting change and adapting to new environments is what keeps certain characters alive (192). Again, more to come later.

Taking another look at Judith Butler's work with melancholy is author Adam Phillips. In "Keeping It Moving: Commentary on Judith Butler's 'Melancholy Gender—Refused Indentification,'" he compares Butler's conclusions about forming an identity to how Plato wanted to ban artists from replicating art. Identity, as it seems, develops from the relationships built between others. In this sense, an identification is merely reflecting a part of another. Individuals come to know themselves based on how they relate to others. A realization of their importance manifests through the loss of another. To Adam Phillips, this loss becomes reassuring even despite the pain experienced when dealing with a loss. As he states:

> The protracted painfulness of mourning confirms something that psychoanalysis had put into question; how intransigently devoted we are to the people we love and hate. Despite the evidence of our dream, our capacity for infinite substitution is meager. In this sense, mourning had been a ballast for the more radical possibilities of psychoanalysis. It is the rock, so to speak, on which Prometheus founders [Phillips].

To experience loss is to understand what the other means, both in the relationship shared with them and fully experiencing their absence.

Additionally, Phillips includes a discussion of gender. In this inclusion, he discusses not only the two sexes but realizing that there are two sexes and what this realization can mean for those who diverge from the standard. However, it is not a physical pain experienced when realizing that there are only two, but of the mind. As he concludes,

> There is a kind of intellectual melancholy in the loss of a third sex that never exists and so can never be mourned; this third, irrational sex that would break the spell (or the logic) of the two, and that is one of the child's formative and repressed fantasies about himself or herself (there is a link between this magical solution to the primal scene and fantasies of synthesis and redemption) [Phillips].

To only think about the two sexes is to create a limitation, a binary, as Phillips explains. This binary system denies personal experiences and understanding of the self. For those who identify outside the binary of two sexes, such a limitation would deny their existence altogether.

Like Phillips is an essay by Andrew Morrison entitled "Psychoanalysis and 'Necessary' Choices: The Shame of Soft Edges." In this essay, Morrison discusses the choices made regarding gender. One can choose to be heterosexual or homosexual, for instance. However, as Morrison discusses, only one choice is deemed acceptable. He writes, "One chooses to be straight, or one chooses to be homosexual; the former is normative and healthy, the latter, deviant and sick" (Morrison). Though the understanding of gender and sexual orientation has changed drastically since the time of Freud, certain behaviors and actions are still considered standard in society. While Morrison does point to how evolution has happened in psychoanalysis, he concludes his remarks with a reminder that regardless of which is selected, one ultimately must choose. Later in his essay, Morrison refers to Butler's assertion that gender is performative and a likeness of an ideal as he states, "heterosexuality representing a reflection of idealized societal norms, rather than a 'normal,' ideal—expectable sexual identity" (Morrison). Though one's sexual identity can be determined by personal choice, this choice may not necessarily reflect what is considered standard. In the next section, I touch upon how such decisions are made in *The Walking Dead*, but just as with sexual orientation, not every opportunity is deemed acceptable.

Zombies Only Care About Your Brains, Not Your Mental or Physical Well-Being

Though my initial exploration of *The Walking Dead* primarily focused on gender representation, I would be remiss to not include a bit about the other fear, anxieties, and tensions that plague the living of this main series and its spinoffs. If zombies are a metaphor for what scares us, *The Walking Dead* Universe provides a multitude of fears beyond what is causing the dead to rise. Later chapters in this book will discuss some of these issues in more detail. For now, my primary goal is to discuss how zombie narratives serve as space for exploring and testing out scenarios depicting representations of our various anxieties. In this sense, *The Walking Dead* Universe becomes a fictional playground of hypothetical models, offering the prospect for viewers to speculate various what-ifs involving the human condition.

In modern terminology, using the word zombie to describe another person supplies a cursory way to explain their behavior. For example, zoning out while mindlessly scrolling through social media posts or not being tuned into an episode or movie that is playing. The metaphor could also be applied to someone merely hearing a conversation without actively listening to what the other party might be attempting to communicate. Their mind is preoccupied or elsewhere. An article by Dr. Matt Johnson in *Psychology Today* demonstrates how the application of zombie could be used to describe someone who is simply doing what is necessary to get through the day, without much thinking or feeling involved, as if what they are doing is an automatic response ("What Zombies Teach Us About the Psychology of Consciousness").

A prime example of how *The Walking Dead* Universe presents hypothetical scenarios of the various fears, anxieties, and tensions that plague society is in its depiction of mental health, specifically depression. While I cannot say with certainty that many, or any, of the survivors depicted in this universe willingly accept their plight of battling the dead in the apocalypse, there are certainly those who capitalized on the upheaval of society. Negan comes to mind when thinking about taking advantage of this circumstance as he built a reputation for being one of the most notorious villains in the franchise. But he is only one example. Then there are those who felt the weight of insurmountable odds as droves of the undead began to rise and devour the living. Some express their struggles out loud while others suffer internally. Writing for *Den of Geek*, a website devoted to covering a myriad aspect of entertainment online, Mark Bonington concludes how at least one extension of *The Walking Dead* Universe reflects a societal tendency not to speak about mental health, especially among men.

Identifying Nick Clark (Frank Dillane) from *Fear the Walking Dead* as a prime example of how mental health is represented but hardly discussed, the author concludes how this character "serves as a metaphor for the way society too often treats mental health, particularly among young men, preferring to deny and silence them rather than admit there is anything wrong" (Bonington). Tying this lack of disclosure into the previous discussion about gender dynamics presented in zombie narratives, it seems all too common that male characters are characters of action while female characters are characters of emotion. Coping with mental health, especially when challenged by a constantly reminder of death and an uncertain future, men like Rick Grimes are often shown behaving in risky behaviors without much thought for their own safety or consequence. While Rick chooses to take out his aggression with an axe, characters like Nick are depicted relying on other harmful behaviors such as drug addiction.

While there are typified behaviors that could easily be identified in analyzing a series like *The Walking Dead* or any of its extensions, the characters presented in these narratives are exceptionally multi-faceted, as they are meant to reflect the very dynamic world in which we live. While there are some characters who very much fit a mold, there are equally many who continuously break those molds, especially when there is space for them to transform over several episodes or seasons of a series. The continuation of a narrative over a decade affords this space as audiences are granted the ability to witness beloved characters fully develop. As a popular culture artifact that is not only meant to reflect society and what ails it, but the viewers of these series also consume and dissect these developments in a mixture of conversations they have with other viewers. As discussed in a moment, viewing a series is now a social event with fans from across the globe coming together in online spaces to have these very conversations. Adding more to this discussion are those who might not only identify with these struggles but find solace in discussing these representations with others.

Participatory Culture and the Undead

Observing television series like *The Walking Dead* or its various extensions no longer remains an isolated activity. Viewers from across the globe post, tweet, hashtag, and so on their opinions about a show as it airs live. As Yun Jung Choi writes in the article "Emergence of the Viewing Public: Does Social Television Viewing Transform Individual Viewers into a Viewing Public?," "television viewers have started using second screens, such as tablet computers or smart phones, to connect to web-based media and SNSs (Social Networking Service) to connect to others who are watching the same program, to be able to share their viewing experiences" (1059). Through social media, watching television has become a social activity unrestricted by location or time as viewers actively participate in the discussion. Coined by Henry Jenkins in his work *Textual Poachers*, the notion of "participatory culture" moves beyond merely enjoying popular culture artifacts. According to Jenkins, the typical response from fans involves "not simply fascination or adoration but also frustration and antagonism, and it is the combination of these two responses which motivates their active engagement with the media" (23). Viewers not only favor a popular culture artifact, such as a television series, but often are moved to comment, dissent, and in some cases, actively create new content to satisfy a need.

Thanks to microblogging services such as *X*, introduced in 2006 as *Twitter*, viewers can actively engage with others in astonishing numbers as new series episodes air each week. Using social media metrics to gauge interaction, *The Walking Dead* repeatedly bests television powerhouses such as Fox's *Empire* and even *Sunday Night Football* with an "average of 3.2 million interactions across Facebook and Twitter per episode," bringing in the largest audience in the 18–49 demographic aside from of sports during its 2016 run in addition to "CBS' 'The Big Bang Theory' and

'NCIS' in total viewers" the year prior (Berg 22; "Empire, Walking Dead Top TV Tweets, Data Shows"; Kissell; Rose; Umstead 31). These numerous exchanges are prime for study since social media "allows audience members to interpret television messages at the social level, which can lead to more diverse discussions about the contents featured in television shows, potentially leading to discussions about public issues" (Choi 1060). Therefore, as viewers actively engage on social media, these conversations reveal a more profound awareness of the interpretations of the character portrayals in the series. More specifically, analyzing the discussions between viewers of *The Walking Dead* offers insight into how viewers relate to the characters and negotiate identities regarding the gender representations apparent within the narrative.

However, despite *The Walking Dead* exiting in the age of active social media engagement, as well as the mind-boggling numbers demonstrating such a lively participatory culture centering on the series, few articles focus on this overlap between social media use and watching *The Walking Dead* (Adolphson; Brojakowski; Christian; Pasztor and Korn; Tenga and Bassett; Teurlings). On the other hand, while dominating Box Office ratings, horror films lack the ability for viewers to participate actively in discussions. Given the darkness of the theater and the numerous reminders to silence phones, using devices to communicate with others during the show is not quite suitable. Moviegoers must wait until after the curtain closes and exit theaters before tweeting, posting, tagging (thanks to hashtags), or whatever other actions associated with using social media. Even still, the active engagement of a virtual conversation on *X* is lost because of the typical "likes" associated with static photographs or short video clips posted on platforms such as *Facebook* or *Instagram*. Even when considering previous analyses of participatory culture and *The Walking Dead*, discussions limit the scope to one season or even just one episode. Besides meme culture, none have discussed how audiences react or interpret gender norms through social media.

Though Jenkins introduces television viewer opinions in *Textual Poachers*, demonstrating their devotion to popular culture artifacts, fans are generally marginalized or utterly absent in larger academic discussions. He argues that to "speak as a fan is to accept what has been labeled a subordinated position within the cultural hierarchy, to accept an identity constantly belittled or criticized by institutional authorities" (Jenkins 23). After reading Jenkins's comments about fan culture and academics, I find it clear that fans and their popular culture texts need more attention paid to them in academic discussions. The makeup of these fans is even more compelling beyond the activity outside the creation of popular culture artifacts such as television shows or comic books. As Cornel Sandvoss states in *Fans*, "fan activities and discourses revolving around popular televisual texts are often driven by female fans" while also "drawing on apparently masculine genres of popular culture such as wrestling, soccer or action and horror films [that] can thus be identified as a subversion of existing gender/norms and their accompanying power relations" (16–17). Despite the overtly masculine characters bolstering traits of violence and gore apparent in the series, *The Walking Dead* extends beyond these qualities by providing strong divergent characters to whom a broader viewing audience can relate.

Combining audience participation through social media with events in the series or character development with a specific focus on gender roles has not been undertaken across the scope of the series. In *The Walking Dead*, one silences the zombies with a blow to their brain. Scholars silence fans by excluding them from academic discourse. Fans using social media candidly discuss (both positively and negatively) roles in the series or the series in general. Additionally, as Roberta Pearson remarks in "Fandom in the Digital Era," digital transformation of communication "has had a profound impact upon fandom, empowering and disempowering, blurring the lines between producers and consumers, creating symbiotic relationships between powerful corporations and individual fans, and giving rise to new forms of cultural production" (84). Unrestrained fans use tweets, posts, and the like to express their favor or dissent of character actions, representations, or series of events.

Viewers of a series establish connections through character identification and relationships with other viewers, thanks to the identification of similar interests in a series via social media. In "Spoiler Alert: Understanding Television Enjoyment in the Social Media Era," Benjamin Brojakowski emphasizes the significance social media has in terms of television viewing enjoyment. Employing the Uses and Gratifications Theory (UGT), which establishes a sequence in seeking out certain media by audiences, Brojakowski writes,

> First, people are active participants in choosing media. Their reasons for choosing a particular media are goal-directed, purposive, and motivated. Second, the media does not use people. People actually use media to satisfy their needs and desires or seek information. Third, social and psychological factors mediate people's communication behavior. Past experiences, paratexts, and interpersonal interactions impact the ways people are drawn to and use media. Fourth, media competes with their forms of communication for selection, attention[,] and use to satisfy people's needs. Last, people are usually more influential than media in this process because individual initiative mediates how media is used [25].

In other words, regarding viewing a series such as *The Walking Dead*, there is an active selection process choosing what to watch on television. On social media, fans seek digital conversations to deliberate or voice opinions in a community united by a mutual interest in the series.

As a participant in social media interaction through posts and tweets, the boundaries dividing viewers disappear to create one extensive viewing community. Explicitly focusing on *The Walking Dead*, despite the numerous analyses mentioned previously, only some use social media as a tool for investigating fan commentary about the series. For the select few who do, the topics vary from violence to the morality of actions. Even still, given the overwhelming number of tweets and interactions generated per episode, some use the series spinoff *Talking Dead* as the focal point for analysis. For example, in an article by Sabrina Pasztor and Jenny Ungbha Korn titled "Zombie Fans, Second Screen, and Television Audiences: Redefining Parasociality as Technoprosociality in AMC's #Talking Dead," the authors conclude "the contemporary act of television viewing as part of a *digital participatory culture*, then, along with the impact of social media and Internet technology on changing perceptions of family, agency, interaction, and community, brings inherent tensions to light" (Pasztor and Korn 184). *Talking Dead*, a live television aftershow led by host Chris Hardwick first appeared on television following the 2011 season premiere of *The Walking Dead* (Ng). At Hardwick's command, using the hashtag #deadlive, fans actively direct comments and questions to the show, which can be answered by guests such as *The Walking Dead* performers, producers, showrunners, and celebrity fans of the series.

Though Pasztor and Korn focus on how social media becomes a tool for establishing a comprehensive viewing community, their analysis needs actual fan commentary. Instead, Pasztor and Korn favor an overarching approach to discussing the transition from letter-writing campaigns and fan-created media that Jenkins heavily utilizes in *Textual Poachers*. However, fans participating in social media are vocal about *The Walking Dead*. Topics of interest to scholars when considering the use of social media involve the loss of characters, consideration of gender through memes, and the gratuitous use of violence in the series. In one such work, a dissertation titled "'We'll Get through This Together': Fan Cultures and Mediated Social Support on AMC's *Talking Dead*," Jeremy Adolphson focuses on the use of *Talking Dead* to discuss the deaths of two specific male characters, T-Dog in the third season and father of Maggie Rhee, Hershel Greene (Scott Wilson) in the fourth season.

According to Adolphson, harnessing the power of social media to fuel the talk show demonstrates the transition and ability to incorporate a more active fan community. He writes, "Social media, as a communication medium, is transforming the potential and potency of fandom through increased affordances of interaction, and also is allowing for a rhetorical reconceptualization of what it means to be a fan" (Adolphson 1). Thus, being a fan becomes more than just an act of watching but one of active participation and discussion. While Adolphson spends most of the writing discussing the power of social media in fandom, the work is limited by examining the reaction to these two deaths, how Chris Hardwick addresses fans on *Talking Dead*, and protocols established for expected behavior or decorum when engaging in social media interactions.

Similarly, in "Violence, Paratexts, and Fandoms: *The Walking Dead* as a Societal Mirror," Jessica Lolli examines the deaths of two leading male characters, the husband of Maggie, Glenn Rhee (Steven Yeun) and Sergeant Abraham Ford. Focusing explicitly on one episode as a case study, the seventh season premiere episode, "The Day Will Come When You Won't Be," Lolli pays specific attention to how audiences draw limits on the level of violence (2). Through posts mostly found on *Reddit*, an online community discussion board of sorts, and posts on *X*, Lolli determines that the "audience's negative feedback resulting from this controversial and violent episode not only facilitates the fan participatory culture and serves as another paratext for *TWD* [*The Walking Dead*], but also acknowledges that there is a conversation that both fans and produces engage in" (33). In other words, not only did fans of the series vocalize their displeasure at seeing two beloved characters perish, but they overtly commented on the intensity of violence for these characters' deaths.

Social media is not only for fans of the series but a way for producers and creators to gauge audience reception of episodes and an ever-growing repository for commentary—both positive and negative. Differing from the work of Adolphson, Lolli also includes how producers of the series, specifically Executive Producer Gale Anne Hurd, comment on fan reactions to disturbing events such as this death scene, which showcases antagonist Negan sadistically bashing in the head of Glenn with a baseball bat, from the seventh season. She writes how Hurd "reacted to the controversy the fans created regarding the level of violence in episode 7.1 at a panel discussing television violence and stated that the producers read what fans had to say about the episode and understood that the level of violence crossed the line" (34). For a television show synonymous with violence and gore, Lolli underscores the powerful connection fans can form with favorite characters and how quickly fans are to dissent when violations, such as the particularly egregious violence committed against these two favored characters, occur. Unfortunately, as with Adolphson, the limited scope of this analysis prohibits any consideration of other characters, especially in their reaction to witnessing this grotesque action. Additionally, absent from both studies is the discussion of gender in *The Walking Dead*.

Despite the limited scope of one episode or one season, these scholars excellently highlight how combining watching television with active participation through X creates a powerful social tool. Shifting away from the interest in fan reactions to violence and loss, the work of Tiffany Christian looks at the use of memes to communicate interpretations of gender roles in *The Walking Dead*. In her article "'Look at the Flowers': Meme Culture and the (Re)Centering of Hegemonic Masculinities Through Women Characters," Christian concludes how the primarily textual focus of previous analyses leaves "unanswered questions about how audiences respond to and build upon the narratives provided"; she closes a gap of sorts by analyzing fan reactions through meme culture (67). Specifically, Christian notes how various "masculine-coded behaviors" from characters such as Carol and Michonne manifest in audience-created textual images, also known as memes (67). Memes, in a sense, are created by taking a digital image, such as a still shot from a film or television series, placing text over the image, and circulating on the Internet through various social media platforms such as X or *Facebook*.

Though memes are primarily static, with text allowing for the image to communicate a particular message, Christian notes how memes align character actions with male action heroes from before the time of *The Walking Dead*. For instance, Carol and her continuous transformation into a lethal killer appear in memes equating her to the skill level of Ellen Ripley from the *Alien* franchise, but according to Christian, ultimately align with male action heroes John Rambo from the *Rambo* franchise or even the Terminator from *The Terminator* franchise (73). However, despite the negative interpretations of her masculine-coded actions, Christian notes the preference of fans to see Carol in a position of strength rather than her initial appearance as the meek and battered housewife (74). For Michonne, her ability to take control appears empowering but, at the same time, "perpetuat[es] a culture of silence around and erasure of real suffering by African American women in order to maintain that image of 'strength'" (Christian 71). Her skills with a katana appearing in memes associating her aptitude with the stereotype of the "Strong Black Woman," Michonne distances herself from her White female counterparts thanks to a reinforced presence of masculinity as an aggressor (Christian 70–71).

Instead of demonizing women for their actions or equating them to hypermasculine fantasies, social media offers viewers an opportunity to gain insight into the thoughts, opinions, and interpretations of those consuming the series. In fact, in an article titled "Social Media and the New Commons of TV Criticism," Jan Teurlings advocates for serious consideration of such opinions. Though limited to the fourth season of *The Walking Dead*, Teurlings notes how such application of industry-specific language into audience commentary demonstrates an incredible level of sophistication. Specifically, viewers of *The Walking Dead* "display quite profound inside knowledge about the industry's working methods, the main players and their creative signatures. In a way, it seems as if these viewers have become semi-professional television critics" (Teurlings 220). Considering the ability to apply industry concepts, my attentive reading of fan commentary offers remarkable insight into how the broader public interprets *The Walking Dead*. The comments included in the following chapters reveal fans' astute capability to engage in conversations about the series. At the same time, these comments offer interpretations of gender expectations, sexuality and sexual identity, heteronormativity, addiction, and so much more. These comments validate the analysis of the incredibly progressive changes for the characters in the series and provide insight into fans' reception of these changes. In this way, the examination of what plagues us moves beyond the analysis of just one person to consider the grander conversation and interpretations made by the driving force of the series, the audience.

Speaking of Zombies: A Reflection

Undoubtedly, the zombie narratives discussed in this book are only a small part of an already extensive history of storytelling. The zombies themselves carry the tremendous weight of having all the fears, tensions, and anxieties placed upon them by the culture that uses them. Thanks to the brilliance of Romero, the zombies in these visual narratives are meant to be scary because they represent everything that scares us. Unfortunately, what scares us appears to be as inexhaustible as the dead themselves with new and emerging frights appearing daily. Still, watching zombie narratives can teach an audience so much about why and how these fears manifest in society as well as how the living handles those fears. In moments of extreme stress and strife, these characters make choices for the good of themselves and those around them. Often, these actions call into question our own actions as we watch these stories unfold. In this sense, our moral compass is tested by our reactions to the events on screen and the conversations we have with others. With social media making these discussions easier to have, audiences turn to places like *Reddit* and *X* to express their thoughts, sometimes finding support and other times starting heated debates. Thankfully, these conversations provide great insight into how audiences receive these depictions and gauge their believability. It is those conversations that will be the focus of this book as these series would not exist without the rabid fanbase of fully astutely sentient viewers are ready to consume them.

2

Badass Apocalyptic Leaders

The Queen, the Widow,
and the First Lady

When *The Walking Dead* debuted its first season in 2010, the series drew an impressively sized audience of six million viewers. Out of those tuning in for the first season, four million landed in the adult 18–49 demographic, making *The Walking Dead* the most-watched drama series in basic cable history for this age group ("AMC's The Walking Dead is the Most Watched Drama Series"; Berg 22; "Empire, Walking Dead Top TV Tweets, Data Shows"; Kissell; Lavin and Lowe 114; Rose; Umstead 31). Although this viewership is undoubtedly remarkable, numbers are only so telling of how viewers received the series. As discussed in the previous chapter, fan participation plays a central role in articulating approval or displeasure for television shows such as *The Walking Dead*. With the power of social media, viewers join a global discussion about the series, sending off thoughts in rapid-fire through tweets and posts focusing on the reinforcement of stereotypical horror tropes apparent in the series. An example of such dissent comes as one viewer asks, "Is it me or has the black guy on walking dead been entirely irrelevant this entire season thus far? #thewalkingdead" (@Hanzi83) about Theodore "T-Dog" Douglas (IronE Singleton). Another calls attention to character Glenn Rhee with the tweet, "Finishing up S2 of Walking Dead. So, what you're saying is: the world has to end for a little Asian guy to get some hot ass? #walkingdead" (@edpachecano) regarding the start of Glenn's relationship with Maggie in the second season.

Collectively on social media, viewers align with the thoughts of scholars in the limitations set upon gender and racial roles depicted in the earlier episodes of the series. One such tweet laments how "Clearly, The Walking Dead writers DO NOT know black women. #TheWalking-Dead" (@BoySoprano) possibly about character Jacqui, the only prominent Black woman in the first season. Another viewer tweets how the "Last ep of Walking Dead was brilliant! If I was one of those women though, I'd just refuse to work unless the men started. #thewalkingdead" (@pixiegigs). Indeed, these six episodes of the first season offer very little character progression or action beyond the reconciliation of Rick and his family. By the second season, the leading group spends a majority of its time attempting to find Carol's lost daughter, Sophia Peletier (Madison Lintz), as well as fighting for a chance to reside at the Greene family farm, a deceptively tranquil location, seemingly untouched by the hordes of undead. That is, unless you look in the barn.

Of course, these episodes have their fair share of scenes featuring women performing domestic chores such as cooking, cleaning, and childcare. Through the first six episodes of the series, the men hunt while the women clean, a sequence typified by the second season. Still, in just these two seasons, viewers behold many new faces, with Maggie Greene (later Rhee) and Michonne being two notable introductions while also witnessing many gruesome and saddening deaths. While characters such as Carol, Maggie, and Michonne appear considerably dissimilar from each other and their placement in the narrative, these characters eventually become dominant figures essential to the storyline, especially starting in the third season. Forced to leave the peaceful setting of the Greene farm and to make a home behind the fences of an abandoned prison, these women begin life anew as they encounter the horrors of the world head-on. Even Amanda Keeler, in the essay "A Postapocalyptic Return to the Frontier: The Walking Dead as Post-Western," notes how the third season marks a turning point for the women of *The Walking Dead*. She writes, "From this point forward, many of the female characters develop into post–Western heroines, working alongside other men and women to ensure everyone's safety" (Keeler 430). No longer dependent on men for safety, not that Michonne ever was, these women emerge as fighters.

This chapter, using both social media comments and my analysis of select episodes beginning with their introductory installments to the final season on the air, discusses the evolution of Carol, Maggie, and Michonne. These women embark on a journey of hardship, loss, and triumph. Additionally, at one point during the series, each of these women identifies as mother, by choice. As the only remaining female character from the first season and therefore receiving a more extended discussion, Carol begins her journey with her separation from her pre-apocalyptic identity as a battered housewife and mother to become one of the strongest women in the series. Maggie starts as the archetypal farmer's daughter evolving to become the matron and protector of her family after the saddening (and shocking) passing of her father and her husband. Her matriarchal obligations later extend beyond her family when she becomes the appointed leader of Hilltop. Finally, Michonne, as the longest-running and leading Black character in the series, evolves from a character stuck in "flat, rigid or stereotypical roles" to challenge the "patriarchal assumptions and gender categories" instituted in the series preceding her arrival in the third season (Abdurraqib 228). Michonne not only demonstrates a zombie-ready superiority to the other women mentioned in this chapter, but her strength aligns her equal ability to her eventual partner and lead series protagonist, Rick Grimes.

The Queen, Kicking Ass and Baking Cookies: Carol Peletier

Hardly uttering a word in the first season, Carol enters *The Walking Dead* as a sheepish mouse of a woman who seems to constantly fear her own shadow. Choosing to pacify her abusive husband, Ed Peletier (Adam Minarovich), Carol "turns to marriage as a form of hope-for protection, though bringing into marriage neither social nor economic power, thus entering that institution also from a disadvantaged position" (Reich 22). Though never shown onscreen, it is without question that Carol endured unspeakable mistreatment in exchange for her protection and the safety of her daughter, Sophia. Not until the devasting loss of her daughter after the horrific death of her husband does Carol find liberation and rebirth in the apocalypse. From this loss, Carol begins her journey as a post-apocalyptic heroine with a penchant for setting oppressors ablaze. Still retaining her motherly intuition and purposefully masking herself with a housewife persona, Carol evolves from a battered victim to a master of manipulation thanks to her incredible awareness of the expectations of her gender. Using her ability to disguise herself and blend in with the people of Alexandria, Carol often escapes notice long enough to fulfill her objective.

The adaptation of Carol in the television series not only long outlives her comic book counterpart but far exceeds the expectations of her character to evolve into anything beyond a hapless damsel in distress. As viewers conclude, the "only thing comic carol and show carol have in common is the name carol" (EvilSporkOfDeath). A character of high complexity, Carol brings a renewed sense of independence and perception. Free to make her own decisions but ever the protector, show Carol, referring to the quote above, decisively acts in what she feels to be the best interest of the group, even though her actions might be perceived as a threat to male authority. Choosing when to strike, when to go into "cardigan mode," a method of disguise Carol employs as a way to appear unassuming to others while the core group resides in Alexandria, when to have a partner, and even when to become a mother again, Carol transforms from passive conformity to a woman of action and authority.

Shedding a Pre-Apocalyptic Identity and the Evolution of an Apocalyptic Heroine

Shifting away from the defenseless and meek housewife, Carol begins a new journey when two crucial aspects of her former self die away. First, with the loss of Ed, Carol frees herself of the constraints placed upon her by the domination and abuse of her controlling husband. Second, with the loss of her daughter, Carol relieves herself of the guilt from her inability to protect Sophia, thus extending Carol to assume the role of a protective motherly figure to her apocalyptic family. When Carol first emerges in the third episode of the first season, her time on screen is limited to a few vague background shots and a couple of short sentences demonstrating her complacency and subservience. Managing to give Shane Walsh a content response to his welfare after a confrontation with Ed, Carol mollifies potentially volatile situations by apologizing profusely as if she were responsible for Shane's actions against Ed. When confessing "[i]t's just the way it is," after Jacqui questions the division of labor as the women tend to laundry, Carol's contribution to the narrative barely extends beyond that of a secondary character ("Tell It to the Frogs" 00:38:05–00:38:09). Instead, Carol mainly directs her attention to being unnoticeable as she quietly and obediently serves her husband, constantly checking over her shoulder as Ed continuously monitors her every move.

Eventually, as the story progresses, Carol navigates through other stages in her development to become a hero in the apocalypse. By the third season, the group establishes a stronghold in an abandoned prison, and, after clearing the site of walkers, they manage to transform the West Georgia Correctional Facility, known as the Prison into a suitable homestead by the fourth season. With Rick taking up farming and other group members finding new roles, Carol finds herself extremely useful compared to her scared-of-her-own-shadow persona from the first two seasons. For Carol, her daring journey begins with her rebirth in the apocalypse, though not in a conventional sense. Instead, her ascension in this world of destruction begins when her pre-apocalyptic signifiers dissolve. Fulfilling a call to adventure to reference Joseph Campbell's monomyth, Rick exiles Carol as punishment for what Rick considers a particularly egregious act, which I will discuss in more detail next.

First, let me preface this discussion with a hypothetical situation. Let's say after countless months of scrounging for food, avoiding failing prey to the undead, and so many nights of restless sleep due to the uncertainty of your safety, you finally come upon a fortified structure that is stable enough to withstand hordes of the undead thanks to a series of security fences lining the perimeter of a prison. Within the perimeter, not only do you find proper shelter ostensibly free of the undead, but the grounds outside the Prison within the security fences provide ample space for raising crops and domesticating animals. At long last are you and your group able to settle down and even though the threat of the undead still linger around the fence, you're safe. What length would you go to protect it? *The Walking Dead* as a series fantastically establishes situations such as this that call for speculation and contemplating the "what ifs" presented within the narrative. For Carol, it seems she would do what others cannot fathom. As a preventative measure, Carol kills two members of the Prison, Karen (Melissa Ponzio) and David (Brandon Carroll), when both fall ill with a potentially fatal illness ("Infected"). Rick, just before her banishment, says, "You're not that woman who was too scared to be alone. Not anymore. You're going to start over, find others, people who don't know, and you're gonna survive out here. You will" ("Indifference" 00:38:54–00:39:15). To this point in the fourth season, Carol survives only by the help of others. Then, with her expulsion from the Prison, Carol crosses the first threshold, where she tests her ability to survive alone (Campbell 34).

In reviewing what others analyzing *The Walking Dead* concluded about Carol's actions, I found that several concluded how unpredictable actions, such as Carol's profound choice to kill Karen and David to save others, threaten the patriarchal authority represented by Rick and also a violation of trust established between herself and those living in the Prison (Lavin and Lowe 121; Vinney and Wiley-Rapoport 212). As Kelly Franklin posits, "The horror that Rick appears to feel, and that some audiences felt, was that Carol was a woman doing this very necessary evil—a task historically relegated to men" (10). In making the executive decision to prevent the spread and potential further infection, an effort proven unsuccessful as the episode shows, Carol not only poses a lethal threat to others in the Prison, but she could potentially usurp Rick and his hegemonic authority.

Using social media to discuss the evolution of Carol since her liberation, viewers transcend into a new dimension of viewership exclusively held by industry professionals through keenly established connections as well as apply business lingo. In this case, viewers debate the decision of Rick to expel Carol for her indiscretion. As one viewer on *Reddit* writes,

> Damn, I really liked Carol. The world before was very soft, nobody really operating solely on the principle of survival. Unfortunately, the world became hard, and so too must the people in it. It sucks to see one of the original characters have to leave because she was too realistic for the group to handle, still tryna hold onto that soft mindset [Vhu].

Not in the minority, comments suggesting Carol acted in the best interest of the group and subsequently undermined Rick not only show how much Carol progressed but potentially marked her removal from the show. Another Reddit viewer writes, "Carol's sure getting a lot of character development ... we all know what that leads to" (N8_the_almost_GR8). I'd like to expand upon this remark just a bit. Historically in this series, characters who demonstrate signs of progression somehow die before their characters can fully develop or show any true potential. For Andrea, her transgressive act of learning to shoot guns rather than perform domestic tasks, in addition to her sexual encounters with both Shane and the Governor, led to her death in the fourth season. For T-Dog, his increasingly vocal persona and shift away from a subdued minority character leads to his death in the third season. Though Carol defies this assumption in forthcoming episodes, it would seem the only character granted permission for any character development in this apocalyptic narrative is Rick Grimes.

Because of Carol's choice to protect the group, her banishment shows how the women in *The Walking Dead* are damned if they do and damned if they don't act. Though she might be working in the best interest of the group, actions have consequences, especially for women. In the article "'Look at the Flowers': Female Evolution in the Face of the Zombie Hordes of *The Walking Dead*," authors Cynthia Vinney and Caryn Wiley-Rapoport note how "[d]espite their evolutions into resilient survivors, both Andrea and Carol are punished for their transgressions of gender stereotypes" (212). These punishments have not gone unnoticed by viewers of the series. One *Reddit* poster comments, quite poignantly, how "Women characters on TV can't fucking win. When she's helpless and annoying nobody likes it, when she kicks ass and takes names she gets called a bitch" (possiblyhysterical). By Carol appearing meek and helpless in the first few seasons, her fellow survivors and fans quickly dismiss her as just another victim of the apocalypse. Then, evolving into a stronger, more action-oriented position, not only does Rick appear threatened by Carol's assertiveness, but some viewers cast her off as insensitive. Exemplifying this negativity toward Carol comes a follow-up comment in reply to the comment mentioned above. Stating how they "wouldn't call what carol is doing kicking ass," the viewers continue by adding how "Michone is kicking some ass, carol is killing sick people and calling kids, who don't stab their dead father's brain, pussies" (initialZEN). Of particular note in this comment is in relation to Carol's tough behavior toward sisters Mika (Kyla Kenedy) and Lizzie Samuels, two girls entrusted to Carol after the death of their father, Ryan Samuels (Victor McCay).

Just before leaving with Rick, Lizzie accidentally refers to Carol as "mom," an action Carol is quick to correct ("Indifference" 00:03:33–00:

03:34). Though she promises to protect the siblings, Carol agrees to only their protection rather than become a substitute parental figure. Only when she chooses to be a parent does this title again become part of her identity. For viewers, her reaction to Lizzie registers cold and threatening. As this *Reddit* poster remarks, "'Don't call me Mom.' Damn, Carol has gotten a lot harder" (BVTheEpic), while another responds, "You would have to be that way, to survive. At least she uses her hardness to do what is necessary for the group" (waryoftheextreme). Regardless of her growing toughness, Carol chooses when and how to act, even if her actions are questionable and, as evidenced by her banishment, threatening for the male authority figures.

Perhaps one of the most painfully shocking moments, wherein Carol decides to execute Lizzie after murdering her sister Mika, essentially sends Carol on the next evolution of her journey. Lizzie, as viewers point out, is disturbingly unbalanced with signs of her apparent lack of comprehension for this apocalyptic setting manifest in her naming and feeding of the walkers ("30 Days Without an Accident"). Ever the protector and never really leaving the proximity of the Prison, Carol reunites with Tyreese Williams (Chad Coleman), Lizzie, Mika, and baby Judith Grimes (Charlotte and Clara Ward). With Tyreese assuming the role of caregiver for Judith and placing the blame for not seeing the signs on herself, Carol knows the responsibility of killing Lizzie falls upon her. At this moment, Vinney and Wiley-Rapoport note, "when Carol dispatches the unstable Lizzie, she assumes leadership due to her desire to protect others in her group, especially baby Judith" (215). Taking Lizzie out to a field of flowers and unable to hold back her tears, she asks Lizzie to "just look at the flowers," a technique Mika used to calm down her sister when Lizzie experiences panic attacks; Carol fires a single shot to bring an end to Lizzie ("The Grove" 00:35:50–00:35:57).

Despite its emotional intensity and perhaps to lighten the mood after experiencing such a wearying moment, this episode was the butt of a joke by television personality Josh Gates (of *Expedition Unknown* and *Destination Truth* fame). Tweeting, "Like I always say: the true cost of the apocalypse will be the serious shortage of quality babysitters. #WalkingDead #JustLookAtTheFlowers," Gates pokes fun at this unsettling moment with a reference to a pigeonholed gender role (@joshuagates). While this tweet could be read in many ways and lacks any identification other than the hashtag #JustLookAtTheFlowers, the implication is that Carol lacks any potential other than being a "quality" babysitter reads overtly sexist. For Tyreese, proves himself as a loyal aid in helping Carol with her successful protection of Judith and her return to her father, Rick, as well as offering his forgiveness for her transgressive deed.

Ultimately, the culmination of Carol's journey and transformation into an "unkillable badass with a ridiculously high body count" (Kurp) comes in the fifth season premiere. As Rick and the others reunite in a trainyard called "Terminus," an apt and somewhat ironic name given the community of cannibals running the place under the direction of Gareth (Andrew J. West), Carol learns about the community from a Termite, referring to the residents within the colony, Martin (Chris Coy). Covering herself in walker guts, a maneuver reminiscent of Rick and Glenn in Atlanta during the first season, Carol disguises herself as one of the dead and approaches Terminus without exposure. As if paying tribute to Romero's *Land of the Dead* film, Carol fires her rifle at a propane tank set outside the compound while launching one of the firecrackers Martin used to deter walkers into the exposed gas. The resulting explosion, an example of the "'shock and awe' display of force ... intended to make zombies submissive" (Lutz 127), derails the bloodletting of Rick and others, allowing their escape. Carol, still covered in walker blood, joins the herd in entering the gates of Terminus as the Termites scramble amidst the chaos (Leon, "'The Walking Dead': Carol's Got a New Man"; "No Sanctuary").

Now having demonstrated her commitment and resilience, her evolutionary journey comes full circle when Rick accepts Carol back into the core group, though not without Rick questioning, "Did you do that?" before embracing her ("No Sanctuary" 00:38:12–00:38:17). Here, thanks to her "deft thinking," as Keeler describes, Carol makes her return into the group dynamic and completes her journey ("A Postapocalyptic Return to the Frontier" 431). Adding yet another layer to this return and reintegration, Carol reunites Rick with his daughter, Judith, a symbolic boon conferred upon the group as they once again become whole. Viewers also seemed to agree with her transformative action; one viewer exclaims how "The Walking Dead tonight was amazing. The excitement, the thrill, and the action. Carol and Rick are bad to the bone!" (@perez_wilmer4). At the same time, another concludes how "The Walking Dead knows how to play with every emotion #TheWalkingDead" (@dantelista06). As this poster asserts, the incredible ability of this series to play on every sentiment undoubtedly lends to the perceived likability of the characters involved. After all, as Keetley notes, "the fate of the survivors is inextricably interwoven with the zombies" (Introduction "'We're All Infected'" 7). As the zombies persist, so too do the living as they advance the narrative into its next season.

Though fans initially, and might I point out, incorrectly, concluded her character development signaled her end, the time dedicated toward expanding character roles beyond that of Rick Grimes, her metamorphosis, and subsequent return were worth the wait. Commenting on this development, Emily Todd VanDerWerff for *Vox* writes, "spending the back half of season four telling various short stories and vignettes about the show's sprawling cast has finally managed to turn many of those archetypes into actual characters ... when the show puts characters in peril—or even kills them off—*you actually give a damn*" (emphasis added). With "No Sanctuary" highlighting the complete transformation of Carol as she single-handedly decimates Terminus, the repeated inclusion of the hashtag #InCarolWeTrust validates watchers' support for this dynamic heroine. Moreover, a keen-eyed *X* user spotted that the hashtag #InCarolWeTrust reached trending status (@KaraRose_LovesU).

Playing House and Baking Cookies in the Apocalypse

Distancing herself from a previous notion of self, stripped of her identity as both a mother and wife, Carol emerges as a renewed, more confident, and capable individual. Most telling of her transformation is her impeccable ability to master gender roles. According to Judith Butler in *Undoing Gender*, gender "is the apparatus by which the production and normalization of masculine and feminine take place along with the interstitial forms of hormonal, chromosomal, psychic, and performative that gender assumes" (42). By using her knowledge as a caretaker, teacher, cook, and other roles adopted before the apocalypse, Carol performs as others would expect of her gender. In her ability to play upon the perception of being a shy and helpless being, she becomes most deadly as those around her mistakenly assume that she offers little more than how she acts. In creating an illusion, Carol manipulates others into perceiving her as less threatening, a skill viewers seem to appreciate. According to one *Reddit* user, "I find it fun how Carol instinctively sees the advantages of playing to gender role expectations, and no one seems to be suspicious of it, as she's one of the characters that subverts them consistently" (monsterlynn). Returning to her housewife identity, Carol poses as helpless to gain trust, which she uses to her advantage.

No other season better demonstrates her ability to perform in a gender role than after the group finds solitude in the Alexandria Safe-Zone during the fifth season. Entering into the fortified walls of Alexandria, Carol switches from her rugged garments to mostly pastel cardigans and crisp khakis while "adopting a humble homemaker persona—perhaps very close to that of the abused wife she was prior to the zombie apocalypse" (Vinney and Wiley-Rapoport 215). In putting on this homemaker guise, Carol blends in well with the other women as they chat about recipes and swap stories about clearing the cupboard in the community pantry; all the while, Carol quietly fulfills her agenda. As Vinney and Wiley-Rapoport conclude, "By appearing to embody a traditional female role, Carol not only makes herself appear unthreatening, she also has a better chance of being accepted in a town that is still concerned with cultural norms that permeated society before the collapse" (218). In this sense, Carol understands the people of Alexandria are living between states of disbelief and even denial that there is anything threatening about the world outside their walls. Though their walls have to this point safeguarded them from danger, their complacency will be their downfall. Using this to her advantage, Carol slips into her cardigans, in essence successfully "constitut[ing] the illusion of an abiding gendered self," as Butler describes (191), to blend in with the complacent housewives and homemakers in Alexandria. In doing so, she gains intel about the weapons cache in the town armory.

Her ability to disguise herself not only allows her to blend in with the people of Alexandria, but unknown to them, this ability will also save them. Without realization, Carol comes to their rescue in the sixth season when an antagonistic group called the Wolves infiltrates their seemingly impenetrable walls. Using the garments from one of the attackers she manages to kill, and painting a W on her forehead with blood, she manages to disguise herself once again. As she did with the walkers in "No Sanctuary," Carol conceals her identity by disguising herself as one of the Wolves, thus allowing her to kill as many intruders as possible. Those using X offer praise for this episode entitled "JSS" as "the best one" (@ cade_pickette) and how this episode "has potential to be the greatest episode of The Walking Dead ... ever" (@awireman). Regarding Carol, she again succeeds in her ability to protect her group. As one poster writes, "Well that was an absolutely insane episode of The Walking Dead. Carol took it to a whole new level! #TWD—watching The Walking Dead" (@ RogerSanchez11). On *Reddit*, users explore deeper into the episode, especially how Carol easily transformed into her role. As one very enthusiastic commenter exclaims,

> Carol is probably the shows strongest characters right now ... she is just so awesome she so easily blends in to the background of the show until TSHTF and she literally turns into a one-woman army ala Rambo and is verrry quick on her feet and gets shit done without a second of hesitation. If I was stuck in Alexandria I'd want Carol as a partner [angiepie02].

Indeed, when "the shit hits the fan" (TSHTF) as angiepie02 so expressively declares, Carol is quick, decisive, and ready to move. Interestingly, on the same thread, one commenter writes, "Sophia dying really changed her character" (Dr_Toast). As previously discussed, shedding her identifiers of mother and wife allows Carol to emerge anew. Perhaps, in losing Sophia, she no longer fears for anyone she truly loves or maybe realizes she has a grander responsibility to protect her group than so many members of her group did for her in the beginning.

As resilient and stealth-like as she now appears, Carol is not ignorant to her killings but rather, unlike the men of the series, shows remarkable indications of remorse. As one *Reddit* poster writes, "It broke my heart when Carol started crying. As much of a hardened badass as she is, it's good seeing that she still isn't completely desensitized to killing" (keshalover1212). Though some speculate Carol's tears are a sign of remorse for instructing Shelly (Susie Spear Purcell) to smoke her cigarettes outside (effectively sending her to her death), Carol's reaction not only shows her emotional vulnerability but also reminds viewers that she is still human. For Carol to go from "cardigan mode" to a lethal force masquerading as the enemy, as *The Daily Beast* contributor Melissa Leon documents, is a "darkly comedic reminder of the two extremes of Carol's character" ("'The Walking Dead': Carol Goes on a Rampage"). Yes, Carol is a mastermind of gender performance, but she is not completely impenetrable.

The latter episodes in the sixth season masterfully communicate the full impact of her ability to kill. Sitting in the darkness of her room, Carol tallies 18 deaths for which she feels responsible, including Lizzie, whom she killed shortly after Lizzie murdered her sister, Mika, Karen and David, the two Carol determinedly executed in her attempt to prevent the spread of a lethal virus at the Prison ("Not Tomorrow Yet"). Additionally, as Leon recounts, "Judging by the beets-and-acorn cookie she leaves at Sam Anderson's (Major Dodson) grave, she also understands the weight of her responsibility in telling a scared, traumatized little boy to essentially shut up and get over the death of his abusive father. Hooray for hindsight" ("'The Walking Dead': Carol's Got a New Man"). Between the tally marks and the cookies, the remorse she demonstrates is palpable. While her Alexandrian love interest, Tobin (Jason Douglas), confesses his fear of her, he intuitively concludes her "motherly instincts" are the driving force behind her abilities (Leon, "'The Walking Dead': Carol's Got a New Man").

Ultimately, Carol is acutely aware of her transformation and the inherent danger she poses. When Carol and Maggie are held captive by three members of the Saviors, Paula (Alicia Witt), Molly aka "Molls" (Jill Jane Clements), and Michelle (Jeananne Goossen), Carol rather convincingly feigns helplessness. While left unwatched, Carol manages to slide her hands out of her restraints and sharpens a cross she so convincingly hides behind. Wielding the cross as a symbol of faith, and thus a disguise, Carol stages piousness as masterfully as she enacts another compelling gender performance. After managing to overpower their captors, Paula realizes the power Carol possesses, stating, "You're good. Nervous little bird.

You were her. But not now, right?" ("The Same Boat" 00:36:55–00: 37:10). The tally marks might indicate her remorse, but her attempt to let Paula flee before ultimately having to kill her offers a glimpse into the mind of a woman tired of causing death. One *Reddit* poster writes that they

> love that they're exploring the psychological toll being a murderous badass can take on the mind. it would be unrealistic (yeah, I know it's a zombie show) for them to have done the things they've done and not be affected by it … we thought she carol as playing possum, but she was coming to grips with what she's become. maybe she tried so hard to become a new person that she's completely lost herself. i think her seeing the wolf give denise a chance at survival was the catalyst to her wanting to re-evaluate her view on life after the world has ended [BettyDraperIsMyBitch].

Her awareness and weary state ultimately influence her departure from Alexandria at the end of the season and arrival in the next chapter of her life as Queen of the Kingdom.

Heavy Is the Head That Wears the Crown

By the ninth season, Carol embarks on yet another transformation as if seeking a middle ground, somewhere between her previously submissive nature but not quite the fearless killer she became over these many seasons. However, her decision to partner with Ezekiel Sutton (Khary Payton), known as King Ezekiel by the people of a colony known as the Kingdom, does not come without thorough contemplation. Temporarily setting her badassery aside, Carol removes herself from others to reside in seclusion on the outskirts of the Kingdom. Though quite reminiscent of her banishment by Rick back in the fourth season, Carol chooses this isolation due to her acute perception of self. According to a viewer on *X*, "I believe shes afraid of what she has become but shes only protecting her people. Shes a leader" (@AlphaObsession). In electing her a life of seclusion, Carol realizes she is the formidable killer Rick saw when he banished her from the Prison. As she explains to Daryl when he pays a visit to her cabin of solitude, "If [the Saviors] hurt any of our people—any more of them—that's what I would do. And there wouldn't be anything left of me after that" ("New Best Friends" 00:39:04–00:39:20). In this disclosure, Carol reveals not only her awareness of her lethal utility but also her understanding of the immensity of loss. In losing her loved ones, she would, in turn, lose her humanity and reason for living.

Eventually, Carol leaves her isolation to not only remain to help protect the Kingdom but as a partner to King Ezekiel. In a talk with Daryl, she confesses, "[King Ezekiel] asked me to marry him.… And part of me wanted to just say 'yes' right then.… I want to help out, take my time, you know?" ("A New Beginning" 00:39:30–00:40:02). Agreeing to take control of the Sanctuary former stronghold of Negan's Saviors, Carol persists in delaying her marriage to the King and keeping her identity not as the Queen, but as herself intact, even if just for a little while. Returning to her moment of revelation about her self-exile to Daryl, her reluctancy to accept the King's proposal seems quite simple. Throughout this narrative, Carol endures such incredible hardship and continuously battles with maintaining her humanity. Not until a botched assault by the onetime followers of Negan does Carol decide to give in to his proposal. Sitting by the campfire, Carol asks, "You still carrying that old ring around? ... Oh, I'm not saying yes. I just thought I'd try it on for a while, you know, while you're gone..." ("The Bridge" 00:39:42–00:39:55). Though she denies the King his opportunity to give his proposal speech, Carol accepts her new role as the Queen. While many *Reddit* comments reflect skepticism of this union, mostly out of the longstanding hope Carol and Daryl will become a couple, as well as other pairings throughout the series, one offers deep insight into the numerous interracial relationships developing. A viewer, keenly aware of this growth, comments how

> It's not just about chemistry, it's about a connection. Rick and Michonne, Carol and Ezekiel, Abraham and Sasha, Jerry and his squeeze, Glenn and Maggie, Jadis and Gabriel ... they found something they connect with. In this post-apocalyptic world, there aren't many humans around, let alone certain races. They are all also traumatized from loss and strife. They are going to find solace in someone they connect with, regardless of injury, race, etc. ... Can't believe I have to even type this all out [earthlings_all].

Despite their outward appearances, the connection between Ezekiel and Carol is irrefutable. Upon the loss of Shiva, his cherished pet tiger, the King confesses that visiting Carol while she recovered at the Kingdom made him "feel real, not a fiction. Real" ("The King, the Widow, and Rick" 00:38:01–00:38:22). In finding Ezekiel, Carol finds a person also in need of a mask to keep people safe. In finding Carol, Ezekiel acknowledges her power and agency but sees a person in a similar plight, needing to portray an identity for the benefit of the community.

While Carol unquestionably evolves into a zombie-killing badass, her nurturing maternal side never truly leaves her, and suffering another devastating loss brings about the dissolution of her relationship with Ezekiel. Visibly shaken by the death of their adopted son, Henry Sutton (Macsen Lintz), Carol removes her ring, a symbol of her marriage to King Ezekiel and part of the identity inextricably linked with her role as a mother. According to Angela Kang, showrunner starting as of the ninth season, the dissolution of their marriage after the loss of their son adds to a sense of reality in the series. Per Kang,

> Whether it's because [of the death] itself ... causes the problem, or it just
> reveals the cracks that were always there, ... or the grief is so much, and people
> can't connect in their grief. That's something that's actually a common thing
> that happens with couples, and we wanted to kind of explore the truth of that
> happening [qtd. in Venable].

While the death of Henry drives an undeniable wedge between them, the loss both Carol and Ezekiel experience in this apocalyptic setting rise above the narrative. It offers viewers a chance to connect to these very authentic, albeit fictional, characters. The intense physical and emotional pain Carol experiences after the loss of Henry severely impacts her well-being, almost to the point of her own demise, which I will discuss in more detail later in this book.

Up to this point in the series, the most transformative character arc belongs to Carol Peletier. Starting as a feeble woman incapable of speaking up for herself, her metamorphosis into a "true survivor" cannot be under-stated (@AlphaObsession). Suffering through severe loss, both dismissal and self-exile from the group, and two marriages, Carol indeed rises above the tests and trials of the apocalypse. To say she is just a woman is to do an incredible disservice. For, as Judith Butler reminds,

> If one "is" a woman, that is surely not all one is; the term fails to be exhaus-
> tive, not because a pregendered "person" transcends the specific paraphernalia
> of its gender, but because gender is not always constituted coherently or con-
> sistently in different historical contexts, and because gender intersects with
> racial, class, ethnic, sexual, and regional modalities of discursively constituted
> identities. As a result, it becomes impossible to separate out "gender" from
> the political and cultural intersections in which it is invariably produced and
> maintained [4–5].

Carol proves she is capable of actions beyond those prescribed to her by her gender. Desperate for companionship as Garland et al. contend, the television version of Carol far exceeds the domesticated housewife starved for attention, as the original graphic novel presents her character (18). Instead, Carol enters exile, first by force and then by will, out of concern for others. Carol wields her experience as a battered housewife and mother to her advantage. Anyone failing to recognize the power of her being and assuming she is all that appears before them demonstrates their disparaging single-mindedness and ignorance. Proving herself to be the capable apocalyptic badass, as Keeler notes, her ability to single-handedly bring down Terminus resulted in her return to the core group and ulti-mate acceptance ("A Postapocalyptic Return to the Frontier" 431; "Gen-der, Guns, and Survival" 237). She decides when to act, she decides when to take control, and she decides when to assume the roles placed upon her. She is more than her gender; she is Carol, Queen of the Apocalypse.

Even as the Queen, a title she seems reluctant to have at times, she is not emotionally impenetrable. It is not until the tenth season that viewers see the extent the loss of her son and her separation from the King have on her state of mind. And death very much weighs on her, especially in the presence of the Whisperers. Literally cloaking themselves in death by wearing the skins of their "guardians," what the Whisperers call the walkers, these individuals not only pose a threat to Carol and her new life as the Queen, but they also pose a threat to everyone they love and everything this group worked unwaveringly to build. Returning from another venture into self-isolation, Carol outwardly exudes a sense of togetherness and self-control. Only after she and Daryl wander outside the borders imposed by Alpha does Carol shed her hardened exterior to show her sensitivity and hunger for revenge. She is not the calm and collected person she was before the loss of Henry. Instead, her thoughts primarily focus on seeking out and destroying Alpha. Fading in and out of periods when Carol struggles emotionally, her rashness leads her friends into danger without careful thought or regard for them or herself. Later in this book, I continue exploring the emotional cost of death in the apocalypse by discussing key differences in how Carol and Alpha approach motherhood and loss.

The Widow, a Watch, and Hilltop:
* Maggie Rhee*

Despite her temporary absence after the departure of Rick Grimes in the ninth season, Maggie Rhee returned to *The Walking Dead* storyline with a powerful narrative in the tenth season. For Maggie, her transformation into leader of the Hilltop Colony and motherhood comes to the forefront after the disruptive shattering of the tranquil illusion created by the Greene family farm. When viewers first meet Maggie, then Greene, at the start of the second season, she appears to know very little about the horrors lying outside the boundaries of the farm, which by outward appearances, is somehow relatively untouched by the apocalypse. Stepping into the position of the Greene family matriarch, Maggie assumes the role of protector in the absence of her father, Hershel Greene, after his intensely brutal murder by the Governor. The idea one must learn how to survive is not far-fetched and should not be held against her or any of the other characters in the series. After all, how can one possibly know how to survive if such an event has not previously taken place? The skills necessary for a life before the apocalypse enable survival for the world as it is at that time. For those needing the necessary skills to survive in the world of *The Walking*

Dead, they must learn. Really, all these characters must learn in some way.

After losing her father and husband, Maggie continues her progression of becoming the only woman to assume a leadership role without the assistance of a man. Seizing control over the Hilltop Colony ahead of the war with the Saviors, Maggie demonstrates her ability as a competent leader in transforming the formerly male-controlled colony into a thriving, self-sustaining community. Additionally, Maggie exercises her influence by extending compassion to former aggressors but only after they prove themselves loyal to her authority. Much like her father, Maggie compassionately and scrupulously considers the ramifications of her actions, such as in her decision to execute Gregory (Xander Berkeley), the interim leader of the Hilltop Colony, for his botched attempt in plotting her murder or sparing Negan after realizing he no longer poses a threat to her or the people of Hilltop.

Not the Farmer's Daughter Anymore

Not appearing physically strong or equipped with weapons from her introduction, Maggie demonstrates qualities beyond innocuous domestic skills such as cooking and cleaning thanks to the wisdom bestowed upon her by her father. As one of the few women to make runs (a responsibility earmarked for men in the previous season), and with the group in desperate need of medical supplies, Maggie volunteers without hesitation ("Cherokee Rose"). Maggie is more than just the quintessential farmer's daughter. Instead, Maggie is vocal, confident, and determined—assets Carol did not possess in the beginning. Maggie also possesses many detrimental qualities such as extreme stubbornness and an initial lack of awareness, especially when it comes to the walkers. For Maggie, as with her incredulous father and the rest of the Greene family, she believes the walkers are people who've fallen ill rather than reanimated dead, their rebirth into the apocalypse occurs after the Greene family secret reveals itself in the middle of the second season.

Much younger and less afraid of her own shadow, Maggie does offer a drastic contrast to a feebler and more submissive Carol. In comparison, viewer comments toward Maggie appear more accepting of Maggie than they are of Carol. I use the word "accepting" quite loosely here. As one anonymous *Reddit* user writes, "I find Maggie Green highly arousing" (Comment on "Episode Discussion: S02E02, 'Bloodletting' [Spoilers]"), while a *X* users posts, "Oh, the girl playing Maggie on walking dead! Hai! My lifelong crush on you continues! #WalkingDead" (@Lady_Heat00). Like Rosita, whom I discuss in more depth in the next chapter, viewers are distracted by her evident attractiveness, commenting on her body and her looks, as they missing the incredibly useful skills Maggie possesses. Unlike Carol, Maggie can identify medications thanks to training from her veterinary father, can ride horses with great ease (even teaching Glenn how to ride), and is emotionally stronger than her sister Beth Greene (Emily Kinney). Still, her lack of exposure to the world outside the family farm is apparent, especially when Maggie and Glenn make runs to the local pharmacy. As Maggie and Glenn approach their destination, Glenn inquires as to how Maggie is doing after witnessing the killing of a walker trapped in a well on the Greene farm. Noting the look on her face, Glenn explains how the group became numb to killing walkers after seeing as much as they have on the road ("Cherokee Rose").

Despite her notable lack of awareness for the violent world outside the farm, Maggie's actions, and growth as a character, both uphold and diverge from the "final girl" trope set forth by Carol Clover. In her work *Men, Women, and Chain Saws*, Carol Clover aptly identifies the actions or characteristics distinguishing the typical victims in horror films from what she coins the "final girl" (35). Based on the qualities outlined by Clover, the "final girl" differs from her female counterparts in many ways. Fundamentally, Clover determines the characteristics of the "final girl" as

> watchful to the point of paranoia, small signs of danger that her friends ignore, she registers. Above all, she is intelligent and resourceful in a pinch ... although she is always smaller and weaker than the killer, she grapples with him energetically and convincingly. ... Her smartness, gravity, competence in the mechanical and other practical matters, and sexual reluctance set her apart from the other girls and ally her, ironically, with the very boys she fears or rejects, not to speak of the killer himself [39].

The "final girl" must be cunning, undauntingly observant, handy, and possibly most important, a virgin. While nothing is known of Maggie before the core group emerges on the farm, Maggie does appear confident and even dominant when pursuing Glenn for sex. As she states, "I'll have sex with you.... It's not like our options are vast these days. And you're not the only one that's lonely" ("Cherokee Rose" 00:29:08–00:30:10). Loneliness, another quality of the "final girl," sets her apart from her sister, Beth, who has her boyfriend, Jimmy (James Allen McCune), accompanying her at the farm. Unlike her sister, however, Beth and Jimmy do not show signs of a physical relationship, thus leaving Beth's innocence unbroken.

Maggie's decision to enter into a physical relationship with Glenn, a transgression signaling an imminent death as in "the slasher film, sexual transgressors of both sexes are scheduled for early destruction" (Clover 33), defies the trope of the "final girl" by her lengthy appearance in the series. Glenn, though he has his group, is also entirely alone as Rick and others refer to him more as an errand boy or their "go-to-town expert" ("Cherokee Rose" 00:07:59–00:08:05). Not knowing much about Maggie before the apocalypse makes determining her sexual experience difficult. However, when the two meet the next day after their first sexual encounter, Maggie's clothing is noticeably different from her, to borrow from Clover, "boyish" wardrobe consisting of jeans, boots, and loosely fitting shirts (40). Wearing a tighter fitting top and noticeably absent bra, Glenn reminds her of the remaining condoms to which she sarcastically replies, "You see eleven condoms, I see eleven minutes of my life I'm never getting back" ("Chupacabra" 00:07:47–00:08:04). Though Glenn persists, Maggie dismisses the conversation by walking away. However, at dinner via a note slid under the table, Maggie solicits Glenn for another encounter, an encounter that never takes place as Glenn's suggested meeting point unveils walkers kept in the barn by Hershel and his family ("Chupacabra").

Awkward exchanges aside, by propositioning Glenn, Maggie asserts her sexual dominance, as she takes control in the choice of when to engage in such an intimate relationship and with whom. Viewers, very aware of this intimacy, draw attention to the treatment of Maggie and Glenn as children by Hershel. First, as Glenn and Maggie are "the only ones doing it at the moment," according to one *Reddit* member comments, many viewers question why the two adults sit with the younger individuals at the "kids' table" (Scoo). Yet, while viewers debate why Maggie and Glenn sit with the younger individuals at the dinner table, there is certainly more to be read in this scene. Both Maggie and Glenn are both incredibly undeveloped as characters. And, per one anonymous poster on *Reddit*,

> It was really the only part of this episode I didn't like. Show really needs stronger female characters. That one was like a big sign yelling "You see what happens when a WOMAN dares do a man's job! People nearly die!" … But still bugs me that for the moment the show just doesn't seem to want any woman to do much more than a 1950s housewife [Comment on "Episode Discussion: S02E05, 'Chupacabra' (Spoilers)."]

Though the union of Maggie and Glenn marks an important moment in the development for both characters, Maggie carries the burden of domestication. As one viewer notes, "daaaaaamn, Glenn hit that ass one time, and got Maggie washing his hat and shit. #walkingdead" (@Trent_Cooley). Defiant as she appears before Glenn, Maggie somewhat remains ignorant of the world outside the farm as she retains hold of domesticated roles.

Finally, moving on from referring to the walkers by name, Maggie emerges fully conscious of the dead and the extreme threat posed by the masquerading tranquility of the farm. In her initial refusal to acknowledge the dead and insisting they have names, Maggie places signifiers on the beings. No longer human, as Glenn sees them, Maggie refuses to see them as anything but the people they once were. In essence, their names signify their human selves, as according to Mark Bracher, "Master signifiers are able to exert such force in messages because of the role they play in structuring the subject—specifically giving the subject a sense of identity and direction" (25). Illusory and dangerous, their names give the walkers a sense of familiarity to the Greene family and absolute refusal to accept their death. Transcending her denial, Maggie challenges Hershel about their collective deficient awareness. The symbolic opening of the barn presents more than just the reveal of a deep-rooted family secret. Maggie, especially, comes into full consciousness as she forcefully accepts the truth that the world is not the same as it was, and the farm is not the serene refuge as Rick and the group hoped.

Maggie Rhee, A Master of Signifiers

As with Carol in the third season, Maggie Greene undergoes a massive transformation in character as she now more fully comprehends and competently kills walkers without issue. At the Prison, she helps dispense walkers to secure their protective border fence, helps clear the halls as the group scouts for supplies, and effectively uses a gun when saving Lori and Carl when walkers overrun the Prison ("Sick"; "Killer Within"). The inability of Hershel to perform up to his fullest ability as the only medical professional leaves her in a precarious and traumatizing situation. As walkers descend upon the Prison, Maggie's aim proves true as she helps Lori and Carl escape back inside the Prison while the rest of the group works to secure it once again. The stress overcomes Lori, inducing labor. Maggie admits, "Carol's the one that practiced that. Dad only taught me the steps.... I have no anesthetic, no equipment ... you won't survive" ("Killer Within" 00:34:03–00:34:12). Reluctantly accepting her call to duty, she assumes the role normally relegated to Hershel. Though successfully retrieving the baby but killing Lori in the process, Maggie takes her first human life while saving another. This scene, one of the darker moments in the series as not only does Lori lose her life, but Carl volunteers to ensure she does not resurrect, became a breaking point for actress Lauren Cohan. According to Cohan,

> I remember after we shot that scene, I threw up; I was so uncomfortable. Because it was so—within the story, so necessary. And it was so ... impactful on the characters and on the viewer. And just the rawness of it, and the real of it. But I look back on the moment, and I was like, 'What does that tell you about yourself? That there was a moment like that that was so pivotal in the show, and so exemplary of The Walking Dead, that was terrifying and made

you want to run away—and ended up being one of the most important things? [qtd. in Bullard]

The realness Cohan describes, along with the gore and pain of loss, makes *The Walking Dead* appear by all accounts so authentic. For a moment, in such a scene, walkers fall from memory while eyes fix upon this heart-breaking scene of a mother sacrificing herself for her child. However, this scene is also incredibly foretelling as Maggie choose to become a mother in the apocalypse, a role plagued with *complications*, to put it lightly, throughout the duration of her upcoming pregnancy.

Though the "final girl" trope would condemn their sexual encounter, the intended marriage of Maggie and Glenn represents a nonconforming turning point for the series as its first interracial union. Until this moment in the series, the couples presented before this time mostly consisted of individuals of similar races. According to Helen Ho in "The Model Minority in the Zombie Apocalypse: Asian-American Manhood on AMC's The Walking Dead," their "sexual relationship … is not deviant, lustful, and will not be punished; rather, the interracial pairing of Asian man/white woman is seen by the show's 'colorblind' characters as merely two human falling in love" (68). Moving beyond race to see the joining of two very human individuals, viewers (unsurprisingly) offer quite a few remarks concerning the details of a rather anticlimactic proposal. One *Reddit* user comments how their "wife was disappointed with the proposal…. I then reminded her that they had survived for over 9 months in a zombie infested world. That's proposal enough. WOMEN AMIRIGHT?!" (Defiant_Griffin), while another poster quips how "Trivial societal customs typically go out the window when you're the last living members of your species" (Comment on "The Walking Dead Episode Discussion S03E15 'This Sorrowful Life'"). Bending the knee or not, the proposal to Maggie and her acceptance marks another identifier for Maggie, an identifier she strongly assumes later when asserting her authority over Gregory, in the seventh season.

By the fourth season, Maggie willingly and openly expresses the desire to begin a family. For Maggie, a child represents a future, a symbol of living rather than just surviving. As Amanda Taylor notes in "Love and Marriage in the Time of *The Walking Dead*," "…their confidence suggests that TWD not only values romance, marriage, and family creation, but sees them as acts of hope" (87). Glenn, on the other hand, with thoughts of the constant danger this world poses, matched with the outcome of Lori's pregnancy, lingers in the past. Another sign Glenn remains in the past is the photograph he carries of his wife. Authors John Greene and Michaela D.E. Meyer assert in their article "The Walking (Gendered)

Dead: A Feminist Rhetorical Critique of Zombie Apocalypse Television Narrative" how the trait of focusing on the past is more closely associated with women, especially in the first season as the reality of the apocalypse was still taking hold. However, the photograph Glenn carries of Maggie contradicts their argument of "men are represented as preparing for the future while women are holding on to the past" (68). When Glenn and Maggie reunite after a forced separation in the fourth season, Maggie has Glenn burn the picture, telling him, "[y]ou don't need a picture of me. You never will again" ("Us" 00:36:41–00:37:04). Maggie is keenly aware that while the picture is of Maggie, the picture is not Maggie. It is a representation, a symbol, a memory—one she is not willing to afford him. Interestingly, viewers use the burning of the picture as a prediction of upcoming death. While one commentor favors Maggie, another writes the "took it as a sign that Glenn will die. She said he'd never need a picture of her again, which I took as foreshadowing of him dying before her" (Comment on "S04E15 'Us' Post-Episode Discussion"). Regrettably, this prediction proves true when Glenn loses his life at the wrath (and bat) of Negan by the seventh season.

Hilltop Has a New Leader

Maggie loses Glenn when Negan takes his prized baseball bat, named Lucille, to Glenn's head in retaliation for Daryl's attempt to subdue their maniacal assailant after his gruesome beating of Abraham ("The Day Will Come When You Won't Be"). Outrage and devastation not only overcome the group, but fans of the series as various tweets and comments on social media condemn the show for killing off these two fan-favorites, as well as to express shock in seeing such over-the-top brutality. As one X viewer comments, "The Walking Dead, you absolutely broke me. I have never felt so empty and bereft of hope after an hour of TV #TWD #TheWaking-Dead" (@Troy_Rudolph). No doubt disparaging, another viewer on *Reddit* offers some hope for Maggie (and Daryl) after such a ghastly endeavor. Stating, "It will be development for him as well as Maggie" the viewer continues, "She's been so tied to Glenn, and now she has to develop her *own distinct character* as opposed to being part of a couple. Individually for both of them it promises to be terrible and interesting" (KAwesome; emphasis added). Reflecting on the comment above, the use of the word "interesting" is putting Maggie's evolution from this gruesome moment lightly. Though visibly distraught, Maggie later assumes authority over Hilltop and partners with Rick, as well as Ezekiel and the Kingdom, to challenge Negan and the Saviors.

At Hilltop, Maggie prepares the residents for the impending war by bestowing upon them her knowledge as a competent fighter. While hiding from the Saviors in the underground food cellar of Barrington House, Maggie offers Daryl forgiveness for his transgression that resulted in the death of Glenn. Considerably tougher now and eagerly seeking revenge for the death of Glenn, Maggie still demonstrates incredible compassion and careful thinking, qualities once possessed by her father. She tells Daryl, "It wasn't your fault…. You're one of the good things in this world. That's what Glenn thought. And he would know, 'cause he was one of the good things, too. And, I wanted to kill that guy, too. I wanted to string them all up and watch them die. But we have to win. Help me win" ("The Other Side" 00:28:01–00:28:47). Her actions and quick thinking all point to her progression as a leader.

As the only female to wield sole control over a colony during the eighth season, she stands apart from both Carol and Michonne despite their influential roles in the narrative. According to Maja Zidarević in their thesis *A Feminist View on Social Issues in* The Walking Dead,

> The only woman who becomes a true leader that actually controls a certain community is Maggie. She becomes leader of the Hilltop Colony and proves herself as even more of a brave, strong and intelligent woman as she stands up to Negan and the Saviors … we can see that the show tends to progress towards gender equality since there are now four co-leaders of the Militia, a coalition against Negan, and those are Maggie, Cyndie (leader of an all-female colony known as Oceanside), Rick and Ezekiel [70].

In other words, while it took nearly eight seasons on television to move a woman into a position of power, Maggie appears to break the glass ceiling for women seeking control and assuming positions of leadership in *The Walking Dead*.

Solidifying her role as leader of Hilltop, Maggie fully exercises her weight and power as a woman in command while also retaining the moral compass bestowed upon her by her late father, Hershel. Unlike Rick, Maggie demonstrates compassion for others. Though her father initially resisted the core group staying on the farm, Maggie actively seeks value in everyone. First, as the colonies can take a few Saviors prisoner, Maggie decides to use them as bargaining tools rather than execute them ("The King, the Widow, and Rick"). Perhaps, in her decision, she receives a boon from a potential ally. Taking Michonne, Enid, and Rosita with her, Maggie meets Georgie, a mysterious leader from an unknown colony flanked by two bodyguards, twin sisters Hilda (Kim Ormiston) and Midge (Misty Ormiston). Not "car[ring] to share this with the weak," as Georgie offers to trade what could be essential information for the future of the Hilltop Colony ("The Key" 00:21:38–00:22:33). Initially hesitant to take the offer of music for knowledge, Maggie eventually gives in to the trade. With a few words of hope, and if, potentially, "people can believe in people again … a sustainable future" can happen ("The Key" 00:23:33–00:23:44). This option for trade puts Maggie and Michonne at odds with each other as Michonne is looking to build a world Carl would approve of while Maggie is looking out for a future for her child and Hilltop. Accepting the offer, Maggie hands over records in exchange for food and "the aforementioned key to a future," a manual for building a sustainable community "so we may have a future from our past" ("The Key" 00:40:09–00:40:27). In their departure, Georgie informs Maggie that she will be able to fulfill her end of the bargain, a sign this book of knowledge will offer a future.

As Maggie looks to a future and Hilltop prepares itself for an assault by a rebel group of the Saviors, it is worth noting from this episode is the reference to Maggie as "the Widow," a name she uses to identify herself ("Do Not Send Us Astray" 00:06:02). While the title "Widow" is indicative of loss and a remembrance of the past, Maggie wields her title with authority. As *Vulture* contributor Richard Rys urges, "Maggie should start using [this title] regularly because it lends a certain air of mystery and intimidation than one really needs when developing a personal brand in the apocalypse" ("The Walking Dead Recap: The Widow Rhee"). Indeed, a title such as "Widow Rhee" (or even just simply "the Widow") carries more weight than the name Maggie. But the connotation implies that Maggie cannot move beyond her association with Glenn. In carrying such a name, Maggie shows that while she focuses on building up Hilltop to be a sustainable colony, she brings with her a bit of the past. The fixation on the past is even more evident when Maggie plots to kill Negan after Rick spares his life in their triumph over the Saviors. For Rick, keeping Negan alive means forcing him to see the world Carl envisioned before his death. For Maggie, the decision to keep Negan alive is a constant reminder of his danger and the loss she suffered in seeing Glenn die ("Wrath"). Perhaps therefore viewers took to *Reddit* to condemn Maggie for her decision to find Glenn when the two become separated after fleeing the Prison instead of seeking out her sister, Beth, during the fifth season. In choosing to find her husband rather than her sister, she unknowingly sacrificed the last time she would see Beth alive. This choice, perhaps, influenced her decision to put her people and family at Hilltop first before offering any help to Rick and those struggling at the Alexandria Safe-Zone.

By the ninth season, Hilltop appears to be flourishing. Rick, paying a visit to Hilltop, asks Maggie to extend her generosity to the Sanctuary, the compound lead by the antagonist Negan. Complimenting her for a thriving community, Rick notes how Hilltop is "thriving because of you. This place is doing better than anywhere else" ("A New Beginning" 00:53:10–00:53:27). Drawing her terms, she tells Rick, "When we were fighting the

Saviors, you told me that soon, you'd be the one following me. But you didn't. 'Cause I wasn't someone to follow. That changes now" ("A New Beginning" 00:55:17–00:55:33). Her reminder to Rick comes from a conversation between the two back in the eighth season. When addressing the unified colonies before taking on the Saviors, Maggie optimistically points to a future in saying, "[W]e have to keep our faith in each other. If we can hold on to that with everything we have, the future is ours" ("Mercy" 00:05:14–00:05:19). Comparatively, Maggie contrasts drastically from the forceful message Rick urges about the "'bigger world' is ours by right" regarding the colonies and their union against a common enemy ("Mercy" 00:02:10–00:02:13). Before setting out for war, Rick acknowledges her abilities and, paying her the ultimate compliment, admits he will be looking to her to follow ("Mercy"). As the de facto leader since the show's inception, Rick was always the one people looked to for guidance and for making decisions.

Unfortunately, though predictably, while Rick renounces his duty when the group fortified the Prison, he never honestly stops being a leader. However, as Corey Hutchinson notes, "The groundwork for her rise to the top has been quietly being laid for a few seasons now, but the big thing here is that Rick isn't just acknowledging her as a leader, but the leader" ("Walking Dead: Will Maggie Take Over as Star If Rick Dies?"), a possible prediction for a world without Rick Grimes. Of course, viewers quickly drew parallels between the leadership styles of Maggie and Rick. One *Reddit*, one viewer concludes how it is "two different logics, one Maggie's and the other Rick's. Rick is the person who decided Negan shouldn't die; it was absolutely not what Maggie wanted. Maggie is the one who decided Gregory should die. So she's consistent yet opposed to Rick's way of thinking" (turkeypants). Aptly, viewers center on Rick's reluctance to abdicate his leadership role, just as he was unable to do when the group resided in the Prison: "Rick told Maggie he's gonna 'follow' her after this is all over. But we know that doesn't happen. I feel like the course of the story this season could lead to a parallel in their leadership style with Rick sparing Negan while Maggie hangs Gregory" (TheGent316). Ultimately, neither would come to fruition as Maggie mysteriously leaves to join Georgie. At the same time, Rick, after he somehow manages to survive impalement by rebar and blowing up a bridge while trying to protect the colonies from an encroaching herd of walkers, departs with Jadis (Pollyanna McIntosh), known by the alias Anne and leader of the Scavengers, to a yet to be revealed location ("Who Are You Now?"; "What Comes After").

The drastic differences between the departures of Rick and Maggie offer more insight into the treatment of gender. For Rick, his exit could only be described as going out in a "blaze of glory" (Brookfield 329). In the essay "No Woman Is an Island: Heroes, Heroines and Power in the Gendered World of Lost," Tarah Brookfield outlines how an exit, like Rick's, comes "in the form of heroic sacrifice" (329). To this extent, watching Rick painfully lift himself off the rebar impaling him, thanks to the aid of his diligent horse, he stumbles slowly onto the bridge he previously asked Maggie's help to repair. With his wound copiously bleeding, Rick passes in and out of consciousness and is visited by the ghosts of Hershel, Shane, and Sasha Williams (Sonequa Martin-Green) as "the result of a long plotline that gives the hero time to contemplate his mortality" (Brookfield 329). Just as Maggie, Michonne, Rosita, Daryl, Carol, and other prominent members of the unified colonies surround and try desperately to help an ailing Rick, he aims his pistol and shoots at a spilled box of dynamite. The blast gives no trace of a body, leaving the group to assume Rick is dead. However, the closing scene reveals Jadis/Anne moving Rick into a helicopter, and the two lift away to a fate unknown ("What Comes After").

While not the end of the series, this scene is eerily reminiscent of Romero's *Dawn of the Dead* as a helicopter takes the remaining survivors away at the end of the film, leaving the audience with a glimmer of hope. Still, the difference in their different partings begs the question of their treatment as characters. For Rick, his exit from the series very much reflects the demeanor of his character, overly aggrandized and unrealistic. I say this mostly due to Rick's tendency for losing his grip on reality, especially the instances when Rick experiences loss and wantonly seeks vengeance of walkers armed with nothing more than a hatchet, a discussion I explore in more depth later in this book. From his unbelievably long string of hallucinations to his embellished act of heroism in sacrificially obliterating the bridge to save the colonies from a herd of encroaching walkers, Rick exits the series with all the ferocity his character brought to the narrative. For Maggie, while her exit certainly does not match the magnitude of her role, it does call attention to the difference between her character and Rick while also opening potential for her return. While Rick is known for his flair for the dramatic, Maggie remains consistently level-headed and in control of herself. While the fate of Rick is uncertain, despite the clues prompting Michonne to track information about his whereabouts down, Maggie's eventual return in the tenth season offers viewers a glimpse of the future and her ability to lead those who follow her.

When Maggie eventually returns to *The Walking Dead* in the tenth season, she brings with her a growing son, Hershel Rhee (Kien Michael Spiller) and a few lingering survivors known as the Wardens. She, unfortunately, also brings trouble as an antagonistic group called the Reapers seek to hunt them down. Reconnecting with Daryl, Maggie unfolds the events taking place during her absence ("Home Sweet Home"). This filler not only allows the group to understand her plight, but such disclosure provides an explanation for her absence following the "quiet" exit at the end of the ninth season. While in all actuality, actress Lauren Cohan left the series to pursue other endeavors (and it appears) reached a bit of a sticking point with negotiating her salary on the series, adding to the narrative in this way closes some gaps and fills in some blanks for the "time jump" experienced between the ninth and tenth seasons (Lisabeth).

Despite this absence and distance from her life at Hilltop, Maggie does not seem to lose any of her loathing for Negan. Constantly butting heads and eventually coming to rely on each other to rescue Hershel in the eleventh season, the dynamic between these two characters creates palpable tension and curiosity about Maggie's intent to see Negan dead. With death being ever present, regardless of it being the constant presence of the walkers (as with Carol) or the absence of a loved one (as with Maggie), how these characters handle death is particularly interesting and explored more in-depth later. For now, I will end my discussion of Maggie by emphasizing the importance of this underrecognized character. Not only does Maggie expertly wield her ability to make difficult choices, but she also commands the respect of those who doubt her ability as a partner, leader, and mother. Her determined character endures the in apocalypse with her transition to *The Walking Dead: Dead City* as she and Negan seek the location of her kidnapped son.

The First Lady of the Zombie Apocalypse: Michonne

Michonne, entering as an already capable fighter for this new apocalyptic world, arrives alone, depicted as an outsider, and shrouded in mystery. Out of these women, not only is Michonne the most adept, but she also enters the story through her relationship with a woman, Andrea. Strikingly different from these other women in more than just her ninja-like skills with a katana, Michonne exudes an exotic appearance. The focus on her hair in locs, athletic build completed with sculpted arms, and dark complexion garnered considerable attention from viewers. Gurira herself identifies herself as Zinmerican based on her Zimbabwean parents and upbringing in Zimbabwe since age five (Lunden). One of only a few women of color in the core group, Michonne "protect[s] herself and others in addition to enduring in a predominately White and male-centered space speaks volumes about her character in a place ... where no character is safe" (Reed 72–73). Indeed, the turbulent world of *The Walking Dead* routinely proves no character is safe, regardless of gender, race, orientation, or significance.

For Michonne, her relationship with Andrea, and later with Carl, permits viewers a chance to see a softer and gentler side of this apocalyptic warrior and explains her perceptively angry persona. Revealing the traumatic death of her son, Andre Anthony, Michonne unburdens herself of the guilt she harbors and rationalizes her apprehension for developing relationships with others. Though her failure to establish relationships confounds her character, Michonne possesses the strength and determination to survive despite her initial entry into the core group as an outsider. Despite her lack of trust in others, her power and fighter-ready capabilities provide viewers the influential female heroine called for by so many on social media. On *Reddit*, one viewer articulates enthusiasm for Michonne's introduction, stating when "I saw it was a tough female character (I haven't read the comics, but I did see 'The Talking Dead' after tonight's episode), I was so excited because there will *finally be a girl I can relate to*" (Ihadacow; emphasis added). Without having said a word, fans on *Reddit* not only express delight for the katana-wielding "GREATEST ZOMBIE KILLER EVER!!!" (BleakGod), but also for a strong female and minority character who comes into the story ready and capable.

Othering in the Apocalypse

Watching the story unfold, viewers quickly picked up on several problems regarding character demographics. From the outset, *The Walking Dead* offers viewers the story of lead protagonist Rick Grimes waking from a coma to find the world is not how he remembers. As such, *The Walking Dead* pretty much begins as a story told through the White, male-controlled perspective of Rick after he sets out for Atlanta to reunite with his family (Reed 70). Then, after rejoining with the Grimes clan and their status at the makeshift camp somewhere on the outskirts of Atlanta goes from bad to worse and forces Rick, as well as the others, to flee in search of refuge. From the gendered division of labor to minority figures rendered inconsequential, this narrative seems to be a zombified–Western as Sheriff Rick gives orders, and the rest obediently follows. For some, such as Carol and Lori, they follow along and live to see another day. Others, such as Jacqui or Dr. Edwin Jenner (Noah Emmerich) from the CDC, decide to join others who "opted out" ("TS-19" 00:08:55–00:08:57). And, of course, *The Walking Dead* does not lack for gory deaths at the hands and teeth of the dead.

Then, this "hooded samurai sword wielding character" enters the narrative (Kahnbrochill). As the quotation shows, the figure is not a woman but a yet-to-be-defined character. For those familiar with the series, the comic, or *Talking Dead*, the character arriving in shadow offers little evidence regarding gender or identity. Instead, carrying a katana and leading two walkers on chains, this figure remains somewhat of a mystery until the third season premiere. By this time, the core group changes drastically from the first two seasons as T-Dog, Jacqui, Dale Horvath (Jeffrey DeMunn), Sophia, Ed, and Shane, to name a few, no longer walk amongst the living. And since both T-Dog and Jacqui departed the narrative, Michonne represents the only prominent Black member in the group after the death of T-Dog and Jacqui and until Sasha enters the story in the third season. Outwardly, Michonne exudes suspicion as she chooses silence when encountering the Governor and Milton Matmet (Dallas Mark Roberts) in Woodbury and then, Rick and the group at the Prison. Using limbless, jawless walkers as a cloak of protection, Michonne effortlessly walks with the dead. So seamless is her ability to walk with the dead that Rick hands over baby Judith to Carl before walking across the prison yard to get closer to this anomaly staring at him through the fence ("Hounded").

Appearing at the very end of the second season, Michonne quite literally enters this apocalyptic narrative as a mystery, a hooded figure cloaked in shadows. Expertly using a katana to dispatch the walker and with two armless walkers following in chains, this genderless specter approaches Andrea just before the screen goes dark ("Beside the Dying Fire"). While viewers know nothing of Michonne until the premiere of the third season, fans familiar with the comic use *Reddit* to cheer her arrival into the narrative. While one *Reddit* user deplores the sexist nature of the show with its focus on Rick Grimes being the sole decision-maker, another poster comments how Michonne "will fix that" (Hero_B). Separating her from her trusty katana, Rick asserts his dominance and brings Michonne within the confines of the Prison. Noticing the constant removal of her katana by her oppressors, one *Reddit* commenter writes, "White guys are constantly taking MIchonne's sword ... there's got to be something freudian about that" (Bittebitte). Indeed, there is a somewhat symbolic meaning behind removing weapons from their owners, and that reference is not limited to just Michonne. In *Guts: The Anatomy of The Walking Dead*, author Paul Vigna notes how "[s]ome of the weapons, like Rick's Colt Python, Daryl's crossbow, or Michonne's katana, act like characters in their own right, and that is not by accident: The weapons are an extension of the characters" (75). With this assertion in mind, and as Bittebitte's comment shows, in separating Michonne from her weapon of choice, her oppressors not only disarm her, but they also symbolically castrate her by asserting their authority to handle the noticeably phallic weapon.

Though her burdens would not reveal themselves until later episodes, Michonne begins her journey with the group as a mysterious outsider: angry, alone, and not to be trusted. Per Cindy Reed in the article "From

One First Lady to Another: The Speculative Worlds of Michelle Obama and The Walking Dead's Michonne," the "representation of her strength could signify the often dehumanizing trope of the strong Black woman, who is responsible for bearing the burdens of others" (72). It comes as no wonder why Michonne again opts for silence while under interrogation by Rick. Commenting on her demeanor, Michonne's unwillingness to divulge information is not missed as one viewer comments, "We all know Michonne is the queen of divulging ZERO information..." (BEyouTH). Supporting this analysis by fans, another poster on *Reddit* follows with, "I'm so tired of Michonne's angry attitude. She couldn't even say thank you to Hershel without looking like she wanted to punch him" (Houdat). With her lack of cooperation and resistance to answering questions along with her zombie-killing capabilities, Michonne enters the narrative unlike any other character. While Michonne needs not for training as her katana-wielding skills show, her inability to trust others lends to her roughened exterior and uncertainty from those she encounters. It is these characteristics, though initially hated by fans, that Michonne perfectly demonstrates the nuances of the Social Penetration Theory model of communication as developed by psychologists Irwin Altman and Dalmas Taylor, which is discussed in more detail below.

Mostly, the lack of a backstory or explanation for Michonne's presumed anger is cause for speculation. Returning to Woodbury and bearing her anger as "her most obvious and defining characteristic" as Samaa Abdurraqib notes in "'Just Another Monster': Michonne and the Trope of the angry Black woman," she seeks her revenge on the Governor for an unknown transgression (229). Though the comics depict the brutal rape of Michonne by the Governor, such a horrendous act could be explained as his retaliation for her failure to adhere to gender norms. Garland et al. in the article "Gender Politics and *The Walking Dead*: Gendered Violence and the Reestablishment of Patriarchy" conclude how Michonne's reluctance to adhere to traditional gender roles cost her a great deal, and as illustrated in the graphic novel, Michonne gets raped while being held captive by the Governor. As they state, "One might argue that the brutal rape of Michonne was a consequence of stepping outside of her assigned gender role by challenging the authority of The Governor" (Garland et al. 20). Instead, the show replaces this brutal scene with the still disturbing but less graphic humiliation of Maggie. Using Glenn as a pawn by threatening his life, Maggie appeases the Governor's commands of remove her clothing and thus use humiliation as a tactic to expose her vulnerability ("When the Dead Come Knocking"). For one viewer, this change from Michonne to Maggie denies Michonne an essential aspect of her character evolution. On the blogging site *Daily Kos*, Chauncey DeVega asserts how the switch robbed Michonne of her "power and complexity" ("Michonne or Maggie? Race, Gender, and Rape on The Walking Dead TV Series"). The writer continues by claiming,

> if you love a character and respect them, then you, the author/creator, must at times let bad things happen to your beloved creation. ... Michonne, who was brutally raped by The Governor in The Walking Dead comic book series, has to suffer in order to have her revenge and triumph over him. Michonne is made by pain; it tempers and refines her like an alloy or fine blade of steel ["Michonne or Maggie? Race, Gender, and Rape on The Walking Dead TV Series"].

While this blog entry provokes a flurry of replies from other viewers, the responses did not necessarily condemn DeVega for such an outrageous assertion as viewers focus on the lack of development for any of the non–White characters in *The Walking Dead* series.

Patricia Hill Collins emphasizes how rape "is a powerful tool of sexual violence because women are forced to 'assume the position' of powerless victim, one who has no control over what is happening to her body" (228). In this way, rape not only demeans women, but as DeVega claims, deprives them of their power. I would like to counter that argument with a question: Does such a brutal method need to be used to make a dynamic character such as Michonne even more compelling? In loud contrast to DeVega's claims, Michonne (or any character for that matter) does not need (nor deserve) to be raped to evolve as a character. Rather, her description by authors such as Garland et al. as a "highly educated and successful woman in the pre-apocalyptic society, ... [Michonne] is the only individual who has been able to successfully navigate a zombie-filled world" (15). A former lawyer before the apocalypse and now a machete-wielding powerhouse, Michonne seemed to transition to her new reality with ease (Garland et al. 14–15). The issue with Michonne is not her anger but the reluctance to let her guard down, to be vulnerable. Michonne is strong and completely capable of survival in this apocalyptic world. Her inability to establish a close relationship is a direct result of the burden she carries, the loss of her son. And who could blame her? Due to their choices, the people she trusted to care for her son as she made a run for supplies lacked the capability of protecting him and themselves from the undead.

Questioning DeVega's claims, one response posits whether "...she not interesting enough a character already..." (capsfan1978). With her acute killing aptitude and mysterious origin, her entry into the narrative causing a stir on social media, and cheers from fans of the comics, I find she is already quite impressive. The same commenter writes, "I think [DeVega] is selling her short. Besides, there is plenty of time for her to continue to develop as a character" (capsfan1978). Though her combative persona is off-putting for those she encounters, Michonne does transform into quite a dynamic character and a welcomed contribution to the core group. Still, I wondered about this undoubtedly purposeful change to the narrative. Based on the graphic novel, the Michonne's unconscionable experience at the hands of the Governor, an experience that included agonizing torture and rape, prove too gruesome for television. It is also not to say that *The Walking Dead* shies away from depictions of sexual assault. There are certainly several instances to consider: Shane's assault of Lori in the first season, Carl's near assault by the Claimers in the fourth season, and Beth Greene's assault by Officer Gorman (Cullen Moss) while she is detained at Grady Memorial Hospital in Atlanta during the fifth season, Jessie Anderson's (Alexandra Breckenridge) abuse by her husband, Pete Anderson (Corey Brill), to name a few.

Instead, what *The Walking Dead* presents is an example of the consequences for engaging in such horrific actions. In other words, despite the post-apocalyptic setting where former governing bodies and established authorities no longer exist, those who commit such cruelties against others do not escape punishment. Speaking to the instances mentioned above, Shane is not only rejected by Lori, but her deep scratches across his neck bring unwanted attention from the rest of the group. Shane later dies after his attempt to usurp Rick as the Grimes patriarch. For the Claimers, Rick uses his teeth to rip out the throat of Joe (Jeff Kober), much to the shock of the group, allowing Michonne and Daryl to kill them off and make their escape. As for Gorman, he is bitten by walker after blackmailing Beth during her attempt to escape and later shot to prevent his reanimation. Pete is not only threatened by an ever-watchful Carol, someone who recognizes the signs of abuse from her own lived experience, but eventually dies in an altercation with Rick.

So, what is to be made of *The Walking Dead* and its depictions of sexual assault? In "Rules for Surviving Rape Culture," Natalie Wilson not only notes the explicit condemnation of assailants but suggests *The Walking Dead* establishing its own rules for combatting violent acts of sexual assault. By not directly showcasing instance of sexual assault but not outright ignoring it either, the argument could be made for *The Walking Dead* to be charting new territory as a forward-thinking series in its increasing approach to feminist-appealing storylines. The decision to replace Michonne's rape and torture by the Governor with Maggie's cringeworthy assault and humiliation for information might have left a gap in explaining Michonne's apparent mistrust of him. Yet the inclusion of storylines that do not sensationalize acts of sexual violence, even in a world without established rules, demonstrates how the series makes it known that such acts do not go without punishment (Wilson 141).

Undoubtedly, with her battle-ready skills and dark complexion, Michonne disrupts the predominant makeup of the core group in the third season. These visual markers, or what Ronald Jackson calls "corporeal zones" in *Scripting the Black Masculine Body: Identity, Discourse, and Racial Politics in Popular Media,* cannot be denied (52). As Jackson states, "There is no such thing as not seeing someone's corporeal zones; one's skin complexion or other markers may not result in unfair treatment by the Other, but they are certainly optic markers" (52). In addition to her different appearance, her attention to physical fitness is in direct contrast to Carol as the attentive den mother and Maggie as the wife of Glenn. This distinction is exemplified after Michonne enters the Prison in the third season. As Carol attends to the makeshift kitchen in the background, Michonne does a series of pushups and crunches with Merle Dixon (Michael Rooker) watching and sarcastically commenting on how Michonne is "smart to stay fit" ("I Ain't a Judas" 00:18:33–00:18:38). Though all three women are undeniably slender, Michonne is the only one of the three to be seen maintaining her physique.

Furthermore, her body, and most notably her arms, appear to be on constant display. Michonne is not only strong internally but exhibits an external strength not associated with Maggie or Carol. As Reed notes, "... Michonne's physical power, coupled with her hair and skin tone makes a statement that even when Black womanhood is present in exclusive places, it is audacious and not easily pushed around ... her looks hold significance beyond the surface" (72). Michonne is not only the only Black female in the narrative, but she is also the only prominent Black female actively participating in a White male-dominated group up to this point in the series. And she will remain the only prominent Black female after the death of Sasha in the seventh season until the introduction of Connie and Kelly in the ninth season. Though Rosita Espinosa (discussed next chapter) is a woman of color, her lighter complexion aligns her more closely with the other prominent White females. As Michonne accustoms herself and becomes one of the core members of the group, she remains distinctly different from the other women. While Maggie and Carol physically evolve into capable fighters as they adapt to their changing world, Michonne emotionally changes as she opens herself up to others and even enters a relationship with none other than the lead protagonist himself, Rick Grimes.

The Unburdening of Disclosure

Though fully competent, Michonne lacks the human companionship bestowed upon her female counterparts, Maggie and Carol. Not until

Michonne lets down her guard with Carl, thus coming to terms with her past, can she begin to form relationships with others, especially men. After reuniting with Carl and Rick, Michonne confides in Carl about her three-year-old son, Andre, a part of her past not previously disclosed to anyone ("Claimed"). Later, when scouting the perimeter of Terminus, Michonne finally reveals the fate of her late boyfriend Mike (Aldis Hodge) and friend Terry (Brandon Fobbs) and her son. Walking with Carl, she explains,

> I was coming back from a run. I saw the fences were down. I heard the moans. It was over. And Mike and Terry, they were high when it happened. They were bit. Could have stopped it. I could have killed them. But I let them turn. I made it so they couldn't bite, couldn't scratch.... It felt like I deserved dragging them around so that I would always know. I found out that they kept me safe. They hid me. The walkers didn't see me anymore. I was just another monster ["A" 00:23:42–00:25:11].

Finally revealing the truth, Michonne finds liberation from the life of isolation she led before meeting her soon-to-be-adopted son, Carl. One *Reddit* user writes how Michonne,

> built up a thorny wall around herself for so long and had slowly started to let people in a little. Then finally after she realizes how badly she needs the people she can trust. She drops the tough-and-distant routine, builds up her comfort level with Carl and completely contrary to her normal attitude, she gets silly for one glorious moment with him [ItsGotToMakeSense].

The slow pace of her disclosure and sharing of her background masterfully fit the time when Carl needed someone to comfort him. Michonne, using a motherly intuition, knew this to be the time to unburden herself for another. This development between Michonne and Carl is exactly why the formatting for *The Walking Dead* as a television series works so well. There is true beauty in how a show can allow its characters to fully embrace changes and disclose aspects in a timeframe that is realistic and does not feel at all forced. Just to put some perspective on the matter, Michonne enters at the end of the second season while this scene with Carl takes place at the end of the fourth season, which is either an absurdly long film or a well-timed series. Michonne's disclosure of specific information comes at her time at her choosing, which makes for a brilliant example of Social Penetration Theory as I mentioned earlier. Essentially, Social Penetration Theory explains how as individuals interact with each other and get to know each other, they engage in a reciprocal process of self-disclosure. Depending on the individuals engaged in the disclosure, the depth (i.e., the level of intimate or sensitive information shared) and breadth (i.e., the variety of subjects covered) of the disclosure ("6.4 Self-Disclosure and Interpersonal

Communication"). For Michonne, her choice of when to reveal or when to withhold information is based primarily on her comfort level with those around her. When she chooses not to disclose specific information, her demeanor is interpreted as cold, angry, standoffish, you name it. Until she can trust those around her, assessing the situation thoroughly, her ability to open up dissolves the impression of the angry Black woman to a person wanting to protect herself from getting too close.

As Michonne unburdens herself, she not only provides comfort for Carl, but she becomes someone he can trust, love, and respect. She becomes a maternal figure to a boy devoid of such companionship. Though Michonne claims she is just another monster, shielding herself with the reanimated corpses of Terry and Mike, it speaks more about Michonne and her understanding of her place in the apocalypse. She removes the jaws of the walkers to keep them from biting. In doing so, she also silences them, just as she takes to silence to hide and to protect herself. By harboring hatred toward these two individuals, Michonne clings to the past by keeping them constantly at her side. Then, in a moment of clarity, she reveals to Carl how "Andrea brought me back. Your dad brought me back. You did" ("A" 00:25:17–00:25:26). Her truth coming out, finding acceptance from Carl and the rest of the group, Michonne no longer needs to walk among the dead but found a place with the living.

Becoming the First Lady

Not only did this scene bring a new layer to her character, but Michonne and Rick as a couple sparked a mashup of their name, "Richonne," complete with a matching hashtag (C. Brown). Unlike Carol and Maggie, who each had relationships at various points throughout the series, this is the first time Michonne becomes intimate with anyone. Although viewers offer varying degrees of acceptance in comments on *Reddit* and *X* about this budding relationship, the debate about Rick and Michonne goes deeper than a conversation about a torrid love story to a discussion about race. While some viewers cheer on the relationship by stating "now that Rick has lost two women to the ZA, I think it's only natural that Rick would turn to someone who can take care of herself" (Damn_Dog_Inappropes), they are not alone when it comes to defending this union despite the makeup of an interracial relationship. As one *Reddit* user comments how, it is "fine not to ship them, but I ship Richonne like Fed Ex. They are the kind of couple that complements each other and brings out the best in each other. They are a really healthy ship without codependency and all that jazz so I'm happy about it" (Sleuth1ngSloth). By allowing herself to begin a relationship with Rick, Michonne finally shows emotional vulnerability, which is a radical change from the mute individual standing at the Prison fence in the third season.

Compared to Maggie or Carol, Michonne guards herself against the countless days spent in isolation stemming from her loss. A glimpse of this reluctance comes in a particular moment during the fourth season when Michonne first refuses to hold baby Judith, and then, after retrieving her from Beth, begins to cry ("Infected"). Even though Michonne later reveals the story of Andre to Carl, this scene ignites speculation from viewers on *Reddit* about her backstory, especially with her relationship towards children. Although this scene shows a hint of her vulnerability, Michonne barely opens herself up to anyone, except, eventually, Carl. Between their conversations revealing her past and her mimicking a walker with a can of spray cheese in the fourth season, Michonne shows Carl a gentler side of her persona as she becomes a surrogate mother to both Carl and Judith. Even before her disclosure about Andre, she is overly protective of Carl as she is unwilling to leave him alone to fend off a group of walkers when he attempts to retrieve a family portrait from the King County Café in the third season ("Clear"). After reuniting with Carol, Tyreese, and Judith following their escape from Terminus, she happily strokes baby Judith's hair ("No Sanctuary"). And, when Deanna (Tovah Feldshuh) bestows Michonne with the role of constable while the group integrates into the community of Alexandria, she is seen by others as a guardian, a trait associated with both a motherly figure and a fatherly protector. And, since Deanna asks both her and Rick to become constables for Alexandria, she is equal in authority and potential as a leader ("Remember").

Not only does their relationship last, but they also blossom an incredibly blended family between Carl, Judith, and later, Rick Grimes, Jr., (RJ) (Antony Azor). While this blended family agonizes over Carl's death in the eighth season and Rick's confession about Judith's birth father in the seventh season, Rick and Michonne do discuss the possibility of a family. Asking Michonne to take a break from developing plans for life, Rick suggestively tells her he "can think of another way to build for the future" ("Warning Signs" 00:07:33–00:07:37). By the expression on Michonne's face, she seems confused by his suggestion at first. After Lori and Jessie fall victim to the ravenous undead, as the comment on *Reddit* about these two women shows, Rick's choice in starting a family with Michonne again reflects her strength and ability as an equal. And, as one anonymous *Reddit* viewer comments, this episode reveals remarkable parallels between characters. According to the viewer,

> I lost my shit when Rick indirectly told Michonne that he wants a baby
> with her, if that's gonna happen then it's good, we will still have the Grimes

blood on the show. The family sequence was lovely, felt like his last day at home.... The dynamic between Carol and Rick was interesting, both of them lost their kids. Sophia'a death made Carol strong, while Carl's death made Rick scared.... If he's the protagonist then it doesn't mean that he's right... [Comment on "The Walking Dead S09E03—Warning Signs—Post Episode Discussion"].

As this comment shows, though Rick is considered the main protagonist, his decisions and actions in the series are not beyond contestation. Instead, with rumors of Rick's exit looming, the legacy will continue through the introduction of a growing family, especially regarding Judith (a force in her own right as later episodes show and discussed later).

Interestingly, while Michonne speaks of a future while in her co-parenting relationship with Rick, his assumed death leads Michonne to regress into the skepticism that kept her alive and eventually brought her to the core group. Unlike Carol using her knowledge of her former weakness to hide, Michonne does not hide her distrust of others. In the world of *The Walking Dead*, roles such as traditional housewife and motherly identities die out since the apocalypse requires developing fighting skills and the ability to kill without emotion. At the same time, one-dimensional masculinist categorizations of zombie-killers also diminish as the apocalypse demands taking care of children. When Judith, now ten, saves a group from walkers, Michonne agrees for them to appeal their case in front of the council of Alexandria, comprised of members from the core group, namely Aaron (Ross Marquand), Father Gabriel Stokes (Seth Gilliam), and Michonne herself. Though many viewers expressed their discontent with Michonne's attitude and apprehension toward these newcomers, others vouched for her decision-making skills. One *Reddit* post notes the rise of her "old world skills kicking in" while reminding others to "...not forget she was a prosecutor before all of this" (pheakelmatters). Revealing a hidden prison tattoo on Magna's hand as evidence the group is not to be trusted, Michonne gives a stern warning to remember the hardships those in Alexandria experienced before she walks triumphantly away from the meeting ("Who Are You Now?"). As one viewer comments on *X*, "I know we were all worried about the Walking Dead once Rick was 'gone' but I think Michonne has it covered. She is powerful and fierce in this episode. #TheWalkingDead" (@TheMariahRamsey). Even in Rick's absence, Michonne maintains her ability through a keen awareness of others and intuition as a lawyer, skills not thought to be as necessary when fighting for survival against the dead.

In addition to distrust, Michonne resumes her practice of speaking to herself as she did after losing her boyfriend. In the third season, her confession to Rick about talking to her dead boyfriend allowed the two to bond when Rick lost his wife Lori ("Clear"). Now, having suffered loss again, Michonne often speaks to Rick, a point not missed by viewers or Judith. Though viewers assume the war between the Saviors, or the loss of Rick is the source of her apprehension of allowing strangers into the community, a flashback reveals an agonizing choice: kill a group of lethally trained children led by her former friend Jocelyn (Rutina Wesley) or lose Judith. In this flashback, a pregnant Michonne welcomes her old friend into Alexandria and, letting down her guard, allows Jocelyn to babysit Judith and other Alexandrian children during a sleepover. Realizing the children are missing, Michonne and Daryl embark upon a rescue mission. Defeating both capture and torment by branding, Michonne and Daryl escape their confinement and, in a gut-wrenching decision, execute the children trying to kill them before they reach Judith ("Scars").

Though some comments on *Reddit* question Michonne, this scene offers a telling moment for Michonne and her angst. As one viewer comments, "when a lifelong friend stabs you in the back, you don't just learn to distrust outsiders. You learn that anyone can turn on you at any time and you need to stand entirely for yourself. And that's what Michonne was aiming for…" (TardsRunThisAsylum). Michonne, as a mother and protector of Alexandria, refuses to let her guard down again. Already losing two sons, two lovers, and perhaps countless friends, she is not ready or willing to lose any more, even if it means forbidding newcomers into their safe zone. Looking at Michonne in the ninth season, though she resumes her skeptical nature, she emerges a different character from when she first entered the narrative. Dubbing her the "most powerful character on The Walking Dead," Johnny O'Dell notes how "even after all this time Michonne still has layers to peel back, like with Magna's group" ("The Walking Dead Season 9"). Peeling back layers is an analogy quite fitting of Social Penetration Theory as layers of the self are revealed only when the person chooses to reveal them (i.e., like peeling the layers of an onion). In the presence of Magna's group, Michonne does not reveal her layers because, well, she does not know them. Only after the group integrate themselves into the community do they get to know Michonne and understand her apprehension about letting them in.

Embodying the characteristics of a strong Black woman, Michonne certainly carries the burdens of others. Between choosing motherhood and assuming leadership, Michonne is not only responsible for her children but the safety of an entire community. Michonne acting as the lead Black female protagonist brings weight to her character extending far beyond her onscreen decisions. From the essay "The Importance of Neglected Intersections: Race and Gender in Contemporary Zombie Texts and Theories," Kinitra Brooks notes:

Too often, the supposed inordinate strength of black women becomes the starting point for all characterizations of black women, be they monstrous or not.... The dehumanization that occurs with this stereotype, ... is a hurdle that must be acknowledged and overcome within contemporary zombie theory. Kirkman and [director Danny] Boyle [of *28 Days Later* fame] successfully initiate a subversion of the stereotype by building upon it, expanding its parameters as they begin to construct multifaceted black women characters who are allowed to possess the full range of their humanity [469; emphasis added].

For Michonne, she not only represents strength and guidance for her daughter and son but viewers looking for, a previously discussed *Reddit* comment shows, "a girl I can relate to" (Ihadacow) to emerge. One who is strong, capable, and even when the world is coming to an end, can maintain her humanity. She is also not one who is willing to give up or risk what took years and lost lives to build.

By the time the Whisperers enter the series, Judith is seen wielding a katana with the ease and expertise of her adopted mother. Still, despite her ability, Judith is still quite young with much to learn about the world and the people in it. For Michonne to take over the role of mother, she not only cares for the survival of her community, but this child she chooses to protect. What is more, the birth of R.J. does not diminish her care for Judith. In the absence of Rick, Michonne tries ever so carefully to keep her emotional struggles out of her children's sight. The burden of being a parent in the apocalypse is not only in ensuring the survival of their children but to maintain a level of emotional stability. According to Kirsh, to support a child's psychological well-being, the personality of the parent must be "high in openness, agreeableness, extraversion, and conscientious" all while being "low in emotional instability" (100). Taking these words into consideration, Michonne has a reason for putting up her walls. While she must be strong for her community, she must also be strong for her children.

If I can say anything about Michonne, it is how much I've enjoyed her character. She's quick, witty, and resolute. With her journey continuing in *The Walking Dead: The Ones Who Live*, Michonne demonstrates the strong mind and skill necessary to persist in the apocalyptic world of *The Walking Dead*. Even more, her choice to locate Rick after finding clues to his potential survival after the bridge explosion midway through the ninth season and leave her children to be cared for by others shows her tremendous growth in the series. She is no longer the silent and untrusting katana-wielding badass introduced to viewers so many years ago. Though she undoubtedly endured tremendous adversities, which led her to build walls, she has come to a place where she is recognized and acknowledged as a leader, a quality she must hide while under the watchful eye of the Civic Republic Military (CRM).

Carol, Maggie, and Michonne: A Reflection

Despite being three very different women, Carol, Maggie, and Michonne share incredibly similar qualities regarding gender roles within *The Walking Dead*. Arguably the weakest of the three, Carol Peletier emerges a true warrior queen. Initially submissive and inept in protecting her daughter, a fault which cost Sophia her life, Carol grows out of her pitiful state to become a protector for a much larger apocalyptic family. After the first two seasons, the women in *The Walking Dead* "who conform to the patriarchal power structures that render women 'the nurturer' are destroyed, while those women who fight against these structures survive" (Erwin 79). Carol fully embodies this defiance in her decision to kill two members of the group to prevent illness from overtaking the Prison, much to the shock of Rick.

Through trial and tribulation, Carol surpasses expectations to survive on her own after expulsion from the group and returns in glorifying fashion to bring down Terminus independently. However, when viewers dub Carol "Rambo" on social media, their association of her assault with the hypermasculine fantasy seems to have merit, but only if she sought this glory. For the women of *The Walking Dead*, they act without expectation of recognition. Instead, Carol acts only to protect others and, through subtle signs of remorse, ponders the implications of her actions, something the men fail to do in the series. Eventually, in the ninth season, Carol exercises her authority when she chooses the time to accept King Ezekiel's numerous proposals. Additionally, after so many years following the death of her daughter and the Samuels sisters, Carol becomes the mother of Henry, King Ezekiel's adopted son. Now fully believing in her capability to protect a child, Carol enters motherhood excitedly and willingly.

Maggie, though noticeably outspoken and fully able to make runs into town without the need of an escort, shows a slight advantage over Carol. Much younger, and to the like of viewers, quite attractive. Her relationship with Glenn and the subsequent reveal of the barn walkers, launch Maggie headfirst into a realization of the state of the world. The dynamic duo of Glenn and Maggie became a symbol of endurance and hope in the apocalypse. In her decision to marry Glenn and to raise a child, Maggie does so without the need for his protection. She is commanding, headstrong, and unlike Glenn, always focuses on the future. After Glenn's death, and eventually raising a child on her own, Maggie presses on.

As the first woman to hold this position without being associated with a man, Maggie destroys the concept that men lead, and women follow. Carol emancipates herself several seasons before acquiescing to her union with the King, and the community often refers to her as the Queen because of her association. While Michonne does not begin a relationship until Rick, the reference as First Lady relegates her to an association with her partner. Furthermore, in assuming her leadership role, Maggie "is a much more explicit indictment of the traditional domestic sphere ... challeng[ing] the audience in a much more direct way because [she] confronts our expectations as to how a woman should behave if she is about to become a mother" (Erwin 90). Rather than sit back in her pregnant state, Maggie acts. When Rick begs for help in assisting the Sanctuary, Maggie refuses to keep her people her first (and practically only) priority. Maggie is not without compassion, as she demonstrates when sparing the Saviors. Instead, she thinks of what is best for those whom she feels responsible, thus circumventing the obligatory need to protect all. Maggie stands for Hilltop, and the Hilltop stands by Maggie.

Behind the walls of Alexandria, Michonne assumes a role equal to her eventual partner, Rick. Michonne, always capable of protecting herself, now bears the responsibility of safeguarding Alexandria. After beginning a relationship with Rick, Michonne rises to become the First Lady of Alexandria. Having already developed a parental relationship with both Carl and Judith, Michonne readily accepts a maternal role once again. Though Rick's departure left Michonne to raise their children alone with baby RJ coming into the narrative after Rick's departure, Michonne maintains her authority as head of security, with the power to override the decisions of the Alexandrian council. Never giving up her search for Rick, Michonne balances losing her partner with the responsibilities of protecting her people. Though her relationship with the other colonies proves strained because of the near loss of Judith, Michonne learns to depend on the other colonies to build a healthier united family (discussed more in the last chapter). From a solo-yet-capable fighter to a strong and commanding leader, Michonne forever reigns supreme as the First Lady of the Zombie Apocalypse.

Yet, while fully recognizing that these women represent three distinct trajectories in the narrative, all three of these women are undeniably linked through their identification as heterosexual women. Though Michonne staves off a romantic connection the longest, her relationship with Rick, Maggie's relationship with Glenn, and Carol's various relationships with Ed, Tobin, and the King seem to fall in line with the overarching criticism of the show for perpetuating a heteronormative stereotype. Entering motherhood (either biologically or through adoption), these three women continue to uphold the perpetuation of woman as a mother and woman as a wife. Despite such perpetuation, these women choose this association themselves rather than accepting motherhood or wifehood because of their gender. The next chapter highlights three unrepresented and underdiscussed characters, Rosita Espinosa, Tara Chambler, and Enid, and their divergence from such an automatic connection to labels with more attention paid to sexual identity, body autonomy, and breaking glass ceilings.

3

Sexual Identity, Body Autonomy, and Glass Ceilings

Tara, Rosita, and Enid

In the previous chapter, I explored ways in which the characters Carol Peletier, Maggie Rhee, and Michonne Hawthorne redefine gender expectations concerning authority and motherhood. For Carol, shedding her pre-apocalyptic identifiers helped transform her from a defenseless housewife to badass Queen of the Kingdom. For Maggie, the loss of her family and husband motivated her to establish a new identity, leader of the Hilltop Colony. For Michonne, her untrusting demeanor faded to reveal incredible vulnerability following her acceptance into the group and burgeoning role as a protector of the Alexandria Safe-Zone and partner to Rick Grimes. However, while these women emerged anew in the apocalypse, they are only a tiny sampling of the dominant and diverging characters presented in *The Walking Dead*. Tara, the first openly gay character, challenges the issue of heteronormativity rampant in the series. For Rosita, as the first prominent Latina character to join the core group, her cunning and aptitude for technical survival skills demonstrate more than just a commodified, hyper-sexualized body. Enid, a naive and often distant teenager, evolves beyond her status as an object of desire to fulfill a lifesaving role as a doctor, a role mostly relegated to men in the series. This chapter is brings critical awareness to not only gender stereotypes but also the representation of neglected demographics often disregarded in television, especially in the horror genre.

Before I explore such powerful identities, a discussion about my selection of these characters is warranted. As the world of *The Walking Dead* flagship series expands beyond Atlanta, new and incredibly multifaceted characters emerge, profoundly impacting the narrative. However, as *The Walking Dead* routinely introduces stereotypes, the characters added to the series offered little in terms of diversity. Case in point, the second season introduced the Greene family, an all–White pastoral bunch. Even still, those introduced to us in the first season at the Atlanta survivor's camp died or "opted out" as Jacqui did, left the camp looking for family as the Morales Family did, or remained in Atlanta as the Vatos, a seemingly hostile protecting senior citizens at an abandoned nursing home, did. Still, there are characters like T-Dog who persisted. Of course, diversity is not limited to what someone looks like but can manifest itself in other ways. As the show continued in its evolution, it seemed the apparent stereotypes introduced at the start of the series began to give way. Thus, I made it my goal to bring attention to these narrative contributions by focusing on Tara, Rosita, and Enid because they not only demonstrate an incredible transformation from their introductions, but they also diverge from conventionalized roles associated with gender expectations, sexual identity, and body autonomy.

Bury the Tropes, Not the Gays: Tara Chambler

I said it before, and I will say it again: *The Walking Dead* is not without its issues, especially introducing and keeping diverse characters. While there were characters of note in the first two seasons, as I mentioned previously, their narrative trajectories were ostensibly cut short by death or other departures. The cycle of minimizing minorities to secondary characters and silencing women, not to mention killing both demographics, perpetuated through the third season. It was not until the fourth season that *The Walking Dead* introduced its first openly gay character. While great news for the LGBTQ+ community to finally have some representation on in this televised narrative, these characters are likely to fall victim to the "bury your gays" trope, which promotes the erasure of gays within a story by killing them off quickly and typically following a moment of happiness or intimacy. In doing so, "LGBTQ fans and their identities … become marginalized, causing a misrepresentation for understanding themselves and others" (Waggoner 1879). Tara Chamber defies convention and represents a group routinely overlooked and under-received on television.

Assertive and foul-mouthed, Tara offers a refreshingly different representation of women in this horror narrative. Her battle-ready skills prove helpful in protecting her family inside the confines of their apartment and later when escaping the Prison with Glenn in the fourth season. Before the apocalypse, Tara's training to become a police officer disrupts the programmed supposition represented by both Rick and Shane as the automatic (male) leaders and saviors in this new world. Additionally, her departure from the safety of their family residence permits Tara to reach an awakening of self. Within the confines of the apartment, her utility lies in protecting her family. But this lack of exposure also limits her acceptance as a gay woman by those closest to her. After leaving a life of isolation behind, Tara symbolically emerges into public awareness, where her status as a gay female is openly discussed and embraced by viewers. Lastly, while not entirely fitting into the category of "[r]esilient but feminine wives and mothers … wait[ing] to be saved by their husbands" (Cady and Oates 316) typified in earlier seasons, a resilient but feminine gay woman defies heteronormativity dominant to this point in the series through her continuation in the narrative, assimilation into the core group, and promotion to interim leader of the Hilltop Colony in Maggie's absence.

A Lesbian in the World of the Undead

Akin to the introductions of both Carol and Maggie, Tara also enters the narrative through a patriarchal lens. However, instead of the triumphant Western hero Rick Grimes, viewers first learn of Tara from the storyline of the Governor after his displacement from Woodbury at the end of the third season. In the episode "Live Bait," the Governor, assuming the name "Brian," finds himself in the company of the Chambler family residing in an abandoned apartment building. Quite outspoken and lacking restraint when addressing the newcomer, Tara asserts her dominance through her pre-apocalyptic role as a police officer in training. Sliding her gun across the table as if to scare him, Tara threatens, "This here is a fully loaded standard issue Smith and Wesson. I'm Atlanta City Police and I have enough artillery in here to kill you every day for the next ten years. You mess with me[,] or my family and I swear to Christ I will put you down. Got it?" ("Live Bait" 00:06:36–00:07:11). As the dominant figure in her family, Tara carries the burden of their protection. However, as the first openly gay character in the series, her role conveys more in terms of presence and identity. Her sexuality not only diverges from the makeup of the core group, but her presence openly challenges heteronormativity in the series.

Unfortunately, constraining terms such as "lesbian cop" or "lesbian sister" litter the *Reddit* threads focused on her introductory episode. By limiting her character to such comments, viewers offered Tara little hope in establishing an identity beyond her sexual identity. Mixed in with the complaints about her shoddy dialogue, a fault many viewers place upon the writers of this specific episode, are comments dismissing Tara as overtly formulaic and a secondary character at best. As one viewer writes, "I hate how lazy the writers are on this show. Female training to be a cop? Lesbian.

Woman in the Army? Lesbian. Can't wait to see the gay hairdresser make an appearance" (Baelorn). Perhaps even more demeaning than the pigeonholing associated with her character are the relentless comments by viewers reducing her character to just "the lesbian" rather than identifying her by name. An example of such labeling becomes apparent as one *Reddit* user openly laments, "The 2 women he meets are just terrible actresses. The lesbian 'cop' was horrible. Every line. Every scene. So. Bad. Lets keep in mind the previous episode the governor shows up to the jail alone. The 2 women and the little girl are goners IMO" (ChunkfaceMcDirtyDick). From this and other similar comments questioning her status as a cop and depriving Tara of an identity, viewers quickly dismissed Tara as bringing nothing more to the narrative outside of her sexuality or, as another posted on *Reddit* concludes, "…Sister = Tara = sorta-cop = not-bang (lesbian)" (HeyHershel).

Quite noticeable in the first three seasons of *The Walking Dead* was its primary focus on re-establishing the heteronormative nuclear family, the failed attempt to usurp control from one dominant White male to another, and the safety of a ubiquitously heterosexual core group. Though the Governor, aka Brian, temporarily usurps Tara's authority, thus perpetuating the "resiliency of the heteronormative nuclear family as the central formation in such stories," as Kathryn Cady and Thomas Oates argue in their article "Family Splatters: Rescuing Heteronormativity from the Zombie Apocalypse" (309), her long trajectory in the narrative disrupts the character demographics previously established. Thus, Tara distances herself from the fate of Alisha (Juliana Harkavy) and Dr. Denise Cloyd (Merritt Wever), two love interests in the series, both characters die after appearing in only one season. Now, I do want to clarify that these characters are not the only gay characters presented in the series, nor would they be the last. The point of my retelling here is to illustrate significant underrepresentation of the LGBTQ+ community in the series.

Returning to Tara and her origins in the narrative, her sexuality completely diverts from her graphic novel counterpart, further disrupting the "bias towards heterosexual couples and white sexually active characters in the series," as Emily Zarka contends (123). Though Zarka proclaims that the sexual politics of *The Walking Dead* are "influenced by gender and race" in the chapter "The Sexualized Heroics of Rick and Michonne" (123), her claims apply only to the graphic novel from which this character originates. In *The Rise of the Governor* graphic novel story arc, Tara's sexuality is not disclosed (Flowers). Therefore, while it could be easy to chastise the television series for not having "any gay, lesbian, bisexual, or transgender characters" midway into the fifth season (Lavin and Lowe 122), the inclusion of Tara as the first openly gay character not only makes her a uniquely important adaptation to the series but groundbreaking for LGBTQ+ roles in television.

The lack of attention to sexual diversity, as Lavin and Lowe lament above, is not wholly without merit, as any instances of Tara's sexuality are quickly overshadowed by other developments in the narrative. Case in point, when Tara and her sister, Lily Chambler (Audrey Marie Anderson), openly discuss Tara's first love, Sam, their conversation is quickly overshadowed when the group abandons their search for a vehicle to flee from a hoard of walkers ("Live Bait"). Even when Tara begins her first relationship with Alisha, she does not refer to her as her girlfriend until after the Governor's unsuccessful attack on the Prison. When the two are shown together on screen before the assault, some viewers complained on *Reddit* that their relationship feels compulsory, as though the writers "decided to put it in at the last second. They didn't develop it like any other relationship on the show. They just threw it in for the heck of it" (dsr541). In other words, by not emphasizing Tara's sexuality or, more overtly, promoting her relationship with Alisha, her character does not come off as convincing. Over the seasons leading up to Tara's introduction, the heterosexual relationships serve a minimal purpose other than to set Rick on his adventure to reunite with his family and perpetuate a continual cycle of establishing the long reign of heteronormative nuclear families.

As a gay character, Tara offers viewers more than a colorfully worded figure. Identifying as both a woman and a lesbian, Tara is as equal in importance and development to the other characters in this series. With comments discussing the impact a gay character has on *The Walking Dead*, alternative views offer different perspectives on how to read Tara as a developing character and the casual nature of her relationships within this series. Refuting the claim about the supposedly forced relationship between Tara and Alisha mentioned earlier, one viewer argues how

> …not making a big deal out of it really normalizes it—there are a few shows on TV now that have gay couples, but Walking Dead isn't going to be like "look at us we have a gay couple too!" … they fu.5nction like some of the background heterosexual couples (wives and husbands that are just there—like the Hispanic family at the Atlanta camp in the first season) which means that we're progressing a bit—gay couples don't need a big hoopla because it's normal. So—I don't think it's forced. I think it just is what it is. Which is nice [Frodoholic].

By not emphasizing or creating a "hoopla," as the comment above claims, Tara possesses an ordinariness about her because of her relationship with Alisha and, later, Denise. X users openly cheered on this coupling, with one exclaiming how "they have a gay couple on the walking dead and I think its wonderful. yay for twd. @WalkingDead_AMC #TheWalkingDead"

(@sempiternal_kat), with another viewer echoing this delight by exclaiming, "FINALLY A LESBIAN COUPLE ON THE WALKING DEAD!!! Just saying. That's the only couple I support on this show! #TheWalkingDead" (@MichelleTelles_). The simplicity of the relationship (if any relationship can be simple in the apocalypse) between Tara and Alisha demonstrates the normalcy of the heterosexual relationships previously established in the series.

More than equality, the inclusion of Tara highlights the very essence of the series. This is a story of *human* survival. And as a story of human survival, nowhere is there any restriction or limitation placed on the demographics of these characters. As one viewer aptly cheers,

> Although the zombie-centered show includes many top-notch action scenes, it's really a show about how people muster, maintain, or misuse strength as they relate to one another during times of crisis. It's an excellent, high-profile show about the human condition, basically, and since queer people are humans, *we should be on it* [Mandanas; emphasis added].

Indeed, *The Walking Dead* is a story about human survival in an apocalyptic world, a comment even the Kirkman gives when describing the narrative as "a continuing story of survival horror" (Cover copy). As the show evolves and new survivors enter the story, the world of *The Walking Dead* expands beyond the scope of the hero sheriff reuniting with his family.

Recognition, Identity, and Acceptance

Tara is also an incredibly vulnerable and flawed character, exemplifying very relatable human qualities and giving her a sense of authenticity. Up to the Prison assault in the fourth season, any consideration of Tara's character development or focus on her relationships is overshadowed by her portrayal as a figure hellbent on revenge. Nevertheless, Tara's sometimes-corny lines and her sharp tongue remind audiences that while she is temporarily eclipsed by the Governor's very prominently displayed male ego, she is still there. Furthermore, as a television show about "how people muster, maintain, or misuse strength as they relate to one another during times of crisis" (Mandaras), she not only owns up to her flaws in judgment but tries to make amends. After helping a weakened Glenn escape from the shambles of the Prison, Tara first profusely apologizes for the attack and Hershel's death before questioning her value in his quest to find Maggie. Fighting back her tears, Tara pronounces, "I mean, I'm a piece of shit. Why would you want my help?" ("Inmates" 00:39:50–00:40:05). As if taking on full responsibility for the Governor and his assault on the Prison, Tara bears incredible guilt for trusting "Brian" and the destruction left in his wake.

Her emergence from seclusion with her family, then into the militant group led by the deceitful Brian, and eventually entering the core group forces Tara into an awakening of self and control over her agency. Despite her remorse and constant questioning of her worth, Tara saves an unconscious Glenn from a small group of walkers. Smashing in the head of one of their assailants with the butt of a gun, Tara encounters a green military truck. Shouting, "Hope you enjoyed the show, assholes," through her panting breath, Abraham, Rosita, and Eugene Porter (Josh McDermitt) emerge from the vehicle. Impressed by her sharp tongue, Abraham questions, "What else you got?" ("Inmates" 00:42:08–00:42:29); a pertinent inquiry worth contemplating. By joining the trio, which subsequently saves Glenn's life, Tara embarks on an evolutionary journey, further distancing herself from the nameless lesbian viewers condemned. Unlike Maggie and Carol, who learn survival skills in their evolution, Tara comes substantially more prepared to handle weapons, setting her apart from the submissive and helpless personas depicted by women in the seasons before the Prison. Emotionally, on the other hand, Tara is woefully unprepared for encountering the callousness of other humans.

While remaining in the confines of the apartment where her family sought refuge, Tara does not possess full awareness of the world and the still living (and very dangerous) beings. Instead, she projects a tough exterior, a trait typically associated with the men of the series. Her projection quickly fades as the once brash Tara cowers in fear when taking part in the assault on the Prison. Interestingly, according to *Autostraddle* contributor Laura Mandanas in the article "The Walking Dead Brings Another Queer Chick Named Tara to TV, We Rejoice," though Tara comes off cocky and tends to exaggerate, her more emotional side is a welcomed divergence. As Mandanas writes, "…it's kind of refreshing to see unjaded characters who are still horrified by the idea of killing people/former-people … and I'm curious if/how her unique experiences as a queer person will come into play." Her unique experience as a queer person ultimately manifests in her longevity. However, viewers express their appreciation for the ordinariness of her character, a far cry from the demeaning comments regarding the unnamed lesbian first seen in the fourth season. On *Reddit*, one viewer writes,

> I think Tara is shaping up to be one of my most favourite characters. She thinks rationally, acts like a normal person, isn't a master at things but is still a great asset, works hard, has had a lot of loss in her life, but still fights on, and even makes jokes to lighten the atmosphere. She legitimately cares about people, and really does try to fit in with the rest of the group [H-K_47].

Far from perfect, her flaws in judgment align her perfectly with the other members of the group who are far from perfect themselves.

Even more humanizing than her self-deprecation and imperfect nature is her need for recognition not as the "lesbian cop" or "lesbian sister," but as Tara. In the same episode where the core group welcomes Tara, she finally receives acceptance from the one person she needs to hear from the most, Maggie. Taking a seat by Maggie, Tara confesses, "I was at the prison. With the Governor. I didn't know who he was or what he could do. And I didn't know who all of you were. I— I just didn't want it to be hidden. That I was there" ("Strangers" 00:35:20–00:35:40). Responding with the words, "You're here with us now" ("Strangers" 00:35:46–00:36:05), Maggie offers Tara an embracing hug signaling acceptance of Tara as a person beyond her transgressive association with the Governor. Tara is both seen and heard. In the chapter "For Love is Strong as Death," Kim Paffenroth explains how "[t]he loving relationships we form with other people, including romantic attachments and ties between parents, children, and siblings, are ... the most fundamental and constant source of meaning and purpose in our lives" (224). Tara becomes a meaningful extension of this apocalyptic blended family.

Emerging from confinement, Tara leaves a secretive existence where only her family knows about her true self. Openly discussing her love for someone named Sam and later entering into a relationship with both Alisha and Denise, Tara distances herself from "[t]he bias[es] of compulsory heterosexuality," as described by Adrienne Reich in "Compulsory Heterosexuality and Lesbian Existence" (13). The first three seasons of *The Walking Dead* lend themselves to many "fairy tales, television, films, advertising, popular songs, wedding pageantry," continuing to perpetuate the ideal of heterosexual relationships as the norm (Reich 24). Interrupting the status quo, Tara brings an uplifting and welcomed change to the heterosexual relationships institutionalized before her arrival into the narrative. Leaving her family and life in seclusion, Tara finds acceptance and validation of herself.

Eluding the Dead Lesbian Syndrome

As one of the few openly gay characters onscreen, Tara becomes more than just a key figure at Hilltop. She is a much-beloved character and a symbol of drastic change from the immature, fist-bumping personality first introduced three seasons earlier. When Tara initially appeared in the fourth season of *The Walking Dead*, she entered the narrative during a time when LGBTQ+ characters were on the rise in scripted broadcast television. According to a *2013 Where We Are on TV* report by GLAAD, formerly the Gay & Lesbian Alliance Against Defamation, the "number of LGBT characters on scripted primetime cable television continued to rise this year with an additional seven regular characters, for a total of 42 in the 2013–2014 season" (3). Considering the 796 characters included in the report for broadcast series regulars, the number of LGBT representations on television appears pathetically minuscule, even with the noted increase (*2013 Where We Are on TV* 12). Not yet a series regular, her presentation as a poorly written and immature woman seemed to mark her for early demise in the eyes of viewers. Nevertheless, she persisted. Her return in the fifth season placed Tara among the 105 LGBT characters on cable television (*2014 Where We Are on TV* 14).

As a gay character in an apocalyptic narrative, Tara must combat the dead while also becoming another victim of the "bury your gays" trope. More specifically, in the case of Tara and other characters like her, they must outlive "Dead Lesbian Syndrome" (Snarker). According to Dorothy Snarker in the article "bury your gays: Why 'The 100,' 'Walking Dead' Death are Problematic," this trope has roots dating back to 1976 with the show *Executive Suite*, a primetime soap opera featuring a large corporate conglomerate based in Los Angeles. Rather than receiving happier endings, an extraordinarily high number of lesbians on television continuously meet tragic ends (Snarker). For those seeking an identifiable character, the lack of representation has an even more detrimental impact, especially for those wanting acceptance at home or elsewhere. In the article "bury your gays and Social Media Fan Response: Television, LGBTQ Representation, and Communitarian Ethics," Erin Waggoner urges an understanding of the implications this extreme absence of LGBTQ+ representation has on viewers. According to Waggoner, "Meaning-making processes are part of the symbolic interaction that occurs when engaging with media. For LGBTQ+ fans, this is especially important in their own meaning-making as representation becomes an important aspect of this process" (1880). Without an excellent depiction to observe, as Waggoner concludes, those looking for a queer icon to identify with are offered little guidance or solid character examples to follow. Tara Chambler signifies a community of individuals frequently underrepresented on television, adding to her already weighty persona.

Nevertheless, while the series makes considerable strides to create an inclusive and diverse cast, deaths can and do happen, even to characters of diverging sexual orientations or identification. When Lizzie shoots Alisha in the head during the assault on the Prison in the fourth season, viewers swiftly point out the quickness of this death. As one anonymous viewer questions, "the one openly gay couple I can recall in the show thus far, and they had to kill her right off the bat?" (Comment on "The Walking Dead S04E08 'Too Far Gone' Post-Episode Discussion Thread"). However, when Tara begged to retreat, Alisha's choice to continue participating in the assault resulted in her death. Furthermore, in the world of *The Walking*

Dead, losses can and do happen regardless of gender, race, or sexual identity. Riley Silverman notes in the article "Immortal LGBT Characters is Not the Solution to 'bury your gays,'" reducing gay characters to mere statistics, such as an *Autostraddle* list created to catalog gay deaths in visual narratives, actually disfavors characters such as Tara rather than promotes awareness. Continuing about the importance of alleviating restrictive dualism (that is, they are either alive or dead), the author concludes how "reducing our stories into binary tallies of whether we live or die does a complete disservice to the potential for three-dimensional, nuanced characters within a genre of storytelling that we yearn to see more of ourselves in" (Silverman). Thus, instead of focusing on potential death, viewers should focus on the contribution these characters give to the storyline.

Unfortunately for Tara and her later love interest, Denise, their romance meets its end and yet another tragic example of the perpetual "bury your gays" trope. Returning from scavenging for medicine at a local apothecary outside of Alexandria with Rosita and Daryl, an arrow shot by a Savior hiding in the woods strikes Denise through her eye, instantly killing her. Though Savior Dwight (Austin Amelio) confesses the arrow was not meant for Denise, her death means more than just being an unfortunate casualty of his bad aim ("Too Far Gone"). In the article "TV Keeps Killing off Lesbian Characters," Bethonie Butler addresses a particularly cruel aspect of the trope. She concludes that "LGBT characters are frequently killed off—often in tragic ways, following a happy event" (B. Butler). The event focused upon by Butler was the death of another openly gay character, Lexa (Alycia Debnam-Carey), from the CW science fiction television series *The 100* (as irony would have it, Lexa was killed off the show to join in the second season filming of *Fear the Walking Dead*). For Denise, her quick death follows the killing of her first walker and recovering a can of orange soda. While killing the walker demonstrates her acquired skill from training with Rosita, the soda was an intended gift for her girlfriend, Tara.

Outraged fans took to social media to express their disapproval of yet another gay character dying so quickly after being introduced in the series (Denise and Alisha die within a few episodes after their introductions). On *X*, one fan claims, "And the bury your gays trope strikes again. I stand with you The Walking Dead fans. LGBT fans deserve better. #RIP-Denise" (@JazzOfLion), while another viewer declares, "THAT WAS THE WORST THING TO EVER HAPPEN TO MY GAY LITTLE HEART I HATE THE WALKING DEAD I'M DONE" (@emma_korte). The continuance of "bury your gays" in this scene cannot be dismissed. Just two weeks before Denise died retrieving a soda for her girlfriend, fans of *The 100* witness the death of Lexa shortly after consummating her relationship with

Clarke Griffin (Eliza Taylor), another female character in the series. Reprimanding show creator Jason Rothenberg for "'queer-bating'" fans with a love story between Lexa and Clarke, fans demanded an explanation for the decision to kill off one of the few lesbian characters on television (B. Butler; Fussell; Murphy, "'The 100' Fans Got Angry about a Queer Woman's Death"). Prompted by this outcry, Rothenberg issued an apology, stating, the "honesty, integrity and vulnerability [actress] Eliza Taylor and [actress] Alycia Debnam-Carey brought to their characters served as an inspiration to many of our fans. Their relationship held greater importance than I ever realized. And that very important representation was taken away by one stray bullet" ("The Life and Death of Lexa"). For Tara, her time to grieve the loss of Denise appears merely ancillary as war with the Saviors looms and the colonies make themselves battle-ready. However, the accidental murder of Denise deepens Eugene's character as he implements a diversionary tactic allowing himself, Rosita, Daryl, and Abraham to escape capture.

As fans openly take to social media to voice their delight or dissent, there are positive notes to take away from such narrative tragedies. Take, for example, this comment about how *The Walking Dead* is "the only show where lgbt characters aren't defined by their sexuality like most shows nowadays and they don't do any queer baiting either" (Fit-Diet-6488). Since the death of Lexa on *The 100*, fans using X and the trending topic "LGBT Fans Deserve Better" became an internationally led fan initiative (B. Butler). Additionally, the Trevor Project, which provides a 24-hour national suicide hotline and other services for LGBT or questioning youths, received fundraising thanks to outraged fans of television shows such as *The 100* (B. Butler; Snarker). While Tara meets her demise at the end of the ninth season, her death means more to the series than another perpetuation of the trope. Tara died not because of her sexual orientation but because of her importance as the interim leader of Hilltop. Contending how "'Story-wise in this case, Alpha's goal was to terrorize the communities and force them to comply with her rules," showrunner Angela Kang explains, "So there's a mix of strategic murders, with Tara, random with Enid, and vengeance-driven with Henry'" (qtd. in Bonomolo, "'The Walking Dead' Criticized"). Though Tara rose prominently to become a scavenger for the Alexandria colony, was strategic in persuading the Oceanside colony to join the war against the Saviors, and later became the leader of Hilltop in the absence of Maggie. Following the death of Paul "Jesus" Rovia (Tom Payne), one of the few other gay figures in the series, her character evolution and contribution to the narrative as a representative of the LGBTQ+ community cannot be understated.

As the outpouring of comments from shocked fans demonstrates, Tara made a definite impact on viewers and a deep connection with members of the LGBTQ+ community. One *X* viewer commented: "I LIT-ERALLY DO NOT CARE ABOUT ANYONE WHO DIED EXCEPT ENID AND TARA WHY DID THE SMARTEST DOCTOR AND ANOTHER HILLTOP LEADER DIE (also @ the walking dead stop killing the gays off) #TheWalkingDead" (@khvlll). Regarding the deaths of LGBTQ+ charac-ters within *The Walking Dead*, these deaths signify more than just a cheap copout for shock value. As Silverman reminds us, television and film will create a world where "we don't judge queer character on simply whether they live or die, but with what they do with their time while they have it" ("Immortal LGBT Characters is Not the Solution to 'bury your gays'"). Compared to her graphic novel roots, her character easily could have been much different. As Robert Kirkman himself reveals, while he maintains complete authority over his zombie-filled intellectual property, he retains control as writers transition the comic storyline to television (Feloni).

Though her subtle disclosure keeps her sexuality lowkey, Tara tran-scends her corny fist-bumping persona to a mature, well-loved leader, friend, and zombie-killing powerhouse and outside of Aaron, the longest-running gay character in the series. While Tara, Jesus, Eric Raleigh (Jordan Woods-Robinson), and Denise are no longer part of the sto-ryline, other openly gay characters remain (mainly Aaron and newcom-ers Yumiko and Magna, who will be discussed in the next chapter). Still, the marginalization of LGBTQ+ representation cannot be excused. Never-theless, the efforts to bring awareness to initiatives like The Trevor Project demonstrate how characters like Tara live on well beyond their television run. And, as fans show, they will not quietly accept any lack of represen-tation or injustices committed against LGBTQ+ characters on television.

A Silent Bombshell to Outspoken Warrior: Rosita Espinosa

Unaware of the circumstances leading up to her arrival in the narra-tive, Rosita quietly enters the world of *The Walking Dead* during the fourth season, accompanied by an outspoken and smug military veteran named Abraham and a squeamish mullet-haired scientist named Eugene. Regret-tably, in the introduction of Rosita, the writers reduce her to a silent prop for the vast majority of the fifth season. Uttering only a few words here and there, Rosita appears to be nothing more than glorified eye candy for both Abraham and viewers. Always overshadowed and underutilized, Rosita mainly stands in the background, her midriff exposed and pigtails topping off her girlified appearance. Not until her separation from Abraham does Rosita gain autonomy, shifting from just being seen to finally being heard.

Later, revealing her effective use of her sexuality, Rosita draws attention to her body to gain valuable, even life-saving skills. Rosita does not quite fulfill the spitfire stereotype unlike other examples of Latina women in television at the time of her introduce to the series. Sexually frivolous and fully aware of her power as a woman, Rosita evolves from using her body to gain an advantage to becoming a nurturing and developed mother.

Additionally, as the only Latina in the main cast, Rosita represents a marginalized group on television. However, her hypersexualized presence in her introductory episode prompted sneering comments from viewers, which primarily focused on her impractical zombie apocalypse attire and one even dubbing her the "Latina croft" (eedna). By all appearances (quite literally in this case), Rosita initially embodies a misguided representation of Latina women. Due in large part to what Isabel Molina-Guzman describes as symbolic colonization, the depiction of Rosita connotes a "homogenized construct" of race and ethnicity (9). Still, as Rosita continues to evolve in the series and separates from being overshadowed by her partner, viewer comments shift away from (although not wholly) her looks to more on what she contributes to the narrative as a robust and capable zombie apocalypse warrior. Though viewers' comments are not devoid of referencing her attractiveness, some viewers embrace Rosita for her action-oriented attitude and, after the revelation of her pregnancy, come to her defense when her sexually prolific history comes under attack.

Symbolic and Apocalyptic Colonization of the Latina Body

Though she barely utters a word upon her entry into the fourth season of *The Walking Dead*, online commentors could not stop posting her appearance. After watching Tara smash in the face of a walker with the stock of a rifle, Rosita sashays across the front of an armored truck, hair in pigtails, and wearing an outfit reminiscent of an oversexed mercenary. Openly disapproving of this choice in wardrobe, one viewer states, "Sure Walking Dead the only Latina character is barely wearing clothes. Name her Lara Croft while you're at it. #TheWalkingDead" (@gabeisidoro). Thanks to her severe lack of depth and almost silent presence, Abraham often dominates their screen time with his embellished and loud personality. With "her visual presence ... work[ing] against the development of a story line," the initial appearance of Rosita implies a certain "to-be-looked-at-ness" as described by Laura Mulvey in her infamous 1975 essay "Visual Pleasure and Narrative Cinema" (364). In other words, Rosita offers viewers and the narrative little in advancing the storyline other than her looks. Quite the opposite of Tara, Rosita is scarcely heard but fully on display.

With her body always prominently displayed, Rosita embodies symbolic colonization, presenting her as a Latina through a manufactured perception of race and ethnicity (Molina-Guzman 9). For the first few episodes after her introduction, Rosita often takes residence in the background, except for the occasional shots where she bends over awkwardly for the camera and thus accentuating her role as a fetish object. Through symbolic colonization, as Isabel Molina-Guzman explains in *Dangerous Curves: Latina Bodies in the Media*, "media practices reproduce dominant norms, values, beliefs, and public understandings about Latinidad as gendered, racialized, foreign, exotic, and consumable" (9). The audience's reception of Rosita, comprising comments regarding her less-than-practical apocalyptic attire, supports the consumable representation of her body. At the same time, these comments complain about her wardrobe, and viewers subsequently pardon this violation because of her evident attractiveness. As one viewer comments, "Rosita's outfit did not look very apocalypse friendly. *However, I'm not complaining*" (Agent-Cooper; emphasis added), while another viewer similarly posts, "Is Rosita going to get any lines? All she has done is stand there and look attractive. *Not that I'm complaining*" (Masenkoe). While these two commentators are among a group who seem appeased by her placement, others are not too content with her treatment as a prop. To illustrate this point, this post on *Reddit* claims,

> Robert Kirkman does not know how to write women. Comic readers can attest to this. ... In Kirkman's world there are basically three types of females: the little girl in need of shelter; the hot piece of ass; the emotionally-dead killing machine. Rosita falls into the second of those categories. The reason she dresses the way she does, is because she's basically nothing more than Abraham's fuck toy. That's how she survives. I don't think Kirkman is deliberately a sexist. I just think he doesn't know shit about women [GaiusMagnus].

The assertion that Kirkman does not know how to write women is understandable when considering how the graphic novel version of Rosita offers very little than her attractiveness. Nevertheless, while Kirkman reserves complete control over his creation, he does not necessarily prohibit changes. At some point in the development of her character, a conscious decision was made to transfer the sexualized Latina image straight from the graphic novel to television.

The debate about Rosita demonstrates an incredible capacity for an audience to determine her worth as a character in the narrative. Mostly, the reception or rejection of her image, the symbolic rupture, "points to the process of interpretation that allows audiences ... as cultural readers to disrupt the process of symbolic colonization" (Molina-Guzman 9). The "'girlification'" of Rosita, a term Brooke Bennett applies to her character in the article

"Tough Women of the Apocalypse: Gender Performativity in AMC's *The Walking Dead*," further emphasizes Rosita's position as an object rather than as a significant character (94). In Bennett's view, "Rosita is not only sexualized [but] turned into an emblem of girlhood—especially via her hairstyle that is seldom seen in adult women" (94). Agreeing with Bennett, the downplay of her incredible zombie-killing dexterity and mechanical know-how, the emphasis on attractiveness places Rosita in a rather debasing and restrictive position as a resourceful and proficient woman.

Ultimately, her role as eye candy for viewers and the object of affection would define Rosita's presence until the dissolution of her relationship with Abraham in the sixth season. Until this separation, only brief moments offer a glimpse at her mental acuity and survival skills while the rest diminish her to a trophy piece standing in the background. In one episode during the fifth season, Rosita demonstrates her knowledge of mechanics and medical skills. However, much like the pivotal but overlooked scenes involving Tara, these moments are often downplayed or interrupted by dramatic changes in the narrative. Interjecting Abraham's rant about the fire truck they attempt to commandeer sputtering out of commission, Rosita informs him, "That feeds the radiator. The intake for the engine is actually on the roof" ("Self Help" 00:27:40–00:27:50). Though Abraham silently acknowledges her insight with a playful smirk and slight nod, this scene is quickly interrupted by the imposing threat of walkers. Earlier in this same episode, after the group fortifies a bookstore for the night, Rosita stitches the injury Abraham sustained to his hand, a skillset she acquired from two former members of their group ("Self Help"). As Abraham and Glenn exchange words about changing the world, Abraham inappropriately discloses he "...really need[s] some ass first" ("Self Help" 00:16:54–00:17:00). Perhaps saving face in his usual macho fashion, Abraham inevitably (and unapologetically) diminishes Rosita to a sex object, a body for pleasure, instead of acknowledging her rather valuable skills.

As the main Latina in the series, Rosita represents a group of individuals often marginalized and, at the same time, commodified by the media. The emphasis, as the remarks from audience members aptly show, is on her body rather than on her mind. As one viewer or *Reddit* sarcastically writes, "She's latin ... don't matter what's happening, She got to look caliente, papi!" (imapotato99). Molina-Guzman comments that ethnic bodies are often "savored, commodified, packaged, and safely distributed for the consumption of audiences throughout the world" (2). Nevertheless, while viewer comments bring attention to this issue, the backpedaling remarks insinuate that these viewers do not necessarily take issue with her appearance to help perpetuate the marginalization of this character as a visually pleasing object of consumption. Consequently, according to Jeffery Brown, in *Beyond Bombshells: The New Actions Heroine in Popular Culture*, "the display of strength and independence associated with the spitfire is typically undermined by the fetishized and racialized sexual exoticism of the stereotypes" (105). The fascination with her fetishized body appears to know no limit when Eugene confesses to Tara how he "enjoy[s] the female form" ("Self Help" 00:17:40–00:17:53). And, as if to solidify her position as an object, Rosita is the only female character in the series actively seen engaging in sex, other than Lori and Shane during the first season.

Despite being the primary Latina character, Rosita does not necessarily embody all the characteristics of the spitfire Latina stereotype. Described by Brown as "hot-tempered, [the] spitfire implies an outspokenness and dangerous sexuality," Rosita demonstrates excellent control over her emotions (104). Rather than use her body to subdue men, she utilizes her sexuality to keep their attention long enough to gain what she needs. In one instance, Rosita attempts to confront Abraham in his disappointment in learning how Eugene lied about his position as a scientist. Though she raises her voice to capture his attention, she decisively quiets herself rather than incite his rage ("Crossed"). In "Knots Untie," after Rosita gifts him a necklace that she competently manufactured from a brake light (again demonstrating her proficiency), Abraham appears grateful but noticeably distant. Though he comments she is "damn near perfection," she draws his attention back to her body by responding, "Show me. In the shower," to keep his interest ("Knots Untie" 00:04:07–00:04:25). In doing so, Rosita redirects the attention back to her body to keep Abraham satisfied and their relationship, for the time being, intact.

Sex, Awareness, and Body Autonomy

Though visibly distraught after the dissolution of her relationship with Abraham in the sixth season, it is in this severance that Rosita finds liberation. In this post-break-up, Rosita commands attention but no longer through her overt sexuality. Devoid of her association with Abraham, she is incredibly more vocal and confident and ultimately gains her autonomy. Her more assertive presence and vocal dominance as a Latina woman become more fully recognized now that she is her own powerful individual. Her use of Spanish becomes fully-fledged when she angrily speaks to Carol about her dislike of Morgan and his apprehension about attacking the Saviors ("Not Tomorrow Yet"). When Rosita encounters Dwight after he kills Denise, Rosita pronounces her name with a distinct inflection and accent ("Twice as Far"). Compared to her introductory episode, where her outfitting could be described as "remarkably similar to Lara Croft in the *Tomb Raider* video game" at best, Rosita appears exceptionally more clothed, and her hair noticeably less girlified (Bennett 93). As a Latina, her recurrence in the series and noticeable growth in character, she simultaneously "break[s] through proverbial glass ceilings in the notoriously white-washed Hollywood" (Murphy).

Though Rosita shifts away from her overt sexualization, her candid disclosure of her past reveals her keen awareness of the power of sex. Appearing to be fully capable and not a damsel in distress in need of a man for rescue, Rosita brings awareness to the ability of women to endure in this post-apocalyptic narrative. Even Serratos comments how not "'only are they part of one of the few series that is inclusive of women of all shapes, sizes, ages and colors ... but they also get to take care of themselves, instead of existing solely as romantic interests or damsels in distress'" (qtd. in Murphy). Just as Carol understands the mastery of a mild and meek enactment of femininity as a tool, Rosita fully understands the power of sex and how easily this action becomes a tool for survival. Her revelation to both Sasha and Denise about how she acquired her skills shows the cognizance of her desirability. Though she dismisses her relationship with Abraham as "just ... a name in a long list of names" after Denise inquires about her ability to fight, it is in her relationship with Abraham, and other men, where she acquired the necessary skills for survival ("Twice as Far" 00:14:25–00:14:30).

Fully capable of protecting herself and others, she has long outgrown her need for Abraham, thus in my opinion, influencing his decision to leave her for Sasha. When embarking on a mission to assassinate Negan, Rosita admits to Sasha how a "lot of guys wanted to protect me, like there was no way I could know how to take care of myself. And I didn't. And I hated the way that felt. So[,] I rolled with it. They didn't even notice I was picking up everything they knew how to do and doing it better" ("The Other Side" 00:35:00–00:35:39). Eventually, as she outgrows their usefulness to her, she moves on and continues surviving. By the time she meets Abraham, Rosita already possesses the skills necessary for survival. Though *Mitú* contributor Araceli Cruz similarly claims her strength undeniably influences Abraham to leave, Rosita needs a companion with whom she sees herself as an equal. In the article "There's a Reason People Are Falling in Love with this Latina from 'The Walking Dead,'" Cruz states, "the various relationships with men who helped shape her fighting mentality and teach her skills that women typically don't care to know. She says that all her ex-boyfriends underestimated her, but that Abraham didn't." Though her relationship with Abraham allowed her to find a partner equal in ability, Rosita did not satisfy Abraham and his desire to find happiness with another.

This disclosure helps deepen her character and allows viewers to gain a new sense of Rosita as a calculating and keenly alert woman. An article by *Gizmodo* author Rob Bricken equates her control with that of an action hero by noting how "[t]he idea of her realizing she was helpless once the zombie apocalypse hit, and then methodically hooking up with guys and learning their skills like some sort of relationship Mega Man in order to learn how to take care of herself is pretty compelling" ("The Walking Dead Did Something I Didn't Think Was Possible"). However, equating Rosita to an action hero, as Bricken argues, does not necessarily explain or rationalize her choice to have sex. Instead, by portraying the damsel in distress, even though she is not, Rosita uses performance as a tool while, as she claims, the sex was for her enjoyment. Although I previously discussed this point above, her decision to use sex is worth repeating as this tool shows her control over her body and emphasizes that her choice to engage in sex is not an expectation or in reciprocation of learning survival skills.

Additionally, her revelation about her jealousy of Abraham finding happiness shows her acceptance of his new relationship and her lack of bitterness toward another woman vying for the affection of Abraham. While her attempt to kill Negan fails, her actions following this incident warrant a serious discussion about how she decisively attempts to execute this villain. Cruz joyously voices how "the only Latina on this show is going to get vengeance against the most hateful villain of the series. It's so awesome to see this woman take matters into her own hands, and not give in while others in her crew seem to be all talk and no action" ("There's a Reason People Are Falling in Love with this Latina from 'The Walking Dead'"). However, a majority of *Reddit* comments demean her action while simultaneously questioning her ability and even blaming her for the death of Olivia (Ann Mahoney), a direct result and retaliation of Negan for the attempt, viewers, either wagered her impending death or pondered the allegations voiced on the post-episode thread.

When Rick, as the main protagonist and touted leader of Alexandria, failed to act against Negan and the Saviors, Rosita stepped up. No denying her actions had consequences, but she is the reason the narrative moved forward. Rosita is the reason Rick finally made the necessary effort to unite the colonies in the battle against their oppressive enemy. Even with the numerous negative comments, her bold move to kill Negan by pressuring Eugene to manufacture a bullet proved essential for narrative progression. As one viewer writes, "I think Rosita's action was integral to the story line. She is the one who showed guts (heh).... Everything that followed that helped to convince Rick that he needs to fight. Rick might not have gotten there without Rosita" (Barghodi). Fueled by the deaths of those closest to her and unwilling to bend to this imposed patriarchal dominance, her missed opportunity becomes a vital provocation for the continued progression of the narrative.

Three Men and a Baby

Even with her noticeable absence in the ninth season, compared to characters such as Michonne, Rosita manages to make a significant transformation—motherhood (though baby Socorro, aka "Coco," does not make an appearance until the tenth season). As a soon-to-be mother but still powerfully capable ass-kicking zombie warrior, Rosita steps further away from the "one-dimensional spitfire stereotype ... or a devoted and saintly maternal figure" (J. Brown 112). Not ever really needing a protector or savior to keep her safe, Rosita carries her self-reliance over to motherhood as her new partner, Father Gabriel Stokes expresses apprehension. Though Rosita actively and positively embraces her fate, she leaves the outcome of their relationship with him. Claiming his trepidation with the pregnancy lies with not being the father, Eugene explains, "It's her decision—pretty much all hers" ("Guardians" 00:14:50–00:15:28). With the news of a baby, Siddiq (Avi Nash) as the actual father, Gabriel as her partner, and Eugene with his all-consuming love for Rosita and as her most extended friendship, all become entangled in this pregnancy. Still, it is Rosita who maintains ultimate control over her body and the fate of her soon-to-be-born child.

Continuing in her trajectory to flip the script on gender norms and expectations, Rosita, in the tenth season, is presented focusing on maintaining her fitness and returning to her peak physical condition. All the while, her three closest male companions (a la *Three Men and a Baby*, as a few comments on X equated this all-male group dynamic) divide responsibilities in caring for baby Coco (@Bronte71; @Kemmybelle; @StarryMag). As the last chapter demonstrated with the presentation of Michonne, the determination to stay fit during the apocalypse is not an entirely new concept. In the 2009 American post-apocalyptic zombie comedy *Zombieland*, the lead protagonist, Columbus, lists cardio as the first rule in surviving the zombie apocalypse (Schwartz). Here in the tenth season, we see Rosita focusing on getting fit after the birth of her daughter and the colonies collaborating on the beach in preparation for any threat from the Whisperers ("Lines We Cross"). Unfortunately for Siddiq, his traumatic experience as the only survivor of the group captured by the Whisperers and his transition from doctor to fatherhood weighs heavily on his mental state. While Kirsh concludes that "traumatic and stressful life events do not always lead to changes in personality," Siddiq's inability to cope with his capture and witnessing the death of his close friends, he fades in and out of reality

(100). Undoubtedly suffering from Post-Traumatic Stress Disorder (PTSD), thus causing Siddiq to have constant flashbacks and relive the horrific events he experienced in the captivity of the Whisperers, Siddiq's emotional status and lack of sleep add to the stressors of being a father (Kirsh 104). Ultimately, Siddiq is able to root out the primary cause of his flashbacks (a Whisperer hidden in plain sight), but this revelation will cost Siddiq his life, and his reanimated corpse nearly costs baby Coco hers ("Open Your Eyes").

Returning to the conversation about Rosita and how she decisively wages her sexuality as a tool for survival, a handful of viewers now take issue with her sexual history. Turning from favor to dissent, viewers condemn Rosita for her choice of partners, mainly directed at Gabriel, and comment on the number of men involved in her life. One even took to pigeonholing her revelation of this pregnancy to Siddiq, stating how "Rosita being pregnant by some dude and Eugene over-hearing it was straight out of a telenovela" (fede01_8). Presumably, because of her identity as a Latina woman, this comment, along with many others, disapproves of her sexual freedom. Nevertheless, some comments defend Rosita and her right to choose how she uses her body and sexuality. One viewer on *Reddit* advocates for Rosita by reminding others how "many years have passed since Rosita showed up. It's been what, 8 or so years in universe? She's been with like all of 4 men in that entire time but y'all act like it's 400" (likeawolf). With the ambiguity of time, the sexuality viewers were happy to see flaunted across the screen now makes Rosita out to be more of a seductive harlot rather than the spitfire Latina. Comparing Gabriel to other men from her previous relationships, Gabriel appears to be a radically different choice as a partner for Rosita. Pondering this choice, a viewer on X writes, "I've finally caught up on the walking dead ... and I can't believe Rosita is messing with the priest.... Saadiq is so fine chileeee #TheWalkingDead" (@StephRoyalty). Entering the narrative in the fifth season after the group escapes from Terminus, Gabriel exudes cowardice and, for at least this viewer, pales in comparison to the appeal of Siddiq. Compared to Abraham and even Spencer Monroe (Austin Nichols), with whom Rosita shares a brief interlude after her split from Abraham, Gabriel markedly does not possess the machismo, weapons savvy, looks, or youth of these former lovers.

Comparatively, the increased presentation of multiracial couples, such as the pairing of Rosita and Gabriel, is a welcome divergence from the series' first few seasons. Despite some viewers taking issue with the pairing, claiming they "don't see any chemistry between them" or how the "only logical explanation is Rosita has a thing for priests," their coupling does not require, nor should require, justification (oursistheendgame;

quinnies). Still, ample viewers are coming to the defense of the couple. Presenting a counterargument to what some refer to as a forced coupling, one viewer wrote, "I want to see Gabriel happy and I love Rosita … so if they (the characters) like it I love it" (Zssmom). Another viewer provided even more insight into the potential for this relationship by reminding others of the trauma both individuals experienced and blaming the producers for the lack of attention in their development. Stating how

> I actually think they have a fun chemistry together, the show just hasn't spent a lot of time developing them otherwise so I get why people don't see it. I didn't care either way until the Stalker episode in season 10 when he saw her struggling mentally and quickly rearranged plans so that she wouldn't have to admit her fear to anyone, then I was completely on board [ravioli0h].

As these fans show, the couple holds value in their ability to lean on each other in times of great uncertainty. Outside of his role as a priest, Gabriel becomes a sympathetic ear for others, including Rosita. Additionally, when considering her relationship with these partners before their coupling, Gabriel has had the longest-standing relationship (outside of Eugene) with Rosita since their meeting before the death of Abraham.

Furthermore, the relationship between Gabriel and Rosita necessitates no elucidation as couples from all backgrounds, abilities, races, and so on came to the forefront in the ninth season. As an interracial couple, one of the many on the show, Rosita and Gabriel join with Carol and Ezekiel, Rick and Michonne, Maggie and Glenn, Yukimo and Magna, Elijah (Okea Eme-Akwari) and Lydia (Cassady McClincy), and the countless other interracial couples in the series. Even more unbelievable is a viewer comment asserting how "The only compelling romance stories to me have been Glenn/Maggie, Carl/Enid and Aaron/Eric" (seneris). All those mentioned in this statement, apart from Glenn, are White. In representing the voiceless sensual woman, Rosita fulfills a sexualized stereotype in the horror genre.

Nevertheless, after the severance of her relationship with Abraham and the increased attention given to her ethnicity, Rosita transforms from an often-silenced young woman to an outspoken Latina heroine capable of speaking her mind. Her hypersexualized body, one utilized as a tool that saved her life, now becomes a vessel that will bring life. Apart from her now fully embracing using her accent and slightly dark skin, giving her an exotic quality, Rosita does not seem to become fully recognized as a Latina until the sixth season. When she enters the narrative flanked by two White men, Rosita's complexion distinguishes her from her escorts but, at the same time, does not align her with them either. As Molina-Guzman explains, "it is the gendered media practices that surround sexual exoticness, racial flexibility, and ethnic ambiguity that position them globally consumable docile bodies subject to the erotic and voracious gaze of the United States" (13). Rosita, who borders on passing as White but still does not fully identify with the White individuals in her company, is less threatening to the power dynamic of the core (primarily White) group.

As a mixed-race actress, Christian Serratos' portrayal of Rosita allows for television shows, such as *The Walking Dead*, to "include different races, and capitalize on the established stereotypes of those ethnicities, without completely jeopardizing an ideal of heroic white womanhood" (J. Brown 113). Now outliving her comic book counterpart, Rosita powered through to the end of the eleventh season as an unstoppable maternal force engrossed in the survival of her daughter. Hoping for an "'epic'" death, Rosita fought to the very end, even with great shock and sadness for fans of this character (qtd. in Drysdale). With the outpouring of comments on *X* calling attention to this "force of nature," claiming Rosita "deserved better," and even a rather disparaging comment that the writers "killed off our sweet Rosita, yet the incredibly useless Walking Dead activist diversity hires—responsible for ruining this entire show—continue to live on" (@BastardGrimm; @futurusticmikec; @joelmiller). Despite their accusations, as the last comment above shows, misdirected remarks about the casting starting in the ninth season, the decision to kill off Rosita was that of Serratos. In an interview with *Entertainment Weekly*, Serratos spoke about this decision bringing herself closure, especially with the various talks of spin-offs and uncertainty following the end of the eleventh season (Ross, "Christian Serratos Asked for That"). For Serratos, she felt "'it really helped me, Christian, have closure. And I really think it made sense for Rosita. I mean, she was so willing to die for her loved ones and die for her child, and I just thought it really made sense for her'" (qtd. in Ross, "Christian Serratos Asked for That"). Even with the end of this character arc, there is optimism for other trailblazing Latinas, such as Princess, to evolve beyond adversity and the chauvinistic rhetoric such characters received from viewers on social media throughout the seasons.

Breaking Hearts to Breaking Glass Ceilings: Doctor Enid

Though prone to escaping the confines of Alexandria to run freely in the woods with the undead, Enid embarks on an incredibly precarious path by stepping into a profession almost unanimously dominated by men. Under the tutelage of Siddiq, Enid becomes the resident doctor at

Hilltop, despite the immense danger. Considering the precarious nature of the vocation, as the preceding doctors in the series demonstrate, accepting such as position almost certainly guarantees a quick death (Dr. Jenner "opted out," the Governor decapitates Hershel, the Saviors kill Dr. Harlan Carson (R. Keith Harris) Rick kills Pete, Dwight shoots Denise in the eye with an arrow, and so on). Before Enid undergoes her transformation from a naïve teenager to a mature caregiver, she forcibly learns the dangers of letting down your guard and becoming attached to others. Her growth over three seasons mirrors the trajectory of three other leading women from the series, Maggie, Michonne, and Rosita. Like Maggie, Enid develops compassion and a willingness to help others, which becomes the driving force for her to assume the role Hershel once held as a caregiver for Maggie. Like Michonne, Enid is reluctant to accept the idyllic setting of Alexandria or to develop meaningful relationships with anyone for fear of suffering more loss. Like Rosita, Enid becomes the fixation of the male gaze and an object of possession.

Unfortunately for Enid, her worth as a character manifests once she assumes her life-saving role as a doctor. Like viewers' reaction to Rosita's purpose in the story, Enid's relevance to the narrative after her introduction was often questioned. For Enid, her growth comes after her realization that her existence implies more than just surviving, a mantra she adopts shortly after the death of her parents. As one viewer on *Reddit* notes, "Her arc abour surviving was pretty interesting. Also, not everyone needs some crazy dramatic storyline to be relevant" (DeadlyShogunate). Even more so, though Enid is not overtly sexualized, she is the object of fixation for Carl Grimes and his romantic adversary, Ron Anderson (Austin Abrams). Seeking refuge and running from the ever-posing threat of the dead, Enid constant journey outside the walls of the Alexandria Safe-Zone speaks volumes about her character. The walls of Alexandria are a cage encircling suburban landscape safely nested inside, a metaphor for a time that once was before the apocalypse. Pitting these two boys against each other, Enid unwillingly becomes the Helen of Troy in the apocalypse. As an object of desire for these two men, or, more appropriately, adolescent teens, Enid temporarily finds herself in the middle of an assertion of patriarchal dominance, which as *The Walking Dead* shows, ends poorly for those involved.

Helen of an Apocalyptic Troy

As a young female, willingly seeking out danger and harboring the pain of watching her parents die, which Carl similarly endures after the birth of Judith, Enid becomes a fixation, a body of adolescent desire. Incredibly disconnected from the world inside the walls of Alexandria,

Enid fails to establish attachments to anyone and yet, quickly becomes the preoccupation of two young adolescents vying for her attention. Favoring the danger outside the walls, Carl, through his voyeuristic spying through the window, watches Enid scaling the wall to wander about on the other side. Assuming the scopophilic gaze, which in this case takes "other people as objects, subjecting them to a controlling and curious gaze," Enid becomes an object of obsession for the young Carl Grimes (Mulvey 59). Stalking her through the woods, as in preying upon her as the walkers unceasingly do throughout the series, Carl relentlessly follows Enid, perplexed by her desire to travel outside the walls, putting them both in obvious danger. Though Enid confesses, "We're supposed to be out here. We're supposed to feel like this. I don't want to forget. And running makes me feel better" ("Try" 00:22:40–00:23:27), Carl perplexingly keeps his gaze fixed on her. Enid exudes the "to-be-looked-at-ness" described by Mulvey (364). However, the obsession with Enid drastically differs from the overtly sexualized presentation of Rosita.

In witnessing the traumatic loss of her parents, Enid begins her journey alone, which forces her to develop skills necessary for survival, including the reluctance to establish meaningful relationships. Seeking out danger becomes a way for Enid to remember her sense of self while also refraining from the complacency provided by Alexandria. Not profoundly caring for others protects her from reliving her previous suffering and the trauma of loss. According to George Hagman in "Surviving the Zombie Apocalypse: Trauma and Transformation in AMC's *The Walking Dead*," trauma may stem from a person "undergoes an experience that violently assaults and disrupts psychological meanings, beliefs, and values that are essential to the sense of self and self-in-relationship" (48). The realness and closeness of these experienced traumas result in Enid building up her emotional wall. Yet, her desire to escape the confines of Alexandria's barrier is deeply metaphoric. Remaining inside the walls, she risks becoming complacent. Outside the walls, she is not only reminded of the adversity she overcame but also of a sense of freedom. She is not one to become attached to another or forget the dangers lurking outside. When the Wolves strike Alexandria, it is here that Ron finds his ego and his ownership of Enid contested when she remains by Carl's side as he pleads with Ron to join them for his safety ("JSS"). As a constant threat, Carl fuels Ron's narcissistic longing to be the only man in Enid's life.

Enid inadvertently finds herself in a perpetual cycle of patriarchal control and dominance set forth by the ever-present authoritative White male figures. In a sense, Enid unknowingly becomes an apocalyptic embodiment of Troy's Helen from Greek mythology, an object so desired men would go to war to have her. Retrieving a handgun from the armory inside Alexandria, which leads to both Ron's death and the near loss of Carl's life, Enid acts as what Mulvey describes in her essay "Visual Pleasures and Narrative Cinema" to be "(passive) raw material for the (active) gaze of man … step[ping] further into the structure of representation, adding a further layer demanded by an ideology of the patriarchal order as it is worked out in its favorite cinematic form—illusionistic narrative film" (or in this case, television) (67). Carl, the son of the main protagonist Rick Grimes, and Ron, the son of the town doctor and abusive drunk, Pete Anderson, continue this patriarchal narrative order by asserting their dominance over each other while fighting for Enid. Enid offering her sympathy to Ron as he deals with the loss of his father means only that, a shoulder to cry on and nothing more. Seeing parallels between this and another love triangle from earlier in the series, viewers concluded how the clash between Carl and Ron over Enid eerily resembles the Lori/Shane/Rick dynamic in the earlier seasons. One viewer reports, "I wouldn't be surprised if he stole Enid just like Shane stole Lori or…. Knowing the makers of *The Walking Dead* it will probably be more extreme though" (gremmygram). The Shane/Lori/Rick dynamic pitted two men against each other to not only possess Lori but also to assert an undeniably, White patriarchal control and dominance over the core group.

Ultimately, with authority over herself and control over her decisions, Enid possesses the right to determine her partner and path. As one viewer replies on *Reddit*, "Enid isn't Ron's property. Don't even appear to be involved. Carl can't 'steal' her like Shane stole Lori (who was married). It's Enid's choice if she's with Ron or Carl, Tara, other, or no one" (cageyfanboy). Just as Lori chooses Shane in the absence of her husband and later decides to end her relationship with Shane in favor of her marriage, Enid equally possesses the right to choose her partner. While evading a group of walkers in the hollowed trunk of a tree, Enid confesses to Carl, "It's their world, we're just living in it" ("Try" 24:50–24:58), a rather fitting statement for more than one reason. Though her original meaning shows her reluctance to move beyond the guilt of surviving the walker attack that claimed her parents, the walkers are not the only figures dominating the storyline. In the male-dominated world of *The Walking Dead*, women routinely appear to be the possessions of men. Not until these dynamic women emerge, characters such as Enid evolve beyond being cared for to caring for others, even with immense risk to their safety, as discussed in more detail next.

Just Surviving Somehow

Before Enid assumes the role of doctor, which subsequently disrupts the predominantly male reign of the position, she must first fully understand her place within the apocalypse's immensity. Following her self-inscribed mantra, "Just Survive Somehow," Enid reluctantly enters the confines of Alexandria, a sure sign of her unwillingness to leave this part of her existence behind. Like the refusal of the call, as Joseph Campbell describes in the monomyth, Enid finds herself walled in "boredom, hard work, or 'culture,'" she "loses the power of significant affirmative action and becomes a victim to be saved" (54). In other words, surviving on her own is all Enid knows after losing her parents and embarking on a treacherous solo journey. As her reluctance to enter the colony of Alexandria and subsequent adventures over the walls at considerable risk to her safety show, Enid fears the complacency Alexandria represents and decisively puts herself in danger as a reminder of her life before losing her freedom.

Glenn, acting as the supernatural aid and becoming a guiding figure, provides Enid with the necessary reasoning for her purpose: hope (Campbell 63). In her journey with Glenn, Enid confronts her fear of loss.

Apprehensive of returning and refusing to admit her fear, Glenn challenges her apprehension, reminding her existence is essential beyond merely being there. "You don't want to lose anything again," Glenn contends, "so you give up and you say, 'That's just what happens' …You honor the dead by going on. Even when you're scared. You live because they don't get to" ("Heads Up" 00:28:54–00:29:00). By continuously refusing to return because she is consumed by the memory of losing her parents to ravenous walkers, Enid is denied closure in their death and acts out her loss with her morbid fascination to be outside the walls of Alexandria. In "Rest in Pieces: Violence in Mourning the (Un)Dead," Laura Kremmel concludes how "[t]he pervasiveness of death in this dangerous new world and the threat of the undead body poses to the living both necessitate and problematize mourning practices, as phrases such as 'surviving the death of a loved one' take on a whole new meaning" (80). In other words, Enid does not yet foresee hope in a world of death. Instead, she places herself in a state of constant dejection brought on by guilt, being the only person in her family to survive.

With a renewed sense of purpose after the death of Glenn, Enid transforms from a cynical teenager to a mature contributor to the success of the colonies. As one viewer writes, "Glenn shows faith and perseverance in the face of awful challenges, but Enid surrenders to loss and fear and gives up a willingness to find a home. She loses faith, quits trying, crumbles to nothing until Glenn pulls her back up" (HiveJiveLive). No longer journeying outside the walls of Alexandria, Enid finds her place alongside Maggie at Hilltop. At Hilltop, Enid finally opens herself up to another; a former Savior named Alden (Callan McAuliffe). As Glenn bestowed the boon of hope on Enid, she will, in turn, give this boon to another, Carol's adopted son

Henry. Enid fulfills her quest to bestow the boon of hope upon Henry, who selfishly hides Lydia while the Whisperers hold Alden and Luke Abrams (Dan Fogler) hostage.

Pleading for the exchange of Lydia for Alden, Enid confesses how "someone else close to me died. Someone special, with a big heart... 'just surviving' it isn't living. And it took me way too long to get what he really meant. You live with it by staying who you are. By not letting the bad things change you" ("Bounty" 00:29:30–00:30:28). In her confession about the death of her parents and revealing her anguish at the loss of Carl, Enid endows Henry with her knowledge and understanding of life's meaning. Described by Campbell as "a symbol of life energy stepped down to the requirements of a certain specific case" (175), bequeathing this boon on Henry saves the lives of two members of the Hilltop. However, unlike the male hero typified in Campbell's monomyth, this female heroine returns from her "mysterious adventure" (28), in her admission, an event she was unwilling to disclose previously. This liberating moment for Enid not only saves the lives of others but allows her to come full cycle in her journey of growth and maturity.

You Become a Doctor, You Risk Your Life

In becoming a doctor, Enid finds her purpose and realization of a life worth living, even in a world where death always encircles these survivors. Stepping into the role of a doctor, a position chiefly held by men in the series, Enid extends the boundaries of gender expectations and prescribed roles of women in horror narratives. Since the sixth season, Enid demonstrates the qualities of a caretaker, foreshadowing the lifesaving role she assumes in the ninth season. Maggie, assuming the part of the matriarch after the loss of her father, regularly watches over and protects her family and the other survivors under her care. In turn, Enid becomes a caretaker for pregnant Maggie. Offering to cover her shift so the pregnant leader can "put up [her] feet and eat some pickles" ("East" 00:18:25–00:19:00), Enid shows signs of a caring nature and concern for the health of others.

In the first few seasons, *The Walking Dead* presents distinct gender binaries where the passive act of caregiving as mothers or homemakers falls upon women. In contrast, the more functional trait of caregiving as doctors and protectors falls upon men. In other words, men care for them while women are cared for in the series. As the show progresses to introduce Denise and later Enid, the concept of caregiving realigns as a trait conveying agency on the part of the caretaker, thus calling into question the association of active roles with masculinity and passive roles as feminine. Instead, the show's continuation allows women to develop into more fully active persons with their agency while challenging established binaries. When Maggie is taken to Hilltop for medical attention, a journey thwarted by the Saviors, Enid leaves Alexandria to join her. Symbolically, as Hershel bequeathed his watch upon Glenn, Maggie gifts the same watch to Enid while reminding her, "I was going to use this for Glenn's [grave marker]. It was my dad's. He gave it to him. But I'm giving it to you" ("Go Getters" 00:41:30–00:42:00). In bestowing the watch to Enid, Maggie symbolically offers Enid a token of honor. The honor, as Enid would come to behold, is stepping into the place of Hershel and the other lifesaving individuals brave enough to take on the role.

Except for Denise, Enid becomes the only other woman to assume the role of a doctor in the series. Until Denise and later Enid, several men—from Dr. Jenner, whom the group encounters in Atlanta, to Hershel, patriarch of the Greene family farm, to Dr. Carson, the resident doctor of Hilltop—fulfilled this critical role within the colonies and before the group arrived at Alexandria. While training under Pete Anderson, Denise forcibly becomes the resident doctor upon Pete's death at the hands of Rick and the subsequent attack on Alexandria by the Wolves ("JSS"). For fans, the decision to amputate Aaron's arm wins their favor of Enid. As one viewer posts, "I'm actually really liking Enid" (kevinsg04), while another follows, "Enid having to cut Aarons hand off was a great scene, highlight of the episode" (SirBamboozled). Her position as a doctor is a far cry from the moody, distant teenager who found herself the center of unwanted teenage obsession who was simply just surviving somehow.

Regardless of gender, sexual orientation, or skillset, doctors in this apocalyptic narrative have an exceptionally high mortality rate. Though Kang maintains that no one character is safe in this apocalyptic narrative (Bonomolo, "'The Walking Dead' Criticized"), Enid (like Tara) is a victim of her influence as an emerging authoritative figure. Mutually concluding her fate, viewers speculate a possible connection between her role as a doctor and her ultimate demise. Offering one of many similar assumptions about Enid on *X*, one viewer writes, "I was worried about Enid as soon as she started training to be a doctor. Doctors on The Walking Dead never make it. #twd" (@ms_jespial). As with Tara, fans took to social media in outrage, claiming, "Enid deserved better. Just Survive Somehow" (Lord_Whis) and expressing, "when they showed her helping out in the fair and doing CPR type stuff i was like aww, look at Enid all grown up and teaching people" (oreides). The impact her character made on the show is overwhelming. Perhaps even more telling than the emotional connection viewers had to her character are the numerous compliments given to the incredible development this forlorn teenager made by her exit from the series.

Enid could easily be left underdeveloped and underutilized as a character original to the show and an unrequited love interest to both Ron and, later, Carl. According to one viewer, "Enid went from just surviving to thriving and realizing that life is more than just survival. ... I'm satisfied with the impact she had on the show and its characters" (zebzoober). As this and other comments show, Enid came full circle as a character in this apocalyptic narrative. A far cry from her bemoaning self and having experienced the loss of someone she truly admired for their kindness, Enid developed relationships with the people of Hilltop and stepped up to one of its most needed roles, a doctor. Still, her death raises questions about how far this character could evolve in her new role. One viewer pointing out how Enid "wasn't left incomplete, but I think she had potential to continue developing into a major character with solid storylines" demonstrates the call for more from beloved, and still growing, characters (SauronOMordor, Comment on "The Walking Dead S09E15"). As death itself is unpredictable, so too can the deaths of characters come without the slightest warning, even if this end means one or more beloved characters.

Tara, Rosita, and Enid: A Reflection

Each of these women contributes significantly to the narrative's progression and pushes boundaries to show women's capabilities in the apocalypse. Katelyn Nacon, the actress playing the role of Enid, remarks how "not all [is] centered around the male heroes. They make all the female characters such badasses, and it's great because you don't necessarily get to see that a lot in popular culture" (qtd. in Bradley, "*The Walking Dead*: Enid Joins the Squad"). While there are badass women in popular culture, they are often overly sexualized. Considering the "warrior women in thongs" motif presented by Susan Douglas in the book *Enlightened Sexism: The Seductive Message That Feminism's Work is Done*, characters such as the initial presence of Rosita confirm the "sexual objectification of women and girls, and suggested that women could be as strong as any man as long as they were poreless, stacked, and a size two" (99). That is, until they separate themselves from being overshadowed by the male-dominance rampant in the series. Unlike other comics featuring women such as Wonder Woman, Ms. Marvel, Storm, or even Harley Quinn, the women in *The Walking Dead* are not necessarily objectified to the degree of their superhuman counterparts. Writing begrudgingly about the series due to killing off beloved gay characters such as Tara and Jesus, *Autostraddle* contributor Jessica Vazquez did compliment *The Walking Dead* for portraying its queer characters respectfully and without hypersexualizing them ("Tara

Chambler's Death on 'The Walking Dead'"). Vazquez admitted to initially feeling elated to finally see what appeared to be one of the first gay characters they can remember in any form of zombie horror to date, only to then be shattered at the revelation of Tara's eventual death in the series ("Tara Chambler's Death on 'The Walking Dead'").

At least for the time some of these iconic characters were part of the narrative, they took on more relatable roles. Tara, Rosita, and Enid did, in many ways, rise above adversity to become dynamos in the apocalypse. Subverting gender expectations, Tara soared to become the interim leader of Hilltop, and Enid to becoming a practicing doctor. Disrupting stereotypes of race and sexuality, Rosita continuously breaks through boundaries thanks to a level head, incredible self-awareness, and motherhood as of the ninth season. Though never surpassing her wisecracking nature, Tara transcends from the unnamed lesbian to one of the most trusted members of the group. Though unlucky with love, Tara not only becomes an integral part of the Hilltop community but is also fully welcomed and embraced by those around her. After her disclosure to Maggie about her appearance at the death of Hershel and in her role as interim leader, she is both seen and heard. Enid finally breaks down her walls of isolation and opens herself up to finding love and being loved by others. Rather than the hapless teenager convinced this world belongs to the dead, she transforms to save the lives of the living, even at a high cost to her own life. While Rosita soldiers on into the final season, the contributions of these three women cannot be minimized or downplayed. Representing marginalized groups on television and offering glimpses of the potential for women to evolve beyond the stereotypes placed upon them in horror genres, these women blaze a trail for viewers looking to find a character to identify with and cheer on.

4

Overlooked Identities
in *The Walking Dead*

Through participatory culture, as discussed in the first chapter, the role of *The Walking Dead* fanbase shifts from not only watching the series but using social media to voice opinions and to challenge producers to make desired changes in the series openly. Challenges such as calling out the lack of diversity, one viewer complains on X how "The real tragedy of the #TWD is the idea that the new world will be populated with white folks and their children. No diversity in the post-apocalyptic world? Damn. #notsurprised" (@AstarrDe). And this comment does not exist in isolation. Entire *Reddit* threads created by fans are dedicated to discussing the lack of representation or diversity in this show, revealing how viewers pick up on these absences and discuss their implications. As if attempting to answer these calls for more representation, the ninth season completely changed the direction of this series by addressing the outcries by viewers about the lack of diversity and yearning for more reflective characters.

While characters such as Rosita and Tara initially placated these cries for diverging gender roles, other strong female roles seemed underutilized and quickly killed off before they fully developed as characters after their introductions in the series (i.e., Andrea, Lori, or even Jacqui). Outside of finding more identifiable characters such as Michonne, fans commented on how much adversity and hardship someone like Michonne overcame by the time she integrated into the core group. Offering up this and other poignant conclusions about how Michonne is an excellent addition because "she's really the first headstrong woman who isn't content with cooking and cleaning and who has experience out in the open world, the world of herds and roamers" in addition to her surviving for "many, many months out in the wild by herself, which I think is an incredible feat" (superzepto). In an article published by the *Los Angeles Times*, author Scott Collins notes how the television audience "itself is diverse—one estimate is that black viewers spend 37% more time watching TV than other racial groups—which has forced network executives to find programming that *reflects the people watching at home*" ("How TV Beats Film"; emphasis added). Continuing to improve and develop more reflective casting, Sarah Barnett, president of the entertainment group for AMC Networks, acknowledges the use of objective external groups, such as ReFrame, to keep track of industry trends (Hill). As an external agency, ReFrame aims to

> provide research, support, and a practical framework that can be used by Partner Companies to mitigate bias during the creative decision-making and hiring process, celebrate successes, and measure progress toward a more gender-representative industry on all levels ["About Us"].

Using such agencies shows how networks such as AMC actively work to include more diverse characters to enhance the variation of its show casts, thus creating a more reflective depiction of the audience.

Additionally, as the largest group watching *The Walking Dead* falls between the coveted 18–49 age demographic, authors Wesley Morris and James Poniewozik remind us how "there are younger viewers for whom diversity—racial, religious, sexual—is their world. That audience wants authenticity" ("Why 'Diversity TV' Matters: It's Better TV. Discuss"). When *The Walking Dead* first debuted in 2010, the coveted age demographic mentioned above fell right between Generation X (born between 1965 and 1980) and the Millennial generation (born between 1981 and 1996). Compared to previous generations, the Millennial generation is the most "racially and ethnically diverse adult generation in the nation's history," with the upcoming generation, known as Generation Z (born between 1997 to 2012) adding even more diversity (Dimock). Suppose the primary viewing audience comprises the most diverse grouping of adults in history, and future generations will only increase this diversity. In that case, it just makes sense that television casts must diversify to reflect their audiences accurately.

Between the number of viewers and the (sometimes unfavorably low) ratings as seasons progressed, *The Walking Dead*, a cable television juggernaut, offers publicists a prime target for advertising. However, realizing how a captive audience brings in dollars, networks such as AMC need to capitalize on its viewership by offering increasingly diverse, and therefore more reflective, characters. My point in this chapter is that with the promotion of Angela Kang ahead of the ninth season and her continuing in this role through the series finale, the increased attention paid to adding a more diverse cast altered the course of the series by rewriting the narrative to further diverge from the storylines captured in the original graphic novel. In this chapter, I examine what I consider to be the central factors responsible for the diversification of *The Walking Dead*, pressure by the fanbase for more representation, and the ascent of Angela Kang to show-runner. Not only would the ninth season bring in its first deaf character, but *The Walking Dead* also departed from the long line of male antagonists to introduce its female adversary, Alpha.

However, as with Tara's introduction in the fourth season, not all change in the series comes with such an open embrace. Some viewers even criticized the show for seeming to impose diversity in the series. For example, one commenter on *X* complained: "I didn't hate, but I didn't really like the latest #TheWakingDead. It seems like they're trying too hard to force diversity into the show, and all I want is a good old-fashioned zombie apocalypse story" (@ProfessorF). Comments by acclaimed actor James Woods expressed his intense disdain for the radical changes made to the ninth season, especially regarding the emerging female storylines. Taking to *X*, Woods expressed his discontent with the series by commenting how *The Walking Dead* became an "'all–chick zombie series' and an 'estrogen fest'" (qtd. in Bonomolo, "'The Walking Dead's Michael Cudlitz"). In response to Woods' tactless remarks about the series, actor Joshua Mikel who played the character Jared, a member of the Saviors, in the seventh and eighth seasons did not let this comment go unanswered. Quipping back, "'Heaven forbid a show feature women as much as men after decades of TV treating women as glorified props,'" Mikel continued by stating he was "Proud of what @WalkingDead_AMC manages in diversity & inclusion'" (qtd. in Bonomolo, "'The Walking Dead's Michael Cudlitz"). No longer glorified props, as Mikel remarked, women take control and continue to persevere despite much public ridicule on social media.

As an open channel of communication, social media not only provides an outlet for viewers to voice their opinions about a series, regardless if they are positive or negative, but also permits *The Walking Dead* crewmembers to offer explanations or, in the case of the comments mentioned above, opportunities to defend the progressive changes made in the series. Replying to a comment by a *X* user for the "'unrealistic and obviously forced'" female characters by proclaiming "'there would be more men alive in an apocalypse than women,'" actor-turned-director Michael Cudlitz tweeted, "Based on the fact that we all know how a 'zombie apocalypse' would unfold........ I mean. You know it's not real, right?? ..." (Bonomolo, "'The Walking Dead': Jeffrey Dean Morgan"; @Cudlitz). Additionally, fan-favorite Norman Reedus commented on how the show is "'being driven by women'" as Angela Kang pushed for "stronger and better represented female characters" (qtd. in Bonomolo, "'The Walking Dead': Jeffrey Dean Morgan"). Norman continued to describe the series by stating how the show felt like a Western, but "'at the same time it's scarier, it's more emotional, it's more heartfelt. There's no posturing. No one's posturing. I will say that the female spirit has put that bad guy in a cage, and it's over there in a cage, and there's a whole bunch of other sh-t happening'" (qtd. in Bonomolo, "'The Walking Dead': Jeffrey Dean Morgan"). With the noticeable changes in the ninth season, specifically with the focus on more female-centric narratives, *The Walking Dead* exudes less of the gun-toting sheriff old–West feel presented in the first season with signs of amplified inclusivity and emerging progression.

In the book *Stealing the Show: How Women are Revolutionizing Television*, author Joy Press describes a showrunner as an "elastic term that encompasses varying degree[s] of creative and managerial control" (9). Additionally, as the "visionary in chief," someone in this position assumes the ability to make changes as they see fit (or necessary) (9). From the events transpiring at the start of the ninth season, Angela Kang appeared to have done just that for *The Walking Dead*. Not new to the crew of *The Walking Dead*, Kang worked her way up through the ranks after starting as an editor during the second season. The transition from an editor to a producer in the third season and later co-executive producer in the fifth season, Kang eventually accepted the offer for showrunner after former showrunner Scott Gimple took over the role of Chief Content Officer (McMahon). Though admitting there would be no show without Andrew Lincoln and concerned over the departure of Lauren Cohan, and eventually Danai Gurira in the tenth season, Kang looked to other roles to expand and to help flourish in their absence. Wanting to "'mess with the rhythm of the show,'" incorporating time jumps helped to move the narrative progression along while also creating other cliffhangers for viewers and gave the show a fresh feel (qtd. in McMahon).

Applauding Kang for "reigniting the excitement I had in the show from earlier seasons," a fan exclaimed how, "I just wanted to express my thoughts and thanks for Angela Kang stepping in and making this show a great watch again" (WontonJr1). This comment is one of many fans offering gratitude to Kang for the new direction of the series. Not only did Kang bring renewed excitement to the storyline after the departure of Rick Grimes and Maggie Rhee, but newly introduced characters during the season also met similar praise. On *X*, one poster exclaimed, "Holy F*ck.... The Walking Dead is off the charts this season. I love the new characters & story line. Well done Angela Kang! #TWD" (@darciCanada). While the much beloved Rick is no longer part of the main story, which caused a flurry of speculation online about his eventual return to the series, the dynamic characters focused upon earlier in this book and including newly introduced characters discussed in this chapter, sustained the narrative by providing audiences with new trajectories and refreshingly divergent angles.

One noticeable difference in this promotion to showrunner came with noticeable increases in female-driven storylines ("Angela Kang–Showrunner/Executive Producer/Writer"; Bonomolo, "'The Walking Dead' Season 9 Will Tell Different"). Not only did Carol and Michonne receive more onscreen attention until Michonne departed the narrative in search of Rick, but the series also would bring back a much beloved and missed character, Maggie (Bonomolo, "'The Walking Dead' Producer"). With so many changes made after her promotion, Gimple even noted how *The Walking Dead* is "a place where you can find great female voices, great female artists and stories that honor female characters, not as a novelty but as intrinsic story value'" (qtd. in Bonomolo, "'The Walking Dead' Season 9 Will Tell Different"). Since its inception, fans witnessed Carol evolve from her battered housewife persona to become Queen of the Kingdom alongside her partner, King Ezekiel, and mother to her adopted son, Henry. Michonne pulled down her guarded walls to eventually form meaningful relationships with others. She became the First Lady of the Alexandria Safe-Zone after beginning a much fan-anticipated romantic relationship with Rick Grimes. Even Maggie emerged as Hilltop's sole leader, making her the only woman in the series to take on such a prominent role without the aid or partnership with a man. These women collectively transform from the individuals the series presents during the first three seasons.

While the show progressed after introducing these dominant and developing female characters, various characters of differing backgrounds, sexuality, and ability continued to appear. Entering the narrative as the first openly gay character in the series, Tara morphed into a crucial member of the core group when she unites the colonies Alexandria and Hilltop with Oceanside, a pivotal partnership in the war against the Saviors, and, in the absence of Maggie and Jesus, became interim leader of Hilltop. Though this ascension cost Tara her life when the narrative brought in the Whisperers (discussed in more depth later in this chapter), her transition from a secondary character to a leader is irrefutably noteworthy. Rosita departed from her status as a quiet yet attractive love interest of Abraham to an outspoken soldier and mother to a daughter, Coco. Her expertise in mechanics and medical training, which she used to help save her group numerous times, often went unnoticed. After her separation from Abraham, Rosita no longer fell under the shadow of such a loud and outspoken character to forge a path of her own. She is the first to attempt any form of retaliation against Negan for his murderous transgressions. Rosita also actively stood against the oppression the Saviors placed upon the colonies. Then, with Enid, her profound teenage angst and self-inflicted guilt from witnessing the death of her parents and overcoming the loss of

Carl faded away as she trained with Siddiq to become a doctor for the people of Hilltop.

Under Kang's direction and with Magna's group's introduction, more female-centric storylines dominate the ninth season. Along with introducing sisters Connie and Kelly came Magna, the new group's leader, Yukimo, Magna's partner, and former music teacher, Luke. While both women exhibit differing abilities (discussed in more detail later in this chapter), Connie and Kelly are also African American. For Magna, her Mediterranean looks and tattooed skin drastically vary from her partner, Yukimo, whose very pronounced British accent and Asian descent alter the core group. Ranging in admiration for Kang filling the void left in the absence of two critical names, Rick and Maggie, with the new characters to cheer for, resurrecting the spirit of the series, some fans reveled in the changes brought to the ninth season. Using *X*, one viewer exclaims, "I'm convinced season 9 might be the best season the walking dead has ever done. Wow! I'm overjoyed with how much has changed and I love the new characters they've bought on to the show! The walking dead is back!! #TheWalking-Dead" (@JDarius28). Another viewer on *X* echoed this sentiment by stating how the six-year time jump after the exit of Rick mid-season "was the perfect opportunity for new characters, relationships, fights, children, etc, and they totally did it #TheWalkingDead #thetalkingdead @Walking-Dead_AMC" (@OscarRamo_). Though not completely filling the cavity left in the absence of Rick and Maggie, the newly instituted characters did help elevate the cast in diversity and intrigue.

Without a doubt, *The Walking Dead* continued to spark debate about the actions and representation of its characters. With comments ranging from praise to dissent about various changes to aspects of the series, fans did not sit idly by as the show continued to bring new trials and tests for these characters. Indeed, those loyal to the original storyline presented in *The Walking Dead* graphic novel or those not particularly fond of changes made to the televised series, such as with the departure of Rick Grimes, used social media as a platform to voice their dissatisfaction, especially with former showrunner Scott Gimple. Undeniably, fans missed Rick. Countless posts on *Reddit* and *X* reflect this sentiment. However, Kang had a job to do, and she did that job well. Pointing out how Kang did "her best to fix Gimples fuck ups," perhaps about Gimple following so closely to the original comic and thus making the show somewhat predictable (Bojalad; Megadog3). Perhaps it is how, as *Vox* contributor Emily St. James sees it, Gimple and the writers "mess[ed] with the *rhythms* of that story," especially leading up to the fifth season ("The Walking Dead's Been Popular"). Even with the missteps that some viewers claim on social media that Gimple took, this fan still admitted how Kang made them "...invested again, holy shit, never thought I'd say that" (Megadog3). Cleverly teasing the introduction of the Whisperers through carefully placed show promotions and keeping fans debating as to whether the zombies are "evolving," a word commonly used by fans when venturing whether or not they actually heard the zombies speak, the potential for a new threat to the lives of those still remaining added to the excitement of the ninth season while also fueling some fans to question if the series jumped the shark by taking such liberties. Regardless of where viewers fell (pro-evolving zombies or pro-new malicious threat), more than just the change in trajectory was noticed going into the ninth season.

Sheriff Little Ass Kicker, Judith Grimes

Considerably different than the previous seasons, *The Walking Dead* progressively made strides to present an extraordinarily diverse cast and bring underrepresented or muted characters to the forefront of the series. In addition to this inclusion came the voice of optimism embodied in the young, ingenious child. As if paying tribute to the earlier seasons, a group of stragglers finds themselves surrounded by an enclosing horde. Circling up with their weapons drawn and ready to fight, gunshots ring out from the woods to clear a path for the group to escape. Once they reach the woods, and away from the danger the walkers pose, Magna and her group encounter this pint-sized oddity. Wielding the Colt Python once used by her father, Rick Grimes, and a miniature katana strapped to her back, the young figure questions about their names. After sharing introductions, the child bends down to retrieve the all-too-familiar campaign hat worn by both her father and her older brother, Carl Grimes, reintroduced the world to Judith Grimes ("What Comes After").

Representing both her father, Rick, and her late brother, Carl, Judith carries with her a hefty burden, keeping the legacy of the Grimes family alive. Wearing the campaign hat Rick bequeathed to Carl and later herself, Judith tries living up to the "brave man" she describes to her brother RJ in later episodes ("Lines We Cross"). Although, as Jonathan Maberry explains in "Take Me to Your Leader," "[w]e can imagine how future generations will describe Rick," Judith provides a description very much befitting a romanticized individual by "transform[ing] Rick from a man into a hero" (32). By focusing only on the glory of the "brave man," Judith instills RJ with a glamorized version of a once incredibly flawed and often dangerous individual. Noticeably absent in her conversation is the story of Carl. Though Judith admits she is starting to forget their voices, she recalls her brother and his vision for the world after the war with the Saviors ("Who Are You Now?")

As previously stated, Carl passed the campaign hat to Judith before his death. In doing so, Carl bestows Judith a reminder of her duty to help others. While "the gun is to 'protect,'" as David Hopkins notes in "The Hero Wears the Hat," "the hat is [to] 'serve'" (207). Therefore, as a representation of Rick and Carl, Judith demonstrates qualities to protect others, an action she demonstrated when saving Magna's group after the time jump mid-ninth season. Additionally, Judith strives to serve others by vying for their acceptance within the community and questioning Michonne about the apparent separation between the colonies after the departure of Rick. When rescued by Judith and brought inside the walls of Alexandria, Magna's group, comprised of her partner Yumiko, sisters Connie and Kelly, and a former music teacher named Luke Abrams, plead their case before the council of Alexandria. Michonne is quite reluctant to allow the group to remain, even going as far as disclosing a prison-style tattoo on Magna's hand and prompting Magna to reveal her cleverly disguised knife. Michonne opens the group up to speculation about the potential threat these unknowns could pose on the colony. Despite this distrust, Judith appeals to Michonne by questioning what Rick would have wanted them to do. Her insight into the group, matched with the kindness bestowed upon her by her late brother Carl demonstrates how the young sage adamantly understands the potential for good in people rather than limiting them to any pre-apocalyptic transgressions ("Who Are You Now?").

Despite knowing the danger posed by allowing newcomers inside Alexandria, she only sees the potential good in people while simultaneously choosing to ignore their possible differences. In a world overrun by the dead and being part of the future generation in the apocalypse, Judith brings a renewed sense of hope for a future; a future predicated on the idea that differences, such as race, gender, sexual orientation, etc., make individuals unique but should not be a reason to create division. Excited about the new direction taken by this show to promote Judith Grimes as a primary focus, one viewer cheerfully exclaims,

> I am so fucking happy. I have been saying this for a while, but if new TV and movies like *Stranger Things* and *IT* can merge great storytelling with child actors, there's no reason why *The Walking Dead* can't. I am excited to see Judith and Hershel take this world by storm ... and the idea of older Henry intrigues me just as well [MerryBandOfPricks].

Integrating the fierceness of a fighter, a quality instilled by her adopted mother Michonne, and an optimistic attitude, a value bestowed upon her by her late brother Carl, Judith brings a refreshing outlook to the fate of the survivors in the apocalypse. For another viewer on *Reddit*, it was how Judith takes on the responsibilities bestowed upon her by her family. "What sold me on Judith," they conclude, "was the serious look she gave at the end, like the world was on her shoulders and she knows it and accepts it, truly a Grimes with a little Shane mixed in" (armokrunner). Judith only knows of a world where zombies constantly threaten survival and that survival is not limited to just the people residing in Alexandria or the other colonies.

Judith's survival represents hope and an opportunity for change as the communities live and learn through mutual interconnectedness. In addition to her optimistic outlook on the apocalypse, Judith also represents a turning point in the narrative. By rescuing Magna and the others, Judith not only challenges Michonne and her authority as head of security, and let us not forget, First Lady of the Alexandria Safe-Zone, but Judith also shows incredible depth in understanding the world they live in now. According to Kang, Judith represents:

> [W]isdom beyond her years, and she's so kind. That's what we were looking for with this character: a child who, despite the fact she grew up in these horrible circumstances that's already so scary and traumatic for the adults, she has an optimism just in the way she approaches the world. Part of that may be genetics. Part of that is she's been raised with love, surrounded by a community of people who are invested in her and raised by Michonne, who has taught her how to be tough [qtd. in Wigler].

Though Judith has only known life in a world of death, she also experienced a world filled with compassion as multiple individuals fought and died for her safety. Extending this benevolence to the other characters present in this book shows how kindness knows no limit but offers a chance for all beings to find acceptance.

With Judith constantly encouraging change, she demonstrates opposition to a world of constant threat and anxiety by promoting acceptance. Just as the ninth season welcomed the inclusion of diverging characters, Judith acceptingly welcomed the stragglers because of their need for recognition. In "Girls, Guns, and Zombies: Five Dimensions of Teaching and Learning in *The Walking Dead*," Anthony Neely argues, "the characters in the show are co-dependent for survival and help each other develop essential skills through active participation in communities of practice" (29). Lacking the formal establishment of schools or organizations as they previously were before the apocalypse, the survivors learn how to survive by working with each other through mutual respect and unified communities. Choosing the precise moment when she felt compelled to divulge this information about her past, Michonne opened up about her experience of nearly losing Judith when she let down her guard to allow a former and trusted friend, Jocelyn, into the colony. Confronting Michonne and her rationale for closing the colony, Judith states, "You're my mom. You chose to be. Because you love me, and I love you.... And loving someone means doing whatever it takes to keep them safe, right? But when did we stop loving Daryl? Aunt Maggie? Carol? The King?" ("Scars" 00:39:45–00:40:06). Though Michonne attempts a rebuttal, claiming their relationship never changed, the foundation of the colonies become divided in this instance of mistrust. As if reverting to building up the emotionally distant walls Michonne hid behind during the third season, Judith challenges her in a way that does not precisely prevent Michonne from completely tearing down these walls but emerges above them just a bit.

Time and time again, *The Walking Dead* proves past experiences influence the actions and decisions of the present. Michonne exemplifies this point in her rejection of outsiders stemming from allowing Jocelyn into the colony. Still, while Michonne makes determinations based on previous experience, Judith only looks to the future and the possibilities acceptance can bring. Returning to Hopkins, he discusses a critical distinction between the world before and after the apocalypse, especially when important decisions, such as welcoming outsiders, are made. In *The Walking Dead*, he states

> the new language is, in part, adjusting to a new morality. This new morality is as much a survival skill as learning to be cautious of any odd noises that might signal the presence of zombies. The traditional morality relied on due process, the hope of rehabilitation, and the possibility of clemency.... In the new world, trust is never entirely given, and judgment is highly subjective. Due process is a waste of time. Rehabilitation is a waste of resources, and clemency might get you killed [Hopkins 205].

Undoubtedly, the morality presented in the ninth season contradicts the traditional morality exhibited in the previous seasons. While Judith undeniably embodies the qualities of Michonne in her steadfastness and ability to wield a katana, she also represents the qualities of her brother. Carl urged for a world where just being is no way to live. However, as Michonne learned from her encounter with Jocelyn, her trust cannot be easily given without risking dire consequences.

As the newest generation grows, so does hope for a peaceful existence in such a chaotic world. As the shifting emergence of roles demonstrates, part of this existence is establishing equality. As men take on the previously assigned tasks of laundry and childcare, a task Eugene seemed all too enthusiastic to take on when baby Coco was born, women routinely take up guard, scavenge for supplies, and, as already covered in the last two chapters, take on the role of a leader. Displaying symbols of authority presented in the campaign hat and Colt Python, both symbols of the social hierarchy of the world before her time, Judith continues to keep the legacy of the Grimes family alive. Even while the symbols of the Grimes' past are on full display, Judith does not necessarily follow in the footsteps of her father. Instead, her presence is a constant reminder of the trials the group survived before arriving at Alexandria and the new realities of this world. Noting this shift on *Reddit*, one viewer concludes, "the whole point of Alexandria as a plot point is to show people who are delusional and think things can still be the way they were" (THE-73est). Indeed, Alexandria was a symbol of a past life where the gender roles of the old world remained intact. That is, until the emergence of characters such as Judith.

Recalling the enlightened words of a dying Bob Stookey (Lawrence Gilliard, Jr.), "Just look at her and tell me the world isn't going to change" ("Four Walls and a Roof" 00:33:42–00:33:45). Regardless of whether fans like it or not, change does happen quite often in this series. Change in time, change in threat, and change in the outlook for a hopeful future. Gale Anne Hurd, a longtime series executive producer, previously noted how the series would take its characters to some dark places. However, as also claimed how the show will "'also give them hope. Hope of a cure and hope of love. We're going to see some pretty interesting relationship stuff'" (qtd. in Goldberg). To add to this thought about emerging from the darkness, Kirkman also mentioned that while the comic book and the series would come to different ends, there would be aspects of hope and humanity involved (D. Taylor). In a time when raising children at the height of uncertainty might seem unfathomable, especially in the apocalypse, these hopeful youth provide the promise of a future. Specifically for Judith, she carries with her the Grimes legacy and the hope there is more to this world than the dead.

Hearing Loss a Damn Superpower: Connie and Kelly

Even with such groundbreaking development for the characters mentioned previously, the predominantly White heterosexual cast showcased over eight seasons did not go unnoticed by viewers. Then, in the ninth season, the look and feel of the series changed with the aggrandized departure of Rick Grimes. Jumping ahead six years since his departure, with the colonies thriving and a renewed hope for a life in an undying world, new predominantly female characters entered the series. According to *ComicBook.com* contributor Cameron Bonomolo, the ninth season of *The Walking Dead* brought forth "multiple new characters ... including comic book fan–favorites" ("'The Walking Dead' Season 9 Will Tell Different").

Favorites such as Magna and Yumiko, who are lovers both within the graphic novel and in the series, and sisters Kelly and Connie, brought new depths of diversity. Connie, the first deaf character introduced into the series, interacts mostly using American Sign Language, another first for the series. As a first, the addition of Connie brought praise for the series from the National Association of the Deaf (Bonomolo, "'The Walking Dead' Season 9 Will Tell Different"; Boucher; Pelletiere).

Furthermore, with Kelly, a character with progressive hearing loss, the direction of the narrative changed to bring more representation to the deaf and hard-of-hearing community (Acuna, "One of the Most Emotional Moments"). According to Kang, "'Rather than fighting against that, we just thought we'd make it part of the story'" (qtd. in Acuna, "One of the Most Emotional Moments"). Reaching out to Angel Theory for permission, the crew incorporated the progression of hearing loss into the narrative (Acuna, "One of the Most Emotional Moments"). In "Lines We Cross," Connie confronts her sister when she notices Kelly's frustration after not hearing a member of the Oceanside Colony's warning about some jagged rocks on the beach. After Kelly defeatedly reveals the progression of her hearing loss to her sister, Connie signs, "It's not a disability, it's a damn superpower" (00:30:50–00:31:01). In quite the personal touch, Kang wrote that specific line into the episode in homage of Theory's mother telling something very similar when Theory experienced a rather difficult time (Acuna, "One of the Most Emotional Moments").

By incorporating this moment into the narrative and promoting the storyline about the hearing impaired, Kang addresses the differing abilities of her characters and embraces those typically underrepresented in apocalyptic stories. As actress Lauren Ridloff noted in an interview on *Good Morning America*, "'I feel that with more representation working behind the camera, the stories that are told in television, film and stage would become more intriguing, truthful and thought provoking'" (qtd. in Pelletiere). As diversity increases offscreen, so do the shared stories onscreen. This distinct quality of representing the deaf and hard-of-hearing community in this genre of storytelling recalls the use of sound, or lack thereof, in horror films such as *A Quiet Place*, where silence magnifies the terror in the narrative. According to supervising sound editor Erik Aadahl, *A Quiet Place* "invert[s] that whole concept, where it's more about the negative space, the quiets, and the shades of quietness, and ultimately, the silence. Where then, when you do play a sound, you're naked" (qtd. in B. Bishop). Throughout *The Walking Dead*, the ability to hear gives survivors a distinct advantage when fleeing or combatting the dead. For both Connie and Kelly, the inability to hear adds unbelievable intensity to these characters. Both sisters often venture outside the walls of

Hilltop despite their differing ability. While this lack of hearing undoubtedly presents a challenge for these characters, they persevere in the face of danger.

Of the characters introduced during the ninth season, they provide a diverging perspective about capabilities in the apocalypse that counters the dissenting commentary regarding the ability of those considered differently abled. In the essay "What Feminism has to Say About World War Z," Jen Rinaldi concludes, "anyone whose body is physically impaired will be susceptible to the [zombie] outbreak … wheelchair users who cannot run away, fat people who cannot run fast, visually impaired persons who cannot see an attack coming, and so on" (13). Intermittently shown throughout the series, elderly survivors only make occasional appearances in the narrative, such as when the core group happens upon a nursing home protected by Guillermo (Neil Brown, Jr.) and the Vatos in the first season ("Vatos"). While the fate of the nursing home is uncertain, figures such as Guillermo and the Vatos understand the severity of the elders' plight. Connie and Kelly prove impairments are not automatically a death sentence. And, with their addition, these new characters enhance the variation of the core group. Noting this representation in the series, a fan on *X* remarks how "The newcomers are such talented actors and very reminiscent of those in the first few seasons. Representation for the deaf community is awesome. I haven't been this excited for #TheWalkingDead in a long time" (@RickAndThangs). Being the only hearing-impaired characters in this series, Connie and Kelly bring attention to differing abilities in the apocalypse.

Along with the applause given to *The Walking Dead* from the National Association of the Deaf, fans of the series voice appreciation for casting such diverse characters. Some viewers echo the sentiment Rinaldi expresses by questioning the possibility of a deaf individual surviving for so long in the apocalypse. Still, the changes in the series earned praise for "[e]xcellent casting" (askylitpichu) to expressions of disbelief that Ridloff "actually is deaf. Props to her. She gotta be one of my favorite new characters" (Nurgus). Continuing with such admiration, viewers on social media platforms appear to welcome the addition, especially for this underrepresented community. For some viewers, adding a deaf character provides an exciting moment for identification. One commenter exclaims: "As a person with hearing loss I love seeing a Deaf character" (waywardgirl25), while another on *X* writes enthusiastically, "@WalkingDead_AMC thank you so much for creating deaf character. I'm deaf and it bring me joy to watch! Thank you! #TheWalkingDead #TWD #Connie" (@justin_proffitt). Ridloff and Theory bring representation to an often-neglected group of viewers, especially those seeking a relatable character.

Not All Villains Are Men: Alpha and the Whisperers

Along with the increased attention paid to diversity in the ninth season, viewers witnessed another monumental change with the introduction of a new antagonistic terror, Alpha. Alpha brings a new level of fear into this already tumultuous story of death and survival because of her disruption from the previously established history of male authority and dominance. "[D]esigned to stir up anxieties about gender, sexuality, and order," as Drew Humphries concludes in "Women Who Kill: *Law and Order, Dexter,* and *The Wire*," Alpha interrupts the status quo established over the previous seasons (297). As her name clearly indicates, Alpha is the predominant figure of her group and asserts terror in her followers by killing without hesitation those who oppose her leadership. In one instance, after Henry observes how the Whisperers remove the skin of the dead and prep the hides for wearing, one Whisperer, Sean (Benjamin Keepers), questions Alpha and her decision to retrieve her daughter, Lydia, from the Hilltop Colony. Demanding that Alpha renounce her leadership of the group, Alpha kills both Sean and his partner Helen (Allie McCulloch) to validate and solidify her supremacy ("Guardians"). Lacking compassion as the other women in the series possesses, Alpha enters the narrative as a hostile and threatening irregularity.

As a female adversary, Alpha is a rarity in horror. Reflecting a reality where women "are complicated, and some that are downright evil. Women deserve to be shown to be as complex and in-depth as male characters are" (McKinney), Alpha matches the brutality of her male predecessors without being deprived of a backstory and development. *The Walking Dead* made sure to provide some context for its characters, assisting the audience understand their history. Alpha comes into the narrative as a mother wanting to assert her superiority in a relationship where she deemed her husband, Frank (Steve Kazee), as weak. Murdering him and possibly others due to her perceived inferiority, she maintains control and authority over herself and her young daughter, Lydia.

Tales of the Walking Dead completely diverges from both *The Walking Dead* and *Fear the Walking Dead* in their formatting and yet manages to accentuate the main series with its presentation of vignettes from the apocalypse focusing on storylines outside the trials of the Rick Grimes ("Tales of the Walking Dead–TV Episode Recaps & News"). As an anthology series of horror-filled short stories, *Tales of the Walking Dead* intentionally "cultivates a different look and feel" (Century). The beauty of this series is in its flexibility, offering the ability to tell different stories set at the start of and during the rise of the dead. Also, viewers of this series can be well-versed or even watch the previous two shows to understand the series, making it brilliant for new viewers to enter *The Walking Dead* Universe (Bankhurst). Since there is no distinct timeline or sequence these short stories need to or must follow, there is excellent potential for favorites from previous episodes of *The Walking Dead* to make an appearance. A perfect example of revisiting a previous character is the episode "Dee," which gives fans more to the story of Alpha and her rise to become the leader of the Whisperers (Bankhurst; Century). We do not get the full story behind the evolution from Dee to her new identity as Alpha, but *Tales of the Walking Dead* made sure to bring in more to expanding her narrative, a treatment some of the most notorious characters in the series received.

For the Governor, his dominance stemmed from a desire to reinstitute the rigid nuclear family structure, a structure exemplified by Rick and the core group inside the Prison. Fans would learn more about the charming Governor and his facade as episodes unfolded, revealing a man who keeps his undead daughter, Penny Blake (Kylie Szymanski), locked in a closet. While hiding this persona from the citizens of Woodbury, he relied on scientist Milton to experiment on the walkers in hopes of finding some redemptive quality, one that could possibly revive his daughter. Michonne saw through the masquerade of Woodbury and the Governor immediately. On the other hand, Andrea seemed all too optimistic that both the city and the man were the answer to finding peace after many days of uncertainty and death. A mistake that would cost her life ("Welcome to the Tombs"). While the Governor did not receive a depiction of his backstory, he did get his own individual narrative arc. After the fall of Woodbury, the arc following the Governor brought fans insight to how he, now known as Brian, sought revenge on Rick and the survivors inside the Prison. Longing for the life he spies Rick living, he sets out to usurp Rick or kill everyone in the process. Though he meets his end during the siege in the Prison, Tara is brought into the narrative and adopted into the core group.

For Negan, his authority focused more on gain: more power, more possessions, and, as evidenced by his many wives, more women. Perhaps one of the biggest cliffhangers in the series, Negan's introduction at the end of the sixth season sent fans into a tizzy as the show ended before revealing the victim of his brutal and maniacal beating with his cherished bat, Lucille ("Last Day on Earth"). Despite his cruelty, the swagger of this character won over fans. Noting how "I personally like him but it's always so frustrating to watch how some people are trying to justify his actions" to favoring specific moments when "he says something borderline asshole or gives an arrogant smirk even during his redemption arc, I like when it feels like he just can't help himself sometimes," fans debate the potential of this character weighed against the egregious actions he committed since his introduction in the sixth season (djord17; Dradus6). Indeed, Negan would carry his arrogance and offensive remarks long after the war with the Saviors ended and even through his, let's call it, redemptive story arc. His tact for wooing women proved useful when he infiltrated the Whisperers and somehow managed to whittle down the hardened exterior presented by Alpha.

Unlike the Governor and Negan, who used their authority as men and superior charisma to subvert power from others, Alpha differs in her aggressive motivation. Differing from the assumption that female killers' "anger derives in most cases not from childhood experience but from specific moments in their adult lives in which they have been abandoned or cheated on by men," as Clover posits (29), Alpha diverges from this prescribed description. Rather than killing her husband because of some torrid love affair or his abandonment, Alpha kills him for his alleged weakness and inability to keep herself or their daughter safe ("Omega"). For Negan and the Governor, neither is responsible for the death of their partners. Fans learn of Negan's history when the character is afforded a backstory episode, which depicts the death of his wife and the potential cause for his ruthlessness ("Here's Negan"). On the other hand, the Governor reveals his wife died in a car accident before the outbreak while in conversation ("Killer Within"). By her continuing to disturb the established male superiority in horror where "men are expected to use horror films as a way to assert their own manliness over their peers and to provide reassurance to their female companions who are expected to display fear" (Michaud), Alpha shows no fear but instead punishes her husband Frank for exhibiting weakness.

No longer attached to a partner, Alpha emerges superior to her formerly dominating male counterpart. No more the weaker sex, Alpha uses her act of violence to rid herself of a man to become a singular protector in place of Frank as the father. As Jack Boozer concludes of the femme fatale in the article "The Lethal Femme Fatale in the Noir Tradition," Alpha "no longer needs the man for violence as she is fully capable of it" (27). Unlike a few of the women previously mentioned, say Carol or Rosita, Alpha does not learn how to defend herself or her daughter from men. And, distinct from all the women previously discussed, Alpha actively uses killing to gain power. Rather than refraining from violence or using violence only when necessary to protect others, Alpha appears to find great satisfaction in killing others.

Additionally, as Alpha shows, she selfishly acts in ways that serve her interests and not for the better of the group. In this way, Alpha varies drastically from Carol in her practice of walking with and dressing as the dead, as well as her self-inflicted abuse to, in her mind, make herself stronger. In essence, Alpha is undeniably "abject terror personified" as she exercises scopic control resulting "not in her annihilation, in the manner of classic cinema, but in her triumph; indeed, her triumph *depends* on her assumption of the gaze" (Clover 35; 60; emphasis added). She not only assumes the gaze of the ever-present threat of the dead but uses this ability to her advantage. Contrasting earlier seasons where Rick and the others are seen covering themselves in walker guts and cautiously meandering through the groups of walkers to escape, Alpha and the Whisperers utilize the dead as a weapon against their foes. In the episodes following her introduction to the narrative, Alpha and the Whisperers continuously wear their masks and walk amongst the dead to pose a threat and keep themselves concealed and safe.

Despite her insistence to carry the title "Alpha," even by her daughter, Alpha somehow manages to show signs of a protective, maternal nature toward her daughter, Lydia. This trait further distances Alpha from the conventional model of a femme fatale. Instead of representing "disappointment embodied," where the traditional Fatale is "[c]hildless, unstable and aggressive ... everything a modern woman is not supposed to be" (Burton), Alpha breaks her own established rules to retrieve Lydia from Hilltop by revealing the identity of the Whisperers. As a group believing to "live with the dead means to live in silence," which Alpha deems is a form of "[n]atural selection," the Whisperers abide by strict rules to conceal their identity ("Guardians" 00:21:30–00:21:42). The Whisperers abide this mantra so well that Alpha even nudges one of the followers to leave her crying baby to the fate of the dead, a task that no one inside Hilltop could fathom ("Guardians").

While the ability to speak freely helps distinguish the dead from the living, viewers even debate the rationale of her actions as a mother and protector when Alpha decides to expose the Whisperers to Hilltop. One viewer declared quite an interest in Alpha on *Reddit* by stating,

> Without mothering instincts, a woman is but a cruel shell. In all seriousness, what's fascinating about Alpha is that she did break her own rules to save her daughter, demonstrating that she does have a mothering instinct—as fucked up as it is. That's going to be an interesting conflict, sociopathic pragmatism going hand in hand with mothering [bracake].

A woman acting in such a violent matter without reason or explanation is deemed cruel. Following this thought about motherhood in all its forms, another viewer concludes, "I think it could really only be a woman to fill that roll. When a woman is evil, she is straight up EVIL. Most women are kind and compassionate because we inherently have a mothering instinct before we even have children" (sick-asfrick). Unlike the femme fatale, a woman acting on behalf of her children can be determined motherly, even with someone as callous as Alpha.

The sociopathic pragmatism described by the previous quote aside, her actions drastically contrast with the motherly persona of women such as Carol, exciting comparison fans debate online. Both women, as mothers, act in ways uncharacteristic of the compassion and kindness typically ascribed to nurturing women. While Carol is cheered on when torching the Saviors for threatening Henry and disguising herself when fighting against the Wolves, viewers condemn Alpha for her actions. One viewer disputes such actions when comparing the actions of both Carol and Alpha. Though calling for patience before throwing out such an assertion, one view pondered how,

> Both were in similar situation (yes different sides of it) and she could see Lydia as Sophia? And maybe think that if Carol was more like Ed (Alpha) Sophia might be alive? But then you realize that Alpha is fucking nuts. I know this might not make sense now, or ever, I just think there could be something there and with Carol not in the comics, they really can do some interesting things with Carol and Alpha I believe [AroundSurviving].

Appropriately drawing a parallel between these two mothers, this viewer sees Carol and Alpha as equally lethal, similarly resilient, and willing to use violence.

Still, while demonstrating great complexity and contrasting views of motherhood, Carol and Alpha differ in their uncharacteristic actions when safeguarding their existence. To demonstrate her authority, Alpha later kills her husband and two members of her group. To protect her adoptive family, Carol kills Lizzie for fear her sociopathic behavior will harm Judith and, quite potentially, others. Carol also torches Terminus and the Saviors when they threaten her family. Even Tobin, Carol's temporary love interest during the sixth season, admits how as a mother, she can act in ways that "just terrify me ... it's the hard stuff, the scary stuff. It's how you can do it. It's strength" ("Not Tomorrow Yet" 00:12:10–00:13:06). The difference between these women lies in their rationale. Carol knows her utility is not in her ability to kill but proactively thwarts further harm from coming to others, a fault she bares in her inability to protect Sophia. Carol also exhibits deep remorse for those who have died. Leaving cookies on Sam's grave, her retreating from the core group on her solo adventures, and even the infamous kill diary demonstrates her guilt for such actions. Quite oppositely, Alpha lacks the remorse that Carol possesses, cares nothing for her disciples, and uses killing to acquire and preserve her power.

Comments debating the emergence and intensity of the most recent threat to the survival of the core group send social media discussions into a tizzy of speculation. Up to the ninth season, viewers saw only two female antagonists: Jadis/Anne as the leader of the Scavengers in the seventh season and Dawn Lerner (Christine Woods) as the militant leader of police officers inhabiting Grady Memorial Hospital during the fifth season. It is not until the eleventh and final season that fans would meet the only other female antagonist, Pamela Milton (Laila Robins). After the Whisperers made their presence known, an overwhelming response from the viewership deemed these antagonists to be the most terrifying villains to enter the series. Their ability to integrate easily with the dead led viewers to wonder if the Whisperers' entry occurred even earlier. Recalling previous seasons, one apt viewer pondered, "way back in Season 3 when Rick saw Morgan again and Morgan said he has 'seen people wearing dead people's faces,' were they setting up the Whisperers back then? #TheWalking-Dead" (@Trevorlloyd92). Alpha, as well as those who follow her, believe the world now belongs to the dead. This sentiment Enid shared when she would sneak over the walls at Alexandria after the death of her parents. To Alpha, the colonies of the Kingdom, Hilltop, the Alexandria Safe-Zone, and Oceanside are "a joke. ...a shrine to a long-dead world" ("The Calm Before" 00:43:16–00:43:21) rather than hope for a future where the living can exist in opposition to the dead. The dichotomy of Carol and Alpha presents differing sides to motherhood that carry over well into the tenth season when Carol utilizes an unlikely ally to bring about the end of Alpha's reign.

As if embodying the terror herself, Carol does what only Carol can do, hatch a plan to bring an end to the Whisperers by using the most significant advantage they have in this fight with the Whisperers, Lydia. Springing Negan from his cell at Alexandria with hopes Carol will leave a good word for him with the colony, Negan infiltrates the Whisperers. Of course, becoming one of the Whisperers does not come easy. Negan ultimately proves himself loyal by ratting out Whisperer named Gamma (Thora Burch), who was first befriended by Aaron reveals more and more about herself, such as her real name, Mary, and the Whisperers while being held at Alexandra ("Stalker"). To reward Negan for this fidelity to Alpha, she persuades him to a secluded area where the two can be alone and engages him in sex ("Squeeze"). Ultimately, her trust in Negan would bring her an end. Despite her second in command, Beta (Ryan Hurst), Alpha follows Negan on the promise of seeing Lydia, whom Negan claims to have for her. Once alone and caught completely off guard, Negan slices Alpha's throat and, after beheading her, presents the severed head to his accomplice, Carol ("Walk with Us").

Reacting to Alpha's final scene, fans took to social media to express their shock. Stating this episode was "Totally worth the wait," and that this was the "First time I have stood & screamed OMG at the TV in a long time," the alarming end to the most intense villain of the series caused a stir online (Juno2018; wolfitalk). Amongst the comments about this scene, Kang appeared to keep the promise of bringing new trajectories and keeping fans guessing. The ability to use the source material from the original graphic novel as inspiration did not bind this showrunner, nor does it appear she needed to keep wholly faithful to its storyline. She also only attempts to draw out storylines as long as needed. One fan echoed this sentiment about the timeline mentioned in the last sentence by praising Kang for "organically telling a story and killing characters off when it feels right rather than having to force plot to make big things happens every mid season or finale" (hunta-gathera). While elements are undoubtedly mirrored and included in various ways, the ability to steer away from the predictable while still honoring the original story and bring fans a show that keeps them guessing demonstrates the mastery of this showrunner and the power of this narrative.

Mental Health and Making Friends: Princess

In this writer's opinion, perhaps the most refreshing addition to *The Walking Dead* is the introduction of Juanita "Princess" Sanchez. Entering the tenth season, Princess, as she prefers to be called, brought a new energy to the series, not to mention some fantastic purple hair and a bright pink coat. So desperate for companionship, Princess staged the dead to mimic a lively and functioning city. After being alone for over a year, Princess takes great delight in greeting Ezekiel, Yumiko, and Eugene as they make their way to a meeting point with a person only known by the name Stephanie ("Look at the Flowers"). Persuading her new friends to follow her to a location where they can access some wheels after she accidentally though trying to be helpful scares away their horses when shooting down some walkers, Princess makes a careless mistake in buying her time with these newly found companions. Much to their displeasure in rooting her intentional delay out, Princess admits to her deceit, citing she only did not want to stop the fun ("The Tower"). Acknowledging the screwed up, Princess confesses more about her crippling loneliness. Stating how the city was "so empty," she realized "this isn't that different from how [she] felt before all of this" ("The Tower" 00:28:08–00:22:14). In her disclosure, the insecurities from her past come pouring out in one of the saddest but most endearing moments with this character.

The introduction of Princess and her internal struggles with mental health is not the first time *The Walking Dead* presented a character with such an affliction. Going back all the way to the first season with Jim (Andrew Rothenberg) struggled with the tremendous guilt caused by him escaping to Atlanta while the walkers distractedly ate his family. His various delusions led him to preemptively dig holes for what would be future victims in a surprise infiltration of the Atlanta survivor's camp ("Vatos"). The Greene family could be included in this discussion as they collectively determine the walkers in the barn to be "sick" rather than dead, a delusion that nearly cost them the safety of their farm. My previous discussion of the Governor harboring his zombified daughter in a closet, occasionally bringing her out to brush her hair, all the while denying to himself that she is dead. Both Rick and Morgan lose their sense of control and care for their wellbeing after witnessing the deaths of their loved ones, a point I will discuss in more detail in the next chapter. Yet, the depiction of Princess battling her inner voices and struggles with PTSD, endear her to not only Eugene but also to fans.

That is not to say that her addition to the narrative escaped its fair share of mixed reactions. From fans on *X* cheering the actress to those commenting on her being just too much, Princess is very much a character that carries a lot of weight. Of those in favor of this addition, one applauded Princess for being "...the best thing to happen to The Walking Dead in a long time. I love her," while another stated, "Paola Lazaro, who plays Princess on The Walking Dead is becoming my favorite actor ever!!! She's incredible!" (@shannonstacey; @tessa). Even more than praise, the addition of Princess brought new levels of representation to the series, one her Puerto Rican heritage and her open struggle with her mental health. When first landing the role, actress Paola Lázaro explained how she requested a modification to her character. Asking for the sake of representation if Princess could be Puerto Rican since, as Lázaro explained in an interview with *Express.co.uk*, "'Rosita [Espinosa] (played by Christian Serratos) is a Hispanic female character who is very strong, and she is Mexican in the show'" (qtd. in Body). Much to her apparent surprise, it seems, the show supported her inquiry about how she could bring this character to life.

In "Splinter," Princess, Yukimo, Eugene, and Ezekiel are captured, separated, and interrogated by a group living in what would later be revealed as the Commonwealth. During her confinement within a railcar, her PTSD is triggered when she gets a splinter (Moran). Her fixating on the annoyingly tiny sliver of wood in her finger, the repetition exacerbates her previous experiences with abuse while triggering her memories of the punishment inflicted on her by her abusive stepfather. Writing about this episode on *Screenrant*, Sarah Moran points out how a repeated action "can often bring up repressed memories, and the splinter reminds Princess of a time she had an infected splinter for which her stepfather blamed and punished her," with the confinement of the train car serving as the small closet her stepfather would lock her in as punishment. Diving deeper into her neurosis and based on the comments given by fans on *Reddit*, this divisive episode not only gave viewers insight into this character but allowed some to identify with someone struggling with their mental health. On *X*, one fan commented on how "...Princess in the walking dead is absolutely precious and imo they handled the topic of domestic abuse well. #TheWalkingDeadUK" (@LordWay69). Similarly, on *Reddit*, fans spoke about understanding her struggle, which Lázaro masterfully and realistically portrayed on screen.

By praising the actress for her performance, one fan even stated how,

> Yeah, I feel like this episode is one of the most accurate representations of what a PTSD episode / trauma response feels like that I've ever seen on television. It's clear to me that someone on the writing team has personal experience with mental health. I think that's why I loved it so much, and I suspect that a lot of the folks that don't also don't have that experience [DreadWolfByTheEar].

The ability to identify and relate to this character based on her struggles endears her as likable and believable. In addition to the accuracy of this representation of PTSD, another fan wrote how they "...never really got why people like to feel 'represented' by a character on a show or video game, but when I watched those few episodes with her, I started to understand" (AnaMain___). Hard as this episode is to watch as her mind turns against her, Princess ultimately overcomes her psychosis to negotiate information out of a Commonwealth officer she manages to (albeit brutally) overpower ("Splinter").

Reflecting on her contributions to *The Walking Dead* and the representation her character brings on screen, Lázaro named the biggest takeaway from being a part of this series is how transparent her character is about her struggles. In an interview with Insider, Lázaro stated, "When I go to conventions, I have people come up to me and thank me for the character. I'm just so thankful that I get to play a character that speaks on" mental health (qtd. in Acuna, "'The Walking Dead' Star Paola Lázaro"). Speaking to the importance of bringing awareness to the issues experienced by these characters, showrunner Angela Kang detailed, "...it sort of makes sense to illuminate a little bit about who she is and where she came from, and the challenges she's faced as somebody who has had to live by herself for a very, very, very long time, and the things that has done to her mental state" (Ross, "'The Walking Dead' Showrunner"). Fans seemed to agree that despite the discord brought by this episode focusing so much on a new character, the ability to speak to the crippling effect isolation has on the mind registered well and, for some, made Princess one pretty significant character.

Overlooked Identities: A Reflection

The Walking Dead transformed when Angela Kang took the helm ahead of the ninth season. Despite fans dreading the potential downward spiral for the series after the departures of both Rick Grimes and Maggie Rhee mid-season, Kang persisted in shocking plot twists and unanticipated outcomes. Excellently put by one viewer on *X*, "Angela Kang has done wonders for #TheWalkingDead. You'd think doing the Whisperers storyline without Rick, Carl, and Maggie would be next to impossible. So far, she's proving that wrong. Go on, girl!" (@DrKnockers05). Though the history of *The Walking Dead* presents numerous instances where White male patriarchy rules the day, the ninth season turned this establishment on its head to bring incredible levels of diversity and complexity in character development. In doing so, the ninth season presents the ability of a television series to take a new direction by promoting emerging female roles.

Women now take the lead, rushing into danger and fighting for a brighter future, even at considerable risk to their safety. As Kang describes, "These characters are in a world where they are constantly engaging with a fight-or-flight response and are also thinking about who they are as people and who they want to be. Is the only way forward to fight and kill, or is there something that makes us uniquely human?" (qtd. in Turchiano). Kang offers a reminder about the tremendous power emotions have when fans become passionately invested in a series such as *The Walking Dead*, and regardless of gender or ability, all life is precious. According to one viewer, the reveal of the victims at the end of the ninth season was not only "emotionally devastating, but also a testament to the genuine heartfelt and tender moments the show can have. The theme of the show has always been pursuing life in such a deadly world, and this episode was no better symbol of just that" (Zomboy716). If the premise is to show people surviving even in such a deadly world and overcoming a devastating loss, the ninth season finale accomplishes this goal.

Under the control of Kang, *The Walking Dead* finally realizes the full promise of the diversity called for by early critics and fans alike. In *The Subversive Zombie*, Aiossa notes how *The Walking Dead* "is trending in the right direction" (138). Still, the core group "deserves to include variations in sexual orientation, religious beliefs, physical stature, attractiveness, and ableism" (131) to grow beyond the disparaging categorizations associated with the series since its inception. For the ninth season, Kang saw fit to bring increased levels of diversity in sexual orientation, varying degrees of ableism, and growing awareness of mental health. Not only that, but the introduction of the Whisperers also brought new levels of anxiety as this group of individuals voluntarily walked with the dead. Instead, the outcomes of the show remind viewers about the incredible fragility of human life. Additionally, by adding characters such as Kelly and Connie as two differently abled characters, Alpha as a threat unlike any other seen on this show, and Princess representing Latin culture, pansexuality, and struggles with mental health, *The Walking Dead* Universe incorporates even more inclusivity. In doing so, Kang and the crew of *The Walking Dead* offer underrepresented individuals a chance for recognition and identification; a change fans vigorously applaud and appreciatively communicate on social media.

Facing the Inescapable
Presence of Death

Be warned. This caution is your spoiler alert. The following statement I am about to make could entirely ruin the series for you. So, turn back now if you are not quite ready for this revelation. All right, I warned you. Here it is. People die in *The Walking Dead*. A lot of people. Surprised, right? Fine, this might not be the most significant revelation given that the entire premise of the series focuses on death and how not to become one of the dead (even the title of the show implies that death is ever-present). Still, despite this commonality of death, it is not without its significance regarding gender. By the end of the eleventh and final season, there are an estimated 1,416 deaths and zombifications since the show began in 2010 ("The Walking Dead Season 11 Census: Alive, Dead, or Zombie? [Updated]"). While I will not go into every death in this chapter, I want to bring attention to a few meaningful instances in the series that demonstrate the variations in dying in the apocalypse, especially along the lines of gender.

Out of eleven seasons demonstrating innumerable shocking and gruesome ways to kill a zombie, at least this series is consistent about how often we are the viewers and the characters within the story are reminded of death. If the zombies themselves do not serve as good enough *memento mori*, perhaps it is the constant struggles of the survivors not to become one of the undead. When unfortunate souls meet their end, those still living ensure they do not rise again by strategically, and sometimes creatively, impaling the brain. I mention creatively for the simple fact that *Talking Dead* dedicates segments to reliving these various zombie deaths, bringing even more attention to just how many "imaginative" ways there are to end a zombie. Depending on the specific character and their affiliation with the core group determines the fate of their remains because here in the apocalyptic world of *The Walking Dead*, "We bury the ones we love, and burn the rest" ("Nebraska" 00:08:42–00:08:45). As a fan of the series, I can attest to shedding more than my fair share of tears and shouting very profanely at my television screen as I watched characters perish because, well, people die in *The Walking Dead*. Of course, as this book discusses, social media proves I am not alone in my solace when beloved characters die, despised characters manage to escape death, even if not for very long, or an episode abruptly ends without any resolution to who might be next. Whether expressed in words, GIFs, or a combination of the two, tweets, forums, and opinion pieces run the gauntlet of emotions that fans of the series convey. Yes, death comes for us all. Even if we watch a fictional depiction of death from the comfort of our homes, we, as viewers, cannot escape this reminder.

As equitable as death seems in the series, the depiction of death proves to be quite a fascinating area of analysis, especially regarding mourning. To process death and adapt to our new reality, Dr. Caitlin Stanaway explains how we cycle through five stages of grief: denial, anger, bargaining, depression, and acceptance. While the cycle of these stages differs for everyone, which I will explore in more depth momentarily, there are some consistencies in the grieving process ("The Stages of Grief: Accepting the Unacceptable"). If the dead refuse to stay dead, how can anyone move on in the apocalypse? Undeniably, the toll death takes on the body, and the mind is detrimental. However, as a leader, protector, parent, or whatever ascribed titles one identifies as in the apocalypse, what happens when the grieving period is prevented due to continuous threats against survival, such as fleeing from a horde of the undead? Perhaps even more detrimental, what happens when the grieving process is outright denied by those refusing to accept their new reality?

Revisiting the discussion about Judith Butler and melancholy discussed earlier in this book helps position the conversations involving coping or dealing with loss. Butler asserts how the refusal of loss, what is known as melancholy, results in "the failure to displace into words; indeed, the place of the maternal body is established in the body, 'encrypted,' to use their term, and given permanent residence there as a dead and deadening part of the body or one inhabited or possessed by phantasms of various kinds" (93). Butler references melancholy through the lens of psychoanalysis, specifically in the context of gender and the understanding of how sex is determined. However, when Butler speaks of the "maternal body as an object of love," I am curious about a broader application to Butler's thoughts on melancholy (Butler 92–93). In *The Walking Dead*, the characters, and the viewers at home, witness loved ones exit their world by dying and, on occasion, observe their reanimation as part of the undead. It is in this period of loss and reanimation that melancholy makes its presence known.

As much as *Talking Dead* likes to relive a highlight reel of crafty zombie killings, it also regularly acknowledges the passing of beloved characters. In this time, viewers collectively mourn these, albeit fictional, losses. Still, while viewers might voice their disapproval of the killing off a favorite character, the specific brutal killing of Glenn comes to mind here, it is not necessarily this loss that connects viewers to the narrative. Instead, it is the very real understanding about the struggle with losing their loved ones. In his chapter "The Pathos of *The Walking Dead*," Kyle William Bishop speaks specifically to the effectiveness of *The Walking Dead* in portraying real and relatable human emotions. Though zombies "obviously function as catalysts for the show's physical action and apocalypse storyline," as Bishop notes, "the core of *The Walking Dead* addresses the essential concerns of dramatic pathos: the struggles, losses, and emotional trauma experienced by the human protagonists" (10). The zombies bring horror, while the surviving humans are the audience's connection to what remains of humanity and a reminder of what the zombies were before they were reanimated.

Despite the hordes of dead roaming the Earth and seeking the flesh of the remaining living, Bishop contemplates if zombies remain the representation of horror they once were, especially when considering George A. Romero's re-envisioning of zombie monsters in his epic film *Dawn of the Dead*. After the so-called "'Zombie Renaissance'" in 2001, as presented by Bishop, the number of zombie narratives and zombie walks has grown exponentially (2). In this transition, Bishop questions the impact of zombies as a monstrosity and something to be feared by the living. Instead, Bishop turns to what he describes as the actual fear apparent in *The Walking Dead* series. He argues, "The real horror is that the monsters used to be people—and they represent what might become of the imperiled protagonists" (Bishop 12). A divergence from the tradition presented by the horror, which focuses on the monster, *The Walking Dead* navigates viewers away from the dead to the endeavor of the living to endure.

Along with the fight for survival, as noted previously, those lucky enough to remain alive are constantly reminded of the loss of life and the people the walking dead once were before the apocalypse. Bishop describes one scene when the main protagonist, Rick Grimes, encounters a father, Morgan Jones, and son, Duane Jones, using the Grimes's former residence as a stronghold and their refusal to leave the area because of Morgan's attachment to his late wife, who just so happens to be one of the undead. As Bishop describes, "[Morgan] laments that he cannot kill the creature she has become, even though her continues existence clearly torments both him and his son [Duane], who spends his nights sobbing uncontrollably" (10). It is unfortunate for both Morgan and Duane to have lost someone they loved, but the loss is never quickly forgotten as the mother makes her nightly appearance at the Jones's stronghold.

As evidenced by the scene with Morgan and Duane, each reoccurrence of their loved one becomes a manifestation of their loss. Loss is never settled fully in *The Walking Dead*. Instead, the survivors must kill what is already dead for fear that becoming a reanimated zombie could further endanger them or any other survivors. While melancholy speaks of loss, a separation must happen for the living to feel the sensation. Instead of allowing that to happen, the deceased come back repeatedly until they are stopped in the only way, which proves helpful, to impale the zombie through the brain. While the zombies are no longer the people they once resembled, their likeness to their former selves proves difficult for the living to overcome. Difficult, but not impossible.

Having witnessed the death of my grandmother firsthand, as well as experiencing the loss of other family members throughout my years, I can relate to the feeling which develops after the death of a loved one. This sense of loss makes for an easy connection and a residual effect as I continue watching *The Walking Dead* episode after episode. Perhaps Bishop had a point in this chapter; the monsters are no longer what is feared. It is who the monsters once were that creates fear. When separated from a loved one by death, their memory embeds itself within us, and we can call upon their image in our minds as we speak their name aloud or reflect on photographs of the past. When discussing the evolution of Maggie from a typified farmer's daughter to leader of the Hilltop Colony, I briefly touched upon the use of photographs as mementos of the past. For Maggie, her burning of Glenn's cherished photograph establishes this awareness of the detriments caused by fixating on the past. Maggie chooses to live in the present, while Glenn clings to a memory from a time long gone.

In *The Walking Dead*, the survivors are constantly reminded of loss. In an environment such as this, melancholy hardly has time to manifest due mainly to the fact that the dead refuse to remain dead. In *Gender Trouble*, Butler explains how experiencing the loss and subsequent refusal to accept this loss of another, especially of a loved one with whom we identify, leaves a subjective impression. In reading these words by Butler, my mind made a connection between loss, the refusal of loss, and this series. As a post-apocalyptic story in which the dead have come back to walk the Earth, the living must scrounge for survival while avoiding falling victim to the ravenous undead. While Butler speaks of melancholy in a discussion of gender, she expresses how melancholy can be experienced in other forms of identification. In an interview with Judith Butler, Vicki Bell enquires about Butler's analogy of melancholia as it relates to sexuality. According to Butler's work, heterosexuality encodes homosexuality, Bell wonders about similarities as they apply to other coded systems such as race.

Interestingly, Butler refers to a cultural institution of melancholia and the perception of love toward another race. As Butler explains during an interview with Vicki Bell, "there is a culturally instituted melancholia because what that would mean is that there is a class of persons whom I could never love or for whom it would be unthinkable for me to love, and they are constituted essentially as the unthinkable, the unlovable, the ungrievable" (170). In this way, culture influences perceptions of who is worthy of love, and those outside the norm cannot be considered worthy of respect because they are not part of that culture. Applying this thought to *The Walking Dead*, the dead do not love the living but merely seek their destruction to satisfy an unquenchable longing for their flesh. For the living, the dead are reminders of the past, of what was once real, but now their death situates them in the realm of the other and, thus, dangerous, and unworthy of love.

Melancholia and The Walking Dead

In a zombie apocalypse, death is inevitable and inescapable as many reanimated corpses meander aimlessly through deserted towns, down once-thriving city streets, and inside abandoned buildings. However, they are only partially with purpose, as a loud noise, movement, or bright light can trigger their attention. These triggers are symbols of life. They are also a dinner bell for the hordes of roaming undead. The hardest part of comprehending the reality the characters now live in every day is that they could quickly become one of the undead. The same can be said for the ones they love. Death is all too real for the characters of the series, but it is not final. In the post-apocalyptic world of *The Walking Dead*, death is only temporary.

Before engaging in the discussion of individual scenes, a conversation about death in *The Walking Dead* needs to take place. Death, while imminent, is not permanent in this post-apocalyptic tale. As Vlad Dima points out, three deaths are experienced in the series in his essay "You Only Die Thrice: Zombies Revisited in *The Walking Dead*." The first is symbolic. When a person develops an awareness of their fate to eventually become a zombie, either by being bitten or dying in another fashion, they have experienced the first death. The second comes as a physical death when the person eventually passes away. The third comes as the death of the zombie. To bring an end to the undead, a traumatic injury to the head must happen (10). However, this process is anything but flawless. As Dima explains, "The three deaths represent the new order of the world and when someone is not allowed for this 'natural' progression, things can go horribly wrong" (11). In navigating their new reality, the characters in the series must adjust to survive. Adapting to the situation helps to stave off becoming one of the undead.

Morgan, Duane, and the Zombie Mother

One instance which demonstrates a lack of adaptation comes during the first episode of the first season, "Days Gone Bye." While the catastrophe, or whatever unknown occurrence caused the zombie outbreak, was still fresh, leading protagonist Rick Grimes awakes from his coma-induced slumber to find his world in disarray. Eventually, after escaping the hospital where he was emitted, he encounters a father and son duo who saves his life and welcomes him into their temporary residence, ironically located inside the Grimes's abandoned home. At first, Morgan and Duane Jones seem to have adjusted to their new reality as they inform Rick of the events unfolding since succumbing to the gunshot wound that placed him in a coma. However, as night comes, so does a tormenting memory from their past. Outside the house stumbles a figure reminiscent of Morgan's late wife, Jenny. Duane recognizes her immediately, flinging himself onto his bed, and starts crying. A curious Rick spies the figure's approach to the house through the peephole in the front door. Lingering for a moment as if coming to some recognition of the house, the figure hovers, even attempting to jiggle the doorknob before losing interest and stumbling away.

Though Morgan knows this repetition of events tortures his young son, he is reluctant to fix the problem. He tells Rick, "I should've put her down, man. I should've put her down. I know that. But, I... You know what? I just didn't have it in me. She's the mother of my child" ("Days Gone Bye" 00:36:15–00:36:32). As Kyle William Bishop summarizes the event in his essay, "'The Pathos of *The Walking Dead*,'" He cannot accept the zombie as a soulless monster with no identity or history; Morgan only sees his zombie wife as the human being she once was" (Bishop 10). The reanimated corpses of formerly recognizable individuals only return to the world of the living as shells. By all appearances, the dead retain many visual qualities of themselves before dying. They might be wearing the same clothes, not showing much or any signs of decay, and pass as functioning while they shamble around. The actions of the dead require a much larger debate in their meaning. Viewers provided their own analysis of this first episode by contemplating theories about muscle memory and retaining some sense of the past as their brains deteriorate. One poignantly called this scene "Creepy as shit" because such actions "made the walkers more tragic— think about Morgan's zombie wife constantly returning to the house" (sabatoa). Another focused more on the intricate details of the episode,

The candlelit dinner scene is outstanding. We go from fear to celebration and joy at the shower scene, to crushing devastation with Morgan and his wife. All these jumps to emotion, yet none of them feel forced. Everything about this episode is just perfect-start to finish [DaNorris1221].

Knowing full well that zombies are no longer human, fans debate the implications of these actions and the consequences when these mixed emotions complicate decisions.

The dead no longer retain any memories or compassion for their loved ones; they long only to eat their flesh. They are no longer their authentic selves but a fabrication and imitation of the person they once were. To Steven Schlozman, this makes a series such as *The Walking Dead* so frightening, how loved ones return as one of the dead. As he explains, "This is the crux of the terror. The walkers, the zombies, the resurrected individuals, are 'shells,' totally impersonal, completely without desires or passions, happiness or misery" (Schlozman 168). The dead cannot feel emotion, they cannot think about their actions, and they cannot return the love others had for them. While the memories of the dead haunt the living, the living must quickly realize how the figure which appears before them and stumbles toward them in wanton desire are not the people they eerily resemble. Schlozman continues this point by noting how "[n]one of those living dead things will fall in love or write poetry. They are, for all intents and purposes, walking manifestations of disease. The walkers exist only to propagate the contagion within" (168). Morgan is fully aware that the figure returning to their encampment every night is not his wife, yet he cannot do what is necessary.

I previously mentioned how photographs demonstrate an interesting point of debate for scholars, especially when considering an association with the past. In the premiere episode, Rick and Morgan contemplate the whereabouts of Rick's family. While Morgan tries to reason with Rick about the likelihood of their survival, Rick uses the absence of their family photographs as evidence that his wife and son were alive when they left. As Rick Grimes explains, "You see the framed photos on the walls? Neither do I... Our photo albums, family pictures—all gone" ("Days Gone Bye" 00:37:40–00:38:38). Laughing as in recognition of a similarity between their wives, Morgan replies, "There I am packing survival gear; she's grabbing photo alb..." ("Days Gone Bye" 00:37:40–00:38:38). In "The Walking (Gendered) Dead: A Feminist Rhetorical Critique of Zombie Apocalypse Television Narrative," authors John Greene and Michaela Meyer conclude how in the aftermath of an apocalypse, "men are represented as preparing for the future while women are holding on to the past" (68). Concentrating on this scene specifically, the authors note that by collecting the photographic memorabilia, women cannot move beyond the idea of what has been. In contrast, men look at and prepare for what is to come.

However, if Greene and Meyer claim photographs keep women stuck in the past, their use by the men of the series provides a counterargument to this assumption. Later in the same episode, Morgan rummages through a box of items to retrieve a small album containing images of his wife and their son before the apocalypse. Flipping through the pages, Morgan is heard whimpering as if on the verge of tears. Propping up one image of his wife on the chair next to him, Morgan positions his rifle and, through the scope, looks for his wife among the undead wandering the streets outside. Finding his target, he breathes deeply before dropping the gun, tears streaming down his face. Steeling himself, Morgan repositions and fixes his aim on what his wife was firmly in the scope but again fails to pull the trigger. Though Morgan laughingly talked about the photo albums earlier in the episode, he cannot bring himself to kill his undead wife. He, too, is stuck in the past, knowing full well that his wife is dead. This action leaves not only Morgan in tears about having come so close to killing her for good and the audience without any resolution as to whether he can pull through his grief to bring an end to Jenny.

After Rick reunites with Morgan in the third season, viewers find some resolution to the issue of the undead wife. After returning to the Grimes' hometown for supplies and a specific memento Carl seeks for his baby sibling, discussed in more detail below, Michonne and Carl set out on a supply run. Rick waits for an unconscious Morgan to awaken in the room where Morgan has taken up residence. The walls are covered in spray-painted and chalked scribbles of words such as "turned" and "clear," which are more telling than Rick initially realizes. Once Morgan wakes, he lunges at Rick with a knife carefully hidden under his cot. Though Rick tries to communicate with Morgan, Morgan's noncomprehensive state prevents him from recognizing the man he once saved about a year prior. It is in this exchange that recalls Freud's description of melancholia provided earlier. Specifically, the "cessation of interest in the outside world, loss of the capacity to love, [and the] inhibition of all activity" manifest in Morgan's transformation of the main street to a boobytrapped filled yard and the spattering of warning signs cautioning wanderers from entering (244). Even Michonne recognizes the danger of this situation as she points these exact details out to Rick, but Rick insists on staying.

It is not until Morgan discloses the events between their last encounter and this moment that he genuinely gives an understanding of Morgan's state of mind, and the audience finally learns the fate of Duane and the woman he once knew as his wife, Jenny. Looking up at Rick from his restrained position on the floor, Morgan tells Rick, "You tried to get me to do it 'cause I was supposed to do it…. But I let it go" ("Clear" 00:27:05–00:27:12). Regrettably, this decision not to kill his wife is what led to the demise of his son, Duane. After this moment, when Morgan can finally do what he needs to, it came at a high cost to the safety of himself and his young son. I want to take a moment to acknowledge the brilliance of this performance by Lennie James. His ability to show a person so broken and saddened after his inability to take care of this lingering threat to their survival results in the punishment Morgan feels necessary to inflict upon himself. As Freud asserts, the "delusional expectation of punishment" is the precise detail viewers discussing this scene picked up on in their online comments (244). On *Reddit*, one poster concluded how,

> From Morgan's statement, "The good people, they die. The bad people die too. The weak people, people like me, we have inherited the earth," that Morgan identifies himself as a weak person. I think Morgan believes that while the good, bad, and strong are off fighting and dying, that the weak like himself are supposed to be stewards to what is remaining in the world. So Morgan makes himself a steward by "clearing" the town and the world around him of walkers and making it a better place for the future [Comment on "The Walking Dead Episode Discussion S03E12 'Clear'"].

Using his torment about losing his son because he could not kill his wife, Morgan commits to clearing the world of the dead to make a future for the living. Another viewer provided similar insight with an additional hopeful outcome for Rick. They wrote, "For now Morgan is punishing himself, stuck in a purgatory until he has cleared enough of the dead out of his life to return to the world of the living. I think Rick left this episode with a renewed psyche" (bandit515). This comment about Rick's renewed psyche will be significant in the following section.

Referring to Morgan's state of mind as discussed previously, the conversation with Rick about his inability to kill Jenny and the consequences resulting from this decision weigh heavily on Morgan, so much so that Morgan takes it upon himself to clear the world of the dead. In the previous chapter, I mentioned how fans picked up on Morgan, claiming he saw "people wearing dead people's faces" ("Clear" 00:22:24–00:22:25). Indeed, the Whisperers fit this very description quite well. However, when thinking about this scene, I contemplate the status of Morgan's recognition of Rick regarding melancholia. Specifically, when Morgan could not bring himself to kill his wife, a person whom he loved and knew by all accounts was dead, it is her likeness to the person she once was that prevented him from pulling the trigger. In essence, Jenny and, by extension, Duane, was a dead person wearing the face of the person Morgan loved very much. With Rick, Morgan is so disillusioned with the real world that seeing a person he vaguely recognizes as Rick very much explains why Morgan shouted these words. Yes, he saw a face he recognized, but he also needed reassurance that the face was not one worn by the dead.

The Melancholic Grimes Family

Out of all the characters introduced in the series, no one better demonstrates melancholy and focuses on the past than the Grimes family. By the time the show enters season three, Rick has reconnected with his wife, Lori, and son, Carl, at a camp outside Atlanta. The group of survivors with whom Lori and Carl have been staying band together, following Rick as their de facto leader, and move away from the city to the rural south. Eventually, after taking temporary refuge on a farm owned by Hershel Greene, they find and take up in an abandoned prison, the West Georgia Correction Facility. Then, in the fourth episode entitled "Killer Within," a pregnant Lori goes into labor during a zombie attack. During the most gut-wrenching events in the series thus far, Hershel's daughter Maggie is forced to perform a C-section on Lori to save the baby. As if deciding to have a baby during the apocalypse is not intense enough, imagine performing an emergency procedure in the middle of a zombie infestation as you are locked away in the bowels of a prison. In my opinion, and without revealing too many details, I will say that this scene was one of the most gruesome moments in the entirety of the show. If my word is insufficient, take it from actress Lauren Cohan who nearly quit the series due to this grisly scene (Chan).

Wrapping up the baby, Maggie urges them to leave the room. "We can't just leave her here," Carl says, "She'll turn" to which Maggie replies by calling out his name with the baby clutched firmly in her arms ("Killer Within" 00:38:34–00:38:40). From the look on Maggie's face, staring incredulity at Carl while knowing what this young boy will have to do. However, at the same time, she seems reluctant to stop him. "She's my mom," Carl says with tears in his eyes and gun in hand, staring Maggie down until she turns to leave (Killer Within 00:38:40–00:38:45). I find this moment with Carl both saddening and momentous for his character. In *Parenting in the Zombie Apocalypse*, Steven Kirsh speaks to Carl's development in a time when someone so young is denied many of the pleasures of life before the apocalypse. Carl knew only so much of the world before the undead started to rise. Now, he has a sibling to care for and protect, one who will never honestly know where they came from or what life could have been without the constant reminder of death. Instead, children in the apocalypse will struggle with coming to know and understanding their identity. Per Kirsh, "a *social destruction* of childhood will take place" when the dead rise as the amenities of developed nations comes to an end and will be replaced with "subsistence living, fear, and a survival mentality will develop" (54). For young Carl, he must learn skills he perhaps never thought about until his family's survival depended on it.

There is a time later in the third season when Carl demonstrates both his nuanced understanding of his new reality as a caregiver and protector of his new baby sibling. In the episode "Clear," Carl plies to obtain supplies for his sibling while Michonne and Rick scout Rick's old hometown for supplies. Exhibiting both a developing "capacity for reflection" in this middle childhood stage, Carl uses his ruse to sneak away from Rick and Michonne to retrieve a family photograph from a local café that he and his parents frequented together as a family. The photograph speaks of a different understanding of their apocalyptic world to Carl. If, as Loir Levy explains in "The Question of Photographic Meaning in Roland Barthes' Camera Lucida," the photograph serves as an "intersection of the past (that-has-been, what actually stood in front of the camera), present (that is, what we see now in the photograph) and future" (402), then the image of the Grimes family represents something different entirely. By retrieving the photograph of his mother for his sibling, Carl is presenting someone from the past. However, Carl is very aware of what the photograph means for their current situation now that they are without Lori. By having a likeness of her in some way, the child will know something of their mother and, in the future, be able to form an identity as the child of Lori Grimes.

Interestingly, as if in defiance, Carl proclaims to Michonne that retrieving the photograph is something he must do on his own. This very rebellious moment illustrates the stubbornness of this youth and his capacity to care for himself in precarious situations. Perhaps most importantly, Carl tries to show he is more than capable without anyone else's help. Unfortunately, his failure to retrieve the photograph from the café on his own shows Carl is not quite ready to walk in the footsteps of his father. Instead, he defeatedly waits outside while Michonne enters the café to recover the photograph and a comical cat statue prize for herself ("Clear"). Though Carl would later become a primary caregiver for his sibling since Rick's role as group leader removes him from being an active participant in the child's upbringing, he does not participate in the same activities that would designate him as parental. As José van Dijck explains in "Digital Photography: Communication, Identity, Memory," "Showing pictures as part of conversation or reviewing pictures to confirm social bonds between friends appears more important than organizing photos in albums and looking at them—an activity they consider their parents' domain" (61). Though both Carl and Lori fixate on the images, an action that Greene and Meyer have focused on in the past, their actions are interpreted quite differently. While Carl is responsible for his sibling and takes it upon himself to educate his new sibling about their mother, their communication helps the child form an identity. At the same time, Lori's actions of organizing the photographs into albums are seen more as savoring the memories of the past.

Returning to the above scene with Carl, Maggie, and the baby, Rick learns of his wife's fate. Walking toward Maggie, holding the baby and Carl by her side, he drops the axe in his hand, shakes his head in disbelief, and later falls to the group in tears as the camera zooms out to end the scene. Fans of the series debated his reactions online, from rationalizing how grief struck Rick to his understanding that he is once again a father. However, in the apocalypse, fans speak to the overwhelming emotions coming from this moment. One exceptionally nuanced fan understood the purpose of this moment: the power of viewer comprehension. As they claim,

> Rick's reaction is based on what you know. His breakdown is a reflection of how you should be feeling inside, knowing that Lori is dead. The framing in that last shot puts Carl further forward, making him bigger, and this places Rick further back in perspective. Naturally, you connect the dots which paint the picture that Carl, who is being shot from a power angle, is responsible for Lori's untimely end, and Rick (who is small and hunched over) is helpless to do anything about. Gold stars all around to the entire Walking Dead crew [JackieBronassis].

Interestingly, this fan emphasizes the change in the dynamic between parent and child when they discuss Carl and Rick. When Carl decided to prevent Lori from turning, his reflective system, as Kirsh calls it, took hold (118). Carl showed incredible clarity and emotional self-regulation through evaluation and judgment of the situation at hand, with his use of appropriate emotions and emotional intensity (Kirsh 121). On the other hand, Rick loses sense of himself and others by jumping recklessly into a dangerous situation to take out his anger on the droves of the undead. Another fan writes how Rick "lost everything all over again. His 'little boy' is now a man that has seen too much. And he's technically still a child, so he's quickly adapted to this environment with which many of the adults are still finding it difficult to cope" (orangejillius). In this sense, the parent and child switch places on an emotional level, one demonstrating restraint and fortitude, even if in a catatonic state of shock, and the other slashing at the undead with reckless abandon.

In "Say the Word," members of Rick's group make plans for a run to find the baby formula. As they set out, Rick walks over to grab his dropped axe and heads back inside. After the group heads out, the scene cuts back to Rick entering through a doorway with his eyes fixed on him. In the background, rumbles of the undead can be heard as Rick slashes at them with his axe. Blood sprays across his shirt, but that does not deter him. The camera pans to follow Rick continuing with his mission, hacking at any of those undead shells shambling across his path. Rick would not be seen again until about twenty minutes into the episode when Glenn tries to revive Rick from this dangerous state of handling the loss of his wife. In this action, Rick embodies what Freud referred to as an unseen and internal struggle. According to Freud, "The melancholic displays something else besides which is lacking in mourning—an extraordinary diminution in his self-regard. Am impoverishment of his ego on a grand scale" (246). While mourning creates the sense of a world of emptiness for the sufferer, melancholy shifts the void to that of the ego. Angry and distraught over his wife's death, Rick seeks an outlet for his rage while simultaneously demonstrating a complete disregard for himself, his son, and his newborn child.

After this point, Rick progresses to the next state of melancholy, which Freud refers to as "hallucinatory wishful psychosis" (244). As mentioned earlier in the discussion of melancholia, hallucinatory wishful psychosis allows the sufferer to reject the loss by allowing moments of temporary delusion. In the episode "Hounded," Rick believes he receives calls from other people on a rotary dial phone. In the first scene, after the opening credits, Rick begs for the voice on the phone to take in his group. "I have a son," he says to the voice on the phone, "I...I have a newborn baby. I'm with a good group of people.... We can pull our weight. We can help you" ("Hounded" 00:03:55–00:04:40). A desperate plea for help shows Rick at his most vulnerable.

Furthermore, by imploring the voice on the phone, Rick demonstrates his lack of belief in himself. Since he cannot protect his wife from an unfortunate death, Rick internalizes his guilt and turns the blame on himself. Then, as an act of defeat and his self-imposed belief that he is incapable of protecting anyone else, he asks for help. As viewers debate Rick's doubt, one fan comments how this scene is "showing his critical thinking skills but still showing hes losing his mind.... Its the thought processes and the little cues that most people don't catch.... He's mentally blocking out those thoughts and voices" (Bloodhound1). However, it is not only his self-doubt that places Rick in this state of melancholy but the reaction of the group he tried his best to protect. When he temporarily surfaces to check on his son, the group steps up to defend those remaining in the Prison and seek out supplies to ensure their continued survival. Provisionally, Rick gives up his command and role of leader to return to his isolation waiting for the phone to ring again. This dive into hallucinatory wishful psychosis would not be the only time Rick experiences a tremendous loss in the series. It would also not be the last time he enacts vengeance on the undead to cope with his loss.

Jumping forward a few seasons to the group's new home in Alexandria, Rick again devolves from his typified persona of a law-enforcing leader to one of questionable action. In the last chapter, I briefly discussed the rivalry between Ron and Carl over Enid. It seems unrequited love not only lost Carl an eye but sent Rick Grimes into a tailspin. In "No Way Out," the residents of Alexandria scramble to fend off the hordes of undead penetrating the colony through the broken walls, thanks to the Wolves. Using a previously measured tactic of smattering themselves in guts, Rick, Carl, and baby Judith make their way through the shambling undead with Rick's new love interest, Jessie Anderson and her two sons, Gabriel and Michonne. By nightfall, with an axe in Rick's hand, the group continues their way across the walker-riddled streets of Alexandria. When the walkers grab hold of a frightened Sam, Jessie very much in the style of Barbra from *Night of the Living Dead* goes catatonic at the sight of her son and is devoured. Blinking in and out of a dreamlike state where Rick sees flashbacks of a smiling Jessie, Rick hacks off Jessie's hand, allowing Carl to escape as the walkers munch down. Retrieving Carl's discarded gun, Ron aims at Rick as the source of his pain and loss. Unfortunately, Ron misses his intended target, hitting Carl in the eye. Managing successfully to get Carl to Denise for medical care, Rick reverts to his perilous melancholic state of mind. Walking casually out the door, the voices calling for him appear to fade as Rick lunges off the patio, hacking recklessly at the dead. Michonne and the others inside the infirmary rush out after him, aiding in his battle to clear the walkers ("No Way Out").

Different than his hallucinatory state when Rick heard voices on the phone, he recognized his peers and their efforts to clear out the streets. In seeing this effort, the citizens of Alexandria gain the confidence they lacked from their initial introduction to the series. As one commenter notes,

> Rick will do whatever it takes to save his son. He will destroy any happiness, any love, anyone that get's in the way of harming Coral. Jessie made Rick feel whole again and filled the hole that Lori left. Him chopping off Jessie's arm and the red filter that was over the memories goes to show that even though it hurts Rick's mental health, he will let his happiness go to save Coral. Rick's rampage is the catalyst that finally gives the people in Alexandria what they really needed: Willpower [ChiefSombrero].

The catalyst necessary for rallying the citizens of Alexandria is what dramatically diverges from the moments following the death of Lori. Rick finally seems to understand the inevitability of death and recognizes what the power of fighting together rather than alone can do for those remaining.

Sacrifice and Sabotage, The Choice Is Yours

The choice to become one of the dead might seem elusive for the characters of the series. However, it is not always so. While the characters cannot necessarily choose not to come back as the undead, they can control certain aspects of their death. Like Morrison's discussion of gender earlier, each group member is infected with whatever makes them return as the undead. As Morrison points out, "One is born, or becomes, either a boy or a girl. One chooses to be straight, or one chooses to be homosexual; the former is normative and healthy, the latter, deviant and sick" ("Psychoanalysis and 'Necessary' Choices: The Shame of Soft Edges"). For the characters within *The Walking Dead*, the choice is not whether they will come back as the undead but how they die. Those who survive can choose to kill their loved ones to prevent their reanimation properly. Alternatively, if their loved one reanimates, they can decide to kill them one final time.

Followers of the television series witnessed this in the final minutes of the second season finale. In "Beside the Dying Fire," Rick reveals information he learned from Dr. Jenner before escaping the destruction of the CDC building in Atlanta. As they discuss a location to camp out for the evening, they start inquiring about a situation earlier in the episode in which a man named Randall Culver (Michael Zegen) was found reanimated as a member of the undead, but he did not have any indication of a bite. It was until this point believed by the group that the only way you could become one of the undead was to be bitten. "We're all infected," Rick explains to the group, "At the CDC, Jenner told me. Whatever it is, we all carry it" ("Beside the Dying Fire" 00:32:12–00:32:33). At first reluctant to believe it himself, it was witnessing the reanimation of his best friend Shane, which solidified this fact for Rick Grimes.

Carol and Alpha

Earlier in this book, I looked at the representation of motherhood in the apocalypse. Of the characters discussed in the book, no two were greater opposites than Carol and Alpha. At times, fans even argued how Carol and Alpha are purposeful opposites because of their approach to loving their children. While both mothers act in what they consider to be the best interest of their children, how they cope with the loss of their children needs more discussion, especially when considering their journeys into the narrative. Both characters enter the narrative as mothers, Carol as Sophia's mother and Alpha as Lydia's mother. While Lydia outlives her mother, Carol outlives two of her children. Recalling back to the earliest seasons, Sophia dies after getting separated after a horde of walkers swarms the group on a desolate highway ("Pretty Much Dead Already"). After overcoming this loss and eventually opening herself up to motherhood again, Carol and Ezekiel lose Henry after he is captured and beheaded by the Whisperers ("The Calm Before"). This second loss results in Carol seeking refuge by herself and separating from the King. Upon her return from a destination unknown, Carol seems every bit the same person she was after the loss of Sophia. Her ability to mask her feelings, as she did so many times when needed, she hides a highly harmful inner struggle.

Not until the episode "Ghosts," does this internal struggle manifest before viewers. Her want of vengeance against Alpha and the numerous losses she endured impact her ability to sleep, thus causing haunting visions of her son. Kirsh notes how "the stressors of apocalyptic living among the dead will increase the adverse psychological and physical outcomes associated with child loss" (204). Using caffeine pills to stay awake, her severe lack of sleep and need for revenge prove detrimental for Carol. Fans commenting on the intensity of this episode praised how well the character depicted her battle with her past. One viewer even noted, "It's weird seeing Daryl as the rational one and Carol as the impulsive one" (paigeap2513). The slip between reality and her haunted past weighs heavily on her and leads those closest to her to question her motives as her reckless behavior increases. At one point, Carol haphazardly takes a shot at Alpha, which results in her group losing access to value hunting land ("Silence the Whisperers"). Later, Carol, followed closely by Daryl, Connie, Kelly, Magna, and Jerry (Cooper Andrews) chases Alpha into a trap, plunging inside a cavern infested with walkers ("Squeeze"). It is until Carol recalls her ability to act in ways no one else can do that we see the cleverness and tact she once possessed.

As the last chapter discusses, Alpha ultimately falls victim to the scheme hatched by Carol to use Negan to lure her to a false sense of security. While Negan's reason for seeking out Alpha is far from altruistic as he desperately seeks redemption, knowing well he will never be fully accepted into Alexandria or the other colonies, Carol uses what could be determined as the least objectionable outcome given the situation. In choosing to release Negan, she delays him from dying because of his actions saving Lydia from a band of Alexandrians who nearly beat her to death ("Silence the Whisperers"). Though her actions would most likely end in expulsion from Alexandria, or worse, Carol already knows a life of solitude. To paraphrase what Rick said to her so many episodes ago, she is no longer that woman who was too scared to be alone. However, if Negan were to fail and be killed by the Whisperers, the colonies would be free of the man who caused them so much harm in the war with the Saviors. Ultimately, Negan succeeds in his deed, and the Whisperers are without a leader, unless you count an Alpha-masked Beta, which is another level of strange. Once Maggie returns to Hilltop and sees her nemesis, Negan, Carol attempts to save Negan again from death by removing him from the colonies. Tempting as Negan finds this isolation and a fresh start, he returns to the colonies, much to the bewilderment of Carol and to the surprise of Maggie, who has returned to the Hilltop Colony after helping Georgie save other colonies. While Negan is determined to stay, Carol feels relieved knowing his potential death at the hands of Maggie will not weigh on her conscious ("Here's Negan"). Her struggle with the loss of life is assuaged by Negan accounting for his own protection.

Rosita and Sasha

Previously, I discussed the representation of the body when discussing the character of Rosita. Undeniably, Rosita demonstrates she is more than just a body to be gawked at or sexualized. Instead, she is keen, ever watching, and fully possesses her identity as a survivor. However, it would be a disservice not to bring up Sasha in this conversation because, much as I feel more could have been done with Sasha's character, these two characters made specific choices regarding how they met their end. Truthfully, the dynamic between Sasha and Rosita was one of my favorites during the series. Here are two powerful female characters at odds with each other due to their love of the same man. They manage to put this discomfort aside for the betterment of their group. When the two join forces to assassinate Negan, the uneasiness of their circumstance becomes a way of bonding. It is, after all, a death that brought these two women together in the first place. Talking to each other, they break down their walls. While Rosita would outlive Sasha in the series, the treatment of their endings provides an exciting example of melancholy regarding how one can choose their ending. This chapter is dedicated to how these characters handle death, or, with the example of Carl above, near death. Their approach to dying speaks volumes about their strength and understanding of their fate for Sasha and Rosita. They also consider those they love in the process of reaching their end.

In "The First Day of the Rest of Your Life," Sasha is captured after unsuccessfully storming the Savior compound. Then, after being unwilling to join the Saviors, their leader, Negan, decides to use her as leverage when he confronts Rick later in the episode. During this season seven finale, Sasha plans to "opt out," a decision only one person made throughout the seasons leading up to this point. Like Jacqui in the first season, Sasha decides to "opt out" on her own. Furthermore, besides Eugene initially refusing to provide Sasha with what she needs to complete her wishes, there is little fighting or resistance. Lastly, the circumstances surrounding this situation are like that of Jacqui. When Sasha realizes she is up against insurmountable odds, she not only decides to "opt out" but to do so on her terms. While listening to Donny Hathaway's "Someday We'll All Be Free" to keep herself calm and distracted in her suffocating enclosure, Sasha swallows a cyanide pill provided by former groupmate turned Savior, Eugene. Much to his surprise, as Negan attempts to open the coffin revealing his captive inside, a reanimated Sasha lunges out, trying to take a bite. With this distraction, Rick's group can draw their weapons and attack their enemy. Sasha's choice to die becomes a saving grace for Rick and the rest of the group. While her death shocked her former family, it became an even more significant shock to their enemy and bought them valuable time to escape.

This decision to "opt out" did not go unnoticed by viewers. Though many viewers on *Reddit* expressed their displeasure about having much of the episode dedicated to Sasha's flashbacks, at least one fan managed to draw an interesting parallel between Sasha and the choice of music. Inquiring, "Did anyone find it interesting that Sasha committed suicide, while listening to Donny Hathaway ... who also committed suicide?!!," this viewer showed their favor for this episode by concluding with how they "Loved seeing her character get an entire episode; this was a great season finale" (ireallyneededthistoo). X viewers seemed to handle Sasha's death quite differently, with expressions of shock over the loss, sadness to have *The Walking Dead* continue without Sasha and appreciation for seeing Sasha with Abraham once again filling the tweets reflecting on this episode. One even wrote about the impact of this episode, claiming how, "Damn I really miss Sasha on The Walking Dead and it has been 4 full days and she is a fictional character" (@Willfull_long). Another fan went as far as to refer to the zombified Sasha as "adorbs," a comment which comes off as awkwardly positive given the dark tone of the episode and the loss of a beloved character (@catgirl422).

Fast forward to the very rushed and jampacked finale of the eleventh season, and we find Rosita is fighting with all her might to recover her kidnapped daughter and get them both to safety as a swarm of undead infests the Commonwealth. After successfully retrieving Coco from her temporary hold and the other missing children from the Commonwealth, Rosita straps her daughter to her body, and the group escapes. Wasting no time, Gabriel, Eugene, and Rosita, all with rescued children strapped tightly to their bodies, flee to the streets only to be met by more walkers. Though Eugene urges her to go first, Rosita declines, and the two men scale the building to the safety of an open window. Turning back to help Rosita, their arms stretched out, trying to grab hold, Rosita falls backward into a pit of walkers. Then the unbelievable, even more unbelievable than a world filled with walkers, happens. Rosita bursts out of the swarm with her machete swinging frantically and manages to scramble to the top of an ambulance before leaping across the walker-laden alley and climbing to the same window by the pole she somehow manages to clutch.

As Rosita watches her daughter sleep, it is not until later that Eugene finds out the devastating truth about her fall. Later in the episode, as those remaining sit down to dinner, Rosita confesses her fate to Gabriel and the others. Laying in a bed beside her sleeping daughter, everyone visits Rosita to say their goodbyes before she peacefully closes her eyes for the last time ("Rest in Peace"). While viewers do not witness Rosita die or anyone take a knife to Rosita preventing her reanimation, as they do with Luke earlier in this same episode, her fate is hotly debated online. Many on *Reddit* expressed disbelief that Eugene would outlive both Rosita and Abraham. At the same time, fans on *X* leaned on the more somber realization that *The Walking Dead* just lost another powerhouse character. However, I wanted to highlight a point about this ending simply because of the gender debate surrounding this character.

On *Reddit*, fans debated the actuality of Rosita's escape from her fall into the horde. One fan wrote how, "When a show decides to ignore the rules of the universe it built just for a 'Yassss queen, you!!!' Moment it ruins the story. Some call it jumping the shark, but this one wasn't that bad" (@Lawndirk). After this and other comments crying foul about this scene, other commentators quickly came to the defense of this scene. Speaking directly to those crying false about the improbability of this scene, one viewer retorted how a "Mother's instinct doesn't give a fuck to the rules of the universe. 'My kid is in danger?!? Fuck physics, I'm saving her!!!'" (leandrombraz). To add to this debate, another viewer provided an almost derisive but poignant opinion about motherhood in such narratives. This viewer stated how, "I always find it kind of weird that the secondary implication with this kind of thing is that a mother that *didn't* manage to lift a car or smash down a wall or whatever to save their child and they ended up dying apparently just wasn't trying hard enough" (duaneap). If anything can be said for Rosita, she did not die due to lack of trying but ultimately, like Sasha, her one-time romantic rival, sacrificed herself to save the life of another.

Death and Dying: A Reflection

In a narrative world filled with uncertainty, perhaps the only constant is death. Despite its regular presence, characters accept death in varying and sometimes dangerous ways. Some, like Sasha, Jacqui, and Dr. Jenner, chose to "opt out" and approached death on their own terms, as much as it could be possible. Others, like the Governor, Lizzie, Clara (Kerry Condon), who kept the zombified head of her husband, and even the Greene family, thought of the dead as not fully gone but potentially redeemable or simply just sick. Then there are those like Carol, Jim, Rick, Morgan, and Siddiq who mentally and physically suffered from the post-traumatic stress of survivor's guilt. Those who survive while others live are not only susceptible to their loss, but this loss manifests in various ways. While some took out their pain in a violent assault on the dead, as Rick did, or became obsessed with digging graves, as Jim did, others suffered internally through hallucinations, sleep deprivation, and a sliding grip on reality. Certainly, as this series demonstrates, no one is completely held to one exact standard or ways of coping with death as a few of these characters were plagued with both internal and external struggles.

Interestingly, mourning and melancholia are not reserved for the characters within the series; the viewers at home experience them. The viewers can follow along as the characters navigate a world belonging to the dead. The slow progression of the show affords viewers the chance to grow an attachment to individual characters, champion their triumphs, and cry over their deaths. Why is this so? As previously discussed, author Paul Vigna offers some insight in his book *GUTS: The Anatomy of The Walking Dead* when he concludes how the characters are so real that they are almost stereotypical. Again, as typical people, the characters are entirely relatable. Without the ability to identify and draw connections with these characters, the ability to develop empathy toward their plight, any want for their accomplishments, and sadness over their losses would not exist.

Mark Bracher offers a similar conclusion when he deliberates differing aspects of desire in his discussion of psychoanalysis in his book *Lacan, Discourse, and Social Change*. Bracher states that "people commonly identify with a particular character when they read a story or watch a movie" (21). More specifically, people do not identify with the characters but with what they represent. Using Vigna's comments about the almost stereotypical commonness of the characters and their status in employment or relationships helps to make them relatable. As a mother, brother, cousin, co-worker, and so on, the viewers at home can find some way to connect to the characters within *The Walking Dead*. Thus, as the characters suffer, the audience feels their pain. When the characters die, the viewers mourn their loss.

Sometimes, the loss of a character is so extreme that viewers quit watching the show. One instance came after the deaths of Abraham Ford and Glenn Rhee during the seventh season premiere. While Abraham was introduced to the series well after it had been on air and had been an excellent source of comic relief with his quick wit and loose tongue, Glenn had been a fixture in Rick's group since the first season. The loss of Glenn carried surmountable weight not as he not only left behind his pregnant wife, Maggie, but in what Glenn represented as a character. On this death, Laura Prudom writes,

> With all due respect to Abraham (and Michael Cudlitz's scene-stealing lines), much of the anguish seems reserved explicitly for Glenn, who has been with the show since the beginning, and, perhaps most importantly, was one of the few Asian-American lead characters on a primetime series—especially since he was never hamstrung by the kind of racial stereotypes that still plague mainstream roles for actors of color ["Did 'The Walking Dead' Finally Go Too Far with Its Latest Kill?"].

Yes, some fans were hysterical over Glenn's departure, so much so that many decided to quit watching the series in retaliation. In their way, the upset viewers were, and still might be to this day, exhibiting their form of melancholia as they found a way to cope. In a sense, it is not their world that no longer means anything; it is the series itself.

Though Freud spoke about melancholia long before *The Walking Dead* debuted on television screens, the subject found a home within the story. As viewers at home watching from the comfort of their living rooms or on their streaming devices, Rick and his group of survivors find ways to adjust to living in a world of the dead. Unfortunately, while death typically comes with finality and a chance for loved ones to mourn their loss, *The Walking Dead* leaves little time for such reflection. At any moment, a deceased loved one could return as a member of the undead. Unless the group thinks quickly or the dying individual has a chance to be proactive, their loved one can come back with only one desire, to consume their flesh.

Those who remain in the realm of the living must do their best to prevent this reanimation from happening. However, it is more than the characters' loved ones coming back from the dead which terrorizes the group. As Kenemore reminds us, "Humans seek to know the unknowable so they can feel normal and healthy. Zombies do not trouble themselves with these paralyzing unknowabilities. Consequently, they are effective killers, able to survive nearly any set of difficult circumstances" (192). To become one with the undead is to become something different, dangerous, and other. As an act of mercy, the survivors must bring themselves to do the unthinkable, kill their loved ones, possibly for a second time. It is only in this way that the survivors can save themselves while at the same time allowing time to mourn their lost loves without fear for their lives.

6

Resurrecting Fears
Through Spinoffs

If the success of *The Walking Dead* demonstrates the ability of Kirkman and producers to develop a cooperative relationship to adapt an already well-established narrative while allowing creative control, then the additions of *Fear the Walking Dead*, *The Walking Dead: World Beyond*, *Tales of the Walking Dead*, *The Walking Dead: Daryl Dixon*, and *The Walking Dead: Dead City* each blazed their own unique paths into the apocalyptic narrative universe, thanks in large part to the popularity of but not being restricted by its preceding narrative. As much as I would like to explore all the series in *The Walking Dead* Universe as thoroughly as I could with the original series, my goal here is to focus on notable themes from each of these series, especially as they are discussed by fans online. Specifically, from the start of *Fear the Walking Dead*, two themes become apparent: drug addiction and a blended family dynamic. Though the series begins in an eerily similar way to *The Walking Dead* flagship series, *Fear the Walking Dead* eases viewers in with believable representations of a contentious family battling with their reluctant consideration of addiction.

While *Fear the Walking Dead* started its narrative by reinforcing a number of apocalyptic tropes, including gender-specific household duties and the mass chaos following the uncertainty of why the dead now walk the earth, it did introduce a revitalizing take on family arrangements, a theme carried over into *The Walking Dead: World Beyond*. An interesting note about this series is its divergence in specific roles, especially since the series follows two female protagonists. A fan on X offered the series praise by stating how "...I really enjoyed having 2 young women (one of whom is Black) be the focus, as well as gay characters and other strong women characters featured. #TWDWorldBeyond" (@evilgrrl). As the series only had two seasons, talks of genocide, militant control, chemical warfare, animal and human testing, women in power, an interracial same-sex couple, child abuse, alcoholism along with reintroducing blended families all occur in a fraction of the main series and its first spinoff. That is not to say that *Fear the Walking Dead* or even the original flagship overlooked or disregarded these issues. The point is how *The Walking Dead: World Beyond* touched upon them in a way that contributed to the overall universe while also remaining its own unique expansion to *The Walking Dead*, especially in such a short time frame. With so many layers of anxieties, fears, and tensions to unpack, *The Walking Dead: World Beyond* deserved more attention and perhaps less complaints than it received.

For those fans who watched *The Walking Dead: World Beyond* in its entirety, the series was littered with easter eggs connecting this narrative to *The Walking Dead* original narrative, *The Walking Dead: The Ones Who Live*, and *The Walking Dead: Daryl Dixon* spinoff, a series completely dedicated to following the journey of fan-favorite Daryl Dixon as he encounters the horrors of the apocalypse abroad. While the setting has drastically changed, as Daryl's journey takes him away from the United States, the way viewers begin the premiere episode did not depart much from a typified zombie narrative introduction. Waking up on the shores of France, which is believed to be the origin of the virus causing the dead to reanimate, viewers once again start the narrative through a male lens. Perhaps a slight divergence is Daryl attempting to remember how he managed to leave his home country, eventually becoming acquainted with a character unlike any other seen in *The Walking Dead* Universe thus far, Coco.

Blended Families and Drug Addiction:
Fear the Walking Dead

Serving as a companion series to *The Walking Dead, Fear the Walking Dead* gives viewers the closest glimpse of life around the time of "the fall" and chronicles its journey from the perspective of Madison Clark (Kim Dickens), a high school guidance counselor and widowed mother of a "dysfunctional family" ("Fear the Walking Dead"). Debuting on August 23, 2015, and providing fans of *The Walking Dead* a prequel of sorts to help establish the start of the apocalypse, *Fear the Walking Dead* attempts to bridge the gap between the notorious bullet that first sent Rick into his coma and after he awakens in an abandoned Georgia hospital (Century). Following the Clark family is a slight detour from *The Walking Dead* in this first attempt at creating an original narrative without relying on the original graphic novel. Extending the universe by giving fans some impression of what caused the dead to rise, *Fear the Walking Dead* eventually caught up to *The Walking Dead* and allowed characters, such as Morgan Jones, to crossover, becoming different and perhaps better versions of their previous selves (Elvy).

The much-anticipated series charted new territory as a completely new storyline housed within the larger universe of *The Walking Dead*. Yet, even with its ability to blaze a new trail, *Fear the Walking Dead* begins in a similar way to the original narrative storyline. The opening scene from the first episode focuses on Nick Clark as he awakens in a what appears to be an abandoned church turned squatters' paradise located somewhere in the suburbs of California. Calling out for his companion, Nick saunters down a staircase looking for signs of life only to stumble upon the blood-covered body of a mangled figure. Startled by this discovery, Nick arms himself with a wrought iron candle stand as he continues into the nave of the church. Much to his surprise, Nick located his companion eating the face off another individual laying behind one of the pews. Managing to evade pursuit by exiting through an open window, a barefoot Nick runs away from the church and into the street before getting hit by a passerby vehicle. While a troubled crowd gathers around, we see Nick slowly come to as the camera pulls away from the accident and tilts upward revealing the busy, noise filled streets of a very lively city ("Pilot").

While there are notable differences between the start of *The Walking Dead* and *Fear the Walking Dead*, the two series opening episodes share a lot of similarities. We see an individual waking up to find their world is not quite the same. Trying to get a sense of their surroundings, they see evidence of a disaster: blood, scattered objects, flickering lights, noises in the distances. Eventually, they encounter one of the dead but are not fully cognizant of their status. By all accounts, the figures they encounter seem to still be human, until the figures start attacking. Ultimately, some event temporarily incapacitates them as the living rush in help their aid. Still, some fans loved the refreshing lead into the series, stating how not every zombie narrative must start "with the main person waking up from hospital (The Walking Dead, 28 Days Later, Dawn of the Dead), so seeing it happen is a breath of fresh air" (Comment on "Fear the Walking Dead–1x01 'Pilot'–Post-Episode Discussion" 11:06 p.m.). By this account, *Fear the Walking Dead* seemed to be on the right track to forge a new path into the apocalypse.

Of course, not all fans were as pleased with the introduction with one viewer calling out the number of tropes represented in the first episode alone. They write how,

> We get the warnings to which no one is paying attention. We get the spread of sickness that people pass off as flu. We get the characters going into dangerous places for no explicable reason, the traffic jam with cops whipping around cars, the angsty teen, the strong fell male lead who's so strong she's stupid and blind, etc.... The great thing about good stories is that they do not re-tread the obvious or remind us of what we already know. They take situations that we've seen before and allow us to experience events that we might not normally

consider or understand [Comment on "Fear the Walking Dead–1x01 'Pilot'—Post-Episode Discussion" 10:19 a.m.]. 9 a.m.

Another poster quickly followed up to confirm this viewer's points by pointing out a clear distinction between the original series and this new addition by stating how this series is not about the zombies but more so focuses on "societal collapse, how familiar structures of our lives can get stretched and finally break you when you apply enough fear" (loklanc).

The familiarity and subtle differences aside, one fan concisely identified one of the most painfully obvious similarities between the opening of *The Walking Dead* and *Fear the Walking Dead*. "TWD Rule 1: Be White" (dacalpha). Despite the potential for *Fear the Walking Dead* to be a blank slate for a new plot in this universe, these apocalyptic narratives irritatingly begin through a White male lens. Fortunately, this introduction is quickly usurped by Madison Clark, matriarch of the Clark family, as she urges daughter, Alicia Clark (Alycia Debnam-Carey), to get ready for the day. While the transition from following a White male lead to Madison is invigorating, we still notice signs of gendered tasks. As Madison grabs clothes to start a load of laundry, her male partner, Travis "Trav" Manawa (Cliff Curtis), is busily fixing the kitchen sink. It is not until the phone rings do we learn the fate of Nick and are introduced to the purpose of Nick's state in the abandoned church: heroin.

In 2021, as many as 1.1 million people reported using heroin and roughly one million people aged 12 or older identified having a heroin use disorder within the last 12 months (NIDA "What is the Scope"). Though deaths from heroin overdoses trended downward between 2020 to 2021, the opioid overdose epidemic still lingers as nearly 220 people died each day from an opioid overdose in 2021 (Centers for Disease Control and Prevention). In February 2024, the National Institute on Drug Abuse, or NIDA, reported 110,000 people die annually as the United States faces its worst drug overdose crisis in its history ("50 Years After Founding"). The representation of Nick as a heroin user provides an angle to this apocalyptic universe not previously encountered and yet one that reflects a timely epidemic occurring across the country. Fans online not only speculated how Nick's companion turned after a potential heroin overdose but also debated the portrayal of Nick as a heroin addict and whether his behaviors are reflected accurately. To one viewer who identified themselves as a recovered addict, they note how "they really failed to portray how a junkie would likely act" and continued by pointing out that "…I'd just use, feel a little better, and then continue not caring about anything … not even the end of the world" (brain_in_vain). While some added to the speculation by debating hospital protocol and the possible introduction of methadone, the contemplation about and inclusion of addiction to the series presents viewers with a diverging narrative focus, especially considering this clear variation from the original narrative.

Where *The Walking Dead* presents a man desperate to find his family, thus reestablishing a White heteronormative nuclear family unit, *Fear the Walking Dead* presents a blended family, with a male authority figure of Māori decent, during what seems to be an all-too-familiar household drama. Interestingly, it is the time in the hospital where the power dynamics between Madison and Trav. Brushing off the doctor trying to speak with her about her son's condition, Madison enters his room and demands the officer questioning him to leave. When the officer asks Trav if she does "all the talking," Madison quickly responds with a forceful "Get the— get out" before the office hands Trav a card and leaves the room ("Pilot" 07:56–08:10). This action could easily be explained by the fact that Trav is not Nick's biological father and therefore has no parental authority over Nick, there is more to the story. Just after Trav urges Nick to listen to his mother, Trav angrily says "You definitely can't help me. You can't do shit. Really. You can't..." ("Pilot" 08:38–08:46). This dismissal of Trav by Nick is echoed when Alicia claims how the issue happening with Nick is none of Trav's business. This strife is only a small example of the challenges faced by this blended family dynamic as Nick's addiction would haunt them long into their escape from an overrun California.

Setting the heroin addiction aside for now, the presentation of a contentious blended family poses an intriguing depiction of the modern American family. In September of 2023, the Pew Research Center released an article detailing the shifting family dynamics of the United States. Of particular interest is the significant decrease in Americans between the ages of 25 to 49 who live with their spouse and one or more children under the age of 18. While 67 percent of Americans fit this description in 1970, only 37 percent do in 2021. Even more interesting is the subtle rise in other family dynamics, such as those cohabiting while living with children and unpartnered individuals living with children. This study also notes the change in certain types of marriage, with a growing number of interracial and interethnic families, like Clark/Manawa family. With same-sex marriage becoming legal in 2015, there is also an increase in same-sex marriages (Aragão et al).

Kim Parker and Rachel Minkin note how there is increased pessimism about the institution of marriage and the family. Noteworthy is the negative view on the inclination toward fewer children being raised by two married parents with about half of the adults in their survey saying this trend will negatively impact the country. While it is not entirely clear what prompted these responses, the tensions apparent in this blended family present a palpable example of the difficulties joining together two families can bring, a tension that is only further reverberated by Trav's son, Chris Manawa (Lorenzo James Henrie).

Much like *The Walking Dead*, fans are divided about the events transpiring in this individual narrative. Though some blame the series for relying on too many tropes, like the comment above, others find the rigid family dynamic to bring a new level to the story. For one, they exclaimed how "it's so jarring to see a family drama like this..." (Maria_LaGuerta), another commented on the episode's believability by stating,

> I'd say it's believable that the father doesn't clue anyone in about his late-night visits because it's clearly a difficult, touchy issue with his *new* family, and he thinks he'll encounter a bunch of strung-out heroin addicts, worst-case scenario. Not blood and guts on the floor and undead junkies. He wanted to connect with his stepson and understand what happened to him, and given what we see of him later as super-teacher, it makes sense [nateday2].

Indeed, in his effort to understand Nick and level with him as a parent, Trav attempts to meet Nick where he is, which is that of a heroin addicted teen struggling with deciphering between a drug-induced hallucination and the now very real threat of an oncoming zombie apocalypse.

In the end, as *Fear the Walking Dead* reached its season finale after eight seasons totaling over 100 episodes, fans online expressed their elation at the return of Skidmark, an adopted cat that managed to endear itself to some of the characters. Still, the overall sentiment from viewers of this series was that it probably ran for far too long. Noting its constant repetition and an abundance of characters, Alan Kelly concluded how this show failed to fully deliver on its promise to bring a pre-apocalyptic narrative with all the suspense and ferocity of *The Walking Dead* ("'Fear the Walking Dead' Should've Ended Seasons Ago"). Yet, *Fear the Walking Dead* presented fears not touched upon in the flagship series with the presentation of the opioid epidemic and its early diverge from the stereotypical American family. Additionally, and worthy of note are its survivors. While *The Walking Dead* had Carol as the only female to make it from the first season to its end, *Fear the Walking Dead* presents the reunification of Madison and Alica, the only two female characters to have survived from the first episode.

Identity, Coming-of-Age, and Resilience: World Beyond

Premiering on Sunday, October 4, 2020, *The Walking Dead: World Beyond* provided fans of *The Walking Dead* with a narrative featuring life about a decade "after the sky fell," a phrase commonly used in the series to describe the start of the apocalypse. Now, it is not lost on this writer that *The Walking Dead: World Beyond* debuted amid Covid-19, a pandemic that seemingly brought the world to a complete stop. Reflecting over this series in comparison to the events during the pandemic experienced here in the States presents many eerie similarities. Inside the world of *The Walking Dead: World Beyond*, we find the Campus Colony surrounded by its protective walls. Though some are allowed to venture beyond this fortification, it is only when necessary. This series also introduces the mysterious CRM; a nefarious militant group hiding behind a façade of saving the world. No one is allowed to know where the CRM is located, and those who go in are not allowed to leave. Their secretive nature stirs distrust amongst some of the characters and rightfully so.

Extending an already intense history of triumph and change, *The Walking Dead: World Beyond* continued down an uncharted path where two young female protagonists, adopted sisters Iris and Hope Bennett, set out to rescue their father, a professor who is biochemist and geneticist, who is working in the labs of the CRM. While some of the characters in this series will "become heroes," others "will become villains" (Ausiello; "The Blaze of Glory" 33:00–33:05). Reminiscent of the novel *Lord of the Flies* by William Golding or what some viewers on *Reddit* said reminded them of the 1986 film *Stand by Me* and even Mystery Incorporated from *Scooby Doo*, the heroes of this story are entirely different in makeup when compared to *The Walking Dead*. With one fan pronouncing how they are "more than intrigued than I have been for FTWD the last two season, so it has that going for it" (sebrebc), I find it interesting that this series ranked the lowest out of all the spinoffs, save *The Walking Dead: The Ones Who Live*, on *Rotten Tomatoes* ("*The Walking Dead* Series Ranked by Tomatometer").

Perhaps it was the "still be intact Monopoly boards" as one viewer griped about on *Reddit* (Weirdguy149), or how this series morphed into what another viewer complained is "a crappy teen angst CW show" on *X* (@TTino74). My confusion in why this spinoff received so much negativity lies in just how much it manages to pack in and bring together so many aspects of *The Walking Dead* Universe. I already mentioned above how in just two short seasons, *The Walking Dead: World Beyond* managed to address a slew of societal tensions, anxieties, and fears. Yet, it also succeeded in paying lowkey tribute to *Dawn of the Dead* with its hopeful yet ambiguous ending by naming one of the main characters Hope, the person whom the CRM deemed their target for bringing control over the rising dead. According to Nico Tortorella, who portrays Felix Carlucci, an openly gay character, this is a show about "'hope and identity'" (qtd. in Tanswell).

Continuing to divert from *The Walking Dead*, this series introduces more diversity right from the start and continued to do so in the nineteen episodes following its premiere. I am probably not the first to call out *The Walking Dead: World Beyond* for perpetuating an already exhausted zombie trope, as seems to be the way with *The Walking Dead* Universe, but we find ourselves coming into the narrative by one of the main protagonists waking up. I do not really know whether the creators of *The Walking Dead* Universe purposefully use this trope as a connection between each iteration, as *The Walking Dead: Daryl Dixon* begins in very much the same way, or purely a coincidence. Still, this introduction into the narrative presents a new twist to waking up in the apocalypse in that we get to take part in the dream. The scenery is gray with what appears to be ash falling from the sky. The dead meander about with their growls increasing in volume. The camera moves around the space before settling on one of the dead. Once our first protagonist, Iris, awakens, it becomes rather obvious that the dream zombie was her. From this opening, we enter this narrative through the eyes of a teenage female.

As the premiere episode progresses, viewers come to know about the world as it is in this timeline through lens of Iris. We not only learn about the events leading to the sky falling but understand how it emotionally and mentally impacted our protagonist. Not only does Iris dream of becoming one of the dead, but she also carries an extreme amount of guilt for not being with her sister, Hope, who witnessed the death of their mother, Kari Bennett (Christina Marie Karis). By the end of the premiere, Iris, Hope, and two new additions to the group, Elton Ortiz (Nicolas Cantu) and Silas Plaskett (Hal Cumpston), start their journey by sneaking outside the walls of the Campus Colony, a move reminiscent of Enid from *The Walking Dead*, to face uncertainty with the goal of reuniting with the Bennett family patriarch, Leonard "Leo" (Joe Holt) ("Brave"). Pausing for a moment to reflect over this plot, it seems understandably similar in nature to the beginning of *The Walking Dead* in that a family tries to reunite in the middle of the apocalypse. Still, the differences between the Bennett family and the Grimes family are quite apparent. While the Grimes family very much depicts stereotypical White nuclear family, the Bennett family is comprised of two African American parents with two adopted daughters, one who is African American and the other who is Caucasian.

Like *Fear the Walking Dead*, *The Walking Dead: World Beyond* is quicker in introducing diverse characters. While Aliyah Royale, who plays Iris Bennett, is African American, Alexa Mansour, who plays her sister Hope, is of Egyptian and Mexican descent ("Alexa Mansour"). Nicolas Cantu, who plays Elton, is Latino and was born in Mexico City (Raquel). Annet Mahendru, who plays Jennifer "Huck" Mallick, was born in Kabul to an Indian father and Russian mother ("Annet Mahendru"; "Home"). Nico Tortorella, who plays Felix, identifies as gender-fluid and an in interview about *The Walking Dead: World Beyond* expressed wanting to play a queer superhero (Tanswell). Toward the end of the first season, the series introduced Will Campbell (Jelani Alladin), Felix's boyfriend, a relationship that caused a bevy of negative comments online. Adding to this already diverse cast, the second season had a director team comprised entirely of women, a decision made by showrunner Matt Negrete after meeting with both men and women ahead of shooting (Hegarty).

Adding even more layers to this series are the two female characters themselves. Iris, as the first character introduced to viewers, is often referred to as Madam President by her peers. While this might not hold much weight outside of attending classes, the reference is noteworthy, nonetheless. She is admired and highly regarded for not only being the daughter of a prominent scientist, one who is supposedly working for the CRM on a journey to "create the science that will being this world back," as Lieutenant Colonel Elizabeth Emily Kublek (Julia Ormond) says during a commemorative speech ("Brave" 37:20–37:23). For Hope, the more rebellious sister, her distrust of the CRM and antics such as distilling copious amounts of alcohol, demonstrate her keen wit and ability that rivals the mind of her father. The premiere episode would reveal another commonality between the flagship and this spinoff, though it took the similarity in a completely new direction. While Carl is forced to keep Lori from reanimating after delivering Judith, Hope accidentally kills Elton's pregnant mother, Amelia Ortiz (Christina Brucato), after Amelia shoots Kari after incorrectly assuming Kari is trying to steal from Amelia. Though at least one fan complained how this scene "sort of felt shoved in," the presentation "is definitely a nice future conflict set up" (Linxxxx); a point demonstrated later in the series.

Forging ahead, *The Walking Dead: World Beyond* takes another step away from the original flagship series by introducing an openly gay character in the first episode, though ever so subtly. Felix can be heard speaking about his partner Will when the Bennett sisters express their concern for their father's well-being, but the two are not shown as couple until later in the first season and only in flashbacks. It is not until the second season that Will and Felix are reunited, a moment that *The Walking Dead* Universe took to defending online after receiving a flurry of hateful comments by stating, "Hi, hello. If LGBTQ+ characters on television (or anywhere) make you uncomfortable or angry, please unfollow us…" and continued by beseeching these individuals to find some introspective (Alter; @TheWalkingDead). Comparing Felix to other gay characters introduced by the flagship series, the revelation of his sexuality became a heated debate on *Reddit*. Some fixated on the derogatory language used during a flashback when Cliff Carlucci (Stirling Gardner), Felix's father, learned of his son's sexuality and proceeded to disown him ("The Blaze of Glory").

Others expressed displeasure at how they felt "pandered to," especially when comparing Felix to Aaron from the main series whose sexuality is "not a big deal ... just part of his story" (Comment on "The Walking Dead World Beyond–01x02 'The Blaze of Glory'—AMC Premiere Discussion" 3:00 a.m.). Another commented on how other introductions felt more organic, that Scott Gimple, who cowrote this premiere episode with Matt Negrete, was simply checking off a box to make sure a gay character had representation (mercutio70). One more followed up with a very impassioned statement about they want being gay "to be accepted in society, not 'tolerated' as a 'unique character trait.' I want it to get to the point where it is as irrelevant as someone's other immutable characteristics (like hair color)" (Comment on "The Walking Dead World Beyond–01x02 'The Blaze of Glory'—AMC Premiere Discussion" 3:14 a.m.). Understandably, when compared to main series, the revelation of Tara, Aaron, and even Jesus as gay was rather indirect. For Tara and Jesus specifically, they both revealed their sexuality in a conversation while Aaron's relationship with Eric Raleigh is unveiled when Eric is rescued by the Grimes clan before they were recruited to the Alexandria Safe-Zone.

While some found the introduction of Felix as a gay character to be forced, others came to the defense of the narrative. One pointed out how there is "more than 1 way to portray a gay character, you know," while another followed up with a more heated response.

Oh fuck off. No, it really wasn't. Maybe it's because I'm tired of shows doing it terribly but the way they did it here actually wasn't bad. He's gay and his father disowns him what's so hard to comprehend? What would be a better way to handle this, huh? If you can't say then stfu.... Maybe for Aaron it wasn't a big deal and it didn't cause him any family troubles but it did for Felix and I don't see what is wrong with them portraying it the way they did [PlamiAG].

Disagree as fans might, the greater point of this debate is not necessarily about how the character was introduced but presents much deeper insight, no one expressed offense about the fact that there was gay representation, apart for one fan who really hoped Elton was gay instead of Felix (LN_Studios). It seems fans on *Reddit* came around to cheering for Felix and Will when they reunified at the end of the first season. As one fan put it, "I tried to see it from felix point of view: he lost hope, he lost huck as close friend (as he obviously hates her now) but found the very person he thought he lost long ago, in the middle of nowhere" (Gorillapatrick). Staving off the "bury your gays" trope, as the pair not only help stop a plot by the CRM to use toxic gas in their experimentation to stop the dead but also find their happy ending, Will and Felix defied expectations placed upon them as gay characters.

Parisian Zombie Strolls and Glamourous Struts: Daryl Dixon

With the decision to set *The Walking Dead: Daryl Dixon* in France, viewers of *The Walking Dead* and *The Walking Dead: World Beyond* might finally learn more about the origin of the virus, as Dr. Edwin Jenner and the after credits scene from *The Walking Dead: World Beyond* alluded (Opie, "World Beyond's finale"). As much it might be interesting to learn that space spores did not cause the dead to rise, thus resurrecting another tired zombie trope, there is more to this narrative worth considering (Zinski). Though this series begins through a White male lens as Daryl wakes on the shores of France, how Daryl came to the shores of France adds a level of mystery and intrigue. Unlike Rick who wakes up from a coma in an abandoned hospital or Nick stirring from a bender in an abandoned church, Daryl is awoken by ocean waves splashing his face as the overturned boat he is tied to eventually washed ashore. Scrambling to separate himself from the boat, Daryl manages to crawl his way to the safety of the sandy beach. Coming upon a sign, he stares at the words as a bit of confusion registers on his face. Continuing to an abandoned boat, he discovers water, a tape recorder, and a series of cassettes, which upon playing reveal that he might be in Marseille. Throughout the night, Daryl continues to listen to the cassettes, piecing together a picture of what happened to the boat's former owner. Collecting whatever supplies he manages to find, Daryl begins to record his own narrative, a scene reminiscent of Rick communicating to Morgan through the walkie-talkies the two share back in Georgia during the premiere episode of the main series.

Presenting an interesting twist to this narrative are the dead themselves. Daryl, encountering a small grouping of the dead in a deserted warehouse, is burned as one of the dead grabs his arm. While the main series presented a few versions of the dead, earlier episodes depicting them as somewhat cognizant as they attempt to climb fences or use rocks to break glass while later episodes bringing in "variants," these new zombies are introduced just before the opening credit sequence, making for a mini-cliff hanger of sorts, as more about these "brûlant" or "burner" zombies is not revealed until much later in the narrative ("L'ame Perdue" 20:48–20:57). With the help of Isabelle Carrière (Clémence Poésy), a former petty thief and drug addict who found safety after becoming a nun with the Union of Hope and joining the Abbey of Saint Bernadette, Daryl learns more about the status of the country in which he now temporarily resides. Along with Isabelle is her nephew Laurent Carrière (Louis Puech Scigliuzzi), thought to be a genius, due to his exposure when he was in-utero. With the urging of Isabelle, Daryl sets on a journey to a place called the Nest to deliver Laurent to Losang (Joel de la Fuente), who sees Laurent as the possible "savoir" for the people of France.

An interesting point of departure in this series is its depiction of France after the fall, especially with how the French underground provides a safe space for survivors to take pleasure in relative normalcy. As Daryl, Isabelle, and Laurent make their way to France, they eventually find themselves in the company of Isabelle's ex-boyfriend, Quinn (Adam Nagaitis), proprietor of the Demimonde nightclub, a party refuge hidden deep within the Paris Catacombs where "the flame of 'la vie Bohème'" still burns ("Paris Sera Toujours Paris" 29:46–29:48). It is here that audiences are introduced to an exceptionally distinct character than previously encountered in *The Walking Dead* Universe, Coco (Paloma). Though their introductions into the narrative vary, LGBTQ+ characters are more commonplace in this narrative franchise. Still, as the first drag queen included, Coco demands considerable attention. As the first season winner of *Drag Race France*, an extension of RuPaul's *Drag Race*, the role of Coco was specifically written into *The Walking Dead: Daryl Dixon* at the request of actor Norman Reedus, a fan of the *Drag Race* series (Wratten).

Before sashaying her way across a catwalk, Coco's voice can be heard calling attention to the next performer set to take the stage in the Demimonde. In a sparkling silver corset bodysuit complete with matching boots and a red feathered coat. Though her introductory scene only lasted for a few seconds, viewers took to social media to share their delight in seeing Paloma make her debut. From shock about how "never did i think i'd see daryl dixon in the same room as a drag queen" (@ spntwt) to excitement about how "...even in a zombie apocalypse, drag thrives! Can't keep a good Queen down, honey!" (Ferril_) to noting how "Paloma has a speaking line too? How fabulous!" (Quanster), this character instantly attracted interest from viewers. Beyond the delight of seeing a drag queen appear in this apocalyptic narrative reported online, fans quickly called attention to the inclusivity presented. On X one specific viewer commented about "...the fact that they mentioned non binary people, yeah, i love this show" (@percysgrant). The dead long have been stripped of any gender identification, but the living remained tightly constricted in gender identification, until now. By calling attention to "Boys, girls, and *everyone in between...*" ("Paris Sera Toujours Paris" 30:16–30:20; emphasis) as part of her entry monologue, Coco not only broke a glass ceiling with the portrayal of drag but also in their identification of gender nonconformity amongst the living, another first for the franchise.

Yet, as delighted as fans appeared to be with Coco, a debate about the portrayal of LGBTQ+ characters still raged online. Starting with the declaration of "…seeing openly queer people (and a drag queen!) in TWDU was truly amazing. Those people exist now, so yes if the world fell, there would still be very few drag queens lmao. Just made me really grateful to see" (ThatChubbyGay) sparked a flurry of comments about the portrayal of queer identities in this series. Responding to this comment, a viewer called out how this comment "…makes it sound like the best we have is a few randos from a club. We have Aaron, Eric, Tara, Denise, Magna, Yumiko, Victor, Althea, Will, and Felix who are all main characters who are queer" (DirectAgentCoulson). To clarify, the first commentor followed up to state how "…while yes we've had queer people in the show, we've never had queer culture which is historically nightlife" (ThatChubbyGay), a comment that led others on *Reddit* to take offense. Though it registers that queer identities were shameful or meant to keep hidden from the public eye, the comment presented about historic nightlife life is not without merit.

LGTBQ+ nightclubs delivered more than just libations, as these locations offered a safe space for queer individuals to find a sense of community and belonging. While it is challenging to pinpoint the exact start of the extensive history associated with queer nightclubs, there are notable dates in the history of these nightclubs in places like New York City and Los Angeles (Babri). Dating back to 1869 in Harlem, New York, masquerade and civil balls, which are more commonly known now as drag balls, began within the Hamilton Lodge. Fast forward to the 1920s and the height of Prohibition, when these clubs were underground, balls attracted thousands of individuals from various races and social classes (Hamel; Pruitt; Velasco). Continuing through the 1960s and 70s, nightclubs in across New York City played a vital role in influencing social action and principles guiding the Gay Liberation Movement, especially with clubs like the Stonewall Inn located in Manhattan (Velasco). To the point about nightlife made by this viewer, the location of Coco on the Demimonde serves for more than just a representation of the LGBTQ+ community. To say that drag survived in the apocalypse is only part of the importance represented in Coco's character. Instead, the secretive location of the nightclub within the Paris Catacombs, matched with the first drag queen to be represented in the series is highly symbolic of an entire history associated with queer culture.

Resurrecting Fears Through Spinoffs: A Reflection

From just the few examples presented in this chapter, the importance of what spinoffs bring to *The Walking Dead* Universe is without question. Though *The Walking Dead* made strides to embody more inclusivity by featuring more diverse character representing the LGBTQ+ community, the deaf community, depictions of mental health, and so on, the main series left room for its various spinoffs to carry the torch to continue expanding the narrative to other communities. In doing so, *Fear the Walking Dead* and *The Walking Dead: World Beyond* spent more time focused on the representation of blended family dynamics while *Fear the Walking Dead* dedicated specific time to recognizing the very serious nature of the opioid epidemic currently plaguing the United States. *Fear the Walking Dead* and *The Walking Dead: World Beyond* also wasted no time introducing leading female protagonists as soon as their debut episodes. Parting ways with the tradition of starting the narrative through the eyes of a White male lead, *The Walking Dead: World Beyond* opened with the world through the perspective of a young, African American female. Not too long after introducing two strong female leads, *The Walking Dead: World Beyond* also dove into the backstory of its leading gay character.

Though paralleling *The Walking Dead* flagship in some ways, *The Walking Dead: Daryl Dixon* presented a fresh look at the apocalypse outside of the United States with its leading protagonist waking on the shores around Marseille, France. In his journey to transport a youth said to the savior of France to the safety of the Nest, this series introduced the first drag queen ever in franchise history, marking another milestone for the LGBTQ+ community.

As characters evolved beyond their conventional limitations, viewers can apply the evolution and change within the series to realistic situations. Considering the "'fertile ground for diverging storylines and characters' that creates intense 'viewer attachments'" as Todd Platts noted in the article "From White Zombies to Night Zombies and Beyond: The Evolution of the Zombie in Western Popular Culture" (231), *The Walking Dead* as a continuous narrative provided viewers a chance to place themselves within the story, discuss the potential consequences, and debate outcomes. Though the characters mentioned above deviated from traditional gender roles, they also presented relatable qualities to maintain viewer engagement and identification. Thereby these characters encouraged the audience to not only "consider the conventional horror link between monstrosity and femininity, but the identity between the oppression of zombies and the oppression of women" (Harper). After all, if zombie narratives embody societal tensions, how else can viewers interpret the meaning of the show but apply these televised situations to the real world? Unquestionably, *The Walking Dead* Universe is a robust media enterprise that will continue to collect record-breaking numbers of viewers. More importantly, in its role as a popular culture artifact where men formerly led and women previously followed, women can now pave the way for surviving in a post-apocalyptic narrative. Unsettling as these changes come for some viewers, comments on social media reflect varying degrees of appreciation for modifying the original storyline and keeping audiences on their toes.

Now taking on a life of its own far beyond the pages of the graphic novel, *The Walking Dead* Universe continued its divergent trajectory to debut a show following a primarily female lead, which differed from *The Walking Dead* ever so slightly. *Fear the Walking Dead*, as an original creation, centered on survivors making their way through new terrain as the start of the apocalypse got underway. Then, *The Walking Dead* Universe expanded an already intense history of triumph and change by adding *The Walking Dead: World Beyond* and its continuation down an uncharted path where women take the lead. Another original creation, *The Walking Dead: World Beyond*, showed the progression of women dominating such narratives and introduced more individuals of diverging backgrounds and sexualities, such as with the casting of gender-fluid actor Nico Tortorella (Pearce).

Perchance this is the true legacy of *The Walking Dead* Universe, one that is meant to shatter records by presenting diverging and more representative characters right from the start. While the universe itself is not entirely post-racial, as Ben Lindbergh writes in "The Legacy of Diversity on 'The Walking Dead,'" but one that seems more "accepting of anyone in their settlements who *isn't* trying to feed on their flesh, regardless of color, creed, gender, or sexual orientation." With the announcements already made about the additional spin-off series, there is hope that these stories will continue down the trajectory already set in place by these latest additions. Kang herself mentioned the potential representation of at least one trans character and multiple Native American characters. With an indigenous Canadian actor already featured in *Fear the Walking Dead*, the representation of differing abilities, such as with Connie and Kelly in *The Walking Dead* and Wendell Rabinowitz (Daryl Mitchell) in *Fear the Walking Dead*, this universe is not devoid of representation (Lindbergh). However, it could be better. Perhaps, this inclusion is indication enough that Kang is not just paying lip service to potential viewers and already dedicated fans. By all appearances, these new installments brought much needed representation and awareness to equality. With more seasons teased for at least two of the remaining spinoffs still on air, it is the hope of this fan that the attention to diverse representation stays true and will manifest in interesting ways.

7

Undead Narrative Body

In the introduction to and throughout this book, I discussed the power of fandom and how watching *The Walking Dead* became a social event, with followers across the globe using *X* to communicate their thoughts on the show and its characters as episodes debuted live on television. Additionally, using *Reddit*, dedicated subscribers take to subreddits to voice their (sometimes rather detailed) opinions and analyze series episodes immediately following or even long after episodes aired. In an article posted on *Den of Geek*, Alec Bojalad noted the astronomical number of subscribers to *The Walking Dead* subreddit. In comparison, the author mentioned that HBO's *Game of Thrones* garnered over 1 million subscribers on *Reddit*, making it practically untouchable as far as numbers go on social media. At the same time, other notable shows, such as FX's *American Horror Story*, accumulated about 67,000 subscribers, and Netflix's *Stranger Things* has about 140,000 subscribers. Still, you have to admit that collecting over 400,000 subscribers to this one subreddit thread about this series is quite impressive.

Moreover, Bojalad discussed how a network such as AMC managed to capitalize on the power of this devoted fandom. Per Bojalad, AMC was able to pull off such a feat by creating "something within a fandom-friendly, entertaining genre that's good" thanks in large part due to the attention earned from its offering of fan-favored shows such as *Breaking Bad* and *Mad Men* ("The Walking Dead: How AMC Harnessed"). Adding to this thought, *The Walking Dead*, like *Game of Thrones*, already had a loyal fanbase of readers thanks to its origin as a graphic novel. Also, like *Game of Thrones*, the creator still pumped out additions to its written counterpart as the series aired on television.

However, shows such as *Breaking Bad*, *Mad Men*, and even the *Reddit* and television juggernaut *Game of Thrones* did not have a post-episode talk show dedicated to conversing about this series (and its spin-off, *Fear the Walking Dead*). Though some gripe about *Talking Dead* being a crutch for *The Walking Dead* to fall on and committing what *Rolling Stone* contributor Noel Murray equates to a cardinal sin committed by this series, others applaud AMC for doing what fans were already doing online, talking (Bojalad; "'The Walking Dead': What the Hell Happened"). Continuing with discussing the power of *The Walking Dead* as a grand narrative body, Frank Rose commented on the ability of the series to remain active between seasons, even episodes, thanks to released clips and images, ongoing discussions and panels, fan events, and as this book thorough discussed, its strong social presence ("The Remarkable Narrative Life of *The Walking Dead*"). Thus, as a narrative platform, companies such as AMC "can create an ecosystem of stories that functions as an exchange of sorts, bringing people together in a marketplace of ideas and information" by straddling multiple existing platforms to expand the story far exceeding its primary dimension (Rose). Using such a platform can and does connect people with the story and allows them to co-create and immerse themselves in unbelievable ways (Rose).

Thinking about *The Walking Dead* as a narrative platform created by AMC and consumed by fans, I would venture a guess to say this series is more than just a story. Still, I must consider the innumerable grumbles about the series regarding its flaws. No, *The Walking Dead* is not perfect, but it does question what makes us want to watch *and* to keep watching. Are we part of a cult following, the viewers who continue to watch to the very end? With that in mind, does *The Walking Dead* even qualify as cult television? Taking a cue from Lorna Jowett and Stacey Abbott, authors of the book *TV Horror: Investigating the Dark Side of the Small Screen*, I decided to do just that, investigate the dark side of the small screen. But first, I wanted to understand better what qualifies as cult television. Of course, finding a solid definition of cult television presented a minor challenge since "[t]he common characteristic is found not in the texts but in their viewers" (qtd. in R. Patterson 8). Thus, the audience shapes our understanding of cult television but assuming the ranks of cult television encompasses more than just the number of viewers or ratings. Instead, as Roberta Patterson asserts in "Observations on Cult Television," "cult television should be predicated on *audience practices*" (8; emphasis added). More than just sitting and watching, viewers actively involve themselves in the viewing process. Thanks to social media platforms such as X, viewing is now a social event with live tweets compiling instantaneously using cleverly developed hashtags (i.e., #thewalkingdead and #TWD). Not only did *The Walking Dead* break television records, but it was also the most tweeted-about series during the 2015–2016 television season, averaging 435,000 tweets per episode ("Empire, Walking Dead Top TV Tweets, Data Shows"; Jarvey; Lynch 8; Umstead 31). Why X, you might ask? Well, listen to one viewer who stated how they are "'always watching the TV show with [their] phone…," because they "…really like to search Twitter hashtags to see how others feel'" (qtd. in Freeman 58). Thoughts, emotions, theories, praise, and the airing of grievances all rapidly manifest in the Twitter-sphere, as it were. It is not just the fans who tweet but those involved in creating *The Walking Dead* themselves. I also like to think the staff working at AMC have quite the knack for providing fans with clues to upcoming episodes and calling out dissenters by encouraging them to "look within and be more accepting" because there "is no place in [this] fandom for hateful discrimination or willful ignorance" (@TheWalkingDead). Period. Full stop.

Cult televisions practices such as that of *The Walking Dead* audience run the gamut of following updates about the series or its characters, commenting on fan sites or social media forums, thoroughly analyzing scenes for easter eggs or hidden clues addressing the fate of beloved characters, dressing as favored characters at conventions, or visiting sets to become immersed in the story (I might have participated in all these activities). As Jane Espenson explains in her chapter "Playing Hard to Get—How to Write for Cult TV," if "you force viewers to participate in order to mine the most enjoyment from a show, then they will feel more invested, and if they enjoy what their effort exposes, they will become the cult you're looking for" (45). Suppose you present viewers with a challenge, directing them to pay that much more attention to the details, giving them clues within the narrative to figure out (easter eggs); those who participate consider themselves one of the select few who "'get'" it (Espenson 45). In that case, that is the cult of cult television.

One way shows like *The Walking Dead* move into the realm of cult television is in their ability to unravel an unending story as a serial narrative. Approaching the telling of an apocalyptic narrative makes perfect sense, especially since, as Jowett and Abbott note, the apocalypse is not instantaneous. Per Jowett and Abbott, "The zombie apocalypse is not a sudden cataclysmic event but a gradually dispersing infection, and even once it has spread globally, the remainder of humanity continue to fight for survival" (31). For *The Walking Dead* specifically, the issue of the dead rising is never solved (or explained) but merely hinted at in its earliest episodes. When viewers first enter the story, the apocalypse is already happening. Diving into the first episode of the original series, *The Walking Dead* presents a world amid chaos. However, the depiction of this chaos does not necessarily follow the patterning of preceding apocalyptic-themed narratives (discussed in more depth below). Instead, *The Walking Dead* opens with a lone police cruiser stopping alongside an overturned semi resting at an intersection. Emerging from the cruise to remove a gas can from the trunk, the figure of a sheriff (later revealed to be lead protagonist Rick

Grimes) cautiously walks amongst a smattering of abandoned vehicles. The scene is as quiet as the dead with little noise other than a few birds chirping in the distance. The sight of the vehicles is the only clue of anything cataclysmic. That is until the sheriff spots the dead inhabitants of the cars' fly-covered bodies. Uttering no words until almost four minutes into the scene, the sheriff addressed the shambling figure of what appears (wrongly) to be a young girl. As if answering his calls, the child-like figure turns to reveal a decaying face and glazed eyes. Snarls grow in volume as it approaches our outwardly discouraged sheriff. In return, he raises his pistol to fire a single bullet into the figure's brain just before *The Walking Dead*'s iconic theme music begins ("Days Gone Bye" 00:00–04:29). This very slowly less than five-minute sequence is how *The Walking Dead* introduced itself to 5.3 million viewers on October 31, 2010 (Vigna 19).

Beyond watching humanity fight back hordes of the undead, the survivors must also deal with everyday dramas (i.e., growing up, heartbreak and loss, providing food and safety, and so on), which do not come to a nicely packaged ending. Instead, some storylines carry over into subsequent episodes or even entire seasons, to analysts such as Espenson, "[s]tory-telling that doesn't reset to status quo after every episode rewards its faithful viewers" (45). In this way, *The Walking Dead* is very much like a soap opera (except with zombies) in that the narrative extends long after the ending credits. Even the "father of the modern zombie and horror master," George A. Romero, himself referred to *The Walking Dead* as a soap opera (a comment with which even creator Robert Kirkman agreed) (qtd. in Davis). Honestly, I cannot recall how I came to know about *The Walking Dead*. I have vague memories of friends telling me about the series and questioning why someone like me has not watched it. Now, let me clarify. By someone like me, I mean someone who completed her master's thesis by analyzing contemporary horror remakes for any modern representations of Carol Clover's "final girl," someone whose childhood memories of arcade games center on *The House of the Dead*, and someone whose favorite time of the year is Halloween. Reflecting on these conversations, I do not remember anyone referring to *The Walking Dead* as a soap opera at any point, and I do not know if that would have made any difference. Yet, I digress.

The Dead, The Slayer, and The Supernatural

So, the survivors within *The Walking Dead* narrative world attempt as best as possible to maintain their lives in what many survivors within the narrative refer to as "after the fall" in a later episode. Based on this setup,

The Walking Dead is "[c]early not *Buffy the Vampire Slayer,*" as Vigna writes in *GUTS: The Anatomy of The Walking Dead* (19). I find this succinct thought from Vigna rather fitting when comparing this opening scene of *The Walking Dead* to other apocalyptic-themed narratives, such as this series by Joss Whedon. Adapted from a film by the same name and written by the same creator, this cult television series followed the events of a young teenage girl named Buffy Summers (Sarah Michelle Gellar) after she relocates to the fictional city of Sunnydale, California, a city that also happens to be situated above the jaws of hell known as Hellmouth (Erin McCarthy; Rodriguez). Wanting to better understand the positioning of its slayer-based apocalyptic-themed narrative, I took a cue from Andrew Tudor's work "Unruly Bodies, Unquiet Minds" to analyze the cold opening sequence for *Buffy the Vampire Slayer.* As Tudor explains,

> Typically, the story opens by establishing an apparently stable situation. Then, this "normality" is interrupted by a destabilizing influence, a monster, say, or supernatural force. And finally, after an extended middle period in which the monster goes on a rampage, order (of some kind) is restored.... The opening scene-setting phase may be severely attenuated, its framework of stability tactility assumed rather than overtly established [34].

Though Tudor notes variations can and do happen, the patterning of these narratives seems set. The difference here, the setup for my short analysis, is how these series draw in their audiences and reveal any positioning for events to transpire within the narrative after their opening credits.

Beginning with a dramatic soundtrack played of a sequence of dimly lit hallways and empty classrooms, *Buffy the Vampire Slayer* jumps into its narrative by revealing a pair of mischievous youths breaking the window into one of the darkened classrooms inside Sunnydale High School. With the intent of making their way up to the roof of the gym, a young dark-haired male and a seemingly frightened blond-haired female wander through an empty hall. Though the female expresses worry about getting caught, the confident male assures her they are alone. Suddenly, a noise in the distance interrupts their romantic endeavors. As the female nervously scans their surroundings, she and the male youth appear to return to their amorous plans for the gym roof. That is, until she turns to face her male companion revealing her notably contorted face, which is more representative of her true vampiric identity, and takes a fatal bite out of the nameless male ("Welcome to the Hellmouth").

Overarchingly, *The Walking Dead* and *Buffy the Vampire Slayer* appear similar in their storylines. Both series feature a banded group of protagonists combatting the forces of evil to protect themselves and others. Additionally, both series rely on the guidance of a White male lead protagonist.

For the teenage slayer, who is still in need of training, Buffy and her band of friends seek guidance and leadership from the high school librarian and Watcher known as Rupert Giles (Anthony Head). In *The Walking Dead*, after reuniting with his family outside of Atlanta and possibly due to his arrival in the sheriff's uniform as a symbol of authority, the group turns to the leadership of Rick Grimes. And, of course, both are fighting embodiments of the undead. However, these series contain their fair share of differences. Most notably, our vampire-slaying heroine or "chosen one" exists in a (let us face it) somewhat unrealistic depiction of a seemingly innocuous town situated on the mouth of hell, where magic is real. Of course, various supernatural creatures beyond vampires wreak havoc on the fictional town of Sunnydale, California. At the same time, the rest of the world seems unaware of these strange happenings (until they uncover a decapitated science teacher in a cabinet or a witch casting spells to advance her position on the cheerleading team). Life goes on as it always has, just with the occasional monster or two popping in to stir trouble. Juxtapose this setup with an attempt to live a supposed everyday life presented in *The Walking Dead*. By the time we meet this group at their campsite on the outskirts of Atlanta, Georgia, we see them complete more routine tasks such as collecting firewood at their camp, doing chores, and listening to the radio for any signs of life amongst the hordes of shambling undead ("Days Gone Bye" 50:26–50:59). While the survivors do not know what exactly caused the fall, they are very aware that life is far from ordinary.

Continuing with this comparison, *The Walking Dead* is also clearly not *Supernatural* despite many similarities. While Jowett and Abbott describe *Supernatural* as a series whose structure "heightens the sense of intimacy between characters, and between characters and the audience" (53), Vigna describes *The Walking Dead* as having a "visceral bond between the viewers and the characters that no other production can replicate" (6). Though Jowett and Abbott laud *Supernatural* as the "ultimate in TV serialized horror" (54), *The Walking Dead* presents a narrative powerhouse that cannot be contained to just one serialized narrative (more about this later). By looking at *Supernatural* specifically, the series starts similarly to *Buffy the Vampire Slayer* despite the eight-year separation between their debuts on television. In *Supernatural*, a darkened yet peaceful evening in Lawrence, Kansas, sets the stage as the Winchester family prepares for bed. Stirred by the sounds emanating from a baby monitor, Mary Winchester (Samantha Smith) stumbles out of bed to find what appears to be a male figure (later revealed to be the demon, Azazel [Fredric Lehne]) standing watchfully over baby Sam Winchester's crib.

Thinking it is her unresponsive husband, she unconcernedly leaves the room to attend to a flickering light down the hall before wandering downstairs to the distant voices radiating from a television screen. Upon finding her sleeping husband in front of said television, she frantically returns to baby Sam's room before letting out a scream that stirs John Winchester (Jefferey Dean Morgan). After John enters Sam's room to find the baby undisturbed, a sense of calm washes over John until he finds drops of Mary's blood on the pillow beside the baby. Following the droplets to the ceiling to find the body of Mary pinned to the ceiling, John falls to the floor as flames engulf Mary's body. Whisking baby Sam out of the crib and handed off to his brother, Dean Winchester (Hunter Brochu), John instructs the child to take his brother outside before returning to unsuccessfully save his wife. The opening sequence ends with the fire department on the scene ("Pilot" 00:00–04:29). This sequence running just over four minutes, helps situate the malevolent supernatural forces manifesting throughout the narrative.

While there is some crossover between *Supernatural* and *The Walking Dead* (*Supernatural* paid tribute to Jeffrey Dean Morgan's exit with a brilliantly placed Lucille easter egg in the twelfth season), the two series clearly diverge in their apocalyptic narrative setup (Lee). As stated previously, *Buffy the Vampire Slayer* and *Supernatural* share more commonalities in their opening sequences. Both series present menial everyday activities such as going to bed, falling asleep in front of the television, or even trying to impress a date for a promiscuous nighttime rendezvous. However, the situations presented before the opening credits of each series position depict very different trajectories for these narratives. For *Buffy the Vampire Slayer* and *Supernatural*, both present distinctly evil supernatural forces intermingled with signs of everyday life. From the constant worry of "getting caught" by any occupants of the high school in the opening of *Buffy the Vampire Slayer* to the arrival of the fire department and inquisitive neighbors in *Supernatural*, there is an energetic presence in these narratives. Also, there is the intensity of the catastrophic and deadly events transpiring in both series openings. For viewers of *The Walking Dead*, our introduction to the lone sheriff moves rather anticlimactic as if to match the deteriorating scenery of the abandoned highway and position this apocalyptic story to be that of a singular individual against the remnants of a slowly decaying world.

Looking within the unyielding existence of *The Walking Dead* Universe itself, *The Walking Dead* represents a mere singular narrative within an undying narrative body or, as William Proctor describes in the chapter "Interrogating *The Walking Dead*," "a minuscule limb within a veritable mass of seething 'undead' hordes" (13). Even with its impressive run and transmedia expansion, *The Walking Dead* brings nothing new to the table regarding the long history of zombie visual narratives.

Challenging the notion set forth by Thomas Leitch that "only movies are remade," Proctor focuses on the makeup of *The Walking Dead*'s narrative origins to discuss its position as an amalgamation of remakes and tributes to the numerous zombie movies to come before its creation. Quoting Jowett and Abbott, the author reemphasizes *The Walking Dead*'s homage to its predecessors within the first six episodes:

> [A] man wakes up in a hospital to find it, and the surrounding town, abandoned while bodies decay in the street (à la *28 Days Later*); a seemingly innocuous man stumbling around in the background of the image is revealed to be the walking dead (*Night of the Living Dead*); a character consoles that he has been bitten and slowly becomes infected (*Land of the Dead*); two survivors smother themselves in zombie blood in order to walk among the undead unnoticed (*Shaun of the Dead*); a scientist trapped alone in his facility tries to find a cure to the infection (*I Am Legend*) [qtd. in Proctor 10–11].

Moreover, Kirkman confesses that "'*The Walking Dead* simply doesn't exist without George A. Romero doing his movies first'" (qtd. in Davis). In fact, Kirkman outlines how Michonne waking in a cell is reminiscent of the introductory scene of Romero's second zombie narrative installment, *Dawn of the Dead*, and how the characters meet Juniata "Princess" Sanchez in Pittsburgh, the hometown of Romero (although, the televised version of these event places the meeting of Princess in Charleston rather than Pittsburgh). Adding to this point is the previously mentioned tribute to the zombie film that started transforming the modern-day concept of the zombie, George A. Romero's. *Night of the Living Dead*. ComicBook.com writer Brandon Davis notes how the character Morgan has a son named Duane, who bears the same name as the actor who portrayed the iconic character Ben ("Robert Kirkman Writes Tribute to 'Walking Dead' Inspiration").

Essentially, the narrative world of *The Walking Dead* is a reanimated creation of composite parts, à la Mary Wollstonecraft Shelley's *Frankenstein*, that come to life and chart a direction all their own. Much like the decaying zombies within the narrative, the disintegration theme threatens society's various foundations. From the onset of many zombie narratives, the collapsing society is typically signaled by the breakdown of its media (an issue depicted in the first episode of *The Walking Dead* when the radio signal between Rick and the campsite fizzles). Using the metaphor of the decaying body quite brilliantly, Allan Cameron notes in "Zombie Media: Transmission, Reproduction, and the Digital Dead," "the zombie body and the 'body' of the medium are metaphorically connected in a reversible relationship ... in which pleasures and fears associated with the breakdown of media are channeled through the spectacle of the disintegrating zombie body" (67). Seemingly formulaic, the setup of many horror narratives presents some form of tension or challenge sparked by signs of increasing uncertainty or mounting fear (i.e., flickering lights, disembodied sounds, and, as previously described, the decline of the media). Andrew Tudor, in "Undying Bodies, Unquiet Minds," notes horror narratives are always "'about' things that threaten us," sparking a response in us to "ask questions about the nature of that threat, the responses it provokes, and the world that it threatens" (Tudor 34). In this sense, horror is a genre that presents us with manifestations of what scares us, and it is up to us to determine why and how we feel this way about it.

Zombies are, as Cameron surmises, "blank media" (70). In the post–Romero era, a zombie as a form of blank media is the perfect metaphor for what scares us. Unlike the vampires who purposefully seek out vengeance against the slayer in *Buffy the Vampire Slayer* or like a demon who feeds his blood to children to serve as potential vessels for the apocalypse in *Supernatural*. Nope. Instead, zombies "have no suppressed identity to conflict with the metamorphosed surface; no agonized recognition that they do terrible things when out of control; no sense therefore of guilt or redemption" (Tudor 33). Instead, the decaying shells of beings that were once human relentlessly seek one thing and one thing only, flesh to consume. Unless you consider how the survivors use zombies as various forms of weaponry, their wandering aimlessly is pretty much all that zombies do in each of *The Walking Dead*'s nearly 200 episodes on air to date. Thinking about it from this angle, zombies are pretty deadly yet predictable. The unpredictability of the other survivors adds to the drama and, therefore, advances the narrative.

A *Case for* The Walking Dead *as Cult Television*

Now, getting back to my other question about how a show like *The Walking Dead* managed such success in spawning its own undead universe, I turn to prolific media analyst Henry Jenkins for guidance. In a contribution to his long-running blog, *Confessions of an Aca Fan*, Jenkins diverges (just slightly) from Jowett and Abbott in what makes *The Walking Dead* a televised success. While Jowett and Abbott pinpoint the serial nature of the apocalypse, Jenkins points to the mastery of Kirkman to both set and break the rules of his own narrative creation. Per Jenkins, "If the comics often shocked readers by abruptly killing off long established characters, here the producers surprised some viewers by refusing to kill a character whose death represented an early turning point in the comics" ("How to Watch Television"). It seems the ability of the narrative to crossover from the pages of the graphic novel or "[strip] away encrusted mythology" adds to the series' success onscreen (Jenkins, "How to Watch Television"). Obviously, the adapted onscreen narrative must be revised to follow the graphic novel as written realistically. The six episodes making up the first season demonstrate this point well. Keeping loyal to the original storyline meant covering a rather expansive world. As stated previously, the graphic novel count is over 200 and the original flagship series only almost meets than number in episodes. However, restricting producers to such a limited scope might not translate well onscreen. Thus, hardcore fans of the graphic novel endured changes to the narrative made by producers who still felt they kept true to the comics and, at the same time, were able to reach a more expansive audience (Jenkins). Quite an audience did it reach. Besting *Saturday Night Football* in the target 18–49 demographic, the fifth season premiere, "No Sanctuary," became the most-watched episode in cable history with a record-setting 17.3 million viewers. Despite the staggering decline in viewers through its final season on the air, *The Walking Dead* maintains its position as AMC's highest-rated scripted series (Bonomolo, "Study Shows Who's Watching *The Walking Dead* the Most").

But why should we care about an apocalyptic zombie visual narrative? And why do people keep watching? These questions need to be addressed. Of the steps Jane Espenson provides for how to write cult television, *The Walking Dead* seems to check all the right boxes: have complex arcs (the Governor, check), under-explain (the cause of the dead to rise, check), make them look (around the corner, in the next room, behind the door … check), make complex people (Carol Peletier … need I say more?, check), stay true to the show's reality (real places harboring real people using authentic language, check) … you see where I am going here (45–53). While Espenson reminds us that not all her suggested steps are needed, they each can undoubtedly help elevate a show into a cult television series. However, there are specific criteria here that I want to highlight. The secret to cult television is its ability to operate like in real life. As Espenson claims, "A lot is made of the fact that many cult TV shows are set in other worlds, but the truth is that cult TV is usually the kind of television that most *resembles* reality…" (47; emphasis added). Thus, as much as critics and scholars grit their teeth at basic tasks such as doing laundry, baking casseroles, tending to the farm, or going to school, these actions are everyday occurrences.

Espenson adds another level to developing cult television that adds a unique quality to a show like *The Walking Dead*, which is how *The Walking Dead* creates a world. This establishment is not a world building in the sense of otherworldly because *The Walking Dead* needs to occur in a distant land during a different time. Indeed, as Espenson notes, shows like *Battlestar Galactica*, *Firefly*, *Star Trek*, and even *Buffy the Vampire Slayer* take place in "special worlds," but these extraordinary worlds are not necessary (51). Instead, it is how viewers of these series identify with the story because "it's easier to tell a complex story about our own world when you view it translated through another world" (Espenson 52). So, while we might not find ourselves fighting off droves of the undead, we can understand what it means to scramble to make ends meet, protect the people we love, endure the pain of loss, and find love even in the most trying of circumstances. For hardcore fans of *The Walking Dead*, series spin-offs are a tribute to those who dedicate their time and attention. As one fan writes about *Tales of the Walking Dead*,

> This series providing a back story to some of the storylines and characters is a huge appreciation to the hard core Dead Fans!! So many franchises don't appreciate the fans who go out of their way to watch each episode live and DVR them when they can't.... They are leaving no story unfinished and throwing so many exciting segways on the way to complete this long and beloved journey. So many franchises never even come close to a full and satisfying outcome for the audience [Hunt].

A comment such as this one got me thinking about how other franchises attempt to appease their fans. However, I am still aware of the plethora of negative comments a show such as *Tales of the Walking Dead* undoubtedly received, and they are out there. Take this one comment posted on the *IMDb* website: "The only thing good about this episode is Terry Crews's and Olivia Munn's chemistry. Other than that, I feel Tales of the Walking Dead, based on this first episode, is pointless and forgettable. Anything to keep the rabid fanbase satiated, I suppose" (jjek911). Hopefully, this universe is not "milking TWD" as another fan claims (fountasalexander), but rather is attempting to provide a tangentially related storyline that attempts to focus anywhere else but within the same canonical limitations of the horror genre (Tudor 34). Instead, I'd like to think of this universe in the way that George Hagman describes it, a form of therapy. Watching from the safety of our homes or other places of comfort, we can temporarily suspend our disbelief, living vicariously through our screens as we identify with the characters and possibly sympathizing with their plights, hoping for their survival. This is exactly what narratives like *The Walking Dead* and its extensions provide us, a story of survival in a fantastical world of trauma (Hagman 55).

Undying Narrative Body: A Reflection

When I set out to analyze *The Walking Dead*, an undead narrative body, I realized the poorness of my metaphor. I say this because *The*

Walking Dead was never actually dead but a thriving narrative embodying its very premise, a tale of survival. It is also a tale of transition, a new reality, and a "definite change from the world where men go to jobs and women stay home" (Vigna 29). Revisiting the criteria outlined by Espenson, the ability to resonate with characters rings so true for *The Walking Dead*. Coming back to *GUTS* by Paul Vigna, the author said it best when he wrote how "the small-town sheriff, the deadbeat redneck, the battered housewife, the army medic, the soldier, the priest, the brainy nerd, the pizza delivery boy, the farmer and his daughters" are so ordinary they are formulaic (5). It is this very commonality that makes these characters so relatable and, for viewers, identifiable. Recognizable locations add to the familiarity developed within the first few episodes of the narrative. As a girl from Georgia, I cannot help but feel a connection with this narrative. The actual skyline of Atlanta makes a prominent appearance during the first season when Rick appears riding on horseback up the abandoned highway leading into the city ("Days Gone Bye" 57:51–58:15). The building introduced as the Centers for Disease Control in the fifth episode in the first season ("Wildfire") is the same building I watched countless students walk for graduation as an instructor with my former college. When Maggie retells the story of hiking to Amicalola Falls during the fourth season, I flashback to my many memories of walking up the slippery trail to the base of the falls with my family and the numerous times I told encouraged myself to climb the over 600 stairs to the top and my youngest sister's tremoring legs when we *finally* reached the summit ("Too Far Gone"). Grady Memorial Hospital, where Beth Greene met Noah (Tyler James Williams) in the fifth season, is the same hospital where my brother recovered from a car accident ("Slabtown"). In Senoia, which is pronounced "suh-noy" for those of you who are not from the area, about an hour south of my hometown in the Northwest of Georgia, an area considered OTP or outside the perimeter, I walked the streets of "Woodbury," passed by the location where Carl sat on the rooftop of an abandoned house eating chocolate pudding as a reward for demonstrating his, albeit naïve, autonomy and sense of accomplishment as Rick devolves into comatose-like sleep after the Governor attacks the Prison ("After"). As "JSS" is my favorite episode of the series to date, I stood by the wall where Enid watched her parents die while taking a *Walking Dead*-themed tour. Attending Walker StalkerCon in Atlanta permitted me to speak with Katelyn Nacon (Enid) and Alanna Masterson (Tara Chambler) about being a part of a series so heavily focused upon in academic circles. For the record, I might have fangirled just a little bit. A close friend even "gifted me" a Cameo, a form of social media allowing the "hire" of celebrities to craft specialized messages, featuring a personalized message from Katelyn Nacon, who congratulated me on the successful defense of my dissertation. Again, for the record, I fangirled just a little bit here, too.

To me, *The Walking Dead* is real. Not in the sense that zombies walk the earth in a literal sense, that is, unless you consider the droves of individuals mindlessly commuting into the city for work, day in and day out. No, it is real in a sense, as Kirkman notes, "'apart from the zombies—it's very grounded, very realistic. So all these bigger threats have to sit in the world and work sort of like real life'" (qtd. in Crecente), which in essence, is the very foundation of what makes cult television to be cult television. Agreeing with Vigna that "you can be a fan of *The Sopranos*, *Game of Thrones*, or *The West Wing*, but most people don't see themselves as mobsters, medieval kings, or presidents" (5). To this extent, and considering the two series discussed previously, this Georgia girl is not a slayer like Buffy, nor is she a demon hunter like the Winchester brothers. She is also "not a witch" (Laing et al.) or Watcher. Instead, she is merely a person who loves a show, someone who cheers on her favorite characters hoping for their survival because she could so easily see herself as one of them despite having taken that *Buzzfeed* quiz that stated I would probably only last six months. This familiarity made *The Walking Dead* so real and kept me coming back each week and streaming the series online more times than I care to admit.

I want to add one more criterion for writing cult television. Cult television gets people talking, talking about plots, talking about theories, talking, and representation or lack thereof. Shows like *The Walking Dead* and its spinoffs lead people to question it and attempt to fill in the blanks later, thanks to in-person and online conversations. These conversations consider how a series changes, adapts or learns to correct itself. As Julie Sanders concludes, "adaptations may express a critical perspective perhaps not easily articulated at the time of the adapted text's production" (qtd. in Jowett and Abbott 65). Based on my research into *The Walking Dead* Universe, scholars and fans alike have much to say. Despite ending after eleven seasons on the air, the sprawling *The Walking Dead* Universe continues through new and diverging television series, online in webisodes and on social media, and in conversations of those viewers both willingly and eagerly watching.

Conclusion

Regardless of what you call them—walkers, biters, geeks, empties, stiffs, hungry ones, creepers, rotters, sickos, freaks, wailers, vessels, delts, infected, or even simply the dead—zombies in *The Walking Dead* present a constant and persistent threat to the living. Still, there is more to *The Walking Dead* than just the zombies. Since its debut on October 31, 2010, *The Walking Dead* has witnessed unbridled success as ground-breaking viewers tuned in to watch a group of displaced humans fight for survival against an undying antagonistic threat. Given the insurgence of zombie narratives over the last decade, zombies are, without a doubt, the monster of the times. Feared because of their distinct otherness manifesting in their empty gaze and mindless deadly consumption, stories about zombies entice audiences with the shock and gore associated with the horror genre. Transcending the silver screen for the television screen, *The Walking Dead* allows spectators to voyeuristically regale in watching from the comfort and safety provided by home or wherever they feel comfortable watching.

The popularity of *The Walking Dead* speaks volumes to its quality as a popular culture artifact with its contribution to the long history of zombie cultural narratives and the development of a compelling storyline. As this book discussed, *The Walking Dead* has long outgrown its graphic novel roots to include a post-episode live aftershow and a variety of spin-offs following various storylines, one of which followed two female leads to "'highlight complicated women'" (Bonomolo, "Third Walking Dead Series Will Be 'Completely Different'"). The countless webisodes, video games, merchandise, a themed cruise, and representation at fan conventions such as the highly attended San Diego Comic-Con are added to this list. Soon, *The Walking Dead* Universe will welcome the addition of three new spin-offs focusing on some beloved and contentious characters' adventures. In its final season on television, which brought nearly 200 episodes between its debut in 2010 until its eleventh season finale near the end of 2022 under the direction of showrunner Angela Kang, *The Walking Dead* flagship series is as unrelenting as the zombies so brilliantly featured within this cinematic quality television story (Turchiano).

The analysis featured in this book highlighted ways characters, especially the women of the series, evolved beyond conventions of gender and sexuality. Much akin to its predecessors in the expansive realm of zombie culture, *The Walking Dead* continuously found itself subject to considerable scholarly discussion regarding the latent perpetuation of stereotypes. Problematic representations of race, social hierarchy, gender, and sexuality are many topics openly deliberated in academic journals or books focused upon the series. However, these discussions failed to do justice to some of the women presented in *The Walking Dead*. As I noted throughout the pages of this book, these featured women offered refreshingly deviant perspectives on motherhood and leadership in a horror narrative that existing scholarship generally failed to recognize. Leaving behind such disparaging clichés as "Dead Lesbian Syndrome" and modifying Carol Clover's "final girl" trope, these women demonstrate how regressive labels are dispensed with and subsequently destroyed thanks to the prolonged run of the series.

While these women broke conventions in many ways, there is much we can learn from them concerning gender when considering social movements such as #MeToo. In their fight for recognition, stance against oppression, and refusal to be silenced, the women of *The Walking Dead* offered insight into the intolerance of gender discrimination. Overcoming loss, sexual humiliation, demeaning abuse, and suppression of their identities, these women persevered until the very end. As part of the dynamic participatory culture surrounding the series, viewers openly, passionately, and even opposingly participated in observing the progression of these influential women and the drastic changes that took place in a world that continually threatened their existence.

As discussed in my second chapter, Carol Peletier, the only female character remaining from the first season, rose like a phoenix from the ashes to be born anew in the apocalypse as the protector she could not be for her daughter, Sophia, or her adopted son, Henry. Before and even after the loss of her abusive husband, Ed, the men in *The Walking Dead* often doubted Carol's survival in the world of the dead. After she usurped the authority of the core group patriarch, Rick Grimes, when she decisively murdered two sickened members of the group, an action she did to save her surrogate family, her expulsion set her on a journey of transformation culminating in the single-handed destruction of Terminus in the fifth season. Finally earning a position of respect and authority in the core group, Carol evolved from meek to mighty by demonstrating triumph in the wake of painful loss and demeaning abuse. Succinctly put, Carol transformed into a zombie-killing badass.

As a single mother, Maggie Rhee afforded viewers a diverging perception of balancing motherhood with a position of power. Shedding the "final girl" trope to promote her status as a mother and compassionate protector, Maggie brought an incredibly feminized quality to her role as a leader. Though youthfully inexperienced when first introduced in the second season, Maggie extended her matriarchal authority to become the sole leader of the Hilltop Colony, a position the inhabitants elected her to after she exposed Gregory's incompetence and deceit. Leaving behind the deceivably perfect world at the Greene family farm, Maggie transformed into a commanding authority figure in the core group. Losing her additional family members and husband along the way, Maggie succeeded in embodying incredible compassion and morality for others. Under her leadership, Hilltop became a flourishing and self-sustaining colony. As the only woman to assume a position of authority without the aid or attachment to a man, she made way for other women, such as Tara, to emerge as dominant, competent leaders.

Becoming the first prominent Black woman to enter the narrative, Michonne left behind a life of isolation to become the head of security and First Lady of the Alexandria Safe-Zone. Losing her partner, Rick, and eventually returning to motherhood furthered her need to be the robust and autonomous fighter associated with her character. Initially, her lack of speaking and incomprehensible mistrust of others proved to limit her development as a character. In denying Michonne a backstory, scholars branded her as another example of the "angry Black woman" stereotype. After eventually revealing her past to Carl, a person with whom Michonne felt a solid maternal connection, and thus showing the brutality of losing her son, Michonne shed her coarsened and silent persona to become an outspoken powerhouse. Though she entered the narrative as the most capable of surviving alone in the apocalypse, her integration into the core group provided her much-needed human companionship. In Michonne becoming a constable for Alexandria in her own right, she took a position ranking her equal in authority to her partner, Rick.

As discussed in my third chapter, the first three seasons offered a mere glimpse into how *The Walking Dead* continued to transcend the gender-laden normativity often placed upon women in the horror genre. Later seasons introduced other examples where women blazed a trail for previously marginalized groups to emerge as prominent figures in the narrative. Tara Chambler, the first openly gay character in the series, brought awareness and representation for the LGBTQ+ community. Despite her entry into *The Walking Dead* through the patriarchal story arc of the Governor, a.k.a. Brian, Tara endured and persevered through the tyranny of male dominance to become vital in uniting groups in their shared goal of resisting oppression. Ultimately, by staying off the "bury your gays" trope to the end of the ninth season, Tara far surpassed expectations of a "token" commodity. As an openly gay character, Tara afforded viewers an identifiable role previously denied to them in the first three seasons.

Rosita Espinosa, the first prominent Latina character in the series, offered another marginalized group representation on screen. Overtly silenced and kept in the backdrop, Rosita initially appeared to be a prop for sexual gratification for her partner, Abraham, and eye candy for the audience to behold in voyeuristic pleasure. However, by utilizing her sexuality to extract information and necessary survival skills from her unsuspecting male pursuers, Rosita empowered herself as a sexualized being. Finding liberation from her larger-than-life White male counterpart, Rosita distanced herself from the exposed pigtailed hypersexualized object of what Laura Mulvey terms the "male gaze" to reveal herself as a fully aware and capable apocalyptic fighter. Rosita passionately embraced her identity as a Latina woman through her use of language and in the naming of her daughter, Socorro. Rosita also fought to the very end to protect her daughter, even when it cost her life. Saddened by her impending demise, Rosita chose to spend her last moments with her family, quietly dying with her daughter resting peacefully by her side.

Enid progressed away from adolescent gullibility to stand tall amongst the female powerhouses leading the colonies. Starting with a depiction as a continuously guilt-ridden teen after witnessing her parents' death, Enid, under extreme protest, learned to survive independently and, eventually, used her quick wit and ability to become a doctor. Like Michonne, Enid initially appeared standoffish and untrusting of the idyllic setting within the walls of Alexandria. Not until unburdening herself of her past did Enid demonstrate her incredible vulnerability and need for companionship. Like Maggie, a person with whom Enid became inextricably linked as a proxy family member, Enid understood the need to care for others and trained as a doctor under the direction of Siddiq. Enid became an invaluable asset to the Hilltop community when she forcibly put her skills to the test.

Comparatively, *The Walking Dead* continues to push the boundaries of gender both on and off-screen "despite themes that some might classify as more masculine—like zombies, survivalist storytelling, and horror" (Bowman) by introducing rather unconventional characters to survive in an apocalyptic narrative. Specifically, starting with the ninth season, the series expanded an incredibly diverse cast to include characters of differing abilities. It also offered viewers a female antagonist, unprecedented for *The Walking Dead*. By introducing sisters Connie and Kelly, *The Walking Dead* extended itself to members of the deaf community by filling a noticeable gap in the representation of an overlooked group. The inclusion of Alpha as the preliminary female antagonist for the series provided an alternative depiction of motherhood compared to highly regarded figures such as Carol. And with the inclusion of Princess in the tenth season, viewers witnessed the quirky but loveable character combat her mental health issues, overcome extreme loneliness, and see Princess find happiness in a relationship with the Chief Officer of the Commonwealth military, Michael Mercer (Michael James Shaw).

As the first woman to hold the role of showrunner, Angela Kang brought with her ascension a renewed outlook for *The Walking Dead* (Bowman). By promoting more female-centric storylines, Kang disrupted the normative male supremacy to present a drastic and refreshing departure from the original trajectory of the graphic novel. By including a pre-teen Judith Grimes, Kang offered viewers an optimistic viewpoint through the eyes of a child who had only known a life where the dead roam. Though she continuously defied her adopted mother, Michonne, Judith represented hope for living in a world where family is chosen. And by introducing Alpha, Kang reflectively presents a woman taking the reins where men previously dominated.

The prolonged run of a series, such as *The Walking Dead*, offered ample narrative space for these characters ample time to develop in psychological detail, one of the many qualities Carol Clover identified as part of the "final girl" archetype. This book discusses that these women only act with purpose and thoughtful consideration. Though other survivors, and even viewers, questioned their motives, women such as Carol perform in ways that serve the best interest of others. Maggie, embodying the cunning of the "final girl," parted from the deified imagery of the virgin when she entered a romantic relationship with Glenn and later became a mother to Hershel. Zombie narratives such as *The Walking Dead* modify the "final girl" archetype, as Natasha Patterson notes in the article "Cannibalizing Gender and Genre," by making "possible alternative visions of femininity, opening up spaces for the female viewers that do not rely significantly on gender stereotypes that anticipate the passivity or masochism of the female viewer" (111). Over the eleven seasons included in this exploration, I demonstrated many ways the women of *The Walking Dead* depart from homogenous portrayals of the damsel in distress typified in the horror genre.

Rather than demonizing women for their nurturing capabilities, *The Walking Dead* glorified women's protective instincts. *The Walking Dead* often challenged the notion of maternity by constantly pitting these featured women against the ever-present threat of the ravenous undead and threats to their makeshift apocalyptic family groups. These women opposed the concept of the traditional nuclear family, which the first few seasons of *The Walking Dead* tended to favor. By raising a child alone, as Maggie demonstrated, or by forming a blended family, as Michonne and Judith exemplified, prescriptive pre-apocalyptic norms seemed to matter less. As the tenth season later revealed, women like Rosita inverted traditional gender roles by leaving men responsible for childcare. Instead, the women focused on physical training, participated in scavenging hunts, or took up security detail. Even despite the crippling loneliness she experienced, Princess managed to weave herself nicely into the group by offering her help to Eugene, Yumiko, and Ezekiel, as they progressed in the mission to meet the mysterious Stephanie and thus be captured by the Commonwealth. Supporting Brooke Bennett's assertion such dramatic changes so quickly after the apocalypse would be "quite silly," the prolonged narrative reflected continuous change as these characters adapted to a world where they could establish new social norms.

More than that, the emergence of the various fears, tensions, and anxieties plaguing the modern world presented a new and refreshing approach to a narrative that originally began through a White heteronormative patriarchal lens. Still, this is not the only aspect of *The Walking Dead* Universe focused upon in this book, though I admittedly spent a fair amount of time discussing it. Initially, I referenced a few scholars who identify zombies as the perfect blank slate to place our fears and anxieties on. I find that the survivors are the perfect example of how society in whatever form handles moments of tension and uncertainty. Issues with food scarcity, housing instability, fuel shortages, sufficient access to medicine, and war are just a few of the tensions I mentioned that take place within this narrative universe. Going on step further, I explored more about what scares us in a narrative like *The Walking Dead* and its spinoffs. Yes, the zombies posed an ever-present threat to survival, but they were not the only threat. Since 2010, *The Walking Dead* Universe touched upon other anxieties and tensions reflective of our world today. Gender equality, motherhood, sexual identity and fluidity, blended family structures, ableism, mental health, death and dying, all found their place in this apocalyptic narrative.

Not only does *The Walking Dead* and its spinoffs distance themselves from the many preceding zombie narratives, but viewers of *The Walking Dead* also engage in a global discussion regarding various standpoints, interpretations, and nonconforming opinions of the series with the help of social media. By participating in active conversations as the show airs in real time or even following the airing of an episode, viewers became part of a continuously dynamic participatory culture surrounding the series; in addition to the conversations about gender taking place online, the emotional outcries when a beloved character dies to exemplify its power to spark conversations amongst its fans. Considering the various comments highlighted in this book, I showcased how intensely detailed conversations about the implications of character actions and representations are no longer restricted to just one community or special intellectual group. Through social media, discussions about representation, motherhood, sexuality, and so on afforded passionate fans an outlet to discuss their thoughts or air their grievances regarding the series.

My investigation of the commentary focused on the show, especially on the characters featured in these chapters, confirmed my reflection on the prevalent stereotypes. Speaking specifically for gender representation, the remark made by a viewer on *Reddit* asserted how women on television "can't fucking win" (possiblyhysterical) indorsed viewers' incredible sophistication and awareness for interpreting female characters. As women continued to traverse new territories within the series, they found themselves in a seemingly inescapable conundrum. Starting with the complaints about women doing laundry while the men protected the group in the early seasons, women in *The Walking Dead* were both underutilized and undermined continuously by men. Then, as the series shifted to promote women who lead and men who follow, grumbles about the "'all–chick zombie … 'estrogen fest'" emerged online (qtd. in Bonomolo, "The Walking Dead's Michael Cudlitz"). Of course, women performing tasks outside of domesticated chores is not the only anxiety focused upon in the ever-growing universe of *The Walking Dead* franchise.

Using social media, viewers highlighted challenges to the norm for horror as *The Walking Dead* continuously promoted more representation onscreen. By pursuing the social media interaction surrounding *The Walking Dead*, I knew I would be confronted with comments both praising and criticizing the series. However, much to my surprise, and sometimes repulsion, were the remarks condemning the series for evolving beyond its comic roots. Why are storylines that prominently feature women so problematic that they cause people to use social media to lambast the show, such as *The Walking Dead*? Suppose *The Walking Dead*'s crew openly express their approval of the series going beyond the male-centric storylines that dominate television, as both series actor and director Michael Cudlitz and actor Joshua Mikel did in retaliation on X. Why are female-centric storylines so controversial? More than that, what about narrative like *The Walking Dead* and its spinoffs make for the perfect environment to test out the fears, anxieties, and tensions that plague our society?

Conceivably, much like the zombies themselves, the characters of *The Walking Dead* Universe complete with their divergent representation present an ubiquitous threat to a patriarchal world that seldom ventures down the path of the hypothetical, making room for other alternatives or positions and giving voice to those who rarely get attention except when times are bad. Though Aiossa poignantly argues that "the zombie apocalypse is not an automatic fix for a flawed society," *The Walking Dead* Universe "certainly invites survivors to devise their own roles, rules, and codes of conduct" as the previous ways of the world die out with the rotting dead (128). Instead of fighting change, I hope that the continued depictions of diverging character identities and abilities will lead viewers to finally embrace the changes occurring within *The Walking Dead* Universe and elsewhere on television. Though beloved characters grow older, make questionable decisions, or even die, they serve as constant reminders of how flawed human society continues to learn, adapt, and evolve.

Perhaps, as Adachi et al. explained in their article "I Can't Wait for the Next Episode!," the draw to continue watching lies in "storylines that are meaningful, thought provoking, and moving, bring[ing] viewers into connection with the characters and enhanc[ing] their intrinsic motivation to watch" (13). As *The Walking Dead* and its spinoffs continued to showcase characters who battle the lingering remnants of a dead world, these essential characters played a critical role in how viewers make meaning. As discussed in this book, fans using social media readily voiced their approval for, dissent against, and other various interpretations for every installment of this narrative universe, conversations that continue to this day as fans return to sites like *Reddit* after rewatching old episodes. One thing I know for sure, and I implore for it to continue, is that fans will continue not to sit by idly or quietly. Take to your posts and tweets, fellow fans, and do not let those who reign over *The Walking Dead* Universe, or any beloved series, forget that you are diligently watching.

Works Cited

"A." *The Walking Dead*, season 4, episode 16, AMC, 30 Mar. 2014. *Netflix*, www.netflix.com/watch/70297539?trackId=200257859.

"A New Beginning." *The Walking Dead*, season 9, episode 1, AMC, 07 Oct. 2018. *Netflix*, www.netflix.com/watch/70177057?tctx=2%2C3%2C%2C%2C.

Abdurraqib, Samaa. "'Just Another Monster': Michonne and the Trope of the Angry Black Woman." *Bad Girls and Transgressive Women in Popular Television, Fiction, and Film*, edited by Julie A. Chappell and Mallory Young, Springer International Publishing, 2017, pp. 227–251.

"About Us." *ReFrame*, www.reframeproject.org/sponsors-1.

"About *Tales of The Walking Dead*: News, Bios and Photos." *AMC*, www.amc.com/shows/tales-of-the-walking-dead/explore--1054256.

Acuna, Kristen. "One of the Most Emotional Moments on 'The Walking Dead's' Season Premiere Is Inspired by a Star's Progressive Hearing Loss and a Line Her Mother Told Her." *Insider*, 09 Oct. 2019, www.insider.com/walking-dead-wrote-angel-theory-hearing-loss-onto-show-2019-10.

_____. "The Long-Awaited Rick and Michonne 'Walking Dead' Spin-Off Finally has an Official Name. Here's the Show's First Teaser Trailer. *Business Insider*, 21 June 2023, www.businessinsider.com/the-walking-dead-rick-and-michonne-trailer-release-date-2023-7.

_____. "'The Walking Dead' Star Paola Lázaro on Saying Goodbye to the Series, the Impact Her Role Has Had on Mental Health Awareness, and Making a Song with a Costar." *Insider*, 3 Apr. 2022, www.insider.com/the-walking-dead-paola-lazaro-interview-2022-4.

Adachi, Paul J.C., et al. "'I Can't Wait for the next Episode!' Investigating the Motivational Pull of Television Dramas through the Lens of Self–Determination Theory." *Motivation Science*, vol. 4, no. 1, Mar. 2018, pp. 78–94. *EBSCOhost*, doi:10.1037/mot0000063.supp.

Adolphson, Jeremy V. "'We'll Get through This Together': Fan Cultures and Mediated Social Support on AMC's *Talking Dead*." *Dissertation Abstracts International Section A: Humanities and Social Sciences*, vol. 79, no. 10–A(E), ProQuest Information & Learning, 2018. *EBSCOhost*, search.ebscohost.com/login.aspx?direct=true&db=psyh&AN=2018-34217-046&site=eds-live&scope=site.

"After." *The Walking Dead*, season 4, episode 9, AMC, 9 Feb. 2014. *Netflix*, www.netflix.com/watch/70297532?trackId=14170289&tctx=2%2C1%2C7e63d72e-8dc4-4d72-a2b1-9acc399588c5-618383686%2CNES_506F923DFFC9D6877B12E8DB196EB0-994911DC4F528C-B3CD55246A_p_1671895135170%2CNES_506F923DFFC9D6877B1 2E8DB196EB0_p_1671895135170%2C%2C%2C%2C70177057.

Agarwal, Apoorv, et al. "Key Female Characters in Film Have More to Talk about Besides Men: Automating the Bechdel Test." *NAACL: North American Chapter of the Association for Computational Linguistics*, Jan. 2015, pp. 830–840. *EBSCOhost*, proxy.myunion.edu/login?url=http://search.ebscohost.com/login.aspx?direct=true&db=edb&AN=109 928370&site=eds-live&scope=site.

Agent-Cooper. Comment on "S04E10 'Inmates' Post-Episode Discussion." *Reddit*,

16 Feb. 2014, 8:06 p.m., www.reddit.com/r/thewalkingdead/comments/1y42sa/s04e10_inmates_postepisode_discussion/cfh6au3.

Aiossa, Elizabeth. *The Subversive Zombie: Social Protest and Gender in Undead Cinema and Television*. McFarland, 2018. Contributions to Zombie Studies.

"Alexa Mansour." *Famous Birthdays*, https://www.famousbirthdays.com/people/alexa-mansour.html.

@AlphaObsession. "#Carol is a true survivor. I believe shes afraid of what she has become but shes only protecting her people. Shes a leader. #TheWalkingDead." *Twitter*, 13 Mar. 2016, 9:00 a.m., twitter.com/AlphaObsession/status/709212478178131968.

Alter, Ethan. "'The Walking Dead' Responds to Homophobic Backlash against an LBGTQ Storyline." *Yahoo!*, 27 Jan. 2021, www.yahoo.com/now/the-walking-dead-homophobic-backlash-lbgtq-storyline-172258698.html?guccounter=1&guce_referrer=aHR0cHM6Ly93d3cuZ29vZ2xlLmNvbS8&guce_referrer_sig=AQAAACZRLodBaBs-9iy2oUqM1oyseYHeDSXNBy-4bMCiQGIgEUUzbZlAvq2ctqcauKNT0OZiMEDAlClNZfDf9EGb1MiB7QMLRRT2XevbzBp65-qBiEuZpfzna3mw3khaek5nuuzwGZ1kk5SajmX9dZzFsucjfMslhIcHqEac5gGRaqYE.

"AMC Keeps On Raising The Dead: New 'The Walking Dead' Spinoff Continues Network's Successful Franchise." *Benzinga.com*, 10 Mar. 2022. *Business Insights: Global*, https://bi-gale-com.ezproxy.snhu.edu/global/article/GALE%7CA696303597?u=nhc_main&sid=ebsco.

"AMC's *The Walking Dead* is the Most Watched Drama Series Among Adults 18–49 in Basic Cable History." *AMC Networks*, 6 Dec. 2010, www.amcnetworks.com/press-releases/amcs-the-walking-dead-is-the-most-watched-drama-series-among-adults-18-49-in-basic-cable-history.

AnaMain___. Comment on "The Walking Dead S10E20—Splinter—POST Episode Discussion." *Reddit*, 21 June 2021, 9:48 a.m., www.reddit.com/r/thewalkingdead/comments/mac8pg/comment/h2jb9oa/?utm_source=share&utm_medium=web2x&context=3.

Andreeva, Nellie. "'Resident Evil' TV Series In Works At Netflix." *Deadline*, 24 Jan. 2019, deadline.com/2019/01/resident-evil-tv-series-in-works-netflix-1202541277.

@AngelaKang (Angela Kang).This photo is out there but here is Rick Grimes and Michonne Hawthorne about to kiss for the first time. To make up for the lack of Andy and..." *X*, 16 Jan. 2022, 6:28 p.m., https://x.com/angelakang/status/1482857349551247362

"Angela Kang—Showrunner / Executive Producer / Writer." *AMC*, AMC Network Entertainment, www.amc.com/shows/the-walking-dead/cast-crew/angela-kang-showrunner-executive-producer-writer.

angiepie02. Comment on "The Walking Dead S06E02—JSS—Episode Discussion." *Reddit*, 19 Oct. 2015, 9:25 a.m., www.reddit.com/r/thewalkingdead/comments/3pancq/the_walking_dead_s06e02_jss_episode_discussion/cw57tgy.

"Annet Mahendru." *IMDb*, IMDb.com, www.imdb.com/name/nm3393732/?ref_=tt_cl_i_7.

"The Apocalypse Worth Spreading, or How to Survive a Zombie Attack | Herman Geijer | TEDxStockholm." *YouTube*, uploaded by TEDx Talks, 21 Jan. 2016, www.youtube.com/watch?v=MriRotjmyjE.

Aragão, Carolina, et al. "The Modern American Family." *Pew Research Center*, 14 Sep. 2023, www.pewresearch.org/social-trends/2023/09/14/the-modern-american-family/.

armokrunner. Comment on "The Walking Dead S09E5—What Comes After—POST Episode Discussion." *Reddit*, 4 Nov. 2018, 9:48 p.m., www.reddit.com/r/thewalkingdead/comments/9u9y0i/the_walking_dead_s09e5_what_comes_after_post/e92vot9.

AroundSurviving. Comment on "The Walking Dead—S09E10 Omega—POST Episode Discussion." *Reddit*, 18 Feb. 2019, 12:53 a.m., www.reddit.com/r/thewalkingdead/comments/arsibn/the_walking_dead_s09e10_omega_post_episode/egpu6he.

askylitpichu. Comment on "The Walking Dead S09E06—Who Are You Now?—Post Episode Discussion." *Reddit*, 11 Nov. 2018, 8:23 p.m., www.reddit.com/r/thewalkingdead/comments/9wac44/the_walking_dead_s09e06_who_are_you_now_post/e9j6d88.

@AstarrDe (I. A. DeShields). "The real tragedy of the #TWD is the idea that the new world will be populated with white folks and their children. No diversity in the post-apocalyptic world? Damn. ...." *Twitter*, 13 Nov. 2018, 9:08 a.m., twitter.com/AstarrDe/status/1062376652557221893.

Ausiello, Michael. "Third Walking Dead Series Gets Title." *TVLine*, 25 Nov. 2019, tvline.com/2019/11/24/the-walking-dead-world-beyond-third-series-title-amc/.

@awireman (Anthony Wireman). "I didn't see that coming!!! This has potential to be the greatest episode of The Walking Dead...ever. #TWD." *Twitter*, 18 Oct. 2015, 6:29 p.m., twitter.com/awireman/status/655918558707326977.

Babri, Nikki. "The Legacy of LGBTQ+ Nightlife." *UCI School of Humanities*, 08 Nov. 2023, https://www.humanities.uci.edu/news/legacy-lgbtq-nightlife.

Baelorn. Comment on "The Walking Dead S04E07 'Dead Weight' Episode Discussion Thread." *Reddit*, 25 Nov. 2013, 12:16 a.m., www.reddit.com/r/thewalkingdead/comments/1rdzkt/the_walking_dead_s04e07_dead_weight_episode/cdmgnal.

Bailey, Matt. "Dawn of the Shopping Dead." *Braaaiiinnnsss!: From Academics to Zombies*, edited by Robert J. Smith?, U of Ottawa P, 2011, pp. 195–207.

Balaji, Murali. "Eating the Dead: AMC's Use of Synergy to Cultivate Zombie Consumption." *Thinking Dead: What the Zombie Apocalypse Means*, edited by Murali Balaji, Lexington, 2013, pp. 227–239.

Baldwin, Martina and Mark McCarthy. *Thinking Dead: What the Zombie Apocalypse Means*, edited by Murali Balaji, Lexington, 2013, pp. 75–87.

bandit515. Comment on "[SPOILERS] What exactly is the meaning of 'clear'?." *Reddit*, 05 Mar. 2013, 12:33 a.m., www.reddit.com/r/thewalkingdead/comments/19o1ur/comment/c8pzes3/?utm_source=share&utm_medium=web2x&context=3

Bankhurst, Adam. "The Walking Dead Is Getting an Anthology Series, Tales of the Walking Dead." *IGN*, 12 Oct. 2021, www.ign.com/articles/the-walking-dead-is-getting-an-anthology-series-tales-of-the-walking-dead.

Barghodi. Comment on "S04E10 'Inmates' Post-Episode Discussion." *Reddit*, 12 Dec. 2016, 2:48 a.m., www.reddit.com/r/thewalkingdead/comments/5hud35/the_walking_dead_s07e08_hearts_still_beating_post/db3d5u0.

Barkman, Ashley. "Women in the Zombie Apocalypse." *The Walking Dead and Philosophy: Zombie Apocalypse Now*, edited by Wayne Yuen, Open Court, 2013, pp. 97–106.

@BastardGrimm. "They killed off our sweet Rosita, yet the incredibly useless Walking Dead activist diversity hires—responsible for ruining this entire show..." *Twitter*, 21 Nov. 2022, 2:55 p.m., twitter.com/BastardGrimm/status/1594781535621812268.

Bell, Vicki. "On Speech, Race and Melancholia: An Interview with Judith Butler." *Theory, Culture & Society*, vol. 16, no. 2, Apr. 1999, pp. 163–174. *EBSCOhost*, proxy.myunion.edu/login?url=http://search.ebscohost.com/login.aspx?direct=true&db=mzh&AN=2000035031&site=eds-live&scope=site.

Bennett, Brooke. "Tough Women of the Apocalypse: Gender Performativity in AMC's The Walking Dead." *Horror Studies*, vol. 10, no. 1, Apr. 2019, pp. 87–104. *EBSCOhost*, search.ebscohost.com/login.aspx?direct=true&db=edb&AN=136582186&site=eds-live&scope=site.

Berg, Madeline. "NFL, 'Walking Dead' Light Up Social Media on Sunday Nights." *Forbes*, Jan. 2017, p. 22. *EBSCOhost*, search.ebscohost.com/login.aspx?direct=true&db=buh&AN=120816272&site=eds-live&scope=site.

Bertram, Colin. "How Women in Horror Movies Keep Us Coming Back for More." *Biography.com*, A&E Networks, 03 Oct. 2018, www.biography.com/news/women-in-horror-movies.

"Beside the Dying Fire." *The Walking Dead*, season 2, episode 13, AMC, 18 Mar. 2012. *Netflix*, www.netflix.com/watch/70248473?trackId=200257859.

"Better than the original? An abridged guide to recent TV drama spinoffs; *Better Call Saul, The Finder, CSI: Cyber*-networks are always reimagining old formulas. Here's what else they've tried besides *Fear of Walking Dead*." *Guardian* [London, England], 18 Aug. 2015. *Gale In Context: Opposing Viewpoints*, link.gale.com/apps/doc/A425895720/OVIC?u=nhc_main&sid=bookmark-OVIC&xid=a2cb8902.

BettyDraperIsMyBitch. Comment on "The Walking Dead S06E13—The Same Boat—Post Episode Discussion." *Reddit*, 13 Mar. 2013, 8:07 p.m., www.reddit.com/r/

thewalkingdead/comments/4ab5s4/the_walking_dead_s06e13_the_same_boat_post/d0yvvee.

BEyouTH. Comment on "The Walking Dead Episode Discussion S03E07 'When the Dead Come Knocking.'" *Reddit*, 26 Nov. 2012, 10:37 p.m., www.reddit.com/r/thewalkingdead/comments/13sb4j/the_walking_dead_episode_discussion_s03e07_when/c76uep1.

Bishop, Bryan. "How the Creators of A Quiet Place Made Silence so Terrifying." *The Verge*, 19 Apr. 2018, www.theverge.com/2018/4/19/17253262/a-quiet-place-sound-design-eric-aadahl-ethan-van-der-ryan-interview.

Bishop, Kyle William. *American Zombie Gothic: The Rise and Fall (and Rise) of the Walking Dead in Popular Culture.* McFarland, 2010. Contributions to Zombie Studies.

_____. Introduction—A Multiplicity of Zombies: How the Walking Dead Conquered Popular Culture. *How Zombies Conquered Popular Culture: The Multifarious Walking Dead in the 21st Century*, McFarland, 2015, pp. 5–21. Contributions to Zombie Studies.

_____. "The Pathos of *The Walking Dead*: Bringing Terror Back to Zombie Cinema." *Triumph of the Walking Dead: Robert Kirkman's Zombie Epic on Page and Screen*, edited by James Lowder, BenBella Books, 2011, pp. 1–14.

Bittebitte. Comment on "The Walking Dead Episode Discussion S03E07 'When the Dead Come Knocking.'" *Reddit*, 25 Nov. 2012, 7:11 p.m., www.reddit.com/r/thewalkingdead/comments/13sb4j/the_walking_dead_episode_discussion_s03e07_when/c76r7ip.

"The Blaze of Glory." *The Walking Dead: World Beyond*, episode 2, season 1, AMC, 11 Oct. 2020. *Amazon Prime*, https://www.amazon.com/gp/video/detail/B0CLHNKGHB/ref=atv_tv_hom_c_YAO5Ct_brws_2_1?jic=32%7CCgdhbWNwbHVzEgxzdWJzY3Jpc HRpb24%3D.

BleakGod. Comment on "The Walking Dead Episode Discussion S02E13 'Beside the Dying Fire' (Spoilers)." *Reddit*, 19 Mar. 2012, 3:29 a.m., www.reddit.com/r/thewalkingdead/comments/r2ltr/the_walking_dead_episode_discussion_s02e13_beside/c42jq8v.

Bloodhound1. Comment on "[SPOILERS 93x06)] Episode Discussion: 'Hounded.'" *Reddit*, 5 Nov. 2012, 11:46 p.m., www.reddit.com/r/thewalkingdead/comments/12oyrf/comment/c6x3qta/?utm_source=share&utm_medium=web2x&context=3.

Body, Jamie. "The Walking Dead Star Details Demand to Change Iconic Character." *Express.co.uk*, 15 Feb. 2022, www.express.co.uk/showbiz/tv-radio/1566230/The-Walking-Dead-Princess-change-Paola-Lazaro.

Bojalad, Alec. "The Walking Dead: How AMC Harnessed the Power of Fandom." *Den of Geek*, 10 Dec. 2017, www.denofgeek.com/comics/the-walking-dead-how-amc-harnessed-the-power-of-fandom/.

Bonington, Mark. "Zombies and Xanax: How Fear The Walking Dead Explores Mental Health." *Den of Geek*, 31 July 2018, https://www.denofgeek.com/tv/zombies-and-xanax-how-fear-the-walking-dead-explores-mental-health/.

Bonomolo, Cameron. "Study Shows Who's Watching *The Walking Dead* the Most." *ComicBook.com*, 5 Mar. 2022, comicbook.com/tv-shows/news/the-walking-dead-final-season-11-ratings-who-is-watching-the-most-study-philo/#:~:text=By%202014%2C%20 The%20Walking%20Dead,television%20among%20adults%2018%2D49.

_____. "Third Walking Dead Series Will Be 'Completely Different' from Other Two Shows." *Comicbook.com*, 9 June 2019, comicbook.com/2019/06/09/third-walking-dead-series-completely-different-first-two-shows.

_____. "'The Walking Dead' Criticized for Killing Another Prominent Gay Character." *ComicBook.com*, 11 Apr. 2019, comicbook.com/thewalkingdead/2019/04/05/the-walking-dead-season-9-criticized-killing-off-gay-character-tara-alanna-masterson.

_____. "'The Walking Dead': Jeffrey Dean Morgan Responds to James Woods' 'Bullsh*t' Sexist Tweet." *ComicBook.com*, 22 Feb. 2019, comicbook.com/thewalkingdead/news/the-walking-dead-jeffrey-dean-morgan-james-woods-tweet-bullshit-michael-cudlitz/#:~:text=%22You're%20a%20terrific%20actor,%22Nice.%22.

_____. "'The Walking Dead' Producer Backing Gender–Based Rebate Plan." *ComicBook.com*, 9 Feb. 2019, comicbook.com/thewalkingdead/2019/02/09/the-walking-dead-producer-gale-anne-hurd-backing-gender-based-rebate-initiative.

_____. "'The Walking Dead' Season 9 Will Tell Different, Female-Driven Stories as Rick

Grimes Exits." *ComicBook.com*, 02 Oct. 2018, comicbook.com/thewalkingdead/2018/10/01/the-walking-dead-season-9-rick-grimes-exit-different-female-driven-stories.

_____. "'The Walking Dead's Michael Cudlitz Shuts Down James Woods Over Sexist 'All-Chick Zombie Series' Remark." *ComicBook.com*, 23 Feb. 2019, comicbook.com/thewalkingdead/2019/02/22/the-walking-dead-michael-cudlitz-shuts-down-james-wood-sexist-tweet-all-chick-zombie-series-andrew-lincoln.

Boozer, Jack. "The Lethal Femme Fatale in the Noir Tradition." *Journal of Film and Video*, vol. 51, no. 3/4, 1999, pp. 20–35. *EBSCOhost*, search.ebscohost.com/login.aspx?direct=true&db=edsjsr&AN=edsjsr.20688218&site=eds-live&scope=site.

"Bounty." *The Walking Dead*, season 9, episode 11, AMC, 24 Feb. 2019. *Netflix*, www.netflix.com/watch/81026627?trackId=155573558.

Boucher, Ashley. "Broadway Actress Lauren Ridloff Cast in 'The Walking Dead' Season 9." *TheWrap*, 16 July 2018, www.thewrap.com/broadway-actress-lauren-ridloff-cast-in-the-walking-dead-season-9.

Bowman, Sabienna. "'The Walking Dead' Season 9 Will Have a Female Showrunner & Here's Why That's So Exciting." *Bustle*, 13 Jan. 2018, www.bustle.com/p/the-walking-dead-season-9-will-have-a-female-showrunner-heres-why-thats-so-exciting-7907398.

@BoySoprano. "Clearly, The Walking Dead writers DO NOT know black women. #TheWalkingDead." *Twitter*, 6 Dec. 2010, 8:58 a.m., twitter.com/BoySoprano/status/11826880894205952.

bracake. Comment on "The Walking Dead S09E11—Bounty—POST Episode Discussion." *Reddit*, 25 Feb. 2019, 7:31 p.m., www.reddit.com/r/thewalkingdead/comments/aug55a/the_walking_dead_s09e11_bounty_post_episode/ehajpkl.

Bracher, Mark. "Desire in Discourse." *Lacan, Discourse, and Social Change: A Psychoanalytic Cultural Criticism*, Cornell UP, 1993, pp. 19–52.

Bradley, Laura. "*The Walking Dead*: Enid Joins the Squad of Women Warriors." *Vanity Fair*, Condé Nast, 18 Nov. 2016, www.vanityfair.com/hollywood/2016/11/walking-dead-season-7-episode-5-enid-katelyn-nacon-interview.

_____. "*The Walking Dead*'s Next Spin-off Will Star Two Female Leads." *Vanity Fair*, Condé Nast, 8 Apr. 2019, www.vanityfair.com/hollywood/2019/04/walking-dead-spin-off-female-leads-lord-of-the-flies.

brain_in_vain. Comment on "Fear the Walking Dead—1x01 'Pilot'—Post-Episode Discussion." *Reddit*, 25 Aug. 2015, 3:14 a.m., https://www.reddit.com/r/FearTheWalkingDead/comments/3i6aae/comment/cueuj79/?utm_source=share&utm_medium=web2x&context=3.

"Brave." *The Walking Dead: World Beyond*, season 1, episode 1, AMC, 04 Oct. 2020. *Amazon Prime*, https://www.amazon.com/gp/video/detail/B0CLHNKGHB/ref=atv_tv_hom_c_YAO5Ct_brws_2_1?jic=32%7CCgdhbWNwbHVzEgxzdWJzY3JpcHRpb24%3D.

Bricken, Rob. "The Walking Dead Did Something I Didn't Think Was Possible." *Gizmodo*, 20 Mar. 2017, io9.gizmodo.com/the-walking-dead-did-something-i-didnt-think-was-possib-1793437964.

"The Bridge." *The Walking Dead*, season 9, episode 2, AMC, 21 Feb. 2016. *Netflix*, www.netflix.com/watch/81026618?trackId=200257858.

Brojakowski, Benjamin. "Spoiler Alert: Understanding Television Enjoyment in the Social Media Era." *Television, Social Media, and Fan Culture*, edited by Alison Slade et al., Lexington Books, 2017, pp. 23–41.

@Bronte71. "#TheWalkingDead 3 men and a baby, Rosita edition." *Twitter*, 07 Oct. 2019, 5:42 a.m., twitter.com/Bronte71/status/1181142839993995265.

Brookfield, Tarah. "No Woman Is an Island: Heroes, Heroines and Power in the Gendered World of Lost." *Journal of Popular Culture*, no. 2, 2013, pp. 315–337. *EBSCOhost*, proxy.myunion.edu/login?url=http://search.ebscohost.com/login.aspx?direct=true&db=edsgao&AN=edsgcl.326243592&site=eds-live&scope=site.

Brooks, Kinitra D. "The Importance of Neglected Intersections: Race and Gender in Contemporary Zombie Texts and Theories." *African American Review*, vol. 47, no. 4, Winter 2014, pp. 461–475. *EBSCOhost*, proxygsu-cht2.galileo.usg.edu/login?url=http://

search.ebscohost.com/login.aspx?direct=true&db=tfh&AN=102090730&site=eds-live&scope=site.

Brown, Christopher. "#Richonne: The Walking Dead's Favorite Shipped Couple Really Happened." *The Inquisitr*, 22 Feb. 2016, www.inquisitr.com/2816542/richonne-the-walking-deads-favorite-shipped-couple-really-happened.

Brown, Jeffery. "Ethnicity and New Action Heroines." *Beyond Bombshells: The New Action Heroine in Popular Culture*, UP of Mississippi, 2015, pp. 78–118.

Bullard, Benjamin. "Lauren Cohan and The Walking Dead Maggie Moment that Made Her Vomit." *SYFY*, 15 Mar. 2019, www.syfy.com/syfywire/lauren-cohan-walking-dead-maggie-vomit-scene.

Burman, Erica. "Contemporary Feminist Contributions to Debates Around Gender and Sexuality: From Identity to Performance." *Group Analysis*, vol. 38, no. 1, Mar. 2005, pp. 17–30. *EBSCOhost*, https://doi-org.ezproxy.snhu.edu/10.1177/0533316405049360.

Burnett, Bob. "2000–2009: America's Lost Decade." *Huffington Post*, Verizon Media, 25 May 2011, www.huffingtonpost.com/bob-burnett/2000-2009-americas-lost-d_b_403887.html.

Burton, Elliott. "Control of the Knife: Transgressing Gender Stereotypes in Bustillo and Maury's Inside." *Offscreen*, vol. 18, no. 6/7, June 2014. *EBSCOhost*, search.ebscohost.com/login.aspx?direct=true&db=edb&AN=98632772&site=eds-live&scope=site.

Butler, Bethonie. "Gender Regulations." *Undoing Gender*. Routledge, 2004, pp. 40–56. search.ebscohost.com/login.aspx?direct=true&db=nlebk&AN=110587&site=eds-live&scope=site.

_____. "TV Keeps Killing off Lesbian Characters. The Fans of One Show Have Revolted." *The Washington Post*, WP Company, 4 Apr. 2016, www.washingtonpost.com/news/arts-and-entertainment/wp/2016/04/04/tv-keeps-killing-off-lesbian-characters-the-fans-of-one-show-have-revolted.

Butler, Judith. *Gender Trouble: Feminism and the Subversion of Identity*. Routledge, Taylor & Francis Group, 2015.

BVTheEpic. Comment on "The Walking Dead Episode Discussion S04E04 'Indifference.'" *Reddit*, 3 Nov. 2013, 7:04 p.m., www.reddit.com/r/thewalkingdead/comments/1puh34/the_walking_dead_episode_discussion_s04e04/cd66hdm.

@cade_pickette (Cade Pickette). "If you missed this episode of The Walking Dead you missed the best one #TWD." *Twitter*, 18 Oct. 2015, 7:17 p.m., twitter.com/cade_pickette/status/655930738160902144.

Cady, Kathryn A., and Thomas Oates. "Family Splatters: Rescuing Heteronormativity from the Zombie Apocalypse." *Women's Studies in Communication*, vol. 39, no. 3, July 2016, pp. 308–325. *EBSCOhost*, doi:10.1080/07491409.2016.1194935.

cageyfanboy. Comment on "What do you thinks gonna happen between Carl, Ron and Enid in season 6?" *Reddit*, 16 Aug. 2015, 8:17 a.m., www.reddit.com/r/thewalkingdead/comments/3ghy9p/what_do_you_thinks_gonna_happen_between_carl_ron/cu4ueg4.

"The Calm Before." *The Walking Dead*, season 9, episode 15, AMC, 24 Mar. 2019. *Netflix*, www.netflix.com/watch/81026631?trackId=155573560.

Cameron, Allan. "Zombie Media: Transmission, Reproduction, and the Digital Dead." *Cinema Journal*, vol. 52, no. 1, Oct. 2012, pp. 66–89. *EBSCOhost*, https://search-ebscohost-com.ezproxy.snhu.edu/login.aspx?direct=true&db=edsjsr&AN=edsjsr.23360281&site=eds-live&scope=site.

Campbell, Joseph. *The Hero with a Thousand Faces*. Commemorative ed., Princeton UP, 2004. *The Paul Rosenfels Community*, www.rosenfels.org/Joseph%20Campbell%20-%20The%20Hero%20With%20A%20Thousand%20Faces,%20Commemorative%20Edition%20%282004%29.pdf.

capsfan1978. Comment on "Michonne or Maggie? Race, Gender, and Rape on The Walking Dead TV Series." *Daily Kos*, 27 Nov. 2012, 10:27 a.m., www.dailykos.com/comments/1164790/48554094#comment_48554094.

@catgirl422 (Catarina Ortiz). "I will say..Isnt Sasha the Cutest Zombie you've ever seen???? Adorbs!! the walking dead." *Twitter*, 6 Apr. 2017, 5:28 a.m., twitter.com/catgirl422/status/849735539708264448.

Centers for Disease Control and Prevention. "Understanding the Opioid Overdose Epidemic." *Centers for Disease Control and Prevention*, 8 Aug. 2023, www.cdc.gov/opioids/basics/epidemic.html.

Champagne, Christine. "From Meek to Mofo: Melissa McBride on Playing *The Walking Dead*'s Most Complicated Zombie–Killer, Carol." *Fast Company*, 6 Feb. 2015, www.fastcocreate.com/3042035/from-meek-to-mofo-melissa-mcbride-on-playing-the-walking-deads-most-complicated-zombie-kille.

Chan, Anna. "Find out Why Lauren Cohan Almost Quit 'Walking Dead'!" *Us Weekly*, 15 Oct. 2017, www.usmagazine.com/entertainment/news/lauren-cohan-almost-quit-the-walking-dead-over-gruesome-scene-w163228/.

"Cherokee Rose." *The Walking Dead*, season 2, episode 4, AMC, 6 Nov. 2011. *Netflix*, www.netflix.com/watch/70248464?trackId=200257859.

Chicago Tribune Staff and KT Hawbaker. "#MeToo: A Timeline of Events." *Chicago Tribune*, 6 Dec. 2018, www.chicagotribune.com/lifestyles/ct-me-too-timeline-20171208-htmlstory.html.

ChiefSombrero. Comment on "The Walking Dead S06E09—No Way Out—Post Episode Discussion." *Reddit*, 14 Feb. 2016, 10:04 p.m. www.reddit.com/r/thewalkingdead/comments/45ugqi/comment/d0093cr/?utm_source=share&utm_medium=web2x&context=3.

Choi, Yun Jung. "Emergence of the Viewing Public: Does Social Television Viewing Transform Individual Viewers into a Viewing Public?" *Telematics and Informatics*, vol. 34, no. 7, Nov. 2017, pp. 1059–1070. *EBSCOhost*, doi:10.1016/j.tele.2017.04.014.

Christian, Tiffany A. "'Look at the Flowers': Meme Culture and the (Re)Centering of Hegemonic Masculinities through Women Characters." *The Politics of Race, Gender and Sexuality in* The Walking Dead: *Essays on the Television Series and Comics*, edited by Elizabeth Erwin and Dawn Keetley, McFarland, 2018, pp. 65–77. Contributions to Zombie Studies.

ChunkfaceMcDirtyDick. Comment on "The Walking Dead S04E06 'Live Bait' Post-Episode Discussion Thread." *Reddit*, 18 Nov. 2013, 12:56 p.m., www.reddit.com/r/thewalkingdead/comments/1qv9zh/the_walking_dead_s04e06_live_bait_postepisode/cdhcs6c.

"Chupacabra." *The Walking Dead*, season 2, episode 5, AMC, 13 Nov. 2011. *Netflix*, www.netflix.com/watch/70248465?trackId=200257858.

Century, Sara. "Tales of the Walking Dead Breaks the TWD Universe Wide Open." *Den of Geek*, 12 Aug. 2022, www.denofgeek.com/tv/tales-of-the-walking-dead-breaks-the-twd-universe-wide-open/.

"Claimed." *The Walking Dead*, season 4, episode 11, AMC, 23 Feb. 2014. *Netflix*, www.netflix.com/watch/70297534?trackId=200257859.

"Clear." *The Walking Dead*, season 3, episode 12, AMC, 3 Mar. 2013. *Netflix*, www.netflix.com/watch/70260058?trackId=200257859.

Clover, Carol J. "Her Body, Himself." *Men, Women, and Chain Saws: Gender in the Modern Horror Film*. Princeton UP, 2005, pp. 21–64.

Collins, Patricia Hill. "Assume the Position." *Black Sexual Politics: African Americans, Gender, and the New Racism*. New York, Routledge, 2006, pp. 215–245.

Collins, Scott. "How TV Beats Film in Giving Women and Minorities Greater Representation on Screen." *The LA Times*, 24 Feb. 2016, www.latimes.com/entertainment/tv/la-et-st-tv-film-diversity-20160224-story.html#.

Colucci, Brian. "Walking Dead Creator Reveals the Series' Tagline Was Always a Lie." *ScreenRant*, 11 Dec. 2022, screenrant.com/walking-dead-creator-robert-kirkman-reveals-tagline-lie/.

Comment on "Diversity and gender roles in The Walking Dead." *Reddit*, 16 Mar. 2015, 10:56 p.m., www.reddit.com/r/thewalkingdead/comments/2yg0m1/diversity_and_gender_roles_in_the_walking_dead/cp9k1nc.

Comment on "Episode Discussion: S02E02, 'Bloodletting' (Spoilers)." *Reddit*, 24 Oct. 2011, 2:14 a.m., www.reddit.com/r/thewalkingdead/comments/lmisn/episode_discussion_s02e02_bloodletting_spoilers/c2tz3e2.

Comment on "Episode Discussion: S02E05, 'Chupacabra' (Spoilers)." *Reddit*, 14 Nov. 2011, 12:43 a.m., www.reddit.com/r/thewalkingdead/comments/mb7e3/episode_discussion_s02e05_chupacabra_spoilers/c2zmshr.

Comment on "Fear the Walking Dead—1x01 'Pilot'—Post-Episode Discussion." *Reddit*, 24 Aug. 2015, 10:19 a.m., https://www.reddit.com/r/FearTheWalkingDead/comments/3i6aae/comment/cudw91p/?utm_source=share&utm_medium=web2x&context=3.

Comment on "Fear the Walking Dead—1x01 'Pilot'—Post-Episode Discussion." *Reddit*, 24 Aug. 2015, 11:06 p.m., https://www.reddit.com/r/FearTheWalking Dead/comments/3i6aae/comment/cueop4l/?utm_source=share&utm_medium=web2x&context=3.

Comment on "S04E15 'Us' Post-Episode Discussion." *Reddit*, 23 Mar. 2014, 10:06 p.m., www.reddit.com/r/thewalkingdead/comments/21737m/comment/cga8r7d/.

Comment on "The Walking Dead Episode Discussion S03E12 'Clear.'" *Reddit*, 3 Mar. 2013, 11:36 p.m., www.reddit.com/r/thewalkingdead/comments/19lxcw/comment/c8pblty/?utm_source=share&utm_medium=web2x&context=3

Comment on "The Walking Dead Episode Discussion S03E15 'This Sorrowful Life.'" *Reddit*, 28 Mar. 2013, 12:07 p.m., www.reddit.com/r/thewalkingdead/comments/1axxb5/the_walking_dead_episode_discussion_s03e15_this/c9450gz.

Comment on "The Walking Dead S04E07 'Dead Weight' Post-Episode Discussion Thread." *Reddit*, 24 Nov. 2013, 8:22 p.m., www.reddit.com/r/thewalkingdead/comments/1re5rf/the_walking_dead_s04e07_dead_weight_postepisode/cdmcdrh.

Comment on "The Walking Dead S04E08 'Too Far Gone' Post-Episode Discussion Thread." *Reddit*, 1 Dec. 2013, 9:38 p.m., www.reddit.com/r/thewalkingdead/comments/1rvtq2/the_walking_dead_s04e08_too_far_gone_postepisode/cdrhk6k.

Comment on "The Walking Dead S09E03—Warning Signs—Post Episode Discussion." *Reddit*, 22 Oct. 2018, 5:12 a.m., www.reddit.com/r/thewalkingdead/comments/9q9eak/the_walking_dead_s09e03_warning_signs_post/e8891m5.

Comment on "The Walking Dead World Beyond—01x02 'The Blaze of Glory'—AMC Premiere Discussion." *Reddit*, 09 Oct. 2020, 3:00 a.m., https://www.reddit.com/r/TWDWorldBeyond/comments/j78h4g/comment/g8710d3/?utm_source=share&utm_medium=web2x&context=3.

Comment on "The Walking Dead World Beyond—01x02 'The Blaze of Glory'—AMC Premiere Discussion." *Reddit*, 11 Oct. 2020, 3:14 a.m., https://www.reddit.com/r/TWDWorldBeyond/comments/j78h4g/comment/g8710d3/?utm_source=share&utm_medium=web2x&context=3.

cosmic_punk. Comment on "What is your all time favorite moment in the walking dead. a part that really spoke to you?" *Reddit*, 20 May 2015, 7:50 a.m., www.reddit.com/r/thewalkingdead/comments/35g8rc/what_is_your_all_time_favorite_moment_in_the/cr4h4gy.

Cover copy. *The Walking Dead, Book One*, by Kirkman et al., Image Comics, 2013.

Crecente, Brian. "Creator Robert Kirkman on 15 Years of 'The Walking Dead.'" *Variety*, Variety, 15 Oct. 2018, variety.com/2018/gaming/features/robert-kirkman-interview-the-walking-dead-anniversary-15-years-1202980789/.

"Crossed." *The Walking Dead*, season 5, episode 7, AMC, 23 Nov. 2014. *Netflix*, www.netflix.com/watch/80010533?trackId=200257859.

Cruz, Araceli. "There's a Reason People Are Falling in Love with this Latina from 'The Walking Dead.'" *We Are Mitú*, 11 July 2017, wearemitu.com/newsfeed/the-walking-deads-rosita-finally-reveals-herself-as-the-true-hero-of-the-living.

@Cudlitz (Michael Cudlitz). "Based on the fact that we all know how a 'zombie apocalypse' would unfold........ I mean. You know it's not real, right?? .... (I'm just...)" *Twitter*, 21 Feb. 2019, 10:02 a.m., twitter.com/Cudlitz/status/1098779931209658368.

@dailylatine. "today's latine is juanita "princess" sanchez from the walking dead (she/her)! she is puerto rican, pansexual, and has ADHD!" *Twitter*, 8 July 2022, 5:29 p.m., twitter.com/dailylatine/status/1545520400653860866.

Damn_Dog_Inappropes. Comment on "Do you guys like Rick and Michonne together? I'm not feeling it really..." *Reddit*, 30 Oct. 2016, 12:01 p.m., www.reddit.com/r/thewalkingdead/comments/5a4q17/do_you_guys_like_rick_and_michonne_together_im/d9e6l05.

DaNorris1221. Comment on "The Walking Dead premiered nine years ago today with the episode Days Gone Bye." *Reddit*, 31 Oct. 2019, 12:44 p.m., www.reddit.com/r/thewalkingdead/comments/dpndgv/comment/f5xfxs2/?utm_source=share&utm_medium=web2x&context=3.

@dantelista06 (Dante Lista). "The Walking Dead knows how to play with every emotion #TheWalkingDead. ..." *Twitter*, 12 Oct. 2014, 9:54 p.m., twitter.com/dantelista06/status/521524473514983424.

@DarciCanada. "Holy F*ck... The Walking Dead is off the charts this season. I love the new characters & story line. Well done Angela Kang! #TWD." *Twitter*, 17 Feb. 2019, 10:15 p.m., twitter.com/DarciCanada/status/1097364021370445824.

Davis, Brandon. "Robert Kirkman Writes Tribute To 'Walking Dead' Inspiration George Romero." *ComicBook.com*, 9 Nov. 2017, comicbook.com/thewalkingdead/news/robert-kirkman-george-romero-walking-dead-/#1.

Dawn of the Dead. Dir. George A. Romero. 1978. United Film Distribution, 2004. DVD.

"The Day Will Come When You Won't Be." *The Walking Dead*, season 7, episode 1, AMC, 23 Oct. 2016. *Netflix*, www.netflix.com/watch/80202475?trackId=14170289&tctx=0%2C0%2C27eae4c4-8905-4a24-9b7f-5f08149bbe42-70981486%2C15513b1d-14b4-4b69-a7a9-bbabd02befd6_58662379X3XX1578936254929%2C15513b1d-14b4-4b69-a7a9-bbabd02befd6_ROOT.

"Days Gone Bye." *The Walking Dead*, season 1, episode 1, AMC, 31 Oct. 2010. *Netflix*, www.netflix.com/watch/70210887?trackId=13752289&tctx=0%2C0%2C284f8c35-8174-4b68-b8a3-f96741bf9795-6956109.

DeadlyShogunate. Comment on "Is Enid the most pointless character and a waste of screen time ever in TWD franchise?" *Reddit*, 15 May 2019, 12:20 p.m., www.reddit.com/r/thewalkingdead/comments/bp1f4w/is_enid_the_most_pointless_character_and_a_waste/ennbk29.

Defiant_Griffin. Comment on "The Walking Dead Episode Discussion S03E15 'This Sorrowful Life.'" *Reddit*, 25 Mar. 2013, 9:44 p.m., www.reddit.com/r/thewalkingdead/comments/1axxb5/the_walking_dead_episode_discussion_s03e15_this/c92ijmt.

DeVega, Chauncey. "Michonne or Maggie? Race, Gender, and Rape on The Walking Dead TV Series." *Daily Kos*, Kos Media, 26 Nov. 2012, www.dailykos.com/stories/2012/11/26/1164790/-Michonne-or-Maggie-Race-Gender-and-Rape-on-The-Walking-Dead-TV-Series.

Dima, Vlad. "You Only Die Thrice: Zombies Revisited in The Walking Dead." *International Journal of Zizek Studies*, vol. 8, no. 2, June 2014, pp. 1–22. *EBSCOhost*, search.ebscohost.com/login.aspx?direct=true&AuthType=ip,shib&db=hlh&AN=99599642&site=eds-live&scope=site.

Dimock, Michael. "Defining Generations: Where Millennials End and Generation Z Begins." *Pew Research Center*, 21 Apr. 2022, www.pewresearch.org/fact-tank/2019/01/17/where-millennials-end-and-generation-z-begins/.

DirectorAgentCoulson. Comment on "The Walking Dead: Daryl Dixon S01E03—Paris Sera Toujours Paris—Episode Discussion." *Reddit*, 25 Sep. 2023, 11:10 p.m., https://www.reddit.com/r/thewalkingdead/comments/16rdxxt/comment/k28fsuy/?utm_source=share&utm_medium=web3x&utm_name=web3xcss&utm_term=1&utm_content=share_button.

djord17. Comment on "I feel like I'm the only one that still hates Negan with a passion." *Reddit*, 1 Mar. 2022, 12:41 p.m., www.reddit.com/r/thewalkingdead/comments/t4bljh/comment/hyxqc9b/?utm_source=share&utm_medium=web2x&context=3.

"Do Not Send Us Astray." *The Walking Dead*, season 8, episode 13, AMC, 25 Mar. 2018. *Netflix*, www.netflix.com/watch/81022964?trackId=200257859.

Douglas, Susan J. "Warrior Women in Thongs." *Enlightened Sexism: The Seductive Message That Feminisms Work is Done*. Times Books, 2010, pp. 76–100.

Dradus17. Comment on "I feel like I'm the only one that still hates Negan with a passion."

Reddit, 1 Mar. 2022, 11:29 a.m., www.reddit.com/r/thewalkingdead/comments/t4bljh/comment/hyxf36x/?utm_source=share&utm_medium=web2x&context=3.

DreadWolfByTheEar. Comment on "The Walking Dead S10E20—Splinter—POST Episode Discussion." *Reddit*, 25 Mar. 2021, 10:14 p.m., www.reddit.com/r/thewalkingdead/comments/mac8pg/comment/gs8wkdg/?utm_source=share&utm_medium=web2x&context=3.

@DrKnockers05. "Damn it, I know I keep going on about her, but Angela Kang has done wonders for #TheWalkingDead. You'd think doing the Whisperers storyline without Rick, Carl, and ...." *Twitter*, 18 Feb. 2019, 4:04 p.m., twitter.com/DrKnockers05/status/1097632877108449281.

Dr_Toast. Comment on "The Walking Dead S06E02—JSS—Episode Discussion." *Reddit*, 18 Oct. 2015, 11:01 p.m., www.reddit.com/r/thewalkingdead/comments/3pancq/the_walking_dead_s06e02_jss_episode_discussion/cw4v95g.

Drysdale, Jennifer. "Christian Serratos Says She's 'Holding It Down' for Latinas on 'The Walking Dead' (Exclusive)" *CBS8*, 30 Mar. 2019, https://www.cbs8.com/article/entertainment/entertainment-tonight/christian-serratos-says-shes-holding-it-down-for-latinas-on-the-walking-dead-exclusive/509-a621a3ce-8c6a-4122-b35d-8cfbaa91c040

dsr541. Comment on "The Walking Dead S04E07 'Dead Weight' Post-Episode Discussion Thread." *Reddit*, 25 Nov. 2013, 2:26 p.m., www.reddit.com/r/thewalkingdead/comments/1re5rf/comment/cdms0cu/?utm_source=reddit&utm_medium=web2x&context=3.

duaneap. Comment on "The Walking Dead S11E24—Rest In Peace—Series Finale—Episode Discussion." *Reddit*, 21 Nov. 2022, 4:11 a.m., www.reddit.com/r/thewalkingdead/comments/z0bauw/comment/ix70rjt/?utm_source=share&utm_medium=web2x&context=3.

earthlings_all. Comment on "The Walking Dead S09E02—The Bridge—Post Episode Discussion." *Reddit*, 15 Oct. 2018, 6:37 a.m., www.reddit.com/r/thewalkingdead/comments/9o8kd5/the_walking_dead_s09e02_the_bridge_post_episode/e7sxn60.

"East." *The Walking Dead*, season 6, episode 15, AMC, 27 Mar. 2016. *Netflix*, www.netflix.com/watch/80031932?trackId=200257858.

@edpachecano (Ed Pachecano). "Finishing up S2 of Walking Dead. So, what you're saying is: the world has to end for a little Asian guy to get some hot ass? #walkingdead ...." *Twitter*, 12 Feb. 2012, 9:58 p.m., twitter.com/edpachecano/status/168922057978036224.

eedna. Comment on "Thoughts on Rosita Espinosa?" *Reddit*, 26 Oct. 2014, 6:40 p.m., www.reddit.com/r/thewalkingdead/comments/2kbmhv/thoughts_on_rosita_espinosa/clkoodu.

Elvy, Craig. "Fear TWD Is Now Better than the Walking Dead." *ScreenRant*, 18 Oct. 2021, screenrant.com/fear-walking-dead-better-twd-reason/.

@emma_korte. "THAT WAS THE WORST THING TO EVER HAPPEN TO MY GAY LITTLE HEART I HATE THE WALKING DEAD I'M DONE." *Twitter*, 20 Mar. 2016, 7:42 p.m., twitter.com/emma_korte/status/711729610405355520.

"Empire, Walking Dead Top TV Tweets, Data Shows." *Spectator*, 2 June 2015. *Infotrac Newsstand*, link.galegroup.com/apps/doc/A416119782/STND?u=vol_m761j&sid=STND&xid=920661d6.

Erwin, Elizabeth. "A Woman's Work is Never Done: Mothering and Marriage." *The Politics of Race, Gender and Sexuality in* The Walking Dead: *Essays on the Television Series and Comics*, edited by Elizabeth Erwin and Dawn Keetley, McFarland, 2018, pp. 78–92. Contributions to Zombie Studies.

Espenson, Jane. "Playing Hard to 'Get'—How to Write Cult TV." *The Cult TV Book: From Star Trek to* Dexter, *New Approaches to TV Outside the Box*, edited by Stacey Abbott, Soft Skull Press, New York, 2010, pp. 45–53.

@evilgrrl. "I watched the first season of The Walking Dead: World Beyond and I liked it a lot. I really enjoyed having 2 young women (one of whom is Black) be the focus, as well as gay characters and other strong..." *Twitter*, 29 Nov. 2020, 4:51 p.m., https://twitter.com/evilgrrl/status/1333166838750986240.

EvilSporkOfDeath. Comment on "Carol's development in this show has been exceptional. She's come a long way." *Reddit*, 5 Nov. 2018, 12:46 a.m., www.reddit.com/r/thewalkingdead/comments/9ua3ad/carols_development_in_this_show_has_been/e9322uc.

"Fear the Walking Dead." *Rotten Tomatoes*, www.rottentomatoes.com/tv/fear_the_walking_dead.

fede01_8. Comment on "The Walking Dead S09E09—Adaptation—Post-Episode Discussion." *Reddit*, 12 Feb. 2019, 7:45 a.m., www.reddit.com/r/thewalkingdead/comments/ap92tq/the_walking_dead_s09e09_adaptation_postepisode/egb3esy.

Feloni, Richard. "Here's How 'The Walking Dead' Creator Plans Out the TV Show and Comics for Years to Come." *Business Insider*, 8 July 2014, www.businessinsider.com/walking-deads-robert-kirkman-on-creative-process-2014-7.

Ferril_. Comment on "Paloma in HBO's The Walking Dead: Daryl Dixon." *Reddit*, 14 Nov. 2023, 4:59 p.m., https://www.reddit.com/r/rupaulsdragrace/comments/17vclzw/comment/k99sr2q/?utm_source=share&utm_medium=web3x&utm_name=web3xcss&utm_term=1&utm_content=share_button.

"The First Day of the Rest of Your Life." *The Walking Dead*, season 7, episode 16, AMC, 2 Apr. 2017. *Netflix*, www.netflix.com/watch/80202490?trackId=14277283&tctx=0%2C15%2C044af544-22bc-4ac6-a8c4-dee08b145b62-51769303.

Fit-Diet-6488. Comment on "All LGBT Characters In The Walking Dead." *Reddit*, 5 June 2022, 9:30 p.m., www.reddit.com/r/thewalkingdead/comments/v5arhe/comment/ibbgj34/.

Flowers, Shaunee. "'The Walking Dead' Star Tom Payne Didn't Say His Character Paul 'Jesus' Rovia Is Gay, So Are We Shipping Him with Sasha Or Maggie?" *The Inquisitr*, 4 Dec. 2016, www.inquisitr.com/3765131/the-walking-dead-star-tom-payne-didnt-say-his-character-paul-jesus-rovia-is-gay-so-are-we-shipping-him-with-sasha-or-maggie.

fountasalexander. Review of *Tales of the Walking Dead: Evie/Joe*, 14 Aug. 2022, *IMDb*, www.imdb.com/review/rw8444762/?ref_=rw_urv.

"Four Walls and a Roof." *The Walking Dead*, season 5, episode 3, AMC, 26 Oct. 2014. *Netflix*, www.netflix.com/watch/80010529?trackId=200257859.

Franklin, Kelly. "The Meek Shall Inherit the Earth? Post-Apocalyptic Heroines in Mad Max: Fury Road and The Walking Dead." *Academia*, pp. 1–19. *Academia*, www.academia.edu/30617280/The_Meek_Shall_Inherit_the_Earth.docx. Microsoft Word file.

Freeman, Matthew. *The World of the Walking Dead*, Taylor & Francis Group, 2019. *ProQuest Ebook Central*, https://ebookcentral-proquest-com.ezproxy.snhu.edu/lib/snhu-ebooks/detail.action?docID=5683716.

Freud, Sigmund. "Mourning and Melancholia." *On the History of the Psycho-Analytic Movement: Papers on Metapsychology and Other Works*, edited by Anna Freud et al. translated by James Strachey, XIV, Hogarth Press, 2001, pp. 243–258.

Frodoholic. Comment on "The Walking Dead S04E07 'Dead Weight' Post-Episode Discussion Thread." *Reddit*, 25 Nov. 2013, 12:23 p.m., www.reddit.com/r/thewalkingdead/comments/1re5rf/the_walking_dead_s04e07_dead_weight_postepisode/cdmrkno.

Fussell, Sidney. "Fans Had a Big Problem with Part of Sunday's 'The Walking Dead.'" *Business Insider*, 21 Mar. 2016, www.businessinsider.com/walking-dead-anti-gay-controversy-2016-3.

@futuristicmikec. "I'm hurt to the core. Rosita you deserved better #twd #twdspoilers." *Twitter*, 21 Nov. 2022, 4:51 a.m., twitter.com/futuristicmikec/status/1594629642312638465.

@gabeisidoro (Gabriel Torres). "Sure Walking Dead the only Latina character is barely wearing clothes. Name her Lara Croft while you're at it. #TheWalkingDead." *Twitter*, 23 Feb. 2014, 7:58 p.m., twitter.com/gabeisidoro/status/437783479984865281.

GaiusMagnus. Comment on "Thoughts on Rosita Espinosa?" *Reddit*, 26 Oct. 2014, 11:15 p.m., www.reddit.com/r/thewalkingdead/comments/2kbmhv/thoughts_on_rosita_espinosa/cljz7zx.

Garber, Megan. "How the Standard for Women in Culture Became Known as the 'Bechdel Test.'" *The Atlantic*, Atlantic Media Company, 25 Aug. 2015, www.theatlantic.com/entertainment/archive/2015/08/call-it-the-bechdel-wallace-test/402259/.

Garland, Tammy S., et al. "Gender Politics and *The Walking Dead*: Gendered Violence and the Reestablishment of Patriarchy." *Feminist Criminology*, 11 Mar. 2016, pp. 1–28. *SAGE Publications*, doi–org.proxy.myunion.edu/10.1177/1557085116635269.

Gavaler, Chris. "Zombies vs. Superheroes: *The Walking Dead* Resurrection of Fantastic Four Gender Formulas." *ImageTexT: Interdisciplinary Comics Studies*, vol. 7, no. 4, 2014. *EBSCOhost*, search.ebscohost.com/login.aspx?direct=true&db=mzh&AN=2015100245&site=eds–live&scope=site.

TheGent316. Comment on "The Walking Dead S08E01—Mercy—Post Episode Discussion for [COMIC] Readers." *Reddit*, 22 Oct. 2017, 9:15 p.m., www.reddit.com/r/thewalkingdead/comments/7850ch/the_walking_dead_s08e01_mercy_post_episode/dor562g.

"Ghosts." *The Walking Dead*, season 10, episode 3, AMC, 20 Oct. 2019. *Netflix*, www.netflix.com/watch/81071681?trackId=14170289&tctx=2%2C0%2Cba70fdc6-5438-4bd4-913d-10f64bbbe30f-1178192225%2CNES_0641F46592C38FACD47EE2A0D7C9E5-994911DC4F528C-A1E94A5CF8_p_1672420924208%2C%2C%2C%2C%2C70177057.

Goldberg, Lesley. "'Walking Dead' Cast Rates Survival Odds, Offers Advice to Characters." *The Hollywood Reporter*, 7 Oct. 2014, www.hollywoodreporter.com/tv/tv-news/walking-dead-cast-rates-survival-738612/.

Gorillapatrick. Comment on "[Early Access Thread] The Walking Dead World Beyond—01x09 & 01x10 'The Deepest Cut; In This Life.'" *Reddit*, 26 Nov. 2020, 8:19 p.m., https://www.reddit.com/r/TWDWorldBeyond/comments/k18syb/comment/gdq0cne/?utm_source=share&utm_medium=web2x&context=3

Gray, Brandon. "Weekend Report: 'Wild Things' Roars, 'Citizen,' 'Activity' Thrill." *Box Office Mojo*, 19 Oct. 2009, www.boxofficemojo.com/article/ed3682206724.

Greene, John, and Michaela D.E. Meyer. "The Walking (Gendered) Dead: A Feminist Rhetorical Critique of Zombie Apocalypse Television Narrative." *Ohio Communication Journal*, vol. 52, 10 Jan. 2014, pp. 64–74. *EBSCOhost*, proxy.myunion.edu/login?url=http://search.ebscohost.com/login.aspx?direct=true&db=edo&AN=103400786&site=eds-live&scope=site.

gremmygram. Comment on "What do you thinks gonna happen between Carl, Ron and Enid in season 6?" *Reddit*, 10 Aug. 2015, 7:07 p.m., www.reddit.com/r/thewalkingdead/comments/3ghy9p/what_do_you_thinks_gonna_happen_between_carl_ron/ctyn26w.

"The Grove." The Walking Dead, season 4, episode 14, AMC, 16 Mar. 2014. *Netflix*, https://www.netflix.com/watch/70297537?trackId=255824129&tctx=0%2C0%2C389bfa80-4acc-46d0-9833-17b4c7e42012-3031362%2C389bfa80-4acc-46d0-9833-17b4c7e42012-3031362%7C2%2C%2C%2C%2C%2C%2C70177057%2CVideo%3A70297537%2CdetailsPageEpisodePlayButton.

"Guardians." *The Walking Dead*, season 9, episode 12, AMC, 3 Mar. 2019. *Netflix*, www.netflix.com/watch/81026628?trackId=200257858.

Hagman, George. "Surviving the Zombie Apocalypse: Trauma and Transformation in AMC's *The Walking Dead*." *Psychoanalytic Inquiry*, vol. 37, no. 1, Jan. 2017, pp. 46–56. *EBSCOhost*, doi:10.1080/07351690.2017.1250589.

Hamel, Jenny. "The Pansy Craze: When Gay Nightlight in Los Angeles Really Kicked Off." *KCRW*, 11 May 2018, https://www.kcrw.com/culture/shows/curious-coast/the-pansy-craze-when-gay-nightlife-in-los-angeles-really-kicked-off.

@Hanzi83. "Is it me or has the black guy on walking dead been entirely irrelevant this entire season thus far? #walkingdead." *Twitter*, 27 Nov. 2011, 8:00 p.m., twitter.com/Hanzi83/status/140988423409373185.

Harper, Stephen. "'They're Us': Representations of Women in George Romero's 'Living Dead' Series." *Intensities: The Journal of Cult Media*, no. 3, Spring 2003, intensitiescultmedia.files.wordpress.com/2012/12/harper-theyre-us.pdf.

"Heads Up." *The Walking Dead*, season 6, episode 7, AMC, 22 Nov. 2015. *Netflix*, www.netflix.com/watch/80031924?trackId=200257859.

Hegarty, Tasha. "The Walking Dead: World beyond Boss Explains Decision to Hire

Only Female Directors." *Digital Spy*, 3 Oct. 2021, www.digitalspy.com/tv/ustv/a37841018/the-walking-dead-world-beyond-boss-female-directors/.

"Here's Negan." *The Walking Dead*, season 10, episode 22, AMC, 4 Apr. 2021. *Netflix*, www.netflix.com/watch/81403753?trackId=14170289&tctx=2%2C0%2Cad570025-2d82-4bfb-87e7-28fc4b8bad8c-1031895645%2CNES_0641F46592C38FACD47EE2 A0D7C9E5-994911DC4F528C-02E0AF576B_p_1672352192750%2C%2C%2C%2C %2C70177057.

Hero_B. Comment on "The Walking Dead Episode Discussion S02E13 'Beside the Dying Fire' (Spoilers)." *Reddit*, 19 Mar. 2012, 10:34 p.m., www.reddit.com/r/thewalking dead/comments/r2ltr/the_walking_dead_episode_discussion_s02e13_beside/c42g 8cv.

HeyHershel. Comment on "The Walking Dead S04E06 'Live Bait' Post-Episode Discussion Thread." *Reddit*, 9 Nov. 2013, 6:42 p.m., www.reddit.com/r/thewalkingdead/comments/1qv9zh/comment/cdid3ou/?utm_source=reddit&utm_medium=web2x& context=3.

Hill, Jarrett. "NBC, AMC, Showtime, Tubi Execs on Future of Inclusive TV." *Variety*, 12 June 2019, variety.com/2019/tv/features/nbc-amc-tubi-showtime-execs-on-inclusion-1203236517.

Hills, Matt. Introduction. *Fan Cultures*, Routledge, 2017, pp. 1–23.

HiveJiveLive. Comment on "The Walking Dead S06E07—Heads Up—Post Episode Discussion." *Reddit*, 24 Nov. 2015, 6:03 p.m., www.reddit.com/r/thewalkingdead/comments/3tw682/the_walking_dead_s06e07_heads_up_post_episode/cxc2t7u.

Hiscott, Rebecca. "The Beginner's Guide to the Hashtag." *Mashable*, 8 Oct. 2013, mashable.com/2013/10/08/what-is-hashtag.

H-K_47. Comment on "S05E07 'Crossed' Post-Episode Discussion." *Reddit*, 23 Nov. 2014, 8:14 p.m., www.reddit.com/r/thewalkingdead/comments/2n85q6/s05e07_crossed_ postepisode_discussion/cmb92tq.

Ho, Helen K. "The Model Minority in the Zombie Apocalypse: Asian–American Manhood on AMC's *The Walking Dead*." *Journal of Popular Culture*, vol. 49, no. 1, 2016, pp. 57–76. *EBSCOhost*, doi:10.1111/jpcu.12376.

"Home." *Annet Mahendru*, www.annetmahendru.com/.

"Home Sweet Home." *The Walking Dead*, season 10, episode 17, AMC, 21 Feb. 2021. *Netflix*, www.netflix.com/watch/81403748?trackId=14170289&tctx=2%2C0%2Cba70fdc6-5438-4bd4-913d-10f64bbbe30f-1178192225%2CNES_0641F46592C38FACD47EE2 A0D7C9E5-994911DC4F528C-A1E94A5CF8_p_1672420924208%2C%2C%2C%2C %2C70177057.

Hopkins, David. "The Hero Wears the Hat: Carl as 1.5-Generation Immigrant and True Protagonist." *Triumph of The Walking Dead: Robert Kirkman's Zombie Epic on Page and Screen*, edited by James Lowder, Smart Pop, 2011, pp. 201–215.

Houdat. Comment on "The Walking Dead Episode Discussion S03E07 'When the Dead Come Knocking.'" *Reddit*, 26 Nov. 2012, 4:37 a.m., www.reddit.com/r/thewalkingdead/comments/13sb4j/the_walking_dead_episode_discussion_s03e07_when/c76uep1.

"Hounded." *The Walking Dead*, season 3, episode 6, AMC, 18 Nov. 2012. *Netflix*, www.netflix.com/watch/70260052?trackId=14272744.

Humphries, Drew. "Women Who Kill: *Law and Order*, *Dexter*, and *The Wire*." *Representations of Murderous Women in Literature, Theatre, Film, and Television: Examining the Patriarchal Presuppositions Behind the Treatment of Murderesses in Fiction and Reality*, edited by Juli L. Parker, Edwin Mellen Press, 2011, pp. 297–321.

Hunt, Robert. Review of *Tales of the Walking Dead*, by Ron Underwood. AMC. September 2022, www.google.com/search?gs_ssp=eJzj4tVP1zc0LCooSTZPzio3YPSSLEnMS S1WyE9TKMlIVShPzMnOzEtXSElNTAEAJYIOMQ&q=tales+of+the+walking+dea d+reviews&rlz=1C1AJZK_enUS785US785&oq=tales+of+the+&aqs=chrome.1.0i355i 433i512j46i433i512j46i131i433i512j69i57j0i512j0i131i433i512j46i512l2j0i512j46i131i 433i512.7311j0j7&sourceid=chrome&ie=UTF-8&stick=H4sIAAAAAAAAAOMwe8 Rowy3w8sc9YSnjSWtOXmPU5eILKMrPSk0uCUoty0wtLxaS5mJzzSvJLKkUEpTi5-LVT9c3NCwqKEk2T84q51nEqliSmJNarJCfplCSkapQnpiTnZmXrpCSmpiiUAQ

xAQBqm-i9ZQAAAA&ictx=1&ved=2ahUKEwjh5tu0ytj6AhUmk2oFHRQDAR
      EQw_oBegUIjgEQAg.
hunta-gathera. Comment on "The Walking Dead S10E12—Walk With Us—POST Epi-
      sode Discussion." *Reddit*, 15 Mar. 2020, 10:05 p.m., www.reddit.com/r/thewalkingdead/
      comments/fjd4x6/comment/fkmaavo/?utm_source=share&utm_medium=web2x
      &context=3.
Hutchinson, Corey. "Walking Dead: Will Maggie Take Over as Star If Rick Dies?" *Screen-
      rant*, 23 Oct. 2017, screenrant.com/walking-dead-season-8-rick-die-maggie-leader-
      star.
"I Ain't a Judas." *The Walking Dead*, season 3, episode 11, AMC, 24 Feb. 2013. *Netflix*, www.
      netflix.com/watch/70260057?trackId=200257859.
Ihadacow. Comment on "The Walking Dead Episode Discussion S02E13 'Beside the Dying
      Fire' (Spoilers)." *Reddit*, 18 Mar. 2012, 8:05 p.m., www.reddit.com/r/thewalkingdead/
      comments/r2ltr/the_walking_dead_episode_discussion_s02e13_beside/c42g8cv.
imapotato99. Comment on "S04E11 'Claimed' Episode Discussion." *Reddit*, 1 Mar. 2014,
      9:19 p.m., www.reddit.com/r/thewalkingdead/comments/1yr14v/s04e11_claimed_
      episode_discussion/cfridi9.
"Indifference." *The Walking Dead*, season 4, episode 4, AMC, 3 Nov. 2013. *Netflix*, www.
      netflix.com/watch/70297527?trackId=200257859.
"Infected." *The Walking Dead*, season 4, episode 2, AMC, 20 Oct. 2013. *Netflix*, www.
      netflix.com/watch/70297525?trackId=200257859.
initialZEN. Comment on "The Walking Dead Episode Discussion S04E04 'Indifference.'"
      Reddit, 1 Dec. 2013, 6:59 a.m., www.reddit.com/r/thewalkingdead/comments/1puh34/
      comment/cdqvn7x/?utm_source=share&utm_medium=web2x&context=3.
"Inmates." *The Walking Dead*, season 4, episode 10, AMC, 16 Feb. 2014. *Netflix*, www.
      netflix.com/watch/70297533?trackId=200257858.
"Insight of the Living Dead | John O'Brien | TEDxMahtomedi." *YouTube*, uploaded by
      TEDx Talks, 21 May 2015, www.youtube.com/watch?v=4Obw0rGt4Ys.
ireallyneededthistoo. Comment on "The Walking Dead S07E16—The First Day of
      the Rest of Your Life—Post Episode Discussion." *Reddit*, 10 Apr. 2017, 1:38 a.m.,
      www.reddit.com/r/thewalkingdead/comments/633zn1/comment/dg29l2v/?
      utm_source=share&utm_medium=web2x&context=3.
ItsGotToMakeSense. Comment on "S04E11 'Claimed' Episode Discussion." *Red-
      dit*, 25 Feb. 2014, 7:18 p.m., www.reddit.com/r/thewalkingdead/comments/1yr14v/
      s04e11_claimed_episode_discussion/cfou64g.
JackieBronassis. Comment on "Rick's reaction to Lori's death." *Reddit*, 6 Nov. 2012, 2:05
      a.m., www.reddit.com/r/thewalkingdead/comments/12oyrf/comment/c6x5gy8/?utm_
      source=share&utm_medium=web2x&context=3.
Jackson, Ronald L. *Scripting the Black Masculine Body: Identity, Discourse, and Racial Pol-
      itics in Popular Media*. State University of New York Press, 2006.
Jarvey, Natalie. "'Walking Dead' Was the Most-Tweeted Show of the 2015–16 TV Sea-
      son." *The Hollywood Reporter*, 6 June 2016, www.hollywoodreporter.com/tv/tv-news/
      walking-dead-was-tweeted-show-899972/.
@JazzOfLion. "And the bury your gays trope strikes again. I stand with you The Walk-
      ing Dead fans. LGBT fans deserve better. #RIPDenise." *Twitter*, 20 Mar. 2016, 8:27 p.m.,
      twitter.com/JazzOfLion/status/711741024696074240.
@JDarius28 (John Darius). "After tonight, I'm convinced season 9 might be the best season
      the walking dead has ever done. Wow! I'm overjoyed with how much has changed and
      I love the new characters …." *Twitter*, 11 Nov. 2018, 8:28 p.m., twitter.com/JDarius28/
      status/1061823118824689664.
Jenkins, Henry. "How to Watch Television: The Walking Dead." *Confessions of an Aca-Fan*,
      Henry Jenkins, 23 Sep. 2013, http://henryjenkins.org/blog/2013/09/how-to-watch-
      television-the-walking-dead.html.
_____. *Textual Poachers: Television Fans & Participatory Culture*. Routledge, 2012.
jjenk911. Review of *Tales of the Walking Dead: Evie/Joe*, 22 Aug. 2022, *IMDb*, www.imdb.
      com/review/rw8475157/?ref_=tt_urv.

@joelmiller. "rosita espinosa is the force of nature." *Twitter*, 21 Nov. 2022, 9:25 a.m., twitter.com/joelmiller/status/1594698615951433729.

Johnson, Dominique Deirdre. "Misogynoir and Antiblack Racism: What *The Walking Dead* Teaches Us about the Limits of Speculative Fiction Fandom." *Journal of Fandom Studies*, vol. 3, no. 3, Sep. 2015, pp. 259–275. *EBSCOhost*, search.ebscohost.com/login.aspx?direct=true&db=edb&AN=110952323&site=eds-live&scope=site.

Johnson, Matt. "What Zombies Teach Us About the Psychology of Consciousness." *Psychology Today*, 03 Nov. 2020, https://www.psychologytoday.com/us/blog/mind-brain-and-value/202011/what-zombies-teach-us-about-the-psychology-consciousness.

@joshuagates (Josh Gates). "Like I always say: the true cost of the apocalypse will be the serious shortage of quality babysitters. #WalkingDead #JustLookAtTheFlowers." *Twitter*, 18 Mar. 2014, 12:04 a.m., twitter.com/joshuagates/status/445818103906070528.

Jowett, Lorna, and Stacey Abbott. *TV Horror: Investigating the Dark Side of the Small Screen*. I.B. Tauris, 2013.

"JSS." *The Walking Dead*, season 6, episode 2, AMC, 18 Oct. 2015. *Netflix*, https://www.netflix.com/watch/80031919?trackId=255824129&tctx=0%2C0%2C389bfa80-4acc-46d0-9833-17b4c7e42012-3031362%2C389bfa80-4acc-46d0-9833-17b4c7e42012-3031362%7C2%2C%2C%2C%2C%2C70177057%2CVideo%3A80031919%2CdetailsPageEpisodePlayButton.

Juno2018. Comment on "The Walking Dead S10E12—Walk With Us—POST Episode Discussion" *Reddit*, 15 Mar. 2020, 10:41 p.m., www.reddit.com/r/thewalkingdead/comments/fjd4x6/comment/fkmdp06/?utm_source=share&utm_medium=web2x&context=3.

Jusino, Teresa. "Alison Bechdel Would Like You to Call It the 'Bechdel-Wallace Test,' ThankYouVeryMuch." *The Mary Sue*, 25 Aug. 2015, www.themarysue.com/bechdel-wallace-test-please-alison-bechdel.

@justin_proffitt (Justin Proffitt). "@WalkingDead_AMC thank you so much for creating deaf character. I'm deaf and it bring me joy to watch! Thank you! #TheWalkingDead #TWD #Connie." *Twitter*, 11 Nov. 2018, 7:19 p.m., twitter.com/justin_proffitt/status/1061805638278410240.

Kahnbrochill. Comment on "The Walking Dead Episode Discussion S02E13 'Beside the Dying Fire' (Spoilers)." *Reddit*, 18 Mar. 2012, 9:05 p.m., www.reddit.com/r/thewalkingdead/comments/r2ltr/the_walking_dead_episode_discussion_s02e13_beside/c42gvns.

@KaraRose_LovesU (Kara Rose). "#myTWD #InCarolWeTrust #TheWalkingDeadTONIGHT Go Carol #TWDReturns Tyreese. ITS ALL TRENDING!!! THE WALKING DEAD IS AMAZING <3 <3 <3 <3 <3 !" *Twitter*, 112 Oct. 2014, 6:33 p.m., twitter.com/KaraRose_LuvsU/status/521473874677215233.

KAwesome. Comment on "The Walking Dead S07E01—The Day Will Come When You Won't Be—Episode Discussion." *Reddit*, 23 Oct. 2016, 8:06 p.m., www.reddit.com/r/thewalkingdead/comments/591uye/the_walking_dead_s07e01_the_day_will_come_when/d951vi7.

Keeler, Amanda. "Gender, Guns, and Survival: The Women of *The Walking Dead*." *Dangerous Discourses Feminism, Gun Violence, & Civic Life*, edited by Catherine R. Squires, Peter Lang Publishing, 2016, pp. 235–256. *Academia*, www.academia.edu/20227144/Gender_Guns_and_Survival_The_Women_of_The_Walking_Dead.

_____. "A Postapocalyptic Return to the Frontier: *The Walking Dead* as Post–Western." *Critical Studies in Television*, vol. 13, no. 4, Dec. 2018, pp. 422–437. *EBSCOhost*, search.ebscohost.com/login.aspx?direct=true&db=edb&AN=133589483&site=eds-live&scope=site.

Keetley, Dawn. Introduction. *The Politics of Race, Gender and Sexuality in* The Walking Dead: *Essays on the Television Series and Comics*, edited by Elizabeth Erwin and Dawn Keetley, McFarland, 2018, pp. 1–9. Contributions to Zombie Studies.

_____. Introduction. *"We're All Infected": Essays on AMC's* The Walking Dead *and the Fate of the Human*, edited by Dawn Keetley, McFarland, 2014, pp. 3–25. Contributions to Zombie Studies.

Kelly, Alan. "'Fear the Walking Dead' Should've Ended Seasons Ago." *Collider*, 29 Oct. 2023, collider.com/fear-the-walking-dead-should-have-ended/.

@Kemmybelle. "Rosita's got a 3 men & a baby situation going on. #TheWalkingDead." *Twitter*, 6 Oct. 2019, 9:29 p.m., twitter.com/Kemmybelle/status/1181018731545165824.

Kenemore, Scott. "A Zombie among Men: Rick Grimes and the Lessons of Undeadness." *Triumph of the Walking Dead: Robert Kirkman's Zombie Epic on Page and Screen*, edited by James Lowder, BenBella Books, 2011, pp. 1–14.

keshalover1212. Comment on "The Walking Dead S06E02—JSS—Episode Discussion." *Reddit*, 18 Oct. 2015, 8:29 p.m., www.reddit.com/r/thewalkingdead/comments/3pancq/the_walking_dead_s06e02_jss_episode_discussion/cw4qaye.

kevinsg04. Comment on "The Walking Dead S09E02—The Bridge—Post Episode Discussion." *Reddit*, 15 Oct. 2018, 8:38 a.m., www.reddit.com/r/thewalkingdead/comments/9o8kd5/the_walking_dead_s09e02_the_bridge_post_episode/e7t4r55.

"The Key." *The Walking Dead*, season 8, episode 12, AMC, 18 Mar. 2018. *Netflix*, https://www.netflix.com/watch/81022963?trackId=255824129&tctx=0%2C0%2C389bfa80-4acc-46d0-9833-17b4c7e42012-3031362%2C389bfa80-4acc-46d0-9833-17b4c7e42012-3031362%7C2%2C%2C%2C%2C%2C70177057%2CVideo%3A81022963%2CdetailsPage EpisodePlayButton.

@khvl1l. "I LITERALLY DO NOT CARE ABOUT ANYONE WHO DIED EXCEPT ENID AND TARA WHY DID THE SMARTEST DOCTOR AND ANOTHER HILLTOP LEADER DIE (also @ the walking dead stop killing the gays ...." *Twitter*, 24 Mar. 2019, 8:22 p.m., twitter.com/khvl1l/status/1110003924294160384.

"Killer Within." *The Walking Dead*, season 3, episode 4, AMC, 12 Nov. 2012. *Netflix*, www.netflix.com/watch/70260050?trackId=14277283&tctx=0%2C3%2C044af544-22bc-4ac6-a8c4-dee08b145b62-51769303.

"The King, the Widow, and Rick." *The Walking Dead*, season 8, episode 6, AMC, 26 Nov. 2017. *Netflix*, www.netflix.com/watch/81022957?trackId=200257859.

Kirkman, Robert. Introduction. *The Walking Dead*, vol. 1, Image Comics, Inc., 2015.

Kirsh, Steven J. *Parenting in the Zombie Apocalypse: The Psychology of Raising Children in a Time of Horror*. McFarland, 2019.

Kissell, Rick. "'The Walking Dead' Tops Nielsen Year–End Lists in TV, Social Media." *Variety*, 30 Dec. 2015, variety.com/2015/tv/ratings/amcs–the–walking–dead–nielsen–year–end–lists–1201668776/.

"Knots Untie." *The Walking Dead*, season 6, episode 11, AMC, 28 Feb. 2016. *Netflix*, www.netflix.com/watch/80031928?trackId=200257859

Kremmel, Laura. "Rest in Pieces: Violence in Mourning the (Un)Dead." *"We're All Infected": Essays on AMC's* The Walking Dead *and the Fate of the Human*, edited by Dawn Keetley, McFarland, 2014, pp. 80–94. Contributions to Zombie Studies.

Kurp, Josh. "The Only Reason Carol is Still Alive on 'The Walking Dead' is Lori." *UPROXX*, 11 Feb. 2016, uproxx.com/tv/carol–lori–the–walking–dead.

@Lady_Heat00. "Oh, the girl playing Maggie on walking dead! Hai! My lifelong crush on you continues! #WalkingDead." *Twitter*, 23 Oct. 2011, 6:40 p.m., twitter.com/Lady_Heat00/status/128284572499722240.

Laing, Kenyon, et al. "EP110 Not a Witch! Crimes (Boston Live Show)." *Wine & Crime*, 14 Mar. 2019, wineandcrimepodcast.com/show_episodes/ep110-not-a-witch-crimes-boston-live-show/.

"L'ame Perdue." *The Walking Dead: Daryl Dixon*, season 1, episode 1, AMC, 10 Sep. 2023. *Amazon Prime*, https://www.amazon.com/gp/video/detail/B0C9T2ZGJ7/ref=atv_hm_hom_c_lZOsi7_2_3?jic=8%7CEgNhbGw%3D.

"Last Day on Earth." *The Walking Dead*, season 6, episode 16, AMC, 3 Apr. 2016. *Netflix*, www.netflix.com/watch/80031933?trackId=14170289&tctx=2%2C0%2Cad570025-2d82-4bfb-87e7-28fc4b8bad8c-1031895645%2CNES_0641F46592C38FACD47EE2A0D7C9E5-994911DC4F528C-02E0AF576B_p_1672352192750%2C%2C%2C%2C%2C70177057.

Lavin, Melissa F., and Brian M. Lowe. "Cops and Zombies: Hierarchy and Social Location in *The Walking Dead*." *Race, Gender & Sexuality in Post–Apocalyptic TV & Film*, Jan. 2015, pp. 113–124. *EBSCOhost*, proxy.myunion.edu/login?url=https://search.ebscohost.com/login.aspx?direct=true&db=edb&AN=114829111&site=eds-live&scope=site.

Lawndirk. Comment on "The Walking Dead S11E24—Rest In Peace—Series Finale—Episode Discussion." *Reddit*, 21 Nov. 2022, 12:01 a.m., www.reddit.com/r/thewalkingdead/comments/z0bauw/comment/ix6wmls/?utm_source=share&utm_medium=web2x&context=3.

leandrombraz. Comment on "The Walking Dead S11E24—Rest In Peace—Series Finale—Episode Discussion." *Reddit*, 20 Nov. 2022, 11:19 p.m., www.reddit.com/r/thewalkingdead/comments/z0bauw/comment/ix74ci5/?utm_source=share&utm_medium=web2x&context=3.

Lee, Ben. "Supernatural Had a Seriously Amazing Walking Dead Cameo." *Digital Spy*, 29 Nov. 2018, www.digitalspy.com/tv/ustv/a823145/walking-dead-supernatural-crossover-lucille-negan/.

Leitch, Thomas M. "Twice Told Tales: The Rhetoric of the Remake." *Literature/Film Quarterly*, vol. 18, no. 3, 1990, pp. 138–48. *EBSCOhost*, https://search-ebscohost-com.ezproxy.snhu.edu/login.aspx?direct=true&db=mlf&AN=1990029709&site=eds-live&scope=site.

Leon, Melissa. "'The Walking Dead': Carol Goes on the Rampage, Kicking Ass and Baking Casserole." *The Daily Beast*, 19 Oct. 2015. *EBSCOhost*, search.ebscohost.com/login.aspx?direct=true&db=edsggo&AN=edsgcl.434426309&site=eds–live&scope=site.

_____. "'The Walking Dead': Carol's Got a New Man––and Is Not Invincible After All." *The Daily Beast*, 5 Oct. 2016. *EBSCOhost*, search.ebscohost.com/login.aspx?direct=true&db=edsgin&AN=edsgcl.450158273&site=eds–live&scope=site.

Levine, Michael, and Damian Cox. "I Am Not Living Next Door to No Zombie: Posthumans and Prejudice." *Critical Philosophy of Race*, no. 1, 2016, pp. 74–94. *EBSCOhost*, search.ebscohost.com/login.aspx?direct=true&db=edspmu&AN=edspmu.S2165869216100047&site=eds–live&scope=site.

Levy, Lior. "The Question of Photographic Meaning in Roland Barthes' Camera Lucida." *Philosophy Today*, no. 4, 2009, pp. 395–406. *EBSCOhost*, proxy.myunion.edu/login?url=http://search.ebscohost.com/login.aspx?direct=true&db=edsgao&AN=edsgcl.215764893&site=eds-live&scope=site.

likeawolf. Comment on "The Walking Dead S09E09—Adaptation—Post-Episode Discussion." *Reddit*, 11 Feb. 2019, 10:09 p.m., www.reddit.com/r/thewalkingdead/comments/ap92tq/the_walking_dead_s09e09_adaptation_postepisode/eg7epax.

Lindbergh, Ben. "The Legacy of Diversity on 'The Walking Dead.'" *The Ringer*, 11 Oct. 2021, www.theringer.com/tv/2021/10/11/22719821/walking-dead-season-11-diversity-angela-kang-jim-barnes.

"Lines We Cross." *The Walking Dead*, episode 1, season 10, AMC, 6 Oct. 2019.

Linxxxx. Comment on "The Walking Dead World Beyond—01x01 'Brave'—Episode Discussion." *Reddit*, 01 Oct. 2020, 8:24 p.m., https://www.reddit.com/r/TWDWorldBeyond/comments/j3hlqh/comment/g7cjlnn/?utm_source=share&utm_medium=web2x&context=3

Lisabeth, Zach. "The Real Reason Lauren Cohan Is Returning to The Walking Dead." *Looper*, 2 May 2022, www.looper.com/199511/the-real-reason-lauren-cohan-is-returning-to-the-walking-dead/.

"Live Bait." *The Walking Dead*, season 4, episode 6, AMC, 17 Nov. 2013. *Netflix*, www.netflix.com/watch/70297529?trackId=200257859.

LN_Studios. Comment on "The Walking Dead World Beyond—01x02 'The Blaze of Glory'—AMC Premiere Discussion." *Reddit*, 28 Oct. 2020, 8:46 p.m., https://www.reddit.com/r/TWDWorldBeyond/comments/j78h4g/comment/gafz24b/?utm_source=share&utm_medium=web2x&context=3.

loklanc. Comment on "Fear the Walking Dead—1x01 'Pilot'—Post-episode discussion." *Reddit*, 25 Aug. 2015, 6:46 a.m., https://www.reddit.com/r/FearTheWalkingDead/comments/3i6aae/comment/cuexicf/?utm_source=share&utm_medium=web2x&context=3.

Lolli, Jessica. *Violence, Paratexts, and Fandoms:* The Walking Dead *as a Societal Mirror.* Fall 2017. Governors State U, Master's thesis. *Open Portal to University Scholarship*, opus.govst.edu/theses/111.

"Look at the Flowers." *The Walking Dead*, season 10, episode 14, AMC, 29 Mar. 2020. *Netflix*, www.netflix.com/watch/81071692?trackId=14170289&tctx=2%2C0%2Cba

70fdc6-5438-4bd4-913d-10f64bbbe30f-1178192225%2CNES_0641F46592C38FACD47 EE2A0D7C9E5-994911DC4F528C-A1E94A5CF8_p_1672420924208%2C%2C%2C%2 C%2C70177057.

Lord_Whis. Comment on "The Walking Dead S09E15—The Calm Before—POST Episode Discussion." *Reddit*, 24 Mar. 2019, 8:35 p.m., www.reddit.com/r/thewalkingdead/comments/b54ylg/the_walking_dead_s09e15_the_calm_before_post/ejb985r.

@LordWay69. "So Princess in the walking dead is absolutely precious and imo they handled the topic of domestic abuse well. #TheWalkingDeadUK." *Twitter*, 22 Mar. 2021, 5:58 p.m., twitter.com/LordWay69/status/1374118352172552192.

Lunden, Jeff. "'Zimerican' Playwright Danai Gurira Brings African Stories to American Stages." *NPR*, 12 Mar. 2016, www.npr.org/2016/03/12/469220332/zimerican-playwright-danai-gurira-brings-african-stories-to-american-stages.

Lutz, John. "Zombies of the World, Unite: Class Struggle and Alienation in *Land of the Dead*." *The Philosophy of Horror*, edited by Thomas Fahy, UP of Kentucky, 2010, pp. 121–136. *Google Books*, books.google.com/books?hl=en&lr=&id=D9yrH1I488sC&oi=fnd&pg=PA121&ots=rTGT2A5YHy&sig=htl6tjx3rOc-J4Pr-4FiSgb_DqY#v=onepage&q&f=false.

Lynch, Jason. "Twitter's Top Shows." *Adweek*, vol. 57, no. 21, June 2016, p. 8. *EBSCOhost*, search.ebscohost.com/login.aspx?direct=true&db=buh&AN=116200607&site=eds-live&scope=site.

Maberry, Jonathan. "Take Me to Your Leader: Guiding the Masses Through the Apocalypse with a Cracked Moral Compass." *Triumph of The Walking Dead: Robert Kirkman's Zombie Epic on Page and Screen*, edited by James Lowder, Smart Pop, 2011, pp. 15–34.

@MamaDeadHead (Sara Large). "Princess is pansexual confirmed! Thanks Hollywood Bobby Kirks and @RyanOttley, I'm a very happy Princess fan today. My favorite comic..." *Twitter*, 26 July 2021, 6:19 p.m., twitter.com/mamadeadhead/status/1419784547433160704.

Mandanas, Laura. "The Walking Dead Brings Another Queer Chick Named Tara to TV, We Rejoice." *Autostraddle*, 23 Nov. 2013, www.autostraddle.com/the-walking-dead-brings-another-queer-chick-named-tara-to-tv-206820.

Manuel Krogstad, Jens. "Optimism Remains on Post-Apocalyptic 'Road.'" *Waterloo-Cedar Falls Courier* (IA), 15 Jan. 2010. *EBSCOhost*, proxy.myunion.edu/login?url=http://search.ebscohost.com/login.aspx?direct=true&db=nfh&AN=2W61801993972&site=eds-live&scope=site.

Maria_LaGuerta. Comment on "Fear the Walking Dead—1x01 'Pilot'—Post-episode discussion." *Reddit*, 25 Nov. 2015, 12:08 a.m., https://www.reddit.com/r/FearTheWalkingDead/comments/3i6aae/comment/cueqlra/?utm_source=share&utm_medium=web2x&context=3.

@TheMariahRamsey (Mariah Ramsey). "I know we were all worried about the Walking Dead once Rick was 'gone' but I think Michonne has it covered. She is powerful and fierce in this episode. #TheWalkingDead." *Twitter*, 11 Nov. 2018, 6:34 p.m., twitter.com/TheMariahRamsey/status/1061809537961861122.

Masenkoe. Comment on "S04E11 'Claimed' Episode Discussion." *Reddit*, 23 Feb. 2014, 7:54 p.m., www.reddit.com/r/thewalkingdead/comments/1yr14v/s04e11_claimed_episode_discussion/cfn26xm.

Mathews, Liam. "Half as Many People Watched *The Walking Dead* Season 9 Premiere as Season 8." *TV Guide*, CBS Interactive Inc., 09 Oct. 2018, www.tvguide.com/news/the-walking-dead-season-9-premiere-ratings-down.

McCarthy, Erin. "33 Fun Facts about *Buffy the Vampire Slayer*." *Mental Floss*, 10 Mar. 2018, www.mentalfloss.com/article/56496/33-fun-facts-about-buffy-vampire-slayer.

McKinney, Kelsey. "Why do all the Best Movie Villains have to be Men?" *Vox*, 29 May 2014, www.vox.com/2014/5/29/5761876/why-do-all-the-best-movie-villains-have-to-be-men.

McMahon, James. "How Angela Kang Resurrected 'The Walking Dead.'" *NME*, 20 Feb. 2022, www.nme.com/features/tv-interviews/angela-kang-the-walking-dead-interview-3162777.

Memmott, Carol. "Among the Walking Dead, Women Stand Tall." *The Toronto Star*, 15

Mar. 2013. *EBSCOhost*, proxy.myunion.edu/login?url=http://search.ebscohost.com/login.aspx?direct=true&db=edsgin&AN=edsgcl.322392862&site=eds-live&scope=site.

"Mercy." *The Walking Dead*, season 8, episode 1, AMC, 22 Oct. 2017. *Netflix*, www.netflix.com/watch/81022952?trackId=200257859.

MerryBandOfPricks. Comment on "The Walking Dead S09E5—What Comes After—POST Episode Discussion." *Reddit*, 5 Nov. 2018, 1:37 a.m., www.reddit.com/r/thewalkingdead/comments/9u9y0i/the_walking_dead_s09e5_what_comes_after_post/e933kgb.

Michaud, Maude. "Horror Grrrls: Feminist Horror Filmmakers and Agency." *Offscreen*, vol. 18, no. 6–7, July 2014, offscreen.com/view/horror-grrrls.

@MichelleTelles_. "FINALLY A LESBIAN COUPLE ON THE WALKING DEAD!!! Just saying. That's the only couple I support on this show! #TheWalkingDead." *Twitter*, 24 Nov. 2013, 8:00 p.m., twitter.com/MichelleTelles_/status/404821975962374144.

Molina-Guzman, Isabel. "Introduction: Mapping the Place of Latinas in the U.S. Media." *Dangerous Curves: Latina Bodies in the Media*, New York UP, 2010, pp. 1–21. *ProQuest Ebook Central*, ebookcentral-proquest-com.proxy.myunion.edu/lib/tui-ebooks/detail.action?docID=865695.

monsterlynn. Comment on "Diversity and gender roles in The Walking Dead." *Reddit*, 9 Mar. 2015, 3:35 p.m., www.reddit.com/r/thewalkingdead/comments/2yg0m1/diversity_and_gender_roles_in_the_walking_dead/cp9k1nc.

Moore, Trent. "*Tales of the Walking Dead* Turns the Franchise into an Ambitious, Mixed-Bag *Twilight Zone*." *Paste Magazine*, 11 Aug. 2022, www.pastemagazine.com/tv/amc/tales-of-the-walking-dead-review/.

Moran, Sarah. "The Walking Dead: Princess Twist Explained (What Does She Have?)." *ScreenRant*, 22 Mar. 2021, screenrant.com/walking-dead-princess-mental-health-twist-explained/.

Moran-Perez, Gillian. "A Timeline of Outbreaks from 2000 to Present." *Daily Sundial*, California State University Northridge, 13 Feb. 2020, sundial.csun.edu/156361/news/a-timeline-of-outbreaks-from-2000-to-present/.

Morris, Wesley, and James Poniewozik. "Why 'Diverse TV' Matters: It's Better TV. Discuss." *The New York Times*, 10 Feb. 2016, www.nytimes.com/2016/02/14/arts/television/smaller-screens-truer-colors.html.

Morrison, Andrew P. "Psychoanalysis and 'Necessary' Choices: The Shame of Soft Edges." *Gender and Psychoanalysis*, vol. 3, no. 4, 1998. *EBSCOhost*, proxy.myunion.edu/login?url=http://search.ebscohost.com/login.aspx?direct=true&db=pph&AN=GAP.003.0387A&site=eds-live&scope=site.

@ms_jespial. "I was worried about Enid as soon as she started training to be a doctor. Doctors on The Walking Dead never make it. #twd." *Twitter*, 24 Mar. 2019, 8:25 p.m., twitter.com/ms_jespial/status/1110004707815247873.

Mulvey, Laura. "Visual Pleasure and Narrative Cinema." *Film Manifestos and Global Cinema Cultures: A Critical Anthology*, by Scott MacKenzie, U of California P, 2014, pp. 359–369.

Murphy, Shaunna. "'The 100' Fans Got Angry about a Queer Woman's Death—and Created an LGBT Fandom Revolution." *Revelist*, 24 Mar. 2016, www.revelist.com/tv/the-100-fans-lexa-death/1109.

———. "'Walking Dead' Star Christian Serratos is Breaking Through Latina Stereotypes." *MTV News*, 4 Dec. 2015, www.mtv.com/news/2616108/christian-serratos-walking-dead-latina-stereotypes.

Murray, Noel. "'The Walking Dead': What Went Wrong and How They Can Fix the Show." *Rolling Stone*, 25 June 2018, www.rollingstone.com/tv-movies/tv-movie-news/the-walking-dead-what-the-hell-happened-to-this-show-627893/.

N8_the_almost_GR8. Comment on "The Walking Dead Episode Discussion S04E04 'Indifference.'" *Reddit*, 3 Nov. 2013, 7:05 p.m., www.reddit.com/r/thewalkingdead/comments/1puh34/the_walking_dead_episode_discussion_s04e04/cd66i8m.

nateday2. Comment on "Fear the Walking Dead—1x01 'Pilot'—Post-Episode Discussion." *Reddit*, 25 Nov. 2015, 5:39 a.m., https://www.reddit.com/r/FearTheWalkingDead/comments/3i6aae/comment/cuewkxl/?utm_source=reddit&utm_medium=web2x&context=3.

"Nebraska." *The Walking Dead*, season 5, episode 8, AMC, 12 Feb. 2012. *Netflix*, www.netflix.com/watch/70248468?trackId=254794450&tctx=4%2C0%2Ca8778421-b046-4705-9a82-88cfde6c7c8b-601075477%2C%2C%2C%2C%2C%2C%2C70177057

Neely, Anthony. "Girls, Guns, and Zombies: Five Dimensions of Teaching and Learning in The Walking Dead." *Dialogue: The Interdisciplinary Journal of Popular Culture and Pedagogy*, vol. 2, no. 1, 2014, journaldialogue.org/issues/issue-2/girls-guns-and-zombies-five-dimensions-of-teaching-and-learning-in-the-walking-dead.

"New Best Friends." *The Walking Dead*, season 7, episode 10, AMC, 19 Feb. 2017. *Netflix*, www.netflix.com/watch/80202484?trackId=200257859.

Ng, Philiana. "It's Official: AMC Orders 'the Walking Dead' Talk Show." *The Hollywood Reporter*, 22 Sep. 2011, www.hollywoodreporter.com/tv/tv-news/official-amc-orders-walking-dead-239170/.

NIDA. "50 Years After Founding, NIDA Urges Following Science to Move Beyond Stigma." *National Institute on Drug Abuse*, 1 Feb. 2024, https://nida.nih.gov/about-nida/noras-blog/2024/02/50-years-after-founding-nida-urges-following-science-to-move-beyond-stigma.

———. "What is the Scope of Heroin Use in the United States?" *National Institute on Drug Abuse*, 14 Dec. 2023, https://nida.nih.gov/publications/research-reports/heroin/scope-heroin-use-in-united-states.

Nilles, Billy. "Why It Took 10 Years for *Zombieland* to Roar Back to Life." *E Online*, 17 Oct. 2019, www.eonline.com/news/1083602/why-it-took-10-years-for-zombieland-to-roar-back-to-life.

"No Sanctuary." *The Walking Dead*, season 5, episode 1, AMC, 12 Oct. 2014. *Netflix*, www.netflix.com/watch/80010527?trackId=14170289&tctx=2%2C0%2Cad570025-2d82-4bfb-87e7-28fc4b8bad8c-1031895645%2CNES_0641F46592C38FACD47EE2A0D7C9E5-994911DC4F528C-02E0AF576B_p_1672352192750%2CNES_0641F46592C38FACD47EE2A0D7C9E5_p_1672352192750%2C%2C%2C%2C%2C70177057.

"No Way Out." *The Walking Dead*, season 9, episode 6, AMC, 14 Feb. 2016. *Netflix*, www.netflix.com/watch/80031926?trackId=14170289&tctx=2%2C0%2Cad570025-2d82-4bfb-87e7-28fc4b8bad8c-1031895645%2CNES_0641F46592C38FACD47EE2A0D7C9E5-994911DC4F528C-02E0AF576B_p_1672352192750%2CNES_0641F46592C38FACD47EE2A0D7C9E5_p_1672352192750%2C%2C%2C%2C%2C70177057.

"Not Tomorrow Yet." *The Walking Dead*, season 6, episode 12, AMC, 6 Mar. 2016. *Netflix*, www.netflix.com/watch/80031929?trackId=200257859.

Nurgus. Comment on "The Walking Dead S09E06—Who Are You Now?—Post Episode Discussion." *Reddit*, 12 Nov. 2018, 7:23 p.m., www.reddit.com/r/thewalkingdead/comments/9wac44/the_walking_dead_s09e06_who_are_you_now_post/e9j9e96.

O'Dell, Johnny. "AMC Updates Release Date Timelines on Walking Dead, Fear, World Beyond." *Skybound*, 5 May 2020, www.skybound.com/shows/the-walking-dead/amc-updates-release-date-timelines-on-walking-dead-fear-world-beyond.

———. "The Walking Dead Season 9 Character Power Rankings: Week Six." *Skybound Entertainment*, 14 Nov. 2018, www.skybound.com/shows/the-walking-dead/the-walking-dead-season-9-character-power-rankings-week-six.

Ogg, Jon C. "Zombies Worth Over $5 Billion to Economy." *NBC News*, 31 Oct. 2011, www.nbcnews.com/id/45079546/ns/business-stocks_and_economy/t/zombies-worth-over-billion-economy/#.XHYBAIhKiUk.

Oliver, Bobby. "The #MeToo Hashtag has Taken Over Social Media. Here's Why." *NJ.com*, Advance Local Media LLC, 16 Oct. 2017, www.nj.com/entertainment/index.ssf/2017/10/me_too_metoo_alyssa_milano_sexual_assault.html.

"Omega." *The Walking Dead*, season 9, episode 10, AMC, 17 Feb. 2019. *Netflix*, www.netflix.com/watch/81026626?trackId=200257859.

"Open Your Eyes." *The Walking Dead*, season 10, episode 7, AMC, 17 Nov. 2019. *Netflix*, https://www.netflix.com/watch/81071685?trackId=255824129&tctx=0%2C0%2C389bfa80-4acc-46d0-9833-17b4c7e42012-3031362%2C389bfa80-4acc-46d0-9833-17b4c7e42012-3031362%7C2%2C%2C%2C%2C%2C70177057%2CVideo%3A81071685%2CdetailsPageEpisodePlayButton.

Opie, David. "The Walking Dead Timeline: Here's How to Watch The Walking Dead Universe in Chronological Order." *Digital Spy*, 22 Jan. 2024, https://www.digitalspy.com/tv/ustv/a38234901/walking-dead-timeline-chronological-order/

———. "World Beyond's Finale Changes The Walking Dead Universe Forever." *Digital Spy*, 6 Dec. 2021, www.digitalspy.com/tv/ustv/a38384796/walking-dead-world-beyond-finale-post-credits/.

orangejillius. Comment on "Rick's reaction to Lori's death." *Reddit*, 5 Nov. 2012, 11:46 p.m., www.reddit.com/r/thewalkingdead/comments/12oyrf/comment/c6x3qta/?utm_source=share&utm_medium=web2x&context=3.

oreides. Comment on "The Walking Dead S09E15—The Calm Before—POST Episode Discussion." *Reddit*, 24 Mar. 2019, 11:15 p.m., www.reddit.com/r/thewalkingdead/comments/b54ylg/the_walking_dead_s09e15_the_calm_before_post/ejbj2e4.

@OscarRamo_ (Oscar Ramo). "I was so impressed with the walking dead doing such a big time jump at mid season and it was the perfect opportunity for new characters, relationships, fights, children ...." *Twitter*, 11 Nov. 2018, 8:26 p.m., twitter.com/OscarRamo_/status/1061825134326136832.

"The Other Side." *The Walking Dead*, season 7, episode 14, AMC, 19 Mar. 2017. *Netflix*, www.netflix.com/watch/80202488?trackId=200257859.

oursistheendgame. Comment on "The Walking Dead S09E12—Guardians—POST Episode Discussion." *Reddit*, 3 Mar. 2019, 8:27 p.m., www.reddit.com/r/thewalkingdead/comments/ax250x/the_walking_dead_s09e12_guardians_post_episode/ehqswgn.

paigeap2513. Comment on "The Walking Dead S10E03—Ghosts—Post-Episode Discussion." *Reddit*, 29 Oct. 2019, 10:11 p.m., www.reddit.com/r/thewalkingdead/comments/dktian/comment/f4jpjpk/?utm_source=share&utm_medium=web2x&context=3.

Paffenroth, Kim. "'For Love Is Strong as Death' Redeeming Values in *The Walking Dead*." *Triumph of The Walking Dead: Robert Kirkman's Zombie Epic on Page and Screen*, edited by James Lowder, Smart Pop, 2011, pp. 218–232.

"Paris Sera Toujours Paris." *The Walking Dead: Daryl Dixon*, season 1, episode 3, AMC, 24 Sep. 2023. *Amazon Prime*, https://www.amazon.com/gp/video/detail/B0C9T2ZGJ7/ref=atv_hm_hom_c_lZOsi7_2_3?jic=8%7CEgNhbGw%3D.

Parker, Kim, and Rachel Minkin. "Public Has Mixed Views on the Modern American Family." *Pew Research Center*, 14 Sep. 2023, https://www.pewresearch.org/social-trends/2023/09/14/public-has-mixed-views-on-the-modern-american-family/.

Pasztor, Sabrina K., and Jenny Ungbha Korn. "Zombie Fans, Second Screen, and Television Audiences: Redefining Parasociality as Technoprosociality in AMC's #Talking Dead." *Television, Social Media, and Fan Culture*, edited by Alison Slade et al., Lexington Books, 2017, pp. 183–200.

Patterson, Natasha. "Cannibalizing Gender and Genre: A Feminist Re-Vision of George Romero's Zombie Films." *Zombie Culture Autopsies of the Living Dead*, edited by Shawn McIntosh and Marc Leverette, Scarecrow Press, 2008, pp. 103–118.

Pearce, Tilly. "The Walking Dead Casts Gender-Fluid Actor Nico Tortorella for New Spin-Off." *Metro*, 6 Aug. 2019, metro.co.uk/2019/08/06/walking-dead-casts-gender-fluid-actor-nico-tortorella-new-spin-off-10525730/?ito=cbshare.

Pearson, Roberta. "Fandom in the Digital Era." *Popular Communication*, vol. 8, no. 1, 2010, pp. 84–95. doi:10.1080/15405700903502346.

Pelletiere, Nicole. "'Walking Dead' Star Opens up on Being First Deaf Actor in Series' History." *Good Morning America*, The Walt Disney Company, 8 Feb. 2019, www.goodmorningamerica.com/culture/story/walking-dead-star-lauren-ridloff-talks-deaf-actor-60853480.

@percysgrant. "and the fact that they mentioned non binary people, yeah, i love this show." *Twitter*, 05 Oct. 2023, 5:05 p.m., https://twitter.com/percysgrant/status/1710038612337737982

@perez_wilmer4 (Wilmer Perez). "The Walking Dead tonight was amazing. The excitement, the thrill, and the action. Carol and Rick are bad to the bone! #TheWalkingDead." *Twitter*, 12 Oct. 2014, 10:26 p.m., twitter.com/perez_wilmer4/status/521517237531074560.

pheakelmatters. Comment on "The Walking Dead S09E06—Who Are You Now?—LIVE

Episode Discussion." *Reddit*, 11 Nov. 2018, 7:37 p.m., www.reddit.com/r/thewalkingdead/comments/9w9sf3/the_walking_dead_s09e06_who_are_you_now_live/e9j3f0j.

Phillips, Adam. "Keeping It Moving: Commentary on Judith Butler's 'Melancholy Gender—Refused Identification.'" *Psychoanalytic Dialogues*, vol. 5, no. 2, 1995, pp. 181–188. *EBSCOhost*, proxy.myunion.edu/login?url=http://search.ebscohost.com/login.aspx?direct=true&db=pph&AN=PD.005.0181A&site=eds-live&scope=site.

"Pilot." *Fear the Walking Dead*, season 1, episode 1, AMC, 23 Aug. 2015. *Amazon Prime*, https://www.amazon.com/gp/video/detail/B0112SZHC4/ref=atv_dl_rdr?deepLinking Redirect=1&autoplay=1.

"Pilot." *Supernatural*, season 1, episode 1, The WB, 13 Sep. 2005. *Netflix*, www.netflix.com/watch/70223016?trackId=255824129.

@pixiegigs. "Last ep. of Walking Dead was brilliant! If I was one of those women though, I'd just refuse to work unless the men started. #thewalkingdead." *Twitter*, 16 Nov. 2010, 5:41 p.m., twitter.com/pixiegigs/status/4710802846130176.

PlamiAG. Comment on "The Walking Dead World Beyond—01x02 'The Blaze of Glory'—AMC Premiere Discussion." *Reddit*, 09 Oct. 2020, 8:27 p.m., https://www.reddit.com/r/TWDWorldBeyond/comments/j78h4g/comment/g89q1g2/?utm_source=share&utm_medium=web2x&context=3.

Platts, Todd K. "From White Zombies to Night Zombies and Beyond: The Evolution of the Zombie in Western Popular Culture." *The Supernatural Revamped: From Timeworn Legends to Twenty-First-Century Chic*, edited by Barbara Brodman and James E. Doan, Fairleigh Dickinson University Press, 2016, pp. 219–235. *EBSCOhost*, search.ebscohost.com/login.aspx?direct=true&db=mzh&AN=2016393443&site=eds-live&scope=site.

_____. "Locating Zombies in the Sociology of Popular Culture." *Sociology Compass*, vol. 7, no. 7, July 2013, pp. 547–560. *EBSCOhost*, doi:10.111/soc4.12053.

possiblyhysterical. Comment on "The Walking Dead Episode Discussion S04E04 'Indifference.'" *Reddit*, 3 Nov. 2013, 8:16 p.m., www.reddit.com/r/thewalkingdead/comments/1puh34/the_walking_dead_episode_discussion_s04e04/cdd2m59.

Press, Joy. "Introduction." *Stealing the Show: How Women Are Revolutionizing Television*, Atria Books, 2018, pp. 1–15.

"Pretty Much Dead Already." *The Walking Dead*, season 2, episode 7, AMC, 27 Nov. 2011. *Netflix*, www.netflix.com/watch/70248467?trackId=14170289&tctx=2%2C0%-2Cba70fdc6-5438-4bd4-913d-10f64bbbe30f-1178192225%2CNES_0641F46592C38FAC D47EE2A0D7C9E5-994911DC4F528C-A1E94A5CF8_p_1672420924208%2C%2C%2C %2C%2C70177057.

Proctor, William. "Interrogating *The Walking Dead*: Adaptation, Transmediality, and the Zombie Matrix." *Remake Television: Reboot, Re-Use, Recycle*, edited by Carlen Lavigne, Lexington Books, 2014, pp. 5–20. *EBSCOhost*, https://search-ebscohost-com.ezproxy.snhu.edu/login.aspx?direct=true&db=nlebk&AN=710115&site=eds-live&scope=site.

@ProfessorF. "I didn't hate, but I didn't really like the latest #TheWakingDead. It seems like they're trying too hard to force diversity into the show, and all I want is a good old ...." *Twitter*, 11 Nov. 2018, 9:35 p.m., twitter.com/ProfessorF/status/1061839862263738368.

Prudom, Laura. "You Can Be Mad about That 'Walking Dead' Death, but You Shouldn't Be Surprised." *Mashable*, 24 Oct. 2016, mashable.com/2016/10/24/the-walking-dead-glenn-death-fans-quit.

Pruitt, Sarah. "How Gay Culture Blossomed During the Roaring Twenties." *History*, A&E Television Networks, 12 June 2019, https://www.history.com/news/gay-culture-roaring-twenties-prohibition.

Pugh, Catherine. "'We Ain't Ashes': Daryl, Carol and the Burning Away of Traditional Gender Roles." *The Politics of Race, Gender and Sexuality in* The Walking Dead: *Essays on the Television Series and Comics*, edited by Elizabeth Erwin and Dawn Keetley, McFarland, 2018, pp. 93–107. Contributions to Zombie Studies.

Pye, Danee and Peter P. O'Sullivan. "Dead _____ Party." *The Walking Dead and Philosophy: Zombie Apocalypse Now*, edited by Wayne Yuen, Open Court, 2013, pp. 107–116.

Quanster. Comment on "Paloma in HBO's The Walking Dead: Daryl Dixon." *Reddit*, 14

Nov. 2023, 4:44 p.m., https://www.reddit.com/r/rupaulsdragrace/comments/17vc1zw/comment/k99q6sv/?utm_source=share&utm_medium=web3x&utm_name=web3xcss&utm_term=1&utm_content=share_button.

quinnies. Comment on "Gabriel and Rosita." *Reddit*, 2 Oct. 2022, 12:46 p.m., www.reddit.com/r/thewalkingdead/comments/xtokv4/comment/iqrpf5s/.

Ramos, Alexandra. "The Walking Dead's Rick and Michonne Series: 5 Things We Know about the Upcoming Spinoff." *Cinemablend*, Future US, 7 Aug. 2022, www.cinemablend.com/television/the-walking-deads-rick-and-michonne-series-things-we-know-about-the-upcoming-spinoff.

Raquel. "Nicolas Cantu Talks 'The Walking Dead: World Beyond' and Latin Representation." *Fangirlish*, 6 Nov. 2021, fangirlish.com/2021/08/12/nicolas-cantu-talks-the-walking-dead-world-beyond-and-latin-representation/.

ravialioh. Comment on "Gabriel and Rosita." *Reddit*, 02 Oct. 2022, 12:14 p.m., www.reddit.com/r/thewalkingdead/comments/xtokv4/comment/iqrkg9n/?utm_source=share&utm_medium=web2x&context=3.

Reed, Cindy N. "From One First Lady to Another: The Speculative Worlds of Michelle Obama and *The Walking Dead*'s Michonne." *Women & Language*, vol. 40, no. 1, Winter2017/2018, pp. 67–82. *EBSCOhost*, search.ebscohost.com/login.aspx?direct=true&AuthType=ip,shib&db=lkh&AN=130764004&site=eds-live&scope=site.

Reich, Adrienne Cecile. "Compulsory Heterosexuality and Lesbian Existence (1980)." *Journal of Women's History*, vol. 15, no. 3, Autumn 2003, pp. 11–48. *EBSCOhost*, doi:10.1353/jowh.2003.0079.

"Remember." *The Walking Dead*, season 5, episode 12, AMC, 1 Mar. 2015. *Netflix*, www.netflix.com/watch/80010538?trackId=200257859.

Resident Evil. Dir. by Paul W.S. Anderson. 2002. Columbia TriStar Home Entertainment, 2003. DVD.

"Rest In Peace." *The Walking Dead*, season 11, episode 24, AMC, 20 Nov. 2022. *Amazon Prime*, www.amazon.com/Rest-in-Peace/dp/B09HYY3967/ref=sr_1_1?keywords=the+walking+dead+season+11&qid=1671912101&s=instant-video&sprefix=the+walking%-2Cinstant-video%2C135&sr=1-1.

Rick K. "5 Awesome Movies Ruined by Last–Minute Changes." *Cracked*, Scripps, 23 May 2008, www.cracked.com/article_16258_5-awesome-movies-ruined-by-last-minute-changes.html.

@RickAndThangs. "Thoughts on 9x06: Judith is incredible. Scarol is back. The newcomers are such talented actors and very reminiscent of those in the first few seasons. Representation …." *Twitter*, 11 Nov. 2018, 8:32 p.m., twitter.com/RickAndThangs/status/1061824078171029504.

Rinaldi, Jen. "What Feminism has to Say about World War Z." *Braaaiiinnnsss!: From Academics to Zombies*, edited by Robert J. Smith?, U of Ottawa P, 2011, pp. 9–19.

"Robert Kirkman's The Walking Dead Panel New York Comic Con 2015 ft. Dan Casey." *YouTube*, uploaded by Skybound, 09 Oct. 2015, www.youtube.com/watch?v=8HADQrPtxbM.

@RobertKirkman (Robert Kirkman). "First, the mentioned tweet is months old and it's been deleted! Second, it was a joke! I would never reveal something like this in a tweet!" *Twitter*, 24 Apr. 2020, 5:33 p.m., twitter.com/RobertKirkman/status/1253799212820512768.

Rodriguez, Edgary. "Buffy the Vampire Slayer: 10 Hidden Details about Sunnydale High You Never Noticed." *ScreenRant*, 19 May 2020, screenrant.com/buffy-the-vampire-slayer-sunnydale-high-details/.

@RogerSanchez11 (Roger Sanchez). "Well that was an absolutely insane episode of The Walking Dead. Carol took it to a whole new level! #TWD—watching The Walking Dead." *Twitter*, 18 Oct. 2015, 8:30 p.m., twitter.com/RogerSanchez11/status/65593389063183232.

Rose, Frank. "The Remarkable Narrative Life of the Walking Dead." *Strategy+Business*, 26 July 2021, www.strategy-business.com/article/The-remarkable-narrative-life-of-The-Walking-Dead.

Ross, Dalton. "Christian Serratos Asked for That Rosita 'Walking Dead' Finale Fate." *EW.com*, 20 Nov. 2022, ew.com/tv/walking-dead-rosita-death-christian-serratos-finale-interview/?utm_source=emailshare&utm_medium=email&utm_campaign=email-share-article&utm_content=20221227.

_____. "'The Walking Dead' Showrunner on That Big Princess Twist." *EW.com*, 21 Mar. 2021, ew.com/tv/walking-dead-princess-angela-kang-showrunner-splinter/.

Rothenberg, Jason. "The Life and Death of Lexa." *Medium*, 24 Mar. 2016, medium.com/@jrothenberg/the-life-and-death-of-lexa-e461224be1db.

Routledge, Clay. "Finding Your Purpose in the Zombie Apocalypse." *The Walking Dead Psychology: Psych of the Living Dead*. Edited by Travis Langley, Sterling, 2015, pp. 246–256.

Rowles, Dustin. "Here's the Single Greatest Decision 'The Walking Dead' Has Ever Made." *UPROXX*, 31 Mar. 2015, uproxx.com/tv/the-walking-dead-decision.

Rys, Richard. "*The Walking Dead* Recap: The Widow Rhee." *Vulture*, 25 Mar. 2018, www.vulture.com/2018/03/the-walking-dead-recap-season-8-episode-13.html.

sabatoa. Comment on "The Walking Dead premiered nine years ago today with the episode Days Gone Bye." *Reddit*, 13 Oct. 2019, 11:48 a.m., www.reddit.com/r/thewalkingdead/comments/dpndgv/comment/f5x896l/?utm_source=share&utm_medium=web2x&context=3.

St. James, Emily. "The Walking Dead's Been Popular for Years. Now It's Also Good." *Vox*, 7 Nov. 2014, www.vox.com/2014/11/7/7172683/the-walking-dead.

"The Same Boat." *The Walking Dead*, season 6, episode 13, AMC, 13 Mar. 2016. *Netflix*, www.netflix.com/watch/80031930?trackId=14170289&tctx=0%2C12%2C696269ee-285c-44a8-bf39-d940aeec0ea4-104200458%2Cd8642ad8-9ca2-4b37-8b80-3ce9b56618ad_132617310X3XX1578687614793%2Cd8642ad8-9ca2-4b37-8b80-3ce9b56618ad_ROOT.

Sandvoss, Cornel. "The Death of the Reader? Literary Theory and the Study of Texts in Popular Culture." *The Fan Fiction Studies Reader*, edited by Karen Hellekson, and Kristina Busse, U of Iowa P, 2014, pp. 61–74. *ProQuest Ebook Central*, ebookcentral.proquest.com.proxy.myunion.edu/lib/tui-ebooks/detail.action?docID=1629507.

SauronOMordor. Comment on "The Walking Dead S09E15—The Calm Before—POST Episode Discussion." *Reddit*, 25 Mar. 2019, 6:03 a.m., www.reddit.com/r/thewalkingdead/comments/b54ylg/the_walking_dead_s09e15_the_calm_before_post/ejbk6hu.

"Say the Word." *The Walking Dead*, season 3, episode 4, AMC, 11 Nov. 2012. *Netflix*, www.netflix.com/watch/70260051?trackId=14277283&tctx=0%2C4%2C044af544-22bc-4ac6-a8c4-dee08b145b62-51769303.

"Scars." *The Walking Dead*, season 9, episode 14, AMC, 17 Mar. 2019. *Netflix*, www.netflix.com/watch/81026630?trackId=200257859.

Schlozman, Steven. "Feel Better? The Uncaring Science of *The Walking Dead*." *Triumph of the Walking Dead: Robert Kirkman's Zombie Epic on Page and Screen*, edited by James Lowder, BenBella Books, 2011, pp. 160–172.

Schwartz, Terri. "Zombieland: Full List of Columbus's (Official) Rules for Surviving the Zombie Apocalypse." *IGN*, 18 Oct. 2019, www.ign.com/articles/2019/10/18/zombieland-rules-full-list-columbus-official-and-deleted-scenes.

Scoo. Comment on "Episode Discussion: S02E05, "Chupacabra" (Spoilers)." *Reddit*, 13 Nov. 2011, 8:18 p.m., www.reddit.com/r/thewalkingdead/comments/mb7e3/episode_discussion_s02e05_chupacabra_spoilers/c2zkwh7.

sebrebc. Comment on "The Walking Dead World Beyond—01x01 'Brave'—Episode Discussion." *Reddit*, 03 Oct. 2020, 8:20 p.m., https://www.reddit.com/r/TWDWorldBeyond/comments/j3hlqh/comment/g7l0mgn/?utm_source=share&utm_medium=web2x&context=3.

"Self Help." *The Walking Dead*, season 5, episode 5, AMC, 9 Nov. 2014. *Netflix*, www.netflix.com/watch/80010531?trackId=14170289&tctx=0%2C4%2C1114d88a-3034-4637-a370-57b603cad349-75438657%2Cd441a338-27aa-47f4-bca5-db2b0f1010e6_79901931X3XX1580951865852%2Cd441a338-27aa-47f4-bca5-db2b0f1010e6_ROOT.

@sempiternal_kat. "they have a gay couple on the walking dead and I think its wonderful. yay for twd. @WalkingDead_AMC #TheWalkingDead." *Twitter*, 24 Nov. 2013, 7:16 p.m., twitter.com/sempiternal_kat/status/404810716764327936.

seneris. Comment on "The Walking Dead S09E12—Guardians—POST Episode Discussion." *Reddit*, 4 Mar. 2019, 4:25 a.m., www.reddit.com/r/thewalkingdead/comments/ax250x/the_walking_dead_s09e12_guardians_post_episode/ehrdv8f.

THE-73est. Comment on "Diversity and gender roles in The Walking Dead." *Reddit*, 09 Mar. 2015, 8:30 p.m., www.reddit.com/r/thewalkingdead/comments/2yg0m1/diversity_and_gender_roles_in_the_walking_dead/cp9umly.

@shannonstacey (Shannon Stacey). "Princess is the best thing to happen to The Walking Dead in a long time. I love her." *Twitter*, 21 Mar. 2021, 10:16 p.m., twitter.com/shannonstacey/status/1373820858016350208.

@Shudder. "The first generation to come-of-age in the apocalypse as we know it..." *Twitter*, 20 Jan. 2011, 11:05 a.m., twitter.com/Shudder/status/1351923884711407617.

"Sick." *The Walking Dead*, season 3, episode 2, AMC, 21 Oct. 2012. *Netflix*, www.netflix.com/watch/70260048?trackId=200257859.

sick-asfrick. Comment on "The Walking Dead S09E11—Bounty—POST Episode Discussion." *Reddit*, 25 Feb. 2019, 1:27 a.m., www.reddit.com/r/thewalkingdead/comments/aug55a/the_walking_dead_s09e11_bounty_post_episode/eh8f78n.

"Silence the Whisperers." *The Walking Dead*, season 10, episode 4, AMC, 27 Oct. 2019. *Netflix*, www.netflix.com/watch/81071682?trackId=14170289&tctx=2%2C0%2Cba70fdc6-5438-4bd4-913d-10f64bbbe30f-1178192225%2CNES_0641F46592C38FACD47EE2A0D7C9E5-994911DC4F528C-A1E94A5CF8_p_1672420924208%2C%2C%2C%2C%2C70177057.

Silverman, Riley. "Immortal LGBT Characters is Not the Solution to 'Bury Your Gays.'" *SYFY WIRE*, 3 Sep. 2019, www.syfy.com/syfywire/immortal-lgbt-characters-is-not-the-solution-to-bury-your-gays.

SirBamboozled. Comment on "The Walking Dead S09E02—The Bridge—Post Episode Discussion." *Reddit*, 15 Oct. 2018, 2:32 a.m., www.reddit.com/r/thewalkingdead/comments/9o8kd5/the_walking_dead_s09e02_the_bridge_post_episode/e7sph6g.

"6.4 Self-Disclosure and Interpersonal Communication." *Communication in the Real World: An Introduction to Communication Studies.* e-book ed., University of Minnesota Libraries Publishing, 2016.

"Slabtown." *The Walking Dead*, season 5, episode 5, AMC, 2 Nov. 2014. *Netflix*, www.netflix.com/watch/80010530?trackId=255824129&tctx=0%2C0%2CNAPA%40%40%-7Cde1f8e9f-6de3-4778-814d-99f7e157fd5c-2988248_titles%2F1%2F%2Fthe%20walking%20dead%2F0%2F0%2CNAPA%40%40%7Cde1f8e9f-6de3-4778-814d-99f7e157fd5c-2988248_titles%2F1%2F%2Fthe%20walking%20dead%2F0%2C%2C%2Cde1f8e9f-6de3-4778-814d-99f7e157fd5c-2988248%7C1%2C%2C70177057.

Sleuth1ngSloth. Comment on "Do you guys like Rick and Michonne together? I'm not feeling it really..." *Reddit*, 29 Oct. 2016, 1:46 a.m., www.reddit.com/r/thewalkingdead/comments/5a4q17/do_you_guys_like_rick_and_michonne_together_im/d9dqrhi.

Smith, Justine. "Dawn of the Dead Had an Alternate Ending That's Even Bleaker than the Original." *Little White Lies*, 31 Aug. 2018, lwlies.com/articles/dawn-of-the-dead-alternate-ending.

Snarker, Dorothy. "Bury Your Gays: Why 'The 100,' 'Walking Dead' Deaths Are Problematic (Guest Column)." *The Hollywood Reporter*, 21 Mar. 2016, www.hollywoodreporter.com/live-feed/bury-your-gays-why-100-877176.

"Splinter." *The Walking Dead*, season 10, episode 20, AMC, 21 Mar. 2021. *Netflix*, www.netflix.com/watch/81403751?trackId=14170289&tctx=2%2C0%2Cba70fdc6-5438-4bd4-913d-10f64bbbe30f-1178192225%2CNES_0641F46592C38FACD47EE2A0D7C9E5-994911DC4F528C-A1E94A5CF8_p_1672420924208%2C%2C%2C%2C%2C70177057.

@spntwt. "never did i think i'd see daryl dixon in the same room as a drag queen." *X*, 24 Sep.2023, 10:45pm, https://x.com/spntwt/status/1706122661099983341?s=20.

"Squeeze." *The Walking Dead*, season 10, episode 9, AMC, 23 Feb. 2020. *Netflix*, www.

netflix.com/watch/81071687?trackId=14170289&tctx=2%2C0%2Cba70fdc6-5438-4bd4-913d-10f64bbbe30f-1178192225%2CNES_0641F46592C38FACD47EE2A0D7C9E5-994911DC4F528C-A1E94A5CF8_p_1672420924208%2C%2C%2C%2C%2C70177057.

"Stalker." *The Walking Dead*, season 10, episode 10, AMC, 1 Mar. 2020. *Netflix*, www.netflix.com/watch/81071688?trackId=14170289&tctx=2%2C0%2Cba70fdc6-5438-4bd4-913d-10f64bbbe30f-1178192225%2CNES_0641F46592C38FACD47EE2A0D7C9E5-994911DC4F528C-A1E94A5CF8_p_1672420924208%2C%2C%2C%2C%2C70177057.

Stanaway, Cailtin. "The Stages of Grief: Accepting the Unacceptable." *Counseling Center*, University of Washington, 8 June 2020, www.washington.edu/counseling/2020/06/08/the-stages-of-grief-accepting-the-unacceptable/.

@StarryMag. "Eugene is a part-time scientist and full time Nanny to Rosita's baby. Between him, Siddiq and Father Gabe, we've got a Three Men and Baby…" *Twitter*, 06 Oct. 2019, 9:29 p.m., twitter.com/StarryMag/status/1181018569154412544.

Steiger, Kay. "No Clean Slate: Unshakable Race and Gender Politics in *The Walking Dead*." *Triumph of the Walking Dead: Robert Kirkman's Zombie Epic on Page and Screen*, edited by James Lowder, BenBella Books, 2011, pp. 99–114.

@StephRoyalty (Steph Royalty). I've finally caught up on the walking dead. and I can't believe Rosita is messing with the priest…. Saadiq is so fine chileeee #TheWalkingDead." *Twitter*, 06 Oct. 2019, 3:41 p.m., twitter.com/StephRoyalty/status/1180931018024538113.

"Strangers." *The Walking Dead*, season 5, episode 2, AMC, 19 Oct. 2014. *Netflix*, www.netflix.com/watch/80010528?trackId=14170289&tctx=0%2C1%2Cebbc0118-56f3-4191-bda5-a2e6d51710a2-544408524%2Cb0a2d15f-b932-4e86-b52a-7936aba359e8_117353771X3XX1580838222560%2Cb0a2d15f-b932-4e86-b52a-7936aba359e8_ROOT.

Sugg, Katherine. "*The Walking Dead*: Late Liberalism and Masculine Subjection in Apocalypse Fictions." *Journal of American Studies*, no. 4, 2015, pp. 793–811. *EBSCOhost*, search.ebscohost.com/login.aspx?direct=true&db=edsgao&AN=edsgcl.440692773&site=eds–live&scope=site.

superzepto. Comment on "Explain what is good about Michonne (other than being 'bad ass')." *Reddit*, 26 Mar. 2012, 6:28 p.m., www.reddit.com/r/thewalkingdead/comments/rejfp/comment/c458set/?utm_source=share&utm_medium=web2x&context=3.

Tabrys, Jason. "How Carol Evolved from Outcast to Unkillable Badass in 'The Walking Dead' Season 5." *UPROXX*, 1 Apr. 2015, uproxx.com/tv/carol–the–walking–dead/.

"Tales of the Walking Dead—TV Episode Recaps & News." *Vulture*, 4 Sep. 2022, www.vulture.com/tv/tales-of-the-walking-dead/.

Tanswell, Adam. "Nico Tortorella on Diversity, Inclusion and 'The World Beyond.'" *Golden Globes*, 13 Mar. 2021, www.goldenglobes.com/articles/nico-tortorella-diversity-inclusion-and-world-beyond.

TardsRunThisAsylum. Comment on "The Walking Dead S09E14—SCARS—POST Episode Discussion." *Reddit*, 19 Mar. 2019, 11:42 a.m., www.reddit.com/r/thewalkingdead/comments/b28hbs/the_walking_dead_s09e14_scars_post_episode/eiw791c.

Tassi, Paul. "There's Only One Character On 'The Walking Dead' The Creator Says He Wouldn't Kill." *Forbes*, 18 Oct. 2015, www.forbes.com/sites/insertcoin/2015/10/18/theres-only-one-character-on-the-walking-dead-the-creator-says-he-wouldnt-kill/#102e7277b695.

Taylor, Amanda. "Love and Marriage in the Time of *The Walking Dead*." *Romancing the Zombie: Essays on the Undead as Significant "Other*," edited by Ashley Szanter and Richards Jessica K., McFarland, 2017, pp. 72–88. Contributions to Zombie Studies.

Taylor, Devon. "Robert Kirkman Says 'Walking Dead' Show and Comic Will Have Different Endings." *Goliath*, 30 Sep. 2016, www.goliath.com/tv/robert-kirkman-says-walking-dead-show-and-comic-will-have-different-endings/.

"Tell it to the Frogs." *The Walking Dead*, season 1, episode 2, AMC, 14 Nov. 2010. *Netflix*, www.netflix.com/watch/70210889?trackId=200257859.

Tenga, Angela, and Jonathan Bassett. "'You Kill or You Die, or You Die and You Kill':

Meaning and Violence in AMC's *The Walking Dead*." *Journal of Popular Culture*, no. 6, 2016, pp. 1280–1300. *EBSCOhost*, doi:10.1111/jpcu.12488.

@tessa. "Paola Lazaro, who plays Princess on The Walking Dead is becoming my favorite actor ever!!! She's incredible!" *Twitter*, 22 Mar. 2021, 11:23 p.m., twitter.com/tessa99778491/status/1374200009294409734.

Teurlings, Jan. "Social Media and the New Commons of TV Criticism." *Television & New Media*, vol. 19, no. 3, Mar. 2018, pp. 208–224. *EBSCOhost*, doi:10.1177/1527476417709599.

ThatChubbyGay. Comment on "The Walking Dead: Daryl Dixon S01E03—Paris Sera Toujours Paris—Episode Discussion." *Reddit*, 25 Sep. 2023, 2:25 p.m., https://www.reddit.com/r/thewalkingdead/comments/16rdxxt/comment/k2654jo/?utm_source=share&utm_medium=web3x&utm_name=web3xcss&utm_term=1&utm_content=share_button.

_____. Comment on Comment on "The Walking Dead: Daryl Dixon S01E03—Paris Sera Toujours Paris—Episode Discussion." *Reddit*, 26 Sep. 2:07 p.m., https://www.reddit.com/r/thewalkingdead/comments/16rdxxt/comment/k2bdspl/?utm_source=share&utm_medium=web3x&utm_name=web3xcss&utm_term=1&utm_content=share_button.

"30 Days Without an Accident." *The Walking Dead*, season 4, episode 1, AMC, 13 Oct. 2013. *Netflix*, https://www.netflix.com/watch/70297524?trackId=255824129&tctx-=0%2C0%2C389bfa80-4acc-46d0-9833-17b4c7e42012-3031362%2C389bfa80-4acc-46d0-9833-17b4c7e42012-3031362%7C2%2C%2C%2C%2C%2C70177057%2CVideo%3A70297524%2CdetailsPageEpisodePlayButton.

@TinaMarieSa. "We're watching The Walking Dead. I have no idea what's going on, but I dig Princess' whole vibe. This is the emotionally unstable Puerto..." *Twitter*, 21 Mar. 2021, 10:00 p.m., twitter.com/TinaMarieSa/status/1373816765990440960.

"Too Far Gone." *The Walking Dead*, season 4, episode 8, AMC, 30 Nov. 2013. *Netflix*, www.netflix.com/watch/70297531?trackId=14170289&tctx=0%2C7%2C9356b49c-de6c-452e-a278-38f8e8b30d8d-74928387%2C5771f3ef-4997-4241-96f2-d2cde7dd3c3e_128073986X3XX1579634812366%2C5771f3ef-4997-4241-96f2-d2cde7dd3c3e_ROOT.

"The Tower." *The Walking Dead*, season 10, episode 15, AMC, 5 Apr. 2020. *Netflix*, https://www.netflix.com/watch/81071693?trackId=255824129&tctx=0%2C0%2C389b-fa80-4acc-46d0-9833-17b4c7e42012-3031362%2C389bfa80-4acc-46d0-9833-17b4c7e42012-3031362%7C2%2C%2C%2C%2C%2C70177057%2CVideo%3A81071693%2CdetailsPageEpisodePlayButton.

@Trent_Cooley. "daaaaaamn [sic], Glenn hit that ass one time, and got Maggie washing his hat and shit. #walkingdead." *Twitter*, 27 Nov. 2011, 7:50 p.m., twitter.com/Trent_Cooley/status/140985939286704128.

"Try." *The Walking Dead*, season 5, episode 15, AMC, 22 Mar. 2015. *Netflix*, www.netflix.com/watch/80010541?trackId=14170286&tctx=2%2C0%2Cd52605e3-35b2-41d3-bbfe-7f50283f9852-108456379%2C6d4cfde9-cff2-4601-8986-d1a0f518d0d9_376660X3XX1581777449662%2C6d4cfde9-cff2-4601-8986-d1a0f518d0d9_ROOT.

@Trevorlloyd92 (Trevor Lloyd). "Wait a minute! Do you think all the way back in Season 3 when Rick saw Morgan again and Morgan said he has 'seen people wearing dead people's faces,' were they setting up ...." *Twitter*, 12 Nov. 2018, 3:25 p.m., twitter.com/Trevorlloyd92/status/1062109240570060812.

@Troy_Rudolph (Troy Rudolph). The Walking Dead, you absolutely broke me. I have never felt so empty and bereft of hope after an hour of TV #TWD #TheWakingDead." *Twitter*, 24 Oct. 2016, 11:57 p.m., twitter.com/Troy_Rudolph/status/790794370203066368.

"TS-19." *The Walking Dead*, season 1, episode 6, AMC, 5 Dec. 2010. *Netflix*, www.netflix.com/watch/70210892?trackId=200257859.

@Ttino74 (Tony Tino). "I'm a #TheWalkingDead fan. I still watch the original and the the others but cannot get into #WorldBeyond Wait:The Walking Dead: World Beyo..." *X*, 25 Oct. 2021, 9:41 a.m., https://twitter.com/TTino74/status/1452631433504178182.

Tudor, Andrew. "Unruly Bodies, Unquiet Minds." *Body & Society*, vol. 1, no. 1, Mar. 1995, pp. 25–41. *EBSCOhost*, https://doi-org.ezproxy.snhu.edu/10.1177/1357034X9500100 1003.

turkeypants. Comment on "The Walking Dead Season Premier Episode Discussion." *Reddit*, 11 Oct. 2018, 1:02 a.m., www.reddit.com/r/thewalkingdead/comments/9mafjf/ the_walking_dead_season_premier_episode_discussion/e7k8l9d.

@TVDoneWright (Adam Wright). "The Walking Dead Lessons: 1) Women can't shoot. 2) Don't give women guns. #TheWalkingSexism #TheWalkingDead." *Twitter*, 13 Nov. 2011, 6:50 p.m., twitter.com/TVDoneWright/status/135912335343759360.

Turchiano, Danielle. "'The Walking Dead' Boss on 'Creative Frenzy' Writing Process but Organized Office." *Variety*, 6 June 2019, variety.com/2019/tv/features/the-walking-dead-angela-kang-writers-office-interview-1203232631.

28 Days Later. Dir. by Danny Boyle. 2006. 20th Century Fox Home Entertainment, 2007. DVD.

2013 Where We Are on TV. GLAAD, 2014, pp. 1–28. *GLAAD*, www.glaad.org/files/2013 WWATV.pdf.

2014 Where We Are on TV. GLAAD, 2015, pp. 1–28. *GLAAD*, www.glaad.org/files/GLAAD-2014-WWAT.pdf.

"Twice as Far." *The Walking Dead*, season 6, episode 14, AMC, 20 Mar. 2016. *Netflix*, https://www.netflix.com/watch/80031931?trackId=255824129&tctx=0%2C0%2C389bfa80-4acc-46d0-9833-17b4c7e42012-3031362%2C389bfa80-4acc-46d0-9833-17b4c7e42012-3031362%7C2%2C%2C%2C%2C%2C70177057%2CVideo3A80031931%2CdetailsPage EpisodePlayButton.

Umstead, R. Thomas. "TV's Social–Media Appeal." *Multichannel News*, no. 23, 20 June 2016, p. 31. *EBSCOhost*, search.ebscohost.com/login.aspx?direct=true&db= edsgao&AN=edsgcl.458812344&site=eds-live&scope=site.

"Us." *The Walking Dead*, season 4, episode 15, AMC, 23 Mar. 2014. *Netflix*, www.netflix. com/watch/70297538?trackId=200257859.

"Vatos." *The Walking Dead*, season 1, episode 4, AMC, 21 Nov. 2010. *Netflix*, www. netflix.com/watch/70210890?trackId=14170289&tctx=0%2C3%2Cc4843074-bc04-4f1f-90aa-5f8742d530b1-248557882%2Cc875b5b9d-dcc2-4af9-80d5-7a92e139574a_3099 893X3XX1585415266980%2Cc875b5b9d-dcc2-4af9-80d5-7a92e139574a_ROOT

Vazquez, Jessica. "Tara Chambler's Death on 'The Walking Dead' Is More than Just Another Buried Gay." *Autostraddle*, 2 May 2021, www.autostraddle.com/tara-chamblers-death-on-the-walking-dead-is-more-than-just-another-buried-gay/.

VanDerWerff, Emily Todd. "The Walking Dead's Been Popular for Years. Now It's Also Good." *Vox*, 7 Nov. 2014, www.vox.com/2014/11/7/7172683/the-walking-dead.

Van Dijck, José. "Digital Photography: Communication, Identity, Memory." *Visual Communication*, no. 7, 2008, 57–76.

Velasco, Matthew. "The History of Gay Nightlife in New York City." *L'Officiel*, 01 June 2023, https://www.lofficielusa.com/politics-culture/history-gay-nightlife-nyc-clubs-drag-ball.

Venable, Nick. "The Walking Dead Showrunner Explains Carol and Ezekiel Shake-Up in Season 9 Finale." *Cinemablend*, 2 Apr. 2019, www.cinemablend.com/television/2469195/ the-walking-dead-showrunner-explains-carol-and-ezekiel-shake-up-in-season-9-finale.

Vhu. Comment on "The Walking Dead Episode Discussion S04E04 'Indifference.'" *Reddit*, 3 Nov. 2013, 8:01 p.m., www.reddit.com/r/thewalkingdead/comments/1puh34/ the_walking_dead_episode_discussion_s04e04/cd67wbv.

Vigna, Paul. *GUTS: The Anatomy of The Walking Dead*, Dey Street Books, 2017.

Vinney, Cynthia, and Caryn Wiley-Rapoport. "'Look at the Flowers': Female Evolution in the Face of the Zombie Hordes of *The Walking Dead*." *The Supernatural Revamped: From Timeworn Legends to Twenty–First–Century Chic*, edited by Barbara Brodman and James E. Doan, Fairleigh Dickinson UP, 2016, pp. 207–218. *EBSCOhost*, proxy.myunion. edu/login?url=http://search.ebscohost.com/login.aspx?direct=true&db=mzh&AN=201 6393442&site=eds-live&scope=site.

Waggoner, Erin B. "Bury Your Gays and Social Media Fan Response: Television, LGBTQ

Representation, and Communitarian Ethics." *Journal of Homosexuality*, vol. 65, no. 13, Dec. 2018, pp. 1877–1891. *EBSCOhost*, doi:10.1080/00918369.2017.1391015.

"Walk With Us." *The Walking Dead*, season 10, episode 12, AMC, 15 Mar. 2020. *Netflix*, www.netflix.com/watch/81071691?trackId=14170289&tctx=2%2C0%2Cba70fdc6-5438-4bd4-913d-10f64bbbe30f-1178192225%2CNES_0641F46592C38FACD47EE2A0D7C9E5-994911DC4F528C-A1E94A5CF8_p_1672420924208%2C%2C%2C%2C%2C70177057.

@TheWalkingDead. "Hi, hello. If LGBTQ+ characters on television (or anywhere) make you uncomfortable or angry, please unfollow us. While we also encourage..." *Twitter*, 25 Jan. 2021, twitter.com/TheWalkingDead/status/1353874101882867712.

"The Walking Dead Season 11 Census: Alive, Dead, or Zombie? (Updated)." *Sling TV*, www.sling.com/whatson/entertainment/horror/walking-dead-who-died-last-season.

"The Walking Dead: The Ride: Thorpe Park Resort." *Thorpe Park*, www.thorpepark.com/explore/theme-park/rides/the-walking-dead-the-ride/.

"The Walking Dead (TV)." *McFarlane*, mcfarlane.com/toys/brands/the-walking-dead-tv/.

"Warning Signs." *The Walking Dead*, season 9, episode 3, AMC, 21 Oct. 2018. *Netflix*, www.netflix.com/watch/81026619?trackId=14170289&tctx=0%2C2%2C48c5580d-f4d6-478f-a6cc-66bdcd787817-642347407%2Cb43325e6-42ee-45ef-be21-883739562397_137966906X3XX1579540922559%2Cb43325e6-42ee-45ef-be21-883739562397_ROOT.

waryoftheextreme.' Comment on "The Walking Dead Episode Discussion S04E04 'Indifference.'" *Reddit*, 3 Nov. 2013, 7:21 p.m., www.reddit.com/r/thewalkingdead/comments/1puh34/the_walking_dead_episode_discussion_s04e04/cd66vt1.

waywardgirl25. Comment on "The Walking Dead S09E06—Who Are You Now?—Post Episode Discussion." *Reddit*, 11 Nov. 2018, 9:13 p.m., www.reddit.com/r/thewalkingdead/comments/9wac44/the_walking_dead_s09e06_who_are_you_now_post/e9j9e96.

Weirdguy149. Comment on "The Walking Dead World Beyond—01x02 'The Blaze of Glory'—Live Episode Discussion." *Reddit*, 11 Oct. 2020, 10:41 p.m., https://www.reddit.com/r/TWDWorldBeyond/comments/j9h9v8/comment/g8k0pb0/?utm_source=share&utm_medium=web2x&context=3.

Welch, Alex. "'The Walking Dead' Finale Leads in 18–49 and Viewer Gains: Cable Live 7 Ratings for March 25–31." *TV by the Numbers*, zap2it.com, 11 Apr. 2019, tvbythenumbers.zap2it.com/dvr-ratings/cable-live-7-ratings-march-25-31-2019.

"Welcome to the Hellmouth." *Buffy the Vampire Slayer*, season 1, episode 1, The WB, 01 Mar. 1997. *Hulu*, www.hulu.com/watch/ec4c4b69-41f5-4595-8e00-4cdda6810c62.

"Welcome to the Tombs." *The Walking Dead*, season 3, episode 16, AMC, 31 Mar. 2013. *Netflix*, https://www.netflix.com/watch/70260062?trackId=255824129&tctx==0%2C0%2C389bfa80-4acc-46d0-9833-17b4c7e42012-3031362%7C2%2C%2C%2C%2C%2C70177057%2CVideo%3A70260062%2CdetailsPageEpisodePlayButton.

"What Comes After." *The Walking Dead*, season 9, episode 5, AMC, 4 Nov. 2018. *Netflix*, www.netflix.com/watch/81026621?trackId=200257859.

"When the Dead Come Knocking." *The Walking Dead*, season 3, episode 7, AMC, 25 Nov. 2012. *Netflix*, www.netflix.com/watch/70260053?trackId=200257858.

"Who Are You Now?" *The Walking Dead*, season 9, episode 6, AMC, 11 Nov. 2018. *Netflix*, www.netflix.com/watch/81026622?trackId=200257859.

Wigler, Josh. "'Walking Dead' Showrunner Explains All Those Post-Time Jump Changes." *The Hollywood Reporter*, 20 Dec. 2019, www.hollywoodreporter.com/live-feed/walking-dead-season-9-episode-6-recap-time-jump-explained-1159977.

"Wildfire." *The Walking Dead*, season 1, episode 5, AMC, 28 Nov. 2010. *Netflix*, www.netflix.com/watch/70210891?trackId=255824129&tctx=0%2C0%2CNAPA%40%40%7Cde1f8e9f-6de3-4778-814d-99f7e157fd5c-2988248_titles%2F1%2F2%2Fthe%20walking%20dead%2F0%2F0%2CNAPA%40%40%7Cde1f8e9f-6de3-4778-814d-99f7e157fd5c-2988248_titles%2F1%2F2%2Fthe%20walking%20dead%2F0%2F0%2C%2C-2Cde1f8e9f-6de3-4778-814d-99f7e157fd5c-2988248%7C1%2C%2C70177057.

@Willful_long (Will Long). "Damn I really miss Sasha on The Walking Dead and it has been 4 full days and she is a fictional character." *Twitter*, 06 Apr. 2017, 2:30 a.m., twitter. com/Willful_long/status/849871800901279744.

Wilson, Natalie. "Rules for Surviving Rape Culture." *The Politics of Race, Gender and Sexuality in* The Walking Dead: *Essays on the Television Series and Comics*, edited by Elizabeth Erwin and Dawn Keetley, McFarland, 2018, pp. 129–141. Contributions to Zombie Studies.

wolfitalk. Comment on "The Walking Dead S10E12—Walk With Us—POST Episode Discussion" *Reddit*, 16 Mar. 2020, 9:10 a.m., www.reddit.com/r/thewalkingdead/comments/ fjd4x6/comment/fknfaea/?utm_source=share&utm_medium=web2x&context=3.

WontonJrl. "Appreciation post for Angela Kang." *Reddit*, 27 Nov. 2018, 10:39 a.m., www. reddit.com/r/thewalkingdead/comments/a0x2t9/appreciation_post_for_angela_ kang.

"Wrath." *The Walking Dead*, season 8, episode 16, AMC, 15 Apr. 2018. *Netflix*, www.netflix. com/watch/81022967?trackId=200257859.

Wratten, Marcus. "Drag Race Winner Paloma Spills Tea on Her Walking Dead Appearance: 'Norman is a Big Drag Race Fan.'" *The Pink News*, 25 Sep. 2023, https://www.thepinknews. com/2023/09/25/drag-race-france-paloma-walking-dead-daryl-dixon-norman-reedus/

Zarka, Emily. "The Sexualized Heroics and Rick and Michonne." *The Politics of Race, Gender and Sexuality in* The Walking Dead: *Essays on the Television Series and Comics*, edited by Elizabeth Erwin and Dawn Keetley. McFarland, 2018, pp. 119–128. Contributions to Zombie Studies.

zebzoober. Comment on "The Walking Dead S09E15—The Calm Before—POST Episode Discussion." *Reddit*, 24 Mar. 2019, 11:38 p.m., www.reddit.com/r/thewalkingdead/ comments/b54ylg/the_walking_dead_s09e15_the_calm_before_post/ejb985r.

Zidarević, Maja. *A Feminist View on Social Issues in* The Walking Dead. 2018, U of Zadar, Undergraduate thesis. *University of Zadar Institutional Repository*, urn.nsk.hr/ urn:nbn:hr:162:373974.

Zinski, Dan. "Walking Dead Creator's Space Spore Origin Theory Was Only a Joke." *ScreenRant*, 26 Apr. 2020, screenrant.com/walking-dead-origin-space-spore-theory-joke/#:~:text=The%20Walking%20Dead%20creator%20Robert,theory%20was%20 just%20a%20joke.

Zomboy716. Comment on "The Walking Dead S09E15—The Calm Before—POST Episode Discussion." *Reddit*, 24 Mar. 2019, 8:35 p.m., www.reddit.com/r/thewalkingdead/ comments/b54ylg/the_walking_dead_s09e15_the_calm_before_post/ejb9825.

Zssmom. Comment on "Gabriel and Rosita." *Reddit*, 02 Oct. 2022, 8:23 p.m., www. reddit.com/r/thewalkingdead/comments/xtokv4/comment/iqtnlgs/?utm_source= share&utm_medium=web2x&context=3.

Index

Firefly 187
"The First Day of the Rest of Your Life" 158
The First Lady of the Alexandria Safe-Zone
    see Hawthorne, Michonne
Fleming, Cailey 20
Flowers, Shaunee 91
Fobbs, Bradon 79
Fogler, Dan 114
Ford, Abraham 43, 59, 67, 94, 98–105, 107–
    108, 122, 159, 160–162, 194
Foree, Ken 15
Forster, Marc 28
"Four Walls and a Roof" 128
France 164, 173–174, 176
Francine (Fran) 15, 27, 29
Frank 131, 133
Frankenstein 185
Franklin, Kelly 29, 51
Freeman, Matthew 180
Freud, Sigmund 21, 33–35, 37, 74, 149, 150,
    154, 162
Fussell, Sidney 98

Game of Thrones 10, 178, 190
Gamma 136
Garber, Megan 32
Gardner, Stirling 172
Gareth 54
Garland, Tammy, et al. 29, 60, 75–76
Gates, Josh 53
Gavaler, Chris 29
gay character 2, 88–92, 95, 96–97, 99, 116–
    117, 122, 163, 169, 171–173, 176, 193–194
gay couple 92, 96
Gay Liberation Movement 175
Geijer, Herman 15
Gellar, Sarah Michelle 182
gender 2, 8, 10–16, 19, 21, 24–25, 27–32, 35–
    38, 42–43, 47, 49, 55–56, 60, 68, 70, 73–76,
    83, 87, 91, 97, 102, 106, 108, 114–115, 117, 119,
    125, 131, 140, 142–143, 145, 148, 156, 160, 163,
    177, 192, 194–197; expectations 10, 27, 45,
    88–89; fluidity 171, 176; identification 30,
    174; nonconformity 174; normativity 10,
    20, 193; norms 40–41, 75; performance 57,
    102; representation 7, 37, 40; roles 3, 10–14,
    17, 19, 24, 29–31, 41, 44, 53, 55, 75, 85, 118,
    128, 176, 196; stereotypes 27, 52, 88, 195
Generation X 119
Generation Z 119
Georgia 164, 173, 183, 189–190
Georgie 32, 68–70, 158
"Ghosts" 157
Giles, Rupert 183
Gilliam, Seth 82
Gilliard, Lawrence, Jr. 128
Gimple, Scott 121–123, 172
girlification 99, 101, 104
GLAAD 95
glass ceiling 68, 87–88, 104, 109, 174
Goldberg, Lesley 128

Golding, William 169
Good Morning America 129
Goossen, Jeananne 57
The Governor *see* Blake, Philip
Grady Memorial Hospital 77, 136, 189
graphic novel 2, 6, 21, 24, 29, 33, 60, 75, 77,
    91, 99, 101, 119, 123, 129, 137, 164, 177, 178,
    186–187, 191, 195
Gray, Brandon 28
Greene, Beth 63, 69, 77, 81, 189
Greene, Hershel 42, 61, 64–65, 68, 71, 75, 93,
    110, 115, 117, 125, 151
Greene, John 2, 66, 148; *see also* Greene and
    Meyer
Greene, Maggie *see* Rhee, Maggie
Greene and Meyer 29, 149, 152; *see also*
    Greene, John; Meyer, Michaela
Greene family 24, 31, 48, 61, 62, 65, 89, 115,
    138, 161, 193
Gregory 62, 66, 70, 193
Griffin, Clarke 97–98
Grimes, Carl 26, 28, 65, 69, 73–74, 77, 79,
    80–82, 86, 108, 110–112, 114, 116, 123–125,
    127, 140, 149, 151–153, 155, 158, 171, 189, 193
Grimes, Judith 20, 53–54, 74, 81–84, 86, 110,
    124–128, 135, 155, 171, 195, 196
Grimes, Lori 31, 65–66, 73, 77, 81–82, 103,
    112, 118, 151–153, 155, 171
Grimes, Rick 6, 18, 21, 24, 26, 30, 33, 36, 38,
    48–54, 58–59, 61, 63, 65, 67–71, 73–75, 77–
    86, 88–93, 105, 108, 110, 112, 115, 121–125,
    128, 131–132, 134, 136, 138, 140, 144, 147–159,
    161–162, 164, 173, 180, 181, 183–185, 189,
    192, 193
Grimes, Rick, Jr. (RJ) 81, 86, 124
Grimes family 73, 124, 128, 151–152, 170, 172
"The Grove" 17, 53
"Guardians" 106, 131, 134
Guillermo 130
Gurira, Danai 2, 72, 121

Hagman, George 29, 111, 188
Halloween 8
Hamel, Jenny 175
The Hamilton Lodge 175
Hardwick, Chris 10, 42–43
Harkavy, Juliana 91
Harlem 175
Harley Quinn 116
Harper, Stephen 27, 176
Harris, Naomie 28
Harris, R. Keith 110
Harrison, Amy 29
Harrison, Andrea 25, 31, 52, 72–74, 80, 118,
    132
hashtag 5, 10–12, 18, 39–40, 42, 53, 55, 80,
    179–180
Hathaway, Donny 159
Hawbaker, KT 12
Hawthorne, Michonne (The First Lady of the
    Alexandria Safe-Zone) 11–12, 14, 20, 26,